THE VEDĀNTA PHILOSOPHY

THE VEDĀNTA PHILOSOPHY

(Original Sūtras and Explanatory Quotations from Upaniṣads, Bhagavadgītā etc. and their English Translation)

By

SRIDHAR MAJUMDAR

BKP

BHARATIYA KALA PRAKASHAN
DELHI (INDIA)

First Edition : 1928
Revised Edition : 2007

Published by **C.P. Gautam**
BHARATIYA KALA PRAKASHAN
3421-A, IInd Floor, Narang Colony, Tri Nagar,
Delhi-110035. Ph.: 27393083, 32967505 (O) 32492129 (R)
E-mail : bkp3421@yahoo.co.in

ISBN :978-81-8090-148-5

Laser Typye Setting by :
A-ONE GRAPHICS
Pitampura, New Delhi-110088.

Printed by :
BDH Printer at Salasar Imaging System, Delhi.

FOREWORD

It is well-known that the Brahma-Sūtra of Bādarāyaṇa has been interpreted by different Ācāryas belonging to distinctly different cults, who became founders of sects and great system-builders. Among those, Rāmānuja and Mādhava have imposed on them two self-consistent philosophical systems called Viśiṣṭādvaita and Dvaita. The cults of Viṣṇu were called Bhāgavata or Pañcarātra and those of Śiva, Pāśupata or Māheśvara, and the followers of these schools sought to prove their orthodoxy by interpreting the Brahma-Sūtra in accordance with their own tenets, indicating their claim to be based on, and regularly evolved from, ancient tradition. These movements unlike the earlier ones do not denominate the Supreme Being as Parama Brahman, but are expressly Vaiṣṇava or Śaiva in their tone, Intense devotion or Bhakti to Śiva or Nārāyaṇa characterises these schools, a devotion that expressed itself in all-absorbing love-a complete self-surrender.

Among the Vaiṣṇava school of interpreters of the Brahma-Sūtra, two other noted Ācāryas besides Rāmānuja and Mādhva, are Ācāryas—Nimbārka and Ballava. Nimbārka's view appears to have been largely influenced by the teachings of Bhāskara who flourished in the first half of the ninth century and who interpreted the Vedānta system from the stand-point of Bhedābheda. This theory was not a new discovery of Bhāskara, but it was held by the ancient teacher Audulomi to which Bādarāyaṇa himself refers in his Brahma-Sūtra.

The learned author of the present work has based his English notes chiefly on the interpretation given by Nimbārka of the Sūtras of Bādarāyaṇa in his own commentary which is known as the "Vedānta-pārijāta-Saurava." The commentary is very brief and it contains no attack on rival theories; but its greatest charm lies in its remarkable perspicuity of diction and clearness of expression.

The metaphysical doctrines as propounded by Ācārya Nimbārka may be summarised here for the benefit of the readers of this book. In this school, Brahman is regarded as both the Efficient and Material cause of the universe, Brahman is both Nirguṇa and Saguṇa, as It is not exhausted in the creation, but also transcends it. The universe is not, according to this view, unreal or illusory but is a true manifestation or Pariṇāma of Brahman. It may, however, be said to be unreal, only in the sense that the present state of its existence is not self-sufficient and that it has no separate existence from Brahman. The universe is both identical with, as well as different from, Brahman, even as a wave or bubble is the same as, and at the same time different from, water. The individual souls are parts of the Supreme Being and are controlled by It. The Emancipation lies in realising the true nature of the Spirit and it is attainable by true devotion or Bhakti. The individuality (जीवत्व) of the finite self is not dissolved even in the state of Mukti. This doctrine of Nimbārka has a fascination of its own, especially for those who do not care to dive deep into the labyrinth of subtle logical and metaphysical arguments, and yet desire to know what the celebrated system of Vedanta has to teach.

The reader of this book will, I am sure, at once be agreeably surprised to find how faithfully and lucidly the author has acquitted himself of this his self-imposed task of labour and love as well. The greatest recommendation of the book is its clearness of expressions and charming sweetness of its style. The aim of the author, as indicated in his preface, in bringing out this publication, is to give a general and clear idea of the system of Vedanta to those English-knowing people who have a desire to learn something of this great system but have no opportunity or ability to study it in the original. The author has it seems, spared no pains in making this absturse philosophy easy of comprehension by the beginners as well by the busy general readers. The method of interpretation and the mode of explanation are so simple and so natural that the book, it may be confidently hoped, will prove of immense usefulness to those for whose sake the author has taken so much pains. With a view to enable the readers to grasp the contents of the different sections, the author has, at the commencement of each new section, given a sketch which cannot but prove a great help to them. One cannot but admire the author's thorough mastery of his subject and painstaking labour which he has brought to bear upon his task.

The author must be congratulated on the noble service he has rendered to his countrymen and to the English-knowing world as well, by the publication of this venerable work. A glossary explaining the difficult terms and expressions appended to the end of the book has greatly enhanced its value.

—Kokileswar Śāstri

PREFACE

Impelled by a strong desire through the grace of my beloved Guru, to get a clear idea of Brahma-Vidyā (knowledge of Brahma), I studied several Upaniṣads and other treatises on the subject, and ultimately turned to the greatest Hindu philosophy, the Vedānta Sūtra, which is, broadly speaking, a synthetic study of these Upaniṣads. In course of my study I had special difficulties in getting at the exact meaning of many words in the Sūtras or aphorisms. Supposing that other persons also may have encountered similar difficulties, I have, in the present book, tried to give in a glossary English equivalents of the technical words used in the Sūtras, in addition to the full explanation of the text comprehending the meaning of each term in English together with the origin all references to the Upaniṣads with their English translations. The reason why I write this book in English and not in my own mother tongue, Bengali—is that it may also be of some use to people outside Bengal, and that other people throughout the English-speaking world may also get a rough idea of the most liberal and at the same time the grandest philosophy of the Hindus. I venture to bring our this publication, being prompted by the consideration that persons, who have an eager desire to study this philosophy but have not the requisite knowledge of Sanskrit, may get the benefit of my labour without undergoing the same for themselves.

A sketch of the whole book, divided into sixteen parts, has also been prepared section by section (Pāda), and appended to the beginning of each section, with a view to give a preliminary idea of the whole section and to show the connecting link between the Sūtras before one enters upon their study, as well as to help the class of readers who want to have a glimpse of the entire Vedānta philosophy without going through the individual Sūtras.

I have endeavoured to present an unbiassed interpretation of the abstruse aphorisms of the Vedānta Sūtra without being influenced by the views of the different commentators, the most illustrious of them being Ācāryas Śaṅkara, Rāmānuja and Mādhva. These commentators have tried to establish theories of their own, such as the uncompromising monism (अद्वैतवाद) of Śaṅkara, the differentiated monism (विशिष्टाद्वैतवाद) of Rāmānuja and the strict dualism (द्वैतवाद) of Mādhva. Ācārya Śaṅkara had in view, while preparing his commentary the purpose of chiefly combating the baneful effects which blind ritualism had brought to bear upon Hinduism. It is only Nimbārkācārya who, as I understand him to be, has been the most unbiased of the commentators; and this induced me principally to follow his line of thought while writing out this book. Ācārya Nimbārka reconciles all the different views, regarding the Lord, taken by Ācāryas Śaṅkara, Rāmānuja, Mādhva and others, and proves that their views are all true in respect of the particular aspect of Brahma dealt with by them, each in his own way; as for instance, Ācārya Śaṅkara has taken Him in His transcendent aspect, while Rāmānuja has taken Him in His immanent aspect principally; but the view, taken by Ācārya Nimbārka, is the adjustment of the different views taken by different commentators; in this all-embracing character lies the greatness of his commentary. I have, however, noted the views of Ācārya Śaṅkara in instances of material difference.

With my humble capacities I have tried my level best to present my expositions as lucidly as possible, with a view to bring the subject within the easy conception of the ordinary reader. It is for the learned public to judge how far I have been successful in my humble endeavours. While placing my work in the hands of my readers, I beg leave to invite their friendly and sympathetic criticism, so that it may come out divested of its glaring fault in the next edition.

In my present attempt I have been immensely helped by the Dārśanik Brahma Vidyā of Śrijut Tārā Kiśore Śarmā Chaudhuri, at present Braja Videhi Mohant Mahārāj Santa Dās Bābāji of Brindāban, who also kindly went through some portions of the manuscript, favouring me with valuable suggestions during his visit to Barisal. He expressed his unqualified satisfaction at my attempt and encouraged its publication, for which my sincerest gratitude is due to him, I have also been occasionally helped by Pandit Jiwānanda Vidyāsāgar's Śaṅkara Bhāṣya, as well as its English translation by the renowned oriental scholar, the late Mr. George Thibaut, of which the copies were kindly lent me by my earnest well-wisher and late professor in College, Babu Rājendra Lāl Banerjee, M.A., B.L., at present Government Pleader of Barisal. Babu Prabhāt Chandra Banerjee, B.A. a colleague of mine, has also rendered me great services by thoroughly revising the manuscript and giving me important suggestions. I am, therefore, greatly thankful to these gentlemen. My son-in-law Srimān Surendra Nāth Bhattāchārya M.A., a brilliant university scholar in Vedānta, at present Professor of Sanskrit, B.N. College, Bankipore has also thoroughly gone through the book, making changes and improvements in several places, and has been mainly instrumental in bringing the book to light by going through the proof sheets and doing everything necessary for its publication. But it is chiefly through the unabated energy of Swāmi Jñānānanda, a member of the same spiritual order with me, in his minutely revising the whole work, making additions and alterations, that it has been at all possible to bring the book to completion. Last of all, I owe it to myself to declare for the information of the public that the colouring of the whole book is from the pen of revered Śrimat Jagadis Mukerjee, the distinguished educationist and unostentatious living saint, of Barisāl, who has been kind enough to spare no pains to give the work a presentable shape; language fails to express my deep debt of gratitude to him for his self-imposed labour extending over several months. I also offer my heartiest thanks to Śrijut Kokileśwar Śāśtri of the Kolkata University for kindly writing the Foreward for my book.

—Sridhar Majumdar

TRANSLITERATION CHART

VOWELS

अ	...	...	a
आ	...	...	ā
इ	...	...	i
ई	...	...	ī
उ	...	...	u
ऊ	...	...	ū
ऋ	...	...	ṛ, Ri
ए	...	...	e
ऐ	...	...	ai
ओ	...	...	o
औ	...	...	au
:	...	...	ḥ

CONSONANTS

क	...	...	k
ख	...	...	kh
ग	...	...	g
घ	...	...	gh
ङ	...	...	ṅ
च	...	...	c
छ	...	...	ch
ज	...	...	j
झ	...	...	jh

ञ	...	...	ñ
ट	...	...	ṭ
ठ	...	...	ṭh
ड	...	...	ḍ
ढ	...	...	ḍh
ण	...	...	ṇ
त	...	...	t
थ	...	...	th
द	...	...	d
ध	...	...	dh
न	...	...	n
प	...	...	p
फ	...	...	ph
ब	...	...	b
भ	...	...	bh
म	...	...	m
य	...	...	y
र	...	...	r
ल	...	...	l
व	...	...	v
श	...	...	ś
ष	...	...	ṣ
ह	...	...	h
क्ष	...	...	kṣ

CONTENTS

CHAPTER IV

CHAPTER I

SECTION—I

This section begins with a hint in Sūtra 1, that the book is meant for those, who have got a genuine desire for knowledge of Brahma, and not for those, who would study philosophy merely for intellectual culture, and that such a desire may arise in those persons alone who have been well acquainted with the religious rites and have realized that they can never yield everlasting bliss. The subsequent Sūtras discuss what this Brahma is.

Sūtras 2.4 show, by reference to Śrutis, that Brahma is the cause of the universe; in other words, the whole universe, consisting of animate and inanimate objects, springs out of, exists in, and finally merges in, Him. Sūtra 3 states that Brahma is known only by the study of Śruti, and by no other means of knowledge. Brahma is represented in Śruti as 'Sat-Cit-Ānanda' (Eternal Existence, consciousness and Bliss). Sūtra 2 establishes His character of eternal existence, as the cause of the universe certainly exists eternally.

Sūtras 5.12 show that none but Brahma is admitted by Śruti to be the cause of the universe. As the cause of the universe is stated in Śruti to exercise His will-power in producing it, He cannot be an insentient principle like the inert Pradhāna of the Sāṅkhya philosophy. It should be noted that Brahma is established here in His character of Pure Consciousness (Cit).

Sūtras 13.20 show that Brahma is All-Bliss (Ānandam) and that by the term Ānandamaya (Bliss Immense) in Śruti is meant neither the individual soul, nor the Pradhāna of Sāṅhya. From Sūtra 13 onward, there are taken up, for discussion, some passages of Śruti regarding 'Ānandamaya', that appear at first sight to indicate something other than Brahma; but the Sūtras prove that they all describe none but Brahma in His various aspects.

Sūtras 21 and 22 point out Brahma as the Innermost Spirit of all, from the highest sun down to the pettiest creature on earth.

Sūtra 23 points out that Brahma is sometimes termed, in Śruti, as Ākāśa,[1] the final destination of the universe.

Sūtra 24 similarly points out that He is Prāṇa (Life-Energy).

Sūtras 25.28 point out that Brahma is termed, in some Śruti, as Jyoti (Light) and as such, comprising the whole universe in His quarter part only, while transcending the creation in His three quarters. So He is not exhausted in the creation, though immanent in it.

Sūtras 29-32 show, by way of corroboration of Sūtra 24, that Brahma is manifested as Prāṇa (Life-Energy); and that it is also proved from the scripture that the individual soul, when he percieves Brahma in himself, thinks and may, therefore, declare, himself as having the powers of Brahma. It has been incidentally shown by Sūtra 32, that there are three ways of meditation of Brahma, according to the capacity of the meditator; namely, (1) as manifested in Jīvātmā, (2) as manifested in Prāṇa and (3) as independently of any manifestation in either.

This section has given a bird's-eye view of the subjects, dealt with in the Brahma-Sūtra, namely, the nature of the Supreme Spirit, of the individual soul and the universe, and their inter-relation, and incidentally gives suggestions on divine meditation. They will be elaborated later on.

अथातो ब्रह्मजिज्ञासा॥१॥

[Here the author of the Sūtras means to say that a genuine desire for the knowledge of Brahma must arise in one before one begins to study Vedānta].

अथ (afterwards), अतः (therefore), ब्रह्मजिज्ञासा (a desire for the knowledge of Brahma).

Explanation—After having acquired a knowledge of Karmas (religious rites) prescribed in the Vedas and having known that their results cannot give everlasting bliss, a time comes when a person becomes indifferent to Karmas; and therefore naturally a desire arises in him for the knowledge of Brahma, (the All-pervading Soul,) Who is above Karma, and is the source of everlasting bliss.

Ācārya Śaṅkara says that even without having the knowledge of Karma-Kāṇḍa (that division of the Vedas which is devoted to the treatment of religious ceremonies), desire for the knowledge of Brahma may arise direct from the study of the Upaniṣads; so in his opinion this Sūtra should not be explained in the way that a desire for the knowledge of Brahma arises after the knowledge of Karmas. He explains that after one acquires the nine principal qualifications for divine meditation, a desire for the knowledge of Brahma arises. These nine principal qualifications are: (1) नित्यानित्यवस्तुविवेकः (discrimination of permanent and transient things), (2) इहामूत्रार्थफलभोगविरागः (aversion to the enjoyment, in this life or the next, of the consequences of one's actions), (3) शमः (control of the mind), (4) दमः (control of the external senses), (5) उपरतिः (cessation from worldly enjoyments), (6) तितिक्षा (endurance of the opposite extremes, such as happiness and misery, pleasure and pain, heat and cold), (7)श्रद्धा (faith in the words of the spiritual guide and of the Upaniṣads) (8)समाधानम् (deep concentration) and (9) मुमुक्षुत्वम् (desire for salvation).

This Sūtra gives a hint as to the fitness of persons for the study of this philosophy; meaning that those, who have got an earnest desire for the knowledge of Brahma, are so fit.

जन्माद्यस्य यतः॥२॥

[Answer to the enquiry after Brahma is given here in brief, and it is shown that Brahma, who is 'सत्' Sat (the Eternal Existence), is the only cause, stay and final resort of the universe].

जन्मादि (origination etc., *i.e.,* origination, continuance and dissolution), अस्य (of this, *i.e.,* of this universe), यतः (from Whom, *i.e.,* from Brahma inquired into in Sūtra I).

Explanation—Brahma, the object of search in Sūtra 1, is He from whom the origination, continuance and dissolation of the universe are brought about.

This Sūtra gives a description of Brahma, Who, being the originator, preserver and (at the end) absorber of this vast universe, must have unlimited powers and properties; so He is omnipotent and omniscient.

The idea of this Sūtra is taken from the Chāndogya Upaniṣad, as well as from the Taittirīya Upaniṣad, as quoted below. Several other Upaniṣads also have similar expressions.

"सर्व्वं खल्विदं ब्रह्म तज्जलानिति शान्त उपासीत।"

(Everything indeed is Brahma, emanating from Him, living and moving in Him and ultimately disappearing in Him, so He is to be worshipped in a calm spirit).

Chāndogya Upaniṣad, Chap. III, 14, 1

"यतो वा इमानि भूतानि जायन्ते । येन जातानि
जीवन्ति । यत् प्रयन्त्यभिसंविशन्ति ।... तद् ब्रह्मेति ।"

(From Whom all these visible things emanate, by Whom they, so emanating, live, and in Whom they disappear and enter, That is Brahma).

Taittirīya Upaniṣad, Bhṛguballi, I, 1

शास्त्रयोनित्वात्॥३॥

[An argument in support of Sūtra 2, is given here].

शास्त्र (scriptures, sacred writings) योनित्वात् (from the proof, because of the proof).

Explanation—It is because of the scriptures being the only proof that the proposition, laid down in Sūtra 2, can be established.

As Brahma is beyond sensuous perception. He can be apprehended only on the authority of the Śrutis or the Vedas (the direct intuitions) of the greatest antiquity, the Smṛtis (the inferential truths) and the Purāṇas *i.e.,* the old mythology, and other scriptures directly following the Śrutis.

तत्तु समन्वयात्॥४॥

[The argument in support of Sūtra 2 is continued].

तत् (that, *the established fact*), तु (but), समन्वयात् (on account of agreement or harmony).

Explanation—But that Brahma, as the only cause of the universe, is the dictum of the scripture, is established, because all the scriptures agree in this respect.

An objection may arise against Sūtra 3 from the standpoint of the Karma portion of the Vedas where the dictum is to enjoin Karma (religious ceremonies). To this, Sūtra 4 rejoins to say that the Vedas, as a whole, agree in aiming mainly at Brahma and not a Karmas. The term 'तु' (but) in the Sūtra implies a rejoinder to the objection that may be raised.

Compare the Śruti:—

"सर्व्वे वेदा यत्पदमामनन्ति तपांसि सर्व्वाणि च यद् वदन्ति।
यदिच्छन्तो ब्रह्मचर्य्यञ्चरन्ति तत्तेपदं संग्रहेण ब्रवीमि ओमित्येतत्॥"

(*Yama instructs Naciketā, saying,* 'Whom all the Vedas proclaim, Whom all religious practices aim at, seeking Whom people observe abstinence from sexual appetite, of Him I speak to thee briefly; Him we call 'Om'.

Kaṭhopaniṣad, Chap. I, 2, 15.

(Dialogue between Yama and Naciketā).

ईक्षतेर्नाशब्दम्॥५॥

[From this Sūtra onward up to Sūtra 12 the principle of the Sāṅkhya Philosophy, where Pradhāna (Primordial Matter) is described as the active cause of the universe, is refuted; and it is shown that Brahma, Who is 'Cit' (All-intelligence) and so has will-power, is the efficient cause of the universe.

An objection may be raised against Sūtra 2-4, where Brahma, the universal spirit, has been stated to be the cause of the universe, as laid down in Śruti; and it may be said, by way of such objection, that the Sāṅkhya Philosophy does not accept this view, but holds that Pradhāna (Primordial Matter) is the ultimate cause of the universe. This objection, *i.e.,* the principle of the Sāṅkhya Philosophy, is refuted by this Sūtra and the following ones (Sūtras 6-12)].

ईक्षतेः (because of the word expressing **'ईक्षण'**, *i.e.,* seeing with consciousness, or simply willing or conceiving), **न** (not, *i.e.*, the Primordial Matter is not the cause of the universe), **अशब्दम्** (not held by Śruti;—**शब्दः**—Śruti).

Explanation—From the application of the words expressing **'ईक्षण'** (will, conception) in the Upaniṣads, to that which is the cause of the universe, it is understood that Śruti does not hold Pradhāna (Primordial Matter) to be the efficient cause of the universe.

The purport is—The Cause (Creator) of the universe, as stated by Śrutis, possesses will-power; hence Pradhāna, which itself is inert and therefore cannot have such will-power, is not the efficient cause of the universe.

To explain this Śūtra some passages from the Upaniṣads should be quoted here, as they have reference to the expression of **'ईक्षण'** (will, conception):—

"सदेव सौम्येदमग्र आसीदेकमेवाद्वितीयम्।

तदैक्षत बहुस्यां प्रजायेयेति, तत्तेजोऽसृजत॥"

(O, my son, this *universe* at first, *before creation,* was One with the only Being, the One without a second. That Being willed 'I will be many, I shall manifest myself;' so He brought forth Tejas (Primordial heat).

Chāndogyopaniṣad, Chap. VI, 2, 2-3.

(Dialogue between Uddālaka and his son, Śwetaketu).

"ओं आत्मा वा इदमेक एवाग्र आसीत्। नान्यत् किञ्चनामिषत्। स ईक्षत लोकान्नुसृजा इति। स इमाँल्लोकानसृजत।"

(At first this *universe* was only one *undifferentiated* Self—*the Universal Soul;* nothing else stirred. He willed 'May I create worlds'. *So* he brought forth these worlds).

Aitareya Upaniṣad, Chap 1, 1, 1-2. There are similar expressions in other Upaniṣads also, such as the Bṛhadāraṇyaka, etc.

गौणश्चेन्नात्मशब्दात्॥६॥

[An argument in support of Sāṅkhya is adduced and refuted].

गौणः (indirect, secondary), चेत् (if); न (not), आत्मशब्दात् (from the word 'आत्मा' *i.e.* soul).

This Sūtra consists of two parts, namely, an objection and its reply. The objection-portion is: गौणश्चेत्; and the reply-7 portion is:—न, आत्मशब्दात्।

Exlanation—It may be argued that 'ईक्षण' (willing), as stated in Sūtra 5, has been applied in the Śruti, indirectly in a figurative sense, to the inert Pradhāna, as inert things are sometimes described as living beings; so Pradhāna can well be accepted as the efficient cause of the universe. But that argument cannot hold, because of the word Ātmā (soul) being applied subsequently in the Śruti to that which is the cause of the universe.

Vide the Śruti:—

"ऐतदात्म्यमिदं सर्व्वं तत् सत्यं स आत्मा तत्त्वमसि श्वेतकेतो।"

(All this *universe* is in essence That; That is the Truth; That is Ātmā (soul); that thou art, O, Śvetaketu).

Chāndogyopaniṣad, Chap. VI, 8, 7. (Instruction of Uddālaka to his son, Śvetaketu).

तन्निष्ठस्य मोक्षोपदेशात्॥७॥

[Further reason is adduced here to prove that Pradhāna is not the cause of the universe].

तत् निष्ठस्य (of the person absolutely devoted to That, *i.e.*, the cause of universe), **मोक्षोपदेशात्** (from the statement of salvation).

Explanation—It is further proved from the statement, in Śruti, that salvation can be attained by one absolutely devoted to the Creator of the universe; consequently the inert Pradhāna is not the Creator of the universe.

The purport is:—It is stated in Śruti that he, who is absolutely devoted to the Creator (Cause) of the universe, obtains his salvation; but it is not reasonable that one obtains his salvation by absolute devotion to blind matter, Pradhāna. So Pradhāna cannot be the creator of the universe.

For the statement alluded to in the Sūtra *vide* the Śruti:—

"तस्य तावदेव चिरं यावन्न विमोक्ष्येऽथ सेम्पत्स्य।"

(He waits only till he is released, and thereupon unites with Brahma).

Chāndogyopaniṣad, Chap. VI 14, 2. Vide the Smṛti also for such statement:—

**"तमेव शरणं गच्छ सर्व्वभावेन भारत।
तत् प्रसादात् परां शान्तिं स्थानं प्राप्स्यसि शाश्वतम्॥"**

(Oh thou descendant of Bharata, take thou shelter in Him in all respects; through His grace you shall get perfect peace and eternal resting place).

Bhagavat Gītā, Chap. XVIII, 62.

हेयत्वावचनाच्च॥८॥

[Another reason is adduced to prove that Pradhāna is not the creator of the universe].

हेयत्व (fitness to be rejected or discarded; inferiority), अवचनात् (from want of such expression in Śruti), च (also).

Explanation—It—the rejection of the Pradhāna theory—is also proved from want of any expression in Śruti to the effect that the cause of the universe is inferior to anything else, and as such, to be rejected for the attainment of salvation.

A seeker after salvation has been taught to fix his whole attention on the Cause; and it is certain that he cannot attain salvation by meditation upon inert Pradhāna. Had Śruti meant Pradhāna to be the cause of the universe, it would have certainly asked the devotee to discard such a cause and to look to something higher for his salvation (certainly pure unconsciousness, *i.e.,* Pradhāna cannot be the end and aim of spiritual culture).But, on the contary, there are instructions in Śruti for divine meditation upon, and thinking oneself as part and parcel of, the First Cause of the universe. Hence Pradhāna cannot be such a cause.

Vide the Śruti:—

"जन्म-मृत्यु-सुख-दुःख-वर्ज्जितं
जाति-नीति-कुल-गोत्र-दूरगम्॥
चिद्विवर्त्त जगतोऽस्य कारणं
तत् सदाहमिति मौनमाश्रय॥"

(Have recourse to silence in always thinking "I am He, Who is not subject to birth and death, joy and sorrow, Who is beyond all classes and canons, lines and races, and Who is the parent of this universe, which again is in itself, an evolution of the spirit, *i.e.*, Brahma"). Brāhmopaniṣad, Chap. III, 7.

प्रतिज्ञाविरोधात्॥९॥

[Further argument, to show that Pradhāna is not the cause of the universe, is adduced].

प्रतिज्ञा (the proposition to be proved), **विरोधात्** (because of antagonism; as it goes against).

Explanation—Pradhāna cannot be taken to be the cause of the universe, as that would be antagonistic to the proposition.

The allusion is to chapter VI of the Chāndogyopaniṣad, where Uddālaka proposed to his son, Śvetaketu, to prove a thing, by the knowledge of which everything becomes known; and he began by saying **"सदेव सौम्येदमग्र आसीदेकमेवाद्वितीयम्"।** (for translation *vide* Sūtra 5). Now if that thing, which is proposed to be so proved and which is implied by **'सत्'** (Sat) in the above quotation, be taken to be Pradhāna, then the proposition—'by its knowledge everything becomes known'—fails; as by the knowledge of Inert Matter the existence of the animate world cannot be explained. Pradhāna, therefore, can, by no means, be construed to be the **'सत्'** (Sat) of the passage quoted, which is established therein as the Cause of the universe.

For the proposition *vide* the Śruti:—

"येनाश्रुतं श्रुतं भवत्यमतं मतमविज्ञातं विज्ञातमिति ....यथा सौम्यैकेन मृत्पिण्डेन सर्व्वं मृन्मयं विज्ञातं स्याद्वाचारम्भणं विकारो नामधेयं मृत्तिकेत्येव सत्यम्।"

(Whereby the unheard is heard, the unconceived is conceived and the unknown is known. ... As for instance, my son, by the knowledge of a lump of earth, all things made of earth are known; they are mere changes of forms, differing in names made of words; the real substance is earth).

Chāndogyaopaniṣad, Chap. VI, I, 3-4.

स्वाप्ययात्॥१०॥

[The argument, to prove that Pradhāna is not the cause of the universe is continued].

स्व(स्वस्मिन्—in self); **अप्ययः (लयः अप्ययात्** from fusion, merging).

Explanation--From the fact that the individual soul merges in Self (the Universal Soul) in sound sleep, it is understood that Self, which is described in Śruti as the Ultimate Reality, the cause of the universe, is not Pradhāna.

It is found in Śruti that when a person is fast asleep the individual soul merges in Self, which is quite different from Pradhāna and is the Reality (**सत् वस्तु**) previously described as the cause of the universe.

Vide the Śruti:—

"यत्रैतत् पुरुषः स्वपिति नाम सता सौम्य तदा सम्पन्नो भवति तस्मादेनं स्वपितीत्याचक्षते स्वं ह्यपीतो भवति।"

[Oh my son, when this individual soul is fast asleep, then he becomes united with the Reality, he obtains the status of Self, it is then called 'merged in Self' (the Universal Soul)].

Chāndogyopaniṣad, Chap. VI, 8, 1.

गतिसामान्यात्॥११॥

[The argument, to prove that Pradhāna is not the cause of the universe, is continued].

गतिः (view); **सामान्यं** (the sameness); **सामान्यात्** (because of the sameness).

Explanation—The view, that the Creator of the universe is an intelligent agent, being the same in all the Śrutis, blind Pradhāna cannot be the Creator.

For the idea in the Śruti vide:—**"सर्व्वे वेदा यत्पदमामनन्ति"**. ..(already quoted and translated under Sūtra 4 of this section).

श्रुतत्वाच्च॥१२॥

[The argument, that Pradhāna is not the cause of the universe, is continued].

श्रुतत्वात् (from Śruti), **च** (also).

Explanation—It is also directly evident from Śruti that Pradhāna is not the Cause of the universe.

Vide the Śruti.—

"ते ध्यानयोगानुगता अपश्यन्
देवात्मशक्तिं स्वगुणैर्निगूढ़ाम्।
यः कारणानि निखिलानि तानि
कालात्मयुक्त्वान्यधितिष्ठत्येकः॥"

(They, i.e., *the Ṛṣis-seers,* by dint of meditation, saw, as the cause, Brahma's Energy inherent in His nature. He alone regulates all the causes acting through time and ego).

Śvetāśvataropaniṣad, Chap. I, 3.

[By Sūtras 2-5 it has been shown that Brahma is the Ultimate Cause of the universe, and it follows, therefore, that He is the Eternally Existing Being (सत्). By Sūtras 5-12 the Pradhāna theory is refuted, and Brahma, the real Cause of the universe, is shown to be All-intelligence. Now the framer of the Sūtras proceeds to point out certain characteristics of Brahma by ascertaining the exact significance of some expressions of Śruti].

आनन्दमयोऽभ्यासात्॥१३॥

[This Sūtra shows that Brahma is Bliss].

आनन्दमयः (Bliss immense), अभ्यासात् (because of frequent repetition).

Explanation—The term 'Ānandamaya' (Bliss immense) signifies Brahma, as it has been frequently applied in Śruti, to Him.

Vide the Śruti:—

"रसो वैसः। रसं ह्येवायं लव्ध्वानन्दी भवति।"

(He, the Universal Soul, is Bliss in itself. He, the individual soul attaining that bliss becomes blissful).

Taittirīyopaniṣad, Brahmaballi, Chap. II, 7, 1.

"आनन्दं ब्रह्मणो विद्वान् न विभेति कुतश्चन।"

(He, who has realized the Joy of Brahma fears none whatsoever).

Taittirīyopaniṣad, Brahmaballi. Chap. II, 9, 1.

"आनन्दो ब्रह्मेति व्यजानात्।"

(*Bhṛgu having recourse to divine meditation,* realised that Brahma is Bliss).

(Taittirīyopaniṣad, Bhṛguballi, 6, 1).

विकारशब्दान्नेति चेन्न प्राचुर्य्यात्॥१४॥

[An objection, against Sūtra 13, is refuted here in this Sūtra].

विकारशब्दात् (from the word **'आनन्दमय'** with the suffix **'मय'** implying change or transformation), **न** (it is not so), **इति** (this) **चेत** (if); **न** (no), **प्राचुर्य्यात्** (because of the sense of immensity).

[The Sūtra consists of both a question and its answer. The question-portion is:—**'विकारशब्दान्नेति चेत्'**। The reply is:—**'न, प्राचुर्य्यात्'**।]

Explanation—It may be argued that the word **'आनन्दमय'** in Sūtra 13 is applied to some emancipated soul, as the suffix **'मयट्'** is used in the sense of change or transformation; and therefore it is not attributable to the universal soul, which is above all transformations. This argument is not acceptable, as the suffix **'मयट्'** is used also in the sense of immensity. Therefore the word **'आनन्दमय'** (Bliss immense) has been certainly applied to denote the universal soul, and not the individual soul.

तद्धेतुव्यापदेशाच्च॥१५॥

[Another argument in support of Sūtra 13, is adduced].

तत् (**तस्य**—its), **हेतु** (cause, source), **व्यपदेशात्** (from expressions), **च** (also).

Explanation—From expressions in Śruti to the effect that the Reality (Brahma) is the source of bliss to the individual soul, it is understood that 'Ānandamaya' (Bliss immense), as stated in Sūtra 13, is Brahma.

Vide the Śruti:—

"एष ह्येवानन्दयति।"

(He, *i.e.*, Brahma, and none else, confers joy upon the individual soul).

Taittirīya, Brahmaballi, Chap. II, 7, 1

मान्त्रवर्णिकमेव च गीयते॥१६॥

[The argument, in support of Sūtra 13, is continued].

मान्त्रवर्णिकं (that which has been stated in the sacred text), **एव** (the very same), **च** (also), **गीयते** (is sung, is stated).

Explanation—The same Brahma, as has been described in the Mantra (the text) of the Taittirīya Śruti under discussion, is also sung (stated) to be Ānandamaya (Bliss Immense) towards the close of the text.

The Mantra, referred to, is:—

"सत्यं ज्ञानमनन्तं ब्रह्म।"

(Brahma is Truth, Knowledge and Infinity).

Taittirīya, Brahmaballi, Chup. II, 1, 2.

नेतरोऽनुपपत्तेः॥१७॥

[The argument, in support of Sūtra 13, is continued].

न (not), **इतरः** (**ब्रह्मेतरः**, other than Brahma),**अनुपपत्तेः** (because of absurdity or unreasonableness; as it is not reasonable).

Explanation—As all the properties, which Śruti has attributed to the Ānandamaya (Bliss Immense), appear to be appropriate only in respect of the Universal Soul, and not in respect of the individual soul, the word "Ānandamaya" cannot mean the latter.

Some of the properties, which the Taittirīya Śruti has attributed to Bliss Immense, are as follows—

"सोऽकामयत बहुस्यां प्रजायेयेति। स तपोऽतप्यत स तपस्तप्त्वा इदं सर्व्वमसृजत्, यदिदं किञ्च। तत् सृष्टवा तदेवानुप्राविशत्।"

(He willed, I will be many, I will manifest myself. He meditated, and meditating created everything existing, and then after creating, entered into them).

Taittirīya, Brahmaballi, Chap. II, 6, 2.

भेदव्यपदेशाच्च॥१८॥

[The argument, in support of Sūtra 13, is continued].

भेदः (distinction); **भेदव्यपदेशात्** (on the ground that Śruti makes a distinction), **च** (and).

Explanation—And on the additional ground that Śruti makes a distinction between the two (describing one as the giver and the other as the receiver, of bliss), the individual soul, as the receiver, cannot be the Ānandamaya (Bliss Immense), Who is the giver.

Vide the Śruti:—

"रसो वै सः (ब्रह्म) रसं ह्येबायं (जीवः) लब्ध्वानन्दौ भवति।" (for translation and reference, *vide* Sūtra 13).

कामाच्च नानुमानापेक्षा॥१९॥

[The argument, in support of Sūtra 13, is continued].

कामात् (from will), **च** (also); **कामाच्च** (and simply by the fiat of His will), **न** (not), **अनुमानं** (a material cause), **अपेक्षा** (waiting for, dependence upon).

Explanation—And simply by the fiat of His will He evolved the universe and needed not the help of a material cause (like the potter). 'Bliss Immense cannot signify the individual soul, who with his limitations, can by no means be conceived to have built the universe without materials.

Vide the Śruti:—

"सोऽकामयत बहुस्यां प्रजायेयेति। स तपोऽतप्यत।
स तपस्तप्त्वा इदं सर्व्वममृजत।"

(For reference and translation *vide* Sūtra 17).

अस्मिन्नस्य च तद्योगं शास्ति॥२०॥

[The argument, in support of Sūtra 13, is concluded].

अस्मिन् (on Him, on Bliss Immense), **अस्य** (his, of the individual soul), **च** (also), **तद्योगं** (**आनन्दयोगं**, union in Bliss), **शास्ति** (teaches; *i.e.*, Śruti teaches).

Explanation—Śruti teaches that the attainment of bliss by the individual soul is dependent on Him; in other words, the individual soul becomes blissfull only on attaining the Ānandamaya (Bliss Immense). So the two are not identical.

Vide the Śruti:—

"रसो वै सः। रसं ह्येवायं लव्ध्वानन्दी भवति।"

(For reference and translation *vide* Sūtra 13).

अन्तस्तद्धर्म्मोपदेशात्॥२१॥

[Brahma is shown to be the In-dwelling Spirit].

अन्तः (**अन्तरात्मा**, the In-dwelling Spirit within the Sun and in the human eye), **तत्** (**तस्य**, His, of Brahma), **धर्म** (essential attributes), **उपदेशात्** (because of the teaching, as Śruti teaches).

Explanation—From the description, in the Chāndogyopaniṣad, of the essential attributes belonging to the In-dwelling Spirit residing in the sun and in the human eye, it is to be understood that He is Brahma and not any individual soul.

Vide the Śruti:—

"य एषोऽन्तरादित्ये हिरन्मयः पुरुषो दृयते.....
स एष सर्व्वेभ्यः पाप्मभ्य उदितः।"

Glorious Being, Who is perceived within the sun, transcends all limitations).

The Chāndogyopaniṣad, Chap. 1, 6, 6-7.

"अथ य एषोऽन्तरक्षिणि पुरुषो दृश्यते सैवर्क्तत् साम तदुक्थम् तद्यजुस्तद्ब्रह्म तस्यैतस्य तदेव रूपं यदमुष्य रूपम्।"

(Again the Being, Who is perceived in the eye, is Rik. He is Sāma, He is Uktha, He is Yajus, He is Brahma. His form is the same as that of the former, *i.e.,* of the Being in the sun).

Chāndogyopaniṣad, Chap. I, 7, 5.

भेदव्यपदेशाच्चान्यः॥२२॥

[An argument, in support of Sūtra 21, is adduced].

भेदव्यवदेशात् (as similar Śrutis make a distinction), च (also), अन्यः (शारीरात् अन्यः, other than the embodied individual soul).

Explanation—And as similar statements in other Śrutis make a clear distinction between Him (the In-dwelling Spirit) and the individuals, it is evident that the In-dwelling Spirit is other than any Jīva, such as the god of the sun, etc.

Vide the Śruti:—

"य आदित्ये तिष्ठन्नादित्यादन्तरो यमादित्यो न वेद, यस्यादित्यः शरीरं य आदित्यमन्तरो यमयत्येष त आत्मान्तर्याम्यमृतः।"

(He, that dwelling in the sun is yet different from it, Whom the sun does not know, Whose body is the sun, Who controls the sun from within, is the Immortal Ātmā, *i.e.,* the Universal Soul, sought for by you, regulating from within).

Bṛhadāraṇyakopaniṣad, Chap. III, 7, 9.

[For the nature of the difference, also *vide* Sūtra 18 of this section].

आकाशस्तल्लिङ्गात्॥२३॥

[Brahma is shown to be Ākāśa].

आकाशः (Ākāśa—the first one of the five primary elements, the sublest of the elements filling all space), **तत्** (**तस्य;** His; of the Universal Soul), **लिङ्गात्** (from discriminating marks).

Explanation—The term Ākāśa has been used in Śruti in the sense of the Universal Soul, as appears from its discriminating marks.

Vide the Śruti:—

"अस्य लोकस्य कागतिरित्याकाश इति होवाच सर्व्वाणि ह वा इमानि भूतान्याकाशादेव समुत्पद्यन्त आकाशं प्रत्यस्तं यन्त्याकाशो ह्येवैभ्यो ज्यायानाकाशः परायणम्।"

('What is the last resort of this universe?' 'Ākāśa', he said, 'because all these created things spring from, and disappear in, Ākāśa; and Ākāśa is the oldest of all these things; Ākāśa is their ultimate resort').

Chāndogyaopaniṣad, Chap. I, 9, 1.

(Dialogue between Śilak and Prabāhaṇa).

अतएव प्राणः ॥२४॥

[Brahma is shown to be Prāṇa (Life-Energy)].

अतएव (therefore, for the same reason) **प्राणः** (the Life-Energy).

Explanation—Just in the same way as stated in Sūtra 23, the expression 'Prāṇa' (Life-Energy) has been treated of, in Śruti, in the sense of Brahma, the Universal Soul, (as appears from its discriminating marks).

Vide the Śruti:—

"प्राण इति होवाच सर्व्वाणिहवा इमानि भूतानि प्राणमेवाभिसंविशन्ति प्राणमभ्युज्जिहते ।"

('It is Prāṇa, *Life-Energy,* said Uśasti, 'all these manifested things merge into Life-Energy, and emerge out of Life-Energy').

Chāndogya, Chap. I, 11, 5.

"प्राणो ब्रह्मेतिहस्माह कौषीतकिः।"

('Prāṇa is indeed Brahma', said Kauṣītaki).

Kauṣītaki-Upaniṣad, Chap. II, 1.

ज्योतिश्चरणाभिधानात्॥२५॥

[The expression 'Jyoti' (light) is next taken up for discussion].

ज्योतिः (light), चरण (a foot, a fourth part, a quarter), अभिधनात् (from the expression).

Explanation— The term 'Jyoti' (Light) of the Chāndogya Śruti (Chap III, 13, 7) is recognised to be the Supreme Being, described in a previous passage, to have foot or part; for there, the Being is said as pervading all heaven by His three parts and the whole visible universe by the fourth part; and here too 'Jyoti' is described as pervading everything above and below heaven.

Vide the Śruti for the term 'Joyti':—

"यदतः परो दिवो ज्योतिर्द्दीप्यते विश्वतः पृष्ठेषु सर्व्वतः पृष्ठेष्वनुत्तमेषूत्तमेषु लोकेष्विदं वाव तद् यदिदमस्मिन्नन्तः पुरुषे ज्योतिः।"

(The Light, Which shines from beyond this heaven all over the worlds, high and low, is the same Light that shines forth from within the man).

Chāndogya, Chap. III, 113, 7.

(Jyoti-Vidyā)

Vide the Śruti for the expression of feet or parts:—

"तावानस्य महिमा ततोज्यायांश्च पुरुषः। पादोऽस्य सर्व्वा भूतानि त्रिपादस्यामृत दिवि।"

(This much is the glory of Brahma, and Brahma Himself is superior far to all of them; the whole creation covers only a fraction of Him; but by far the largest portion, the imperishable three fourths, belong to heaven—*His transcendental aspect*).

Chāndogya, Chap. III, 12, 6.

(Gāyatrī-Vidyā).

This Supreme Spirit, Brahma, is subsequently represented as Light in the Śruti "**यदतः परो दिवो...**" quoted previously.

छन्दोऽभिधानान्नेति चेन्न तथा चेतोऽर्पणनिगदात्तथाहि दर्शनम्॥२६॥

[An objection raised against Sūtra 25, is refuted].

छन्दः (the metre known as Gāyatrī), **अभिधानात्** (from the expression), **न** (not; not Brahma), **इति** (this), **चेत्** (if); **न** (no), **तथा** (like that); **चेतः** (the mind), **अर्पण** (use, application); **चेतोऽर्पण** (application of the mind; meditation by directing attention), **निगदात्** (**कथनात्**, from the expression; from the instruction),**तथाहि** (like that; moreover), **दर्शनम्** (instances in other Śrutis).

[This Sūtra consists of both an objection and its reply. The objection portion is '**छन्दोऽभिधानान्नेतिचेत्**'; and the reply portion is '**न, तथा चेतोऽर्पणनिगदात्तथाहि दर्शनम्**'।].

Explanation—If it be argued that the expression of foot or part, referred to in Sūtra 25, is applicable to the metre (known as Gāyatrī), and not to Brahma, that argument cannot stand, as there is instruction in the Śruti, of meditation by directing attention to Gāyatrī, which, therefore, cannot stand for metre but for Brahma; moreover, there are instances in other Śrutis also to that effect.

Vide the Śruti:—

"**एतं ह्येव बह्वृचा महत्युकथे मीमांसन्त एतमग्नावध्वर्य्यव एतं महाव्रते छन्दोगाः।**"

(*It is the Supreme Being under the name of Gāyatrī,* Whom the Bahvṛca-priests worship as Mahat-Uktha, *i.e.* Mahā-Prāṇa, the Adhvaryu-priests as Agni (Fire), and the Chāndoga-priests as Mahābrata (the greatest rite).

भूतादिपादव्यपदेशोपपत्ते श्चैवम्॥२७॥

[An argument, in support of Sūtra 25, is adduced].

भूतादि (the elements etc., *i.e.,* the elements, the earth, the body and the heart), व्यपदेश (expression), उपपत्तेः (because of the proof; as it is rightly deduced from the above reason), च (also), एवम् (so).

Explanation—There are expressions in Śruti indicating that Gāyatrī consists of four parts, namely, the elements, the earth, the body and the heart; and from such expressions also, it is deduced that Gāyatrī is so, *i.e.,* Brahma.

It will also appear from the reasoning that the element, the earth, the body and the heart can, by no means, be represented as the four Verses of Gāyatrī, but they can be understood only to mean the four-fold manifestations of the Supreme Being.

उपदेशभेदान्नेति चेन्नोभयस्मिन्नप्यविरोधात्॥२८॥

[Another objection, against Sūtra 25 is raised and refuted].

उपदेश (expression), भेदात् (on account of difference), न (not), इति (this), चेत् (if), न (no), उभयस्मिन् (in both, in either), अपि (even, assuredly), अविरोधात् (there being no contradiction).

The Sūtra consists of both an objection and its reply. The objection portion is 'उपदेशभेदान्नेति चेत्'; and the reply-portion is 'नोभयस्मिन्नप्यविरोधात्'।

Explanation—If it be argued that there is a difference of expression (consisting in case-ending) in the Gāyatrī-Śruti and in the Jyoti-Śruti regarding the word 'दिव्' (heaven); then the reply is 'No, the argument is not tenable, as there is no material contradiction between the two expressions'.

The reference is to the following passages:—

"यदतः परो दिवो ज्योतिर्दीप्यते..." (the Joyti-Śruti); and

"तावानस्यमहिमा ...त्रिपादस्यामृतं दिवि" (the Gāyatrī-Śruti).

Quoted and translated under Sūtra 25.

In the first passage the word 'दिव्' (heaven, the unrevealed portion of Brahma) has been used in the oblative, *i.e.*, the fifth case-ending; and in the second passage in the locative, *i.e.*, the seventh case-ending. So it may be argued that there being this difference in case-endings in the use of the word 'दिव्' in the above two passages, they do not indicate the Same (Brahma). But the argument cannot stand; as by going through the whole of both the passages, it appears that they do not conflict with each other in indicating the same Supreme Spirit, though they differ in form.

प्राणस्तथाऽनुगमात्।।२९।।

[The expression 'Prāṇa' is again taken up for discussion].

प्राणः (Life-Energy), **तथा** (likewise; like that stated in the Śrutis quoted before; in connection therewith), **अनुगमात्** (owing to the similarity of expressions in all parts of the Śruti under discussion).

Explanation—Likewise, the Life-Energy has been treated of in the Kauṣītaki-Śruti (in the instruction of Indra to Pratardana) in the sense of Brahma, as will appear, when the full text is taken into consideration.

The reference is to chapter III of the Kauṣītaki-Upaniṣad, where Indra teaches Pratardana to worship his (Indra's) Prāṇa; and considering the whole of the chapter, it will appear that Brahma has been meant by Prāṇa, spoken of therein.

[Though the conclusions in Sūtras 24 and 29 are identical; the facts, from which the conclusions have been drawn, and the lines of argument in support thereof, are different].

न वक्तुरात्मोपदेशादिति चेदध्यात्मसम्बन्धभूमाह्यस्मिन्।।३०।।

[An objection to Sūtra 29 is refuted].

न (not, that is not the case), वक्तुः (of the speaker), आत्म (self), उपदेशात् (as it is an instruction), इति (this), चेत् (if); अध्यात्म (spiritual), सम्बन्ध (connection), भूमा (plenty), हि (certainly), अस्मिन् (in this).

[The Sūtra consists of two parts: one part is in the form of an objection, *viz.* 'वक्तुरात्मोपदेशादिति चेत्; and the other part is in the form of a reply, *viz.*, 'न, अध्यात्मसम्बन्धभूमाह्यस्मिन्'।].

Explanation—If it be argued that the speaker (Indra) has instructed (Pratardana) to worship himself (Indra) and not Brahma; the reply is that it is not so, because there is plenty of references to the Supreme Spirit in Indra's teaching to Pratardana.

For reference vide the Śruti:—

"मामेव विजानीह्येतदेवाहं मनुष्याय हिततमं मन्ये।"

(Know me alone; this I consider to be the most beneficial for men).

Kouṣītaki, Chap. III, 1b.

"प्राणोऽस्मिं प्रज्ञात्माय; तं मामायुरमृतमित्युपास्स्व।"

(I am Prāṇa, the Intelligent Soul; worship me as Life Eternal).

Kauṣītaki, Chap. III, 2.

"स एष प्राण एव प्रज्ञात्मानन्दोऽजरोऽमृतः।"

(This Prāṇa is undoubtedly the Intelligent Soul, Bliss itself, not subject to decay or death).

Kauṣītaki, Chap. III, 8c.

शास्त्रदृष्ट्या तूपदेशो वामदेववत्॥३१॥

[The objection, raised in Sūtra 30, is further refuted].

शास्त्र (sacred writings, Śruti), दृष्टया (by the insight); शास्त्रदृष्ट्या (because of the divine insight as attested by Śruti), तु (but), उपदेशः (declaration), वामदेववत् (like Vāmadeva).

Explanation—The declaration (referred to in Sūtra 30), made by Indra calling himself one with Brahma, is justified because of his divine insight; and such insight is attested by Śruti, as in the case of Vāmadeva.

So Indra taught Pratardana to know of his (Indra's) self (*vide* **'मामेव विजानीहि....'**) quoted and translated under Sūtra 30); just like the sage Vāmadeva, who, after realising Brahma in himself, declared that he became Manu, he became the sun.

Vide the Śruti:—

"तद्धेतत् पश्यन्नृषिर्वामदेवः प्रतिपेदेऽहं मनुरभवं सूर्य्यश्चेति।"

(Realising that *Brahma,* the sage Vāmadeva declared, 'I became Manu and the sun').

Bṛhadāraṇyaka, Chap. I, 4, 10.

जीवमुख्यप्राणलिङ्गान्नेति चेन्नोपासात्रैविध्यादाश्रितत्वादिह तद्योगात्॥३२॥

[Another objection to Sūtra 29 is raised and refuted].

जीव (the individual soul), **मुख्यप्राण** (the main life-energy), **लिङ्गात्** (from the discriminating marks), **न** (not), **इति** (this), **चेत्** (if); **न** (no, that argument cannot stand), **उपासा** (**उपासना**, worship, divine meditation), **त्रैविध्यात्** (because of the three ways; as there are three ways), **आश्रितत्वात्** (on account of their acceptance elsewhere in Śruti; as they have been prescribed also elsewhere in Śruti), **इह** (here; in this case; in the case of the instruction of Indra to Pratardana), **तद्योगात्** (for their application; as they have been applied).

[The Sūtra consists of an objection and its reply. The objection-portion is **'जीवमुख्यप्राणलिङ्गान्नेतिचेत्'**; and the reply-portion is **'न, उपासपत्रैविध्यादाश्रितत्वादिह तद्योगात्।**]

Explanation— If it be argued that as the discriminating marks, used in the instruction of Indra to Pratardana in the

Kauṣītaki-Śruti, directly and clearly apply to the individual being and to the main life-energy, Brahma is not indicated thereby; the reply is:—No, that argument cannot stand, as there are three ways of worship of, or meditation on Brahma, (He may be meditated on:—(1) as manifested in Jīvātmā, (2) as manifested in Prāṇa or vital principle, and (3) as independently of any manifestation in either), such as have been prescribed elsewhere in Śruti, and as have also been prescribed here in the instruction of Indra to Pratardana. So it is maintained that the individual soul and the main life-energy have been treated of, in Śruti, to stand for Brahma.

For reference *vide* the quotations and their translations under Śutra 30 of this section.

SECTION—II

Doubts may arise as to the exact meaning of certain expressions of Śruti—whether they indicate Brahma or something else. Those expressions are taken up for discussion in this and the next sections.

In this section it is proved, that the different expressions, employed in different Śrutis for divine meditation, indicate the same Infinite Spirit, Brahma.

In the portion of the Chāndogya Upaniṣad known as the Śāṇḍilya Vidyā, it is taught, that as the form and the character of a person in his next life are determined by his desires and thoughts of the present one, he should constantly desire for, and meditate upon, a Being Who is ideally perfect, and Who functions through his life-energy, and Who is All-Light, *i.e.,* Brahma, so that he may become of the same nature with Him.

In Sūtras 1-8 of this section it is proved, that the above-mentioned expressions, the ideal of perfection, the Light and the Life-energy, all point to the Supreme Being.

Sūtra 9-12 show that the Devourer of the whole world comprising the animate and the inanimate, in the Kaṭha Śruti, indicates Brahma.

Sūtras 13-18 state that the Indwelling Spirit of the eye, in the Chāndogya-Upaniṣad indicates neither a reflected image nor any individual soul, but Brahma.

Sūtras 19-21 show that the Controller Within (**'अन्तर्यामी'**), described, in the Bṛhadāraṇyaka-Upaniṣad, as pervading and guiding the five elements (earth, water, fire, air and ether) and also heaven, sun, moon, stars etc., is no other than Brahma.

Sūtras 22-24 say that the Invisible, Imperceptible, Formless, Omnipresent, All-pervading, Everlasting and Extremely Subtle 'Puruṣa' (Spirit) of Muṇḍaka Śruti is Brahma.

Sūtras 25-33 state that by instructing to worship Vaiśvānara, Śruti has taught to worship neither the element fire, nor the Fire-god, but the Infinite Spirit.

The opinions of different sages, namely Jaimini, Aśmarathya and Bādari, have also been cited here to show, that to facilitate divine meditation according to the capacity of the meditator, the Infinite Spirit is sometimes conceived as finite and as possessing trunk, head, foot and other limbs and organs.

सर्व्वत्र प्रसिद्धोपदेशात्॥१॥

[An expression from the Chāndogya Śruti is taken up for discussion].

सर्व्वत्र (everywhere, *i.e.*, in all the Upaniṣads), **प्रसिद्ध** (the well known), **उपदेशात्** (from description; because it is described).

Explanation—The passage under discussion denotes Brahma, and not the individual soul; becuase Brahma, Who is well known in all the Upaniṣads, is recognised to be described here.

Vide the Śruti:—

"सर्व्वं खल्विदं ब्रह्म तज्जलानिति शान्त उपासीताथ खलु क्रतुमयः पुरुषो, यथाक्रतुरस्मिंल्लेंके पुरुषो भवति, 'तथेतः प्रेत्य भवति' स क्रतुं कुर्व्वीत मनोमयः प्राणशरीरो भारूपः।"

(All this universe is indeed Brahma, emanating from Him, living and moving in Him, and ultimately disappearing in Him. He is to be worshipped in a calm and serene spirit. A man in his present life is the outcome of his previous thoughts and desires; and he becomes in after-life what he now resolves to be, while in this world. So he ought to have recourse to meditation upon Him, Who is ideally perfect, Who functions through one's very Life-Energy and Who is All-Light).

Chāndogya, Chap. III, 14, 1 and 2.

This can only mean the Supreme Being referred to in all the Śrutis.

विवक्षितगुण्णोपपत्तेश्च॥२॥

[An argument, in support of Sūtra 1, is adduced].

विवक्षित (sought to be applied) **गुण** (attributes); **उपपत्तेः** (for the justification), **च** (and).

Explanation—And because the attributes, sought to be applied by the Śruti quoted above, justly belong to Brahma, it must be admitted that the passage refers to Brahma.

For attributes referred to, vide:—

"सत्यसङ्कल्प आकाशात्मा सर्व्वकर्म्मा सर्व्वकामः सर्व्वगन्धः सर्व्वरसः सर्व्वमिदमभ्यात्तोऽवाक्यनादरः।"

(Whose desires prove true; Who is all-pervading as Ākāśa; from Whom proceed all actions, all desires, all scents, all tastes; Who is All-embracing; Who is voiceless and unattached).

Chāndogya, Chap. III, 14, 2.

These attributes are possible in Brahma only.

अनुपपत्तेस्तु न शारीरः॥३॥

[The argument, in support of Sūtra 1, is continued].

अनुपपत्तेः (not being justifiable), **तु** (on the other hand), **न** (not), **शारीरः** (the embodied soul).

Explanation—On the other hand, as the attributes stated in the Śruti quoted under Sūtra 2, and other epithets, such as **'ज्यायान् पृथिव्याः, ज्यायान् दिवः'** (superior to the earth, even superior to heaven) occurring further on in the same text, cannot certainly apply to any Jīva (individual soul), in whatever stage of perfection he may be, the subject of discussion cannot be any Jīva.

कर्म्मकर्त्तृव्यपदेशाच्च॥४॥

[An argument, in support of Sūtra 3, is adduced].

कर्म्म (object, the passive person), **कर्त्तृ** (the agent, the subject of the action, the active-person), **व्यपदेशात्** (from expressions), **च** (and).

Explanation—And the object and the subject of the action, 'to attain', being clearly pointed out, in the Śruti, as the Universal Soul and the individual soul respectively, it appears that the embodied soul is not denoted by the quotation under Sūtra 1.

For the action referred to vide:—

"इतः प्रेत्याभिसम्भवितास्मीति।"

(Leaving this world, may I attain Him).

Chāndogya, Chap. III, 14, 4.

In the quoted extract, 'I' (the embodied soul) has been spoken of as an agent desiring to attain Him (Brahma) Who is stated to be the object of the action 'to attain'.

शब्दविशेषात्॥५॥

[The argument, in favour of Sūtra 1, is continued].

शब्दः (word, expression), **विशेषः** (distinction); **शब्दविशेषात्** (from the distinctive word or expression).

Explanation—From the clear and distinct expression in the same connection, it appears that Brahma is meant by the passage under discussion (in Sūtra 1).

For the distinctive expression referred to, vide:—

"एष म आत्मान्तहृदय एतद्ब्रह्म।"

(This Soul dwells in the depth of my heart. It is Brahma).

Chāndogya, Chap. III, 14, 4.

स्मृतेश्च॥६॥

[The argument, in support of Sūtra I, is continued].

स्मृतेः (from Smṛti), **च** (also).

Explanation—From Smṛti also, it is evident that the embodied soul is markedly different from the subject-matter of the text under discussion.

Vide the Smṛti:—

"ईश्वरः सर्व्वभूतानां हृद्देशेऽर्ज्जुन तिष्ठति।

भ्रामयन् सर्व्वभूतानि यन्त्रारूढ़ानि मायया॥"

(Oh Arjuna! The Lord resides in the heart of all individual beings and turns them round and round on the wheel of His Māyā).

Bhagavad Gīta, Chap. XVIII, 61.

अर्भकौकस्वात्तद्व्यपदेशाच्च नेति चेन्न निचाय्यत्वादेवं व्योमवच्च॥७॥

[An objection, to Sūtra 1, is raised and refuted].

अर्भकौकस्त्वात् [**अर्भकं** (small) **ओकः** (**स्थानं**, space) **यस्य तस्य भावः तस्मात्**; because of its occupying a small space; because of limitation of space], **तत्** (**तस्य**; of that; to that effect), **व्यपदेशात्** (from an expression; because there is an expression), **च** (also), **न** (not, *i.e.*, the objection cannot stand), **इति** (this), **चेत्** (if); **न** (no, *i.e.*, the objection cannot stand), **निचाय्यत्वात्** (because of conception; for the sake of easy conception; so that it may be easily conceived), **एवं** (so), **व्योमवत्** (like the sky; like the empty space or the vacuum), **च** (also).

[The Sūtra consists of two parts, namely an objection and its reply. The objection-portion is:—**अर्भकौकस्त्वात्तद्व्यपदेशाच्च नेति चेत्**; and the reply-portion is :—**न, निचाय्यत्वादेवं व्योमवच्च।**]

Explanation—It may be argued that the subject of discussion is not Brahma (the Infinite Spirit), as there is an expression to the effect that it occupies a small space (within the heart). But the argument cannot stand, as the expression has been put in this way to facilitate the conception of the Infinite

Spirit; just as the infinite empty space is spoken of as the small space of the air-hole.

For the expression referred to, vide—

"एष म आत्मान्तर्हृदयेऽणीयान् व्रीहेर्वा यवाद्वा सर्षपाद्वा।"

(This Soul is within my heart, smaller than a grain of paddy or barley, or a mustard seed).

Chāndogya, Chap. III, 14, 3.

सम्भोगप्राप्तिरितिचेन्न वैशेष्यात्॥८॥

[Another objection is raised and refuted here].

सम्भोगप्राप्तिः (perception of pleasure and pain, subjection to enjoyment and suffering), **इति** (this), **चेत्** (if); **न** (no, that cannot be) **वैशेष्यात** (because of the distinction).

[This Sūtra consists of an objection and its refutation. The objection portion is:—**सम्भोगप्राप्तिरिति चेत्**; and the refutation portion is:—**न, वैशेष्यात्**।].

Explanation—It may be apprehended that the expression (referred to in Sūtra 1, *i.e.,* in the portion, of the Chāndogya Śruti, known as the Śāṇḍilya-Vidyā) is not applicable to Brahma; for, being connected with the heart of the living being, He may be subject to enjoyment and suffering. But this apprehension is groundless, as in spite of His connection with the heart of the inidividual soul. He is distinct from the latter; He is above pleasure and pain, wheras the individual soul is subject to enjoyment and suffering in consequence of his own actions.

Vide the Śruti—

"द्वा सुपर्णा सयुजा सखाया समानं वृक्षं परिषस्वजाते।
तयोरन्यः पिप्पलं स्वाद्वत्यनश्नन्नन्योऽभिचाकशीति॥"

(Two birds are living together as friends on the same tree, *i.e., the body.* One of them, *i.e., the individual soul,* eats the tasteful fruit, *i.e., enjoys the fruit of his works;* and the other, *i.e., the Universal Soul,* witnesses without eating anything, *i.e.*, without partaking of the fruit).

Muṇḍakopaniṣad, Chap. III, 1, 1.

Sūtras 1-8, have established that the subject of discussion, in the quoted portion of the Chāndogyopaniṣad (Chap. III, 14), is Brahma, the Universal Soul, and none else.

अत्ता चराचरग्रहणात्॥९॥

[A passage, from the Kaṭha Śruti, is now taken up for discussion].

अत्ता (the devourer, the eater), **चराचर** (the animate and the inanimate, the whole universe), **ग्रहणात्** (because of His taking; as He takes or devours; as He withdraws in Himself).

Explanation—The term 'Attā' (the Eater) indicates Brahma; as He takes in or eats up the whole universe comprising both the animate and the inanimate, *i.e.*, as He withdraws in Himself the entire universe at the time of dissolution.

For the reference vide—

**"यस्य ब्रह्मच क्षत्रञ्च उभे भवत ओदनः।
मृत्युर्यस्योपसेचनं क इत्था वेद यत्र सः॥"**

(Who feeds on both, Brāhmaṇa and Kṣatriya, *i.e.*, *withdraws in Himself the whole world,* Whose supplementary article of food is death; who knows what He is and where He dwells?).

Kaṭhopaniṣad, Chap. I, 2, 25.

प्रकरणाच्च॥१०॥

[An argument, in support of Sūtra 9, is adduced].

प्रकरणात् (from the context), **च** (also).

Explanation—That the devourer is Brahma, is also known from the context of the passage (the 2nd Vallī of chapter I of Kaṭhopaniṣad, dealing with Brahma, Who is there expressed in a passage, as 'महान्तं विभुमात्मानम्' (The Great, the All-pervading—The Self).

गुहां प्रविष्टावात्मानौ हि तद्दर्शनात्॥११॥

[Another passage, of the Katha Śruti, is taken up for discussion].

गुहां (recess, the recess of the heart), प्रविष्टौ (entered), आत्मानौ (two 'selfs'—the Higher Self or परमात्मा and the lower self or जीवात्मा; the Universal Self and the individual self), तद्दर्शनात् (being so represented), हि (यतः; as; because).

Explanation—Two are the 'selfs', described as entered in the recess of the heart, the Universal or Higher Self (Brahma), and the individual or lower self (Jīva); as these two have been represented in the Kaṭhopaniṣad as such.

Vide the Śruti:—

"ऋतं पिबन्तौ सुकृतस्य लोके गुहां प्रविष्टौ परमे परार्द्धे।
छायातपौ ब्रह्मविदो वदन्ति पञ्चाग्नयो ये च त्रिणाचिकेताः॥"

(Seated within the most sacred, inmost recess of the heart, are the two 'selfs' enjoying the fruit of their own work, who are spoken of being intimately connected as Light and shade, by those who know Brahma and by those who worship five fires, as well as by those householders who offer sacrifices to the Naciketā fire thrice a day).

Kaṭhopaniṣad, Chap. I, 3, 1.

That the Śruti quoted above denotes the Universal and the individual souls, is verified by the following two Śrutis. Of these two Śrutis, the first indicates the Universal Soul, and the second the individual soul, most clearly and in similar language, both as residing within the heart.

The first Śruti is:—

"तं दुर्दर्शं गूढ़मनुप्रविष्टं गुहाहितम्"

(Him, Who is very difficult to be realised, Who is All-pervading, and Who is hidden and seated within the depth of the heart).

Kaṭhopaniṣad, Chap. I, 2, 12.

The second Śruti is—

"या प्राणेन सम्भवत्यदिति र्देवतामयी।

गुहां प्रविश्य तिष्ठन्ती या भूतेभिर्व्यजायत॥"

(*The individual soul,* who manifests himself with Life-energy, who is the perceiver, who is endowed with the functions of the senses, and who resides within the recess of the heart, and who was born with the elements).

Kaṭhopaniṣad, Chap. II, 1, 7.

विशेषणाच्च॥१२॥

[An argument, in support of Sūtra 11, is adduced].

विशेषणात् (from attributes), **च** (also).

Explanation—From the attributes used in Śruti in this connection, it also appears that the passage, quoted under Sūtra 11, speaks of the two selfs—one the individual self, and the other the Universal Self; for they have been described, one as the worshipper and the other as the object to be worshipped.

Vide the Śruti:—

"यः सेतुरीजानानामक्षरं ब्रह्मयत्परम्"

(Who is the Immutable Highest Brahma and Who is the Support of sacrificers).

Kaṭhopaniṣad, Chap. I, 3, 2.

अन्तर उपपत्तेः॥१३॥

[The form of worship in another part of Chāndogya (Chap. IV, part 15), taking the spirit within the eye as a symbol for the Universal Soul, is taken up as the subject for discussion].

अन्तरः (the interior; *i.e.,* the Spirit in the interior of the eye), **उपपत्तेः** (from the appropriateness of the attributes applied).

Explanation—The Spirit, in the interior of the eye, indicates Brahma, because, then and then only will the attributes, applied to It, be appropriate.

For reference vide the Śruti:—

"**य एषोऽक्षिणि पुरुषो दृश्यत एष आत्मेति होवाचैतदमृतमभयमेतद्-ब्रह्मेति।**"

('This Spirit, which is perceived within the eye, is self,' said he, 'It is immortal, It is beyond the region of fear, It is Brahma').

Chāndogya, Chap. IV, 15, 1.

स्थानादिव्यपदेशाच्च॥१४॥

[An argument, in support of Sūtra 13, is adduced].

स्थानादि (location etc.; *i.e.,* location, name and form), **व्यपदेशात्** (from the statement), **च** (also).

Explanation—In other Śrutis, location etc., *i.e.,* location, name and form are attributed to Brahma Himself to facilitate meditation. By a reference to those clear statements it is evident that the Spirit, beaming through the pupil of the eye, as stated in Sūtra 13, is also Brahma.

The Statements are:—

(For location).

"**यश्चक्षुषि तिष्ठन्**" (Who residing in the eye)

Bṛhadāraṇyaka, Chap. III, 7, 18.

(For name).

"**तस्योदिति नाम**" (His name is 'Ut'—the Uplifter).

Chāndogya, Chap. I, 6, 7.

(For form).

"**एष.........हिरण्यश्मश्रुः**" (He possesses a beard of light).

Chāndogya, Chap. I, 6, 6.

सुखविशिष्टाभिधानादवेच॥१५॥

[The argument, in support of Sūtra 13, is continued].

सुखविशिष्ट (the Blissful One), **अभिधानात्** (from the denomination), **एव** (to be sure), **च** (and).

Explanation—And (in the same Chāndogya Śruti, in the dialogue between Satyakāma and his disciple, Upakośala) the Spirit, referred to in Sūtra 13, has been denominated as the Blissful One, but as the individual soul cannot be styled so, it shows that the Spirit, referred to, surely indicates Brahma.

Vide the Śruti—

"प्राणो ब्रह्म, कंब्रह्म खंब्रह्म"

(Brahma is Life, He is Bliss, boundless Bliss—boundless as the sky).

Chāndogya, Chap. IV, 10, 5.

[This is said in explanation of the nature of the Spirit within the eye. In this connection, a review of Sūtra 13, Sec. I, Chap. I may be made].

अतएवच तद्ब्रह्म॥१६॥

[The argument, in favour of Sūtra 13, is continued].

अतएव (therefore; as it has been described to be so in the same Śruti), **च** (also), **तद्ब्रह्म** (that is Brahma).

Explanation—It (the Spirit dwelling in the eye), is Brahma, also because It has been described, in the same portion of the Chāndogya Śruti referred to in Sūtra 15, as Boundless Bliss.

Vide the Śruti—

"यद्वाव कं तदेवखं, यदेव खं तदेव कम्।"

(What is Bliss, that is Ākāśa, the *Infinite;* what is Ākāśa, that is Bliss).

Chāndogya, Chap. IV, 10, 5.

श्रुतोपनिषत्कगत्यभिधानाच्च॥१७॥

[The argument, in support of Sūtra 13, is continued].

श्रुत (heard, acquainted with), **उपनिषत्** (the knowledge of Brahma), **गति** (path), **श्रुतोपनिषत्कगति** (the path taken by those who are acquainted with Upanishad, *i.e.,* the knowledge of Brahma), **अभिधानात्** (from description), **च** (also).

Explanation—Also from the description, in Śruti, of the path taken (for the acquisition of the World of Brahma) by those who are acquainted with Upaniṣad (*i.e.,* the knowledge of Brahma), it appears that the worshipper of the Spirit dwelling in the human eye takes the same path (the path of the gods), as is taken by the worshipper of Brahma; so it is clear that the Spirit dwelling within the human eye is Brahma.

For the path taken by the worshipper of Brahma, vide the Śruti—

"अथोत्तरेण तपसा ब्रह्मचर्य्येण श्रद्धया विद्ययात्मानमन्विष्यादित्यमभिजायन्ते, एतद्वै प्राणनामायत्नमेतदमृतमभयमेतत् परायणमेतस्मान्न पुनरावर्त्तन्ते।"

(Those, who seek Ātmā—*self*—by penance, continence, faith and knowledge, attain to Sun by the northern passage (the path of the gods). This is the receptacle of the Prānas (the Prāṇa in its five-fold aspects); this is immortal, beyond the region of fear, the highest resort from which there is no return (to this world).

Praśnopaniṣad, Chap. I, 10.

For the same path taken by the worshipper of the Spirit dwelling in the human eye, vide—

"य एष अक्षिणि पुरुषो दृश्यत एष आत्मेति होवाचैतदमृतमभयमेतद् ब्रह्मेति।.....सर्व्वेषु लोकेषु भाति य एवं वेद।...अथ यदु चैवास्मिञ्छव्यं कुर्व्वन्ति यदि च नार्च्चिषमेवाभिसम्भवन्ति।.... एष देवपथो ब्रह्मपथ, एतेन प्रतिपद्यमाना इमं मानवमावर्त्तं नावर्त्तन्ते।"

('The Spirit which appears to be within the eye is Self',

said he 'It is Immortal, beyond the region of fear; It is Brahma....He shines forth in all the worlds, who worships this *Spirit*....Now, whether obsequies are performed for him or not, he *at once* proceeds by the path of the solar rays...This is the path of the gods, leading to Brahma; by choosing this path there is no return to this mortal world').

Chāndogya, Chap. IV, 15, 1 and 4-6.

अनवस्थितेरसम्भवाच्च नेतरः॥१८॥

[The argument, in support of Sūtra 13, is continued].

अनवस्थितेः (for non-existence; as it is not felt to exist), **असम्भवात** (for impossibility; as it is impossible), **च** (also), **न** (not), **इतरः** (**ब्रह्मेतरः**; other than Brahma, *i.e.,* Jīva).

Explanation—As the individual soul is not felt to exist always in one organ of the body, such as the eye, and as it is impossible for the same to possess the attributes, such as immortality etc., applied to the Spirit within the eye, Sūtra 13 does not suggest Jīva, the individual soul; nor does it mean the reflected image, since its appearance in the eye is not constant, but variable; therefore it indicates none other than Brahma.

अन्तर्याम्यधिदैवादिलोकादिषु तद्धर्म्मव्यपदेशात्॥१९॥

[A passage, from the Bṛhadāraṇyaka Śruti, is now taken up for discussion].

अन्तर्यामी (the regulator within), **अधिदैवादिलोकादिषु** (in the spheres of the gods etc).; **तत्** (**तस्य**, His, of Brahma), **धर्म्म** (attributes); **व्यपदेशात्** (from the statements); **तद्धर्म्मव्यपदेशात्** (from the attributes assigned to Him).

Explanation—He, Who is described (in the Bṛhadāraṇyaka Upaniṣad) as regulating, from within the gods, the Jīvas and the elements, is no other than Brahma, as can be understood from the attributes assigned to Him.

Vide the Śruti:—

"यः पृथिव्यां तिष्ठन् पृथिव्याअन्तरो, यं पृथिवी न वेद, यस्य पृथिवी शरीरं यः पृथिवीमन्तरो यमयत्येषत आत्मान्तर्याम्यमृतः।"

(Who, residing in the earth, is yet aloof from it; Whom the earth does not know, Whose body is the earth; Who being within, guides the earth; He is thy *asked for* Everlasting Ātmā, the Universal Soul, the Controlling Spirit within).

Bṛhadāraṇyaka Chap. III, 7, 3.

नच स्मार्त्तमतद्धर्म्माभिलापात्॥२०॥

[An argument, in support of Sūtra 19, is adduced].

न (neither), च (also), स्मार्त्तम् (Pradhāna which is spoken of in the Smṛti, *i.e.,* in Sāṅkhya) अतद्धर्म्म (attributes not applicable to the Pradhāna; *i.e.,* the attributes of an intelligent being), अभिलापात् (because of the statement).

Expanation:—The expression (the Controlling Spirit within), referred to in Sūtra 19, does not indicate Pradhāna; because the Controlling Spirit is stated to possess attributes (such as hearing, seeing etc). inapplicable to blind matter.

Vide the Śruti—

"अन्तर्याम्यमृतोऽदृष्टो द्रष्टाऽश्रुतः श्रोता।"

(The Indwelling Controlling Spirit is immortal, the Unseen Seer, the Unheard Hearer).

Bṛhadāraṇyaka, Chap. III, 7, 23.

शारीरश्चोभयेऽपि हि भेदेनैनमधीयते॥२१॥

[The argument, in support of Sūtra 19, is continued].

[न (nor does)], शारीरः (the embodied soul), च (so also, *i.e.*, as in the case of Sūtra 20), उभये (both, referring to the Kāṇva and the Mādhyandina schools), अपि (also), हि (as because), भेदेन (by way of difference), एनम् (him, the embodied soul), अधीयते (read, indicate).

Explanation—Nor does the expression 'अन्तर्यामी' (the Controlling Spirit within) in Sūtra 19, mean the embodied soul, because both the Kāṇva and the Mādhyandina schools of Śruti read It as different from the embodied soul.

[The Kāṇvas use the expression 'य विज्ञाने तिष्ठन्' (He Who resides in the intellect), while the Mādhyandinas read it as 'य आत्मनि तिष्ठन्' (He Who resides in the soul)].

अदृश्यत्वादिगुणको धर्म्मोक्तेः॥२२॥

[Some expressions, from the Muṇḍaka Śruti, are now taken up as the subject for discussion].

अदृश्यत्वादि (invisibility and the like), गुणकः (possessing the properties), धर्म्म (characteristics), उक्तेः (from the utterance; from the statement); धर्म्मोक्तेः (because of the statement of attributes).

Explanation—The One, possessing the properties of invisibility and the like (as described in the Muṇḍaka-Upaniṣad), is Brahma; because this One is stated to possess the characteristics of Brahma.

For the properties of invisibility and the like, vide the Śruti—

"यत्तदद्रेश्यमग्राह्यमगोत्रमवर्णम्...."

(That which is invisible, *i.e.,* imperceptible by the senses, incomprehensible, without origin, beyond caste or class).

Muṇḍakopaniṣad, Chap. I. 1, 6.

For the characteristics of Brahma, vide:—

"यः सर्व्वज्ञः सर्व्ववित्..."

(Who is all-knowing, all-perceiving..."

Muṇḍakopaniṣad, Chap. I, 1, 9).

विशेषणभेदव्यपदेशाभ्यां च नेतरौ॥२३॥

[An argument, in support of Sūtra 22, is adduced].

विशेषणभेदव्यपदेशाभ्यां (as there are expressions of epithets and distinctions) च (also), न (not) इतरौ (the other two; matter and the individual soul).

Explanation—As the Śruti uses epithets and distinctions by which Brahma is differentiated from Jīva on one hand and from matter on the other, it is understood that the One (referred to in Sūtra 22) can be neither of them (*i.e.,* Jīva and matter).

To show clearly that the One (referred to in Sūtra 22) is not the individual soul, Śruti distinguishes the one by special adjuncts (such as 'Omnipresent etc.'). And to show, that the One is not matter, Śruti makes a difference between the One and matter by using the expression—

"अक्षरात् परतः परः"

(Puruṣa, the Spirit is higher than the highest immutable matter). Muṇḍakopaniṣad, Chap. II, 1, 2.

रूपोपन्यासाच्च॥२४॥

[The argument, in support of Sūtra 22, is continued].

रूप (form)] उपन्यासात् (from the description)] च (also).

Explanation—From the description of the forms (given in the Muṇḍaka Śruti) of the Invisible Spirit (referred to in Sūtra 22)] it is clear that the Spirit is no other than Brahma, for such forms are possible in Him only.

For the description of the forms referred to, vide the Śruti:—

"अग्निर्मूर्द्धा चक्षुषी चन्द्रसूर्य्यौ दिशः श्रौत्र वाग्विवृताश्च वेदाः।
वायुः प्राणो हृदयं विश्वमस्य पद्भ्यां पृथिवी ह्येष सर्व्वभूतान्तरात्मा॥"

(Whose head is the bright sky, Whose eyes are the sun and the moon, Whose ears are the quarters of the horizon, Whose utterances are the Vedas, Whose breath is the air, Whose heart is the universe, and from Whose feet the earth has sprung; He is the Indwelling Spirit of all the living beings.

Muṇḍaka, Chap. II, 1, 4.

वैश्वानरः साधारणशब्दविशेषात्॥२५॥

[This Sūtra undertakes to prove that the word 'Vaiśvānara', used in Śruti for worship, indicates Brahma].

वैश्वानरः (the digestive heat in the stomach, as well as Brahma, the Universal Manhood, Universal Ego—the sum total of all the created beings), **साधारणशब्द** (common word), **विशेषात्** (from the distinctive attributes).

Explanation—It has been prescribed in Śruti to worship 'Vaiśvānara'- Though it is a common name for fire and the Universal Ego, *i.e.,* Brahma, yet here in Śruti it is specially used to mean the latter, specified, as it is, by the distinctive attributes, such as—'Whose head is the bright sky, etc.'

Vide the Śruti:—

"तस्य ह वा एतस्यात्मनो वैश्वानरस्य मूर्द्धैव सुतेजाः ..."

(Of that Vaiśvānara Soul the head is the shining firmament).

Chāndogya, Chap. V, 18, 2.

स्मर्य्यमाणमनुमानं स्यादिति॥२६॥

[An argument, in support of Sūtra 25, is adduced].

स्मर्य्यमाणम् (mention made in Smṛti), **अनुमानं** (indication), **स्यात्** (is), **इति** (because).

Explanation—Vaiśvānara is Brahma, *i.e. qualified Brahma;* because mention made in Smṛti of similar attributes to Brahma, is an indication to such a conclusion.

[This is, of course, a circumstantial evidence only].

For the reference vide the Smṛti—

"यस्याग्निरास्यं द्यौ र्मूर्द्धा खंनाभिश्चरणौ क्षितिः।
सूर्य्यश्चक्षुर्दिशः श्रोत्रं तस्मै लोकात्मने नमः॥"

(I bow to Him, the Soul of the worlds, of Whom fire is the

mouth, heaven the head, the sky the navel, the earth the feet, the sun the eye, and the quarters of the horizon are the ear).

Also vide—

"अहं वैश्वानरो भूत्वा प्राणिनां देहमाश्रितः।
प्राणापानसमायुक्तः पचाम्यन्नं चतुर्विधम्॥"

(I, residing within the body of the animate being in the shape of the digestive heat and being united with inhaled and exhaled airs, digest four kinds of food).

Bhagavad-Gītā, Chap. XV, 14.

शब्दादिभ्योऽन्तःप्रतिष्ठानान्नेति चेन्न तथा दृष्ट्युपदेशादसम्भवात् पुरुषमभिधीयते॥२७॥

[The argument, in support of Sūtra 25, is continued].

शब्दादिभ्यः (from the word etc.; from the word 'Vaiśvānara' and the other expressions attending it, which ordinarily mean the gastric heat) **अन्तःप्रतिष्ठानात्** (from existence within; from the description of its being situated within the stomatch) **न** (not, *i.e.*, not Brahma)] **इति** (this)] **चेत्** (if); **न** (no, *i.e.*, the objection cannot stand)] **तथा** (as that, *i.e.*, as Brahma)] **दृष्टि** (regard)] **उपदेशात्** (from instruction; as there is instruction in Śruti)] **असम्भवात्** (for impossibility; as it is impossible)] **पुरुषम्** (Spirit)] **अभिधीयते** (is designated).

[This Sūtra consists of an objection and its refutation. The objection-portion is:—**शब्दादिभ्योऽन्तःप्रतिष्ठानान्नेति चेत्**; and the refutation-portion is:—**न तथा दृष्ट्युपदेशादसम्भवात् पुरुषमभिधीयते।**]

Explanation—If one objects by saying, that as there is the word 'Vaiśvānara' with other expressions attached to it to indicate the ordinary fire, and as it is stated in Śruti to be situated within the body, it does not mean Brahma, but the gastric heat; the reply would be:—no, the objection cannot stand, because there is instruction in Śruti to regard Vaiśvānara as Brahma, and because It is termed in Śruti as Puruṣa (Spirit)] which term is inapplicable to the gastric heat.

The purport is as follows—

It may be argued, that as the term 'Vaiśvānara' ordinarily means the gastric heat or the common fire, and as it is stated in Śruti to exist within the body, it does not mean Brahma, but the animal heat. This argument cannot stand, first because Śruti teaches us to regard 'Vaiśvānara' in the light of Brahma while engaged in meditation, secondly because 'Vaiśvānara' is termed in Śruti as Spirit; and thirdly because both these conditions are inapplicable to the gastric heat or ordinary fire.

अतएव न देवता भूतं च॥२८॥

[The argument, in support of Sūtra 25, is continued].

अतएव (therefore; for the reasons as stated in Sūtra 27), **न** (not), **देवता** (a deity, the deity named Fire), **भूतं** (an element, the element fire), **च** (or).

Explanation—For the reasons stated in Sūtra 27, the term 'Vaiśvānara, as referred to in Sūtra 25, means neither the deity presiding over the fire, nor the element, fire.

साक्षादप्यविरोधं जैमिनिः॥२९॥

[The argument, in support of Sūtra 25, is continued].

साक्षात् (directly, *i.e.,* from the derivative meaning of the word; from the original significance of the word 'Vaiśvānara', literally meaning the Universal Ego—the Universe and at the same time man—the sum total of all the 'selfs' of the universe—the Universal Self), **अपि** (also), **अविरोधं** (no incongruity), **जैमिनिः** (Jaimini, the author of the Pūrva-Mīmāṁsā philosophy).

Explanation—Jaimini says, that taking the direct meaning (the literal signification of the word 'Vaiśvānara', originally meaning the Universal Self of all 'Selfs'), there is no incongruity in indicating Brahma by the word 'Vaiśvānara'.

अभिव्यक्तेरित्याश्मरथ्यः॥३०॥

[The argument, in support of Sūtra 25 is continued].

अभिव्यक्तेः (because of manifestation; as He manifests Himself), **इति** (this), **आश्मरथ्यः** (the sage Āśmarathya).

Explanation—The sage Āśmarathya says, that for the benefit of the worshipper the Infinite Spirit—the Universal Ego—manifests Himself in infinite individuals, being localised in limited places, such as the body or the heart of the human being. So there is no incongruity in using the word 'Vaiśvānara' (even when standing for the gastric heat) to signify Brahma.

अनुस्मृतेर्वादरिः॥३१॥

[The argument, in support of Sūtra 25, is continued].

अनुस्मृतेः (**अनुस्मृत्यर्थम्, ध्यानार्थम्;** for the sake of meditation), **वादरिः** (the sage, Bādari).

Explanation—The sage Bādari says, that for the sake of divine meditation, the Infinite Spirit is conceived sometimes as a small body, such as occupying the space of half a cubit (**प्रादेशमात्रम्**) etc., and sometimes as a person possessing head, foot and body and other limbs and organs. So Vaiśvānara may well stand for Brahma.

सम्पत्तेरिति जैमिनिस्तथाहि दर्शयति॥३२॥

[The argument, in support of Sūtra 25, is continued].

सम्पत्तेः (for union with the object of meditation in order to realise union with the Infinite Soul), **इति** (this), **जैमिनिः** (Jaimini, the sage who is the author of Pūrva Mīmāṁsā), **तथाहि** (similarly, in the same method), **दर्शयति** (Śruti shows; Śruti prescribes).

Explanation—The sage Jaimini says, that in order to realise union with the Infinite Soul, different parts of the meditator's own body are conceived as those of the Infinite Soul, and Śruti also prescribes the same method of divine meditation.

Vide the Śruti:—

"मूर्द्धानमुपदिशन्नुवाच एष वा अतिष्ठा वैश्वानर इति।"

(*The teacher* said pointing to his own head 'This is the highest Vaiśvānara, *i.e., the head of the Vaiśvānara*').

Vājasaneyi Brāhmaṇa.

आमनन्ति चैनमस्मिन्॥३३॥

[The argument, in support of Sūtra 25, is concluded].

आमनन्ति(वदन्ति, speak, teach **),** **च** (also), **एनम्** (this—Vaiśvānara in the light of Brahma), **अस्मिन्** (in this body).

Explanation—Śrutis also teach that this Vaiśvānara, referred to in Sūtra 25, is to be worshipped in the light of Brahma, in this body, (*i..e.,* the worshipper's own body).

From this also it appears that the word 'Vaiśvānara' is used in Śruti to signify Brahma.

Vide the Śruti;—

"स यो हैतमग्निं वैश्वानरं पुरुषविधं पुरुषे.....अन्तःप्रतिष्ठितं वेद"

(He who worships this Vaiśvānara Fire personified and located within the body *of the worshipper).*

SECTION—III

Some other expressions, prescribed for divine meditation in different Śrutis, not already discussed in section II, are now taken up for discussion to prove that they all indicate the same Infinite Spirit, Brahma.

Sūtras 1-7 show that the Spirit, Who is the abiding place of the universe, as described in the Muṇḍaka Śruti, is Brahma.

Sūtras 8 and 9 state that 'Bhūmā' (the Vast One), of the Chāndogya Śruti, is Brahma.

Sūtras 10-12 say that 'Akṣara' (the Imperishable One), of the Bṛhadāraṇyaka Śruti, is Brahma.

Sūtra 13 says that the 'Indwelling' Spirit, of the Praśnopaniṣad, is Brahma.

Sūtras 14-23 show that 'Daharākāśa. (the small cell *within the heart*), of the Chāndogya Śruti, is Brahma.

Sūtras 24 and 40-41 show that the Spirit, of the size of the thumb ('अंगुष्ठमात्र पुरुष'), of the Kaṭha Śruti, signifies Brahma.

Sūtras 25-28 and 31-39 raise a side issue and decide that deities and all classes of men excepting the Sūtras are equally entitled to practise Brahma-Vidyā (the meditation on Brahma), as prescribed in the Vedas. By the word 'Sūtra' is meant the class of men in whom no desire for the knowledge of Brahma has arisen (vide notes at the end of Sūtra 39).

Sūtras 29 and 30 establish the conclusion that the Vedas are eternal.

Sūtra 42 says that 'Ākāśā', in the Chāndogya Śruti, is no other than Brahma.

Sūtras 43 and 44 state that the Being, spoken of in the Bṛhadāraṇyakopaniṣad, Chap. IV, 3, is Brahma, the Universal Soul, as different from, and superior to, the individual soul, who, unlike the Supreme Being, passes through the stages of sound sleep and death; and this conclusion is corroborated by the expressions, **'सर्व्वस्याधिपतिः'** (the Lord of all) and **'सर्व्वस्येशानः'** (the Ruler of all), occurring further on in the 4th Brāhmaṇa of the same chapter and referring to the Universal Soul.

द्युभ्वाद्यायतनं स्वशब्दात्॥१॥

[An expression, from the Muṇḍaka Śruti, is taken up for discussion].

द्यु (heaven), **भू** (earth), **आदि** (et cetera; and such other worlds), **आयतनं (आश्रयः,** stay; support; the abiding palce), **स्व** (own), **शब्दात्** (from the word).

Explanation—The Spirit,Which is described in the Muṇḍaka Śruti (quoted below) to be the abiding place of heaven, earth and such other worlds, is Brahma; as can be understood from a word which is Brahma's own name proper, *i.e.,*.. the word 'Ātmā' (Self) occurring in the same passage.

For reference vide the Śruti—

यस्मिन् द्यौः पृथिवी चान्तरिक्षमोतं मनः सह प्राणैश्च सर्व्वैः।
तमेवैकं विजानथात्मानमन्या वाचो विमुञ्चथामृतस्यैष सेतुः॥

(He, in Whom heaven, earth, sky and mind together with all the senses are woven—realise that Absolute Ātmā alone; away with other utterances; this *Absolute Ātmā* is the causeway for deliverance from death).

Muṇḍakopaniṣad, Chap. II, 2, 5.

मुक्तोपसृप्य-व्यपदेशात्॥२॥

[An argument in support of Sūtra 1 is adduced].

मुक्त (the emancipated), उपसृप्य (प्राप्य; the attainable goal), व्यपदेशात् (*He* being stated).

Explanation—The abode, referred to in Sūtra 1, being stated (in the said Muṇḍaka-Upaniṣad) as the attainable goal of the Emancipated souls, must mean Brahma.

For the expression vide the Śruti:—

"यदा पश्यः पश्यते रुक्मवर्णं कर्त्तारमशिं पुरुषं ब्रह्मयोनिम्।
तदा विद्वान् पुण्यपापे विधूय निरञ्जनः परमं साम्यमुपैति॥"

(When the seer sees the Glorious Lord, the maker and the cause of the universe, the Great God, then the Enlightened Seer has his virtues and vices washed away and becoming purified attains the excellent state of equilibrium, *i.e., the highest tranquility)*.

(The Glorious Lord is the same as the Abode, referred to in Sūtra 1).

Muṇḍaka, Chap. III, 1, 3.

नानुमानमतच्छब्दात्॥३॥

[The argument, in support of Sūtra 1, is continued].

न (not), अनुमानम् (that which is inferred, *i.e.,* the matter of the Sāṅkhya philosophy), अतच्छब्दात् (for want of any expression indicative of matter).

Explanation—The Abiding place, referred to in Sūtra 1, does not indicate matter; for there is no such expression, in the said Muṇḍaka Śruti, as can be construed to indicate matter.

प्राणभृच्च॥४॥

[The argument in support of Sūtra 1 is continued].

प्राणभृत् (the animate being; the living being, the individual soul), च (also), [न—not to be understood].

Explanation—The abiding place, referred to in Sūtra 1, is not also to be taken mean the individual soul, (though possessed of selfhood and intelligence unlike the matter of Sāṅkhya); for there is no word in the said Muṇḍaka Śruti to that effect.

भेदव्यपदेशाच्च॥५॥

[The argument, in support of Sūtra 4 is continued].

भेद (difference), **व्यपदेशात्** (from expressions), **च** (moreover).

Explanation—Moreover, the animate being, *i.e.,* the individual soul, cannot be the Abode (referred to in Sūtra 1); for the same (Muṇḍaka) Śruti draws a clear distinction between the former and the said abode.

For, the distinction referred to, vide the verse of the Śruti, quoted and translated under Sūtra 1, where the individual soul is the agent to know, and the abode, *i.e.,* the Universal Soul, is the objecct to be known.

प्रकरणात्॥६॥

[The argument, in support of Sūtra 1, is continued].

प्रकरणात् (from the context).

Explanation—From the context it is known, that the abode, referred to in Sūtra 1, indicates Brahma, and not the individual soul.

स्थित्यदनाभ्याञ्च॥७॥

[The argument in support of Sūtra 1, is concluded].

स्थिति (existence), **अदनम्** (eating, enjoying, undergoing the consequences of actions), **च** (also); **स्थित्यदनाभ्याञ्च** (also from expressions denoting existence and enjoyment *as stated in the Muṇḍaka Śruti*).

Explanation—The Muṇḍaka Śruti states that the individual soul, existing in the body, enjoys the consequences of the previous actions, while the Universal Soul co-exists with the former merely as a witness without enjoying any consequences, as He is bound by no previous actions. From these two expressions—co-existence and enjoyment—the difference between Jīva (the individual soul) and Brahma (the Universal Soul), Who is again identical with the 'Abode', is clear; and therefore it is also evident, that the 'Abode', referred to in Sūtra 1, is not the individual soul, but the Universal Soul, Brahma.

For the statement in the Muṇḍaka Śruti vide—

"द्वा सुपर्णा सयुजा सखाया समानं वृक्षं परिषस्वजाते।
तयोरन्यः पिप्पलं स्वाद्वत्त्यनश्नन्नन्योऽभिचाकशीति॥"

(Two birds—*the individual soul and the Universal Soul*—inseparable friends, reside on the same tree, *i.e., the body;* one of them, *the individual soul,* enjoys the tasteful fruit, *i.e., the consequence of his previous actions;* and the other, *the Universal Soul,* without enjoying anything, looks on, *i.e., remains as witness).*

Muṇḍaka, Chap. III, 1, 1.

भूमा सम्प्रसादादध्युपदेशात्॥८॥

[An expression, from the Chāndogya Śruti, is taken up for discussion].

भूमा (the Vast—the Infinite—the Perfect One); सम्प्रसादः (the undisturbed peace or bliss; *hence* the state of sound sleep *when that bliss is enjoyed; here it means the Vital principle which alone remains awake during that state),* अधि (above, beyond); सम्प्रसादादधि (beyond the bliss enjoyed in sound sleep; *hence* being above Prāṇa—*the Vital principle),* उपदेशात् (from the instruction; from the description; as it is described).

Explanation—Bhūmā (the Vast One) signifies Brahma, because it is described in Śruti to be above Prāṇa, which is here represented by the bliss enjoyed during sound sleep.

Bhūmā is to be comprehended as the Highest Bliss, the highest state of self (the 4th state) according to the Chāndogya Śruti, beyond Prāṇa which is here represented by the undisturbed peace enjoyed during the state of sound sleep (the third state); because in this state, the functions of the mind and the senses all remain suspended, Prāṇa alone being awake, which is here termed as 'Samprasāda'. This third state, the state of sound sleep though it confers unperturbed peace, is incapable of imparting the highest permanent bliss, which is the fourth state.[2]

That Bhūmā is, according to Śruti, above and beyond Prāṇa may be shown by the way in which Bhūmā is described in the Chāndogyopaniṣad. The sage Sanatkumāra, asked by Nārada to instruct him in the knowledge of Brahma, taught him the worship of Brahma, beginning with a very crude form and through successive stages ending at last with the finest, *i.e.,* the worship of Bhūmā (the Infinite). Immediately before the teaching of this highest form, he makes mention of the worship of Brahma in the form of Prāṇa. This shows that Bhūmā is meant to signify the highest state of self—the next above Prāṇa. Moreover, there are passages in the same chapter to show directly, that Bhūmā is superior to Prāṇa (vide the Chāndogya Śruti, Chapter VII, parts 23-26).

धर्म्मोपपत्तेश्च॥९॥

[An argument, in support of Sūtra 8, is adduced].

धर्म्म (nature), **उपपत्तेः** (from applicability, as they apply to), **च** (also).

Explanation—The Vast One mentioned in Sūtra 8, signifies none other than Brahma, also becuase the character attributed to it applies to Brahma only.

For the character attributed, vide:—

"यो वै भूमा तत् सुखं नाल्पे सुखमस्ति, भूमैव सुखम्।"

(What is Bhūmā, *the Infinite,* is Bliss; there is no satisfaction in what is limited. The Infinite only is Bliss).

Chāndogya, Chap. VII, 23, 1.

Also vide:—

"यो वै भूमा तदमृतम्।"

(What is infinite is Imperishable).

Chāndogya, Chap. VII, 24, 1.

In tne same manner Śrutis can be quoted to show other attributes, namely, the True, the Omnipresent, Self of everything (as assigned to the Vast One), that can be applicable only to Brahma. So Bhūmā (the Perfect One) is none else but Brahma.

अक्षरमम्वरान्तधृतेः॥१०॥

[An expression, from the Bṛhadāraṇyaka Śruti, is taken up for discussion].

अक्षरम् (the Imperishable One), अम्बर (Ākāśa), अन्त (up to), धृतेः (because of holding, because of sustaining).

Explanation—The Imperishable One (referred to in the Bṛhadāraṇyaka Śruti) indicates Brahma, because of His supporting everything even including Ākāśā (which, in Śruti, is spoken of as the first thing created).

Vide the Śruti:—

"'कस्मिन्नु खल्वाकाश ओतश्च प्रोतश्चेति।'

'सहोवाचैतद्वै तदक्षरं गार्गि ब्राह्मणा अभिवदन्ति॥"

('In and through whom does Ākāśā abide?'—*enquired Gargi*. He, *Yājñavalkya,* replied 'O Gārgi! Brāhmaṇas, *i.e., persons knowing Brahma*, call Him the Imperishable One, Who is the warp and woof of Ākāśā itself).

Bṛhadāraṇyaka, Chap. III, 8, 7-8.

साच प्रशासनात्॥११॥

[An argument, in support of Sūtra 10, is adduced].

सा (she; धृतिः, referred to in Sūtra 10, *i.e.,* that supporting of Ākāśā is by Brahma) **च** (also), **प्रशासनात्** (from the effective control).

Explanation— The Imperishable One sustaining Ākāśā, referred to in Sūtra 10, indicates Brahma, as it can also be understood from the effective control exercised by Him (as stated in the Bṛhadāraṇyaka Śruti).

For the effective control, vide—

"एतस्य वा अक्षरस्य प्रशासने गार्गि सूर्य्याचन्द्रमसौ विधृतौ तिष्ठतः।"

(Through the effective control of the Imperishable One, O Gāgri, the sun and the moon are held suspended *in mid air)*.

Bṛhadāraṇyaka, Chap. III, 8, 9.

अन्यभाव-व्यावृत्तेश्च॥१२॥

[The argument, in support of Sūtra 10, is concluded].

अन्यभाव (any other interpretation than Brahma, such as the matter of Sāṅkhya and the individual soul), **व्यावृत्तेः** (because of preclusion), **च** (also).

Explanation—The Imperishable One, referred to in Sūtra 10, indicates Brahma; any other interpretation, such as Pradhāna or Jīva, being also precluded; as it appears from subsequent expressions which are applicable neither to Pradhāna nor to Jīva.

For the subsequent expressions, referred to above, vide the Śruti—

"तद्वा एतदक्षरं गार्ग्यदृष्टं द्रष्टृश्रुतं श्रोत्रमतं मन्त्रविज्ञातं विज्ञातृ, नान्यदतोऽस्ति द्रष्टृ नान्यदतोऽस्ति श्रोतृ नान्यदतोऽस्ति मन्तृ नान्यदतोऽस्ति विज्ञात्रेतस्मिन्नु खल्वक्षरे गार्ग्याकाश ओतश्च प्रोतश्चेति।"

(The Imperishable One, O Gārgi, remains unseen though seeing, unheard though hearing, unconceived though conceiving, unknown though knowing; than This, there is none other, capable of seeing, hearing, conceiving and knowing; in and through this Imperishable One, to be sure, O Gārgi, Ākāśā remains woven).

Bṛhadāraṇyaka, Chap. III, 8, 11.

ईक्षतिकर्म्मव्यपदेशात् सः॥१३॥

[An expression from the Praśnopaniṣad is taken up for discussion].

ईक्षति (seeing, realising), **कर्म्म** (object), **व्यपदेशात्** (from the statement), **स** (He).

[Here 'He' stands for the Being spoken of as the object of meditation in the Śruti **"यः पुनरेतं त्रिमात्रेणैवोमित्येतेनैवाक्षरेण परं पुरुषमभिध्यायीत...."** (who, again meditates upon the Supreme Being with the help of the entire word 'Om' consisting of three syllables)].

Explanation—This 'He' is Brahma, because He is stated to be the object of the action 'seeing' (realisation). The object of meditation may be imaginary, but the object of seeing must be real. Therefore, as the Being, referred to in the above quoted Śruti, has been stated to be the object of 'seeing', He is no other than Brahma.

Vide the Śruti:—

"यः पुनरेतं त्रिमात्रेणैवोमित्येतेनैवाक्षरेण परं पुरुषमभिध्यायीत.....स एतस्माज्जीवघनात् परात्परं पुरिशयं पुरुषम् ईक्षते।"

[He, who, on the other hand, meditates upon the Supreme Being with the help of the entire word 'Om' consisting of three syllables (अ, उ, म्), sees—*realises*—the Supreme Being lying latent in the body, and higher far than the concrete individual soul).

Praśnopaniṣad, Chap, V, 5.

दहर उत्तरेभ्यः॥१४॥

[Another expression from the Chāndogya Śruti is taken up for discussion].

दहरः (small; here it stands for **'दहराकाशः'**, the small cell—the heart), **उत्तरेभ्यः** (from subsequent expressions).

Explanation—The small cell within, referred to in the Chāndogya Śruti, signifies Brahma, as can be understood from subsequent statement in the same Śruti.

For the small cell, referred to, vide:—

"यदिदमस्मिन् ब्रह्मपुरे दहरं पुण्डरीकं वेश्म दहरोऽस्मिन्नन्तराकाशस्तस्मिन् यदन्तस्तदन्वेष्टव्यं तद्वाव विजिज्ञासितव्यमिति।"

(In this Brahmapura (the city of Brahma—the human body) there is a small lotus-house, the heart; and that, which lies filling the space of its narrow cell, must be sought for and inquired into).

Chāndogya, Chap. VIII, 1, 1.

For the subsequent statements vide:—

"यावान् वा अयमाकाशस्तावानेषोऽन्तर्हृदय आकाश, उभे अस्मिन् द्यावापृथिवी अन्तरेव समाहिते।"

"एष आत्मापहतपाप्मा विजरो विमृत्युर्विशोको विजिघत्सोऽपिपासः सत्यकामः सत्यसंकल्पः।"

(This internal Ākāśā—*the Akāśa within the heart*—is as much extensive as this Ākāśā *without*, and both heaven and earth find room for themselves within It.

This Ākāśā is soul, free from all imperfections, without decay, death, sorrow, hunger and thirst, and with desires and purposes that ever come true).

Chāndogya, Chap. VIII, 1, 3, 5.

गतिशब्दाभ्यां तथाहि दृष्टं लिङ्गञ्च॥१५॥

[An argument, in support of Sūtra 14 is adduced].

गति (going; goal), **शब्द** (word); **गतिशब्दाभ्यां** (from the *revealed* word **'ब्रह्मलोक'** which means **ब्रह्म एव लोकः**, and from its being the goal), तथा (तद्वत्, in that way), हि (यतः, as, because), दृष्टं (seen; found), लिङ्गं (distinctive mark), च (also).

Explanation—The small cell, referred to in Sūtra, 14 stands for Brahma, because it is described as the goal of all individual souls (as the resting place where all individual souls daily resort during sound sleep), and also because it is termed 'Brahma-Loka' (Brahma-world), meaning Brahma Who is the Loka (the abiding place, the goal or destined place to be attained by individual souls). That the said goal of the individual souls is Brahma, and that the term 'Brahma-Loka' is a distinctive mark of Him, are corroborated by clearer statements in other Śrutis.

Vide the Śruti—

"इमाः सर्व्वाः प्रजा अहरहर्गच्छन्त्येतं ब्रह्मलोकं नावन्दन्त्यनृतेन हि प्रत्यूढ़ाः।"

(All these creatures, everyday going into this Brahma-Loka—the Universal Soul—*during sound sleep*, do not know Him, being deluded by deceptive appearances).

Chāndogya, Chap. VIII, 3, 2.

For a similar statement found elsewhere in the scripture, vide the Śruti quoted under Sūtra 10, section I, Chap. I.

Again, here is quoted a passage to show the use of the word 'Brahma-Loka, as the distinctive mark of Brahma:—

"एष एव परमआनन्द एष ब्रह्मलोकः"

(This is the Highest Bliss—this is the Brahma-Loka—the state of Brahma).

Bṛhadāraṇyaka, Chap. IV, 3, 33.

Here Brahma-Loka is said to be the highest Bliss (Bliss Infinte), which is a distinctive term indicating Brahma.

धृतेश्च महिम्नोऽस्यास्मिन्नुपलब्धेः॥१६॥

[The argument, in favour of Sūtra 14, is continued].

धृतेः (because of holding, or supporting), च (also), महिम्नः (from the glory or greatness), अस्य (Its, *i.e.*, of this Daharākāśa), अस्मिन् (in this, *i.e.*, in Brahma), उपलब्धेः (as it can be understood).

Explanation—Daharākāśa, referred to in Sūtra 14, indicates Brahma, as the glory of supporting all the worlds, can be reasonably true only in respect of Brahma.

For the reference vide the Śruti—

"स सेतुर्विधृतिरेषां लोकानामसम्भेदाय"

(He is the causeway and support of these worlds in order to avert chaotic disorder).

Chāndogya, Chap. VIII, 4, 1.

"एतस्य वाऽक्षरस्य प्रशासने गार्गि सूर्य्याचन्द्रमसौ विधृता तिष्ठतः।"

(For translation and reference, see under Sūtra 11 of this section).

प्रसिद्धेश्च॥१७॥

[The argument in support of Sūtra 14, is continued].

प्रसिद्धेः (as it is a well-known fact) च (also).

Explanation—As it is a well-known fact in Śruti, that Brahma is indicated by the term Ākāśā, so 'Daharākāśa' also stands for Brahma.

For reference vide the quotation and translation under Sūtra 23, section I, Chapter I.

इतरपरामर्शात् स इति चेन्नासम्भवात्॥१८॥

[The argument, in support of Sūtra 14, is continued].

इतर (ब्रह्मेतर, other than Brahma, *i.e.*, Jīva, the individual soul), परामर्शात् (owing to conjunction), सः (he, *i.e.*, the individual soul), इति (this), चेत् (if), न (no, not so), असम्भवात् (because of impossibility).

[This Sūtra consists of an objection and its reply. The objection-portion is:—इतरपरामर्शात् स इति चेत्; and the reply-portion is:—न, असम्भवात्।]

Explanation—It may be argued, that the 'Dahara' of Brahmapura is understood to be in conjunction with 'Samprasāda', the individual soul (vide the Śruti quoted below), and so 'Dahara' may stand for the individual soul, and not for the Universal Soul. The reply is: It cannot be so, because the attributes of 'Dahara', stated in Chāndogya, Chap. VIII, 1, 3 and 5 (quoted under Sūtra 14 last), cannot be the characteristics of the individual soul.

For reference, vide:—

"ऐष सम्प्रसादोऽस्माच्छरीरात् समुत्थाय परं ज्योतिरूपसम्पद्य स्वेन रूपेणाभिनिष्पद्यत एष आत्मेति।"

(This blissful individual soul *in the tranquil state of sleep,* leaves this gross body and entering into the Transcendent Light, recovers his own proper form; and this is the Supreme Soul).

Chāndogya, Chap. VIII, 3, 4.

An objection may be raised, that on account of the term 'Samprasāda', which is used in the Śruti to denote the individual soul in the state of sound sleep, the term 'Daharākāśa', which is the subject matter of the chapter, also indicates rather the individual soul than the Universal Soul; but to refute this objection we say that this suggestion is unacceptable, as the attributes applied to 'Daharākāśa' are incongruous with the character of jīva.

For the attributes vide the third quotation and its translation under Sūtra 14 of this section.

उत्तराच्चेदाविर्भूतस्वरूपस्तु॥१९॥

[The argument, in support of Sūtra 14, is continued].

उत्तरात् (from the subsequent part *of the Śruti*), **चेत** (if), **आविर्भूत** (manifest, revealed), **स्वरूपः** (the true nature), **तु** (but).

[The Sūtra consists of two parts, namely an objection and

its reply. The objection-portion is:—उत्तरात् चेत्; and the reply-portion is:—आविर्भूतस्वरूपस्तु।]

Explanation—If it be argued, that 'Daharākāśa' indicates the individual soul and not Brahma, because of an almost similar passage in the subsequent part of the Śruti (Chāndogya, Chap. VIII, 7 ff)., where the same attributes, as referred to in the preceding Sūtra 18 (namely, to be above sin, without infirmity, without death, etc)., have been asigned to the individual soul; then the reply is, that there the individual soul has been described as revealed in his true character, which is also the character of Brahma. So there is no impropriety there in the description; and there is nothing to show that the attributes belong to the individual soul while in the state of bondage, when he is under the influence of passion and vices, and subject to births and deaths and infirmities of age; and the individual soul cannot, therefore, be indicated by the expression 'Dahara'.

अन्यार्थश्च परामर्शः॥२०॥

[The argument, in support of Sūtra 14, is continued].

अन्यार्थः (for another purpose), च (and), परामर्शः (reference).

Explanation—And the reference to Jīva (see ante Sūtra 18) is for another purpose, namely, to show his transfigured stated after emancipation, which is his normal condition.

अल्पश्रुतेरिति चेत्तदुक्तम्।

[The argument, in support of Sūtra 14, is concluded].

अल्प (small, limited), श्रुतेः (because of Śruti); अल्पश्रुतेः (because Śruti calls it small); इति (this), चेत् (if), तत् (that), उक्तम् (already answered); तदुक्तम् (the reply has already been made).

[The Sūtra consists of two parts, namely an objection and

its reply. The objection-portion is:—**अल्पश्रुतेरिति चेत्;** the reply-portion is:—**तदुक्तम्।]**

Explanation—It may be argued, that as 'Dahara' in Śruti denotes smallness in compass, it cannot mean Brahma. This objection has been anticipated and replied to in Sūtra 7, section II, Chapter I.

अनुकृतेस्तस्य च॥२२॥

[A passage, from the Muṇḍaka Śruti, is taken up for discussion].

अनुकृतेः (from imitation, from the following), **तस्य** (the word '**तस्य**', the first word of the 4th line of the Śruti quoted below, meaning 'of Him' *i.e.*, of Brahma), **च** (and).

Explanation—And everything in the universe shines by reflected light borrowed from Him, Who is perfect and suffers no change; so 'Dahara' cannot be Jīva, he being subject to ebb and flow.

For the expression vide the Śruti:—

"दिव्ये ब्रह्मपुरे ह्येष व्योम्नि आत्मा प्रतिष्ठित"

* * * *

"न तत्र सूर्य्यो भाति न चन्द्रतारकं नेमा विद्यातो भान्ति कुतोऽयमग्निः।
तमेव भान्तमनुभाति सर्व्वं तस्य भासा सर्व्वमिदं विभाति॥"

(This soul is indeed installed in the heavenly sky of Brahmapura—*Which must be identical with Dahara.* There the sun shines not, nor the moon, nor the stars, nor these flashes of lightning, what to speak of the fire? Everything shines after Him, the Self-Luminous One; and by His light all this is illuminated).

Muṇḍaka, Chap. II, 2, 7 and 10.

अपितु स्मर्य्यते॥२३॥

[An argument, in support of Sūtra 22, is adduced].

अपितु (moreover), स्मर्य्यते (is stated in Smṛti).

Explanation—Moreover, it is stated in Smṛti. The description, of individual souls as being reflections of the Universal Soul, and of Universal Soul as being the Universal Light, is found in Smṛti:—

"न तद्भासयते सूर्य्यो न शशाङ्को न पावकः।
यद्गत्वा न निवर्त्तन्ते तद्धाम परमं मम॥"

(Neither the sun, nor the moon, nor the fire illumines that place, where once entered persons never return: that is my highest abode).

Bhagavat Gītā, Chap. XV, 6.

Again:—

"यदादित्यगतं तेजो जगद्भासयतेऽखिलम्।
यच्चन्द्रमसि यच्चाग्नौ तत्तेजो विद्धि मामकम्॥"

(The light in the sun, which illumines the whole world, that in the moon and that in the fire, know, that all those lights are mine).

Bhagavat Gītā, Chap. XV, 12.

शब्दादेव प्रमितः॥२४॥

[An expression, from the Kaṭhopaniṣad, is taken up for discussion].

शब्दात् (from the word; from the revealed word **'ईशान'**, *i.e.*, the Ruler in the passage quoted below from the Kaṭhopaniṣad), एव (itself), प्रमितः (measured, *i.e.*, described as having the size of the thumb).

Explanation—The Spirit, described in the Kaṭha Śruti as having the size of the thumb, is Brahma, as can be understood from the revealed word 'Iśāna' (the Ruler).

For reference vide the Śruti:—

"अङ्गुष्ठमात्रः पुरुषो मध्य आत्मनि तिष्ठति।
ईशानो भूतभव्यस्य........॥"

(The Spirit, having the size of the thumb resides within the heart. He rules over the past and the future).

Kaṭhopaniṣad, Chap. II, 1, 12.

हृद्यपेक्षया तु मनुष्याधिकारत्वात्॥२५॥

[A qualifying explanation, of Sūtra 24, is adduced, and the privilege for divine meditation begins to be discussed].

हृदि (in the heart), **अपेक्षया** (in consideration of), **तु** (but), **मनुष्याधिकारत्वात्** (because of the privilege of men).

Explanation—Though the Universal Soul is all-pervading, yet He has been described as of the size of the thumb in consideration of the fact that the Spirit, referred to in Sūtra 21 above, dwells in the heart of human beings, which is generally as big as the thumb. But why a man's heart only and not that of any other animal also? The reply is that man alone has the privilege of divine meditation.

तदुपर्य्यपि वादरायणः सम्भवात्॥२६॥

[The description, of the privilege of divine meditation, is continued].

तदुपरि (above them, *i.e.*, higher than men), **अपि** (also, even), **वादरायणः** (the sage Bādarāyaṇa), **सम्भवात्** (as it is possible).

Explanation—The sage Bādarāyaṇa holds, that the gods also, who are higher than men, have the privilege of meditation on Brahma, as it is possible for them; *i.e.*, as they possess all the requisites of divine meditation.

विरोधः कर्म्मणीति चेन्नानेकप्रतिपत्तेर्दर्शनात्॥२७॥

[An objection, against Sūtra 26, is raised and refuted].

विरोधः (incongruity), **कर्म्मणि** (in the sacred rite), **इति** (this), **चेत्** (if), **न** (no; *i.e.*, the objection cannot stand), **अनेक** (several), **प्रतिपत्तेः** (of assumption), **दर्शनात्** (as shown by Śruti).

[The Sūtra consists of two parts—an objection and its refutation. The objection-portion is:—**विरोधः कर्म्मणि इति चेत्**; and the refutation-portion is:—**न अनेक-प्रतिपत्तेः दर्शनात्**].

Explanation—An objection may be raised, that as divine meditation is impossible without assuming a physical form, the deities, if they have the right for divine meditation, are to be admitted to possess such bodies; but their appearance with a body or form is incongruous with simultaneous appearance in different places where rites are performed and they are invoked. This objection is groundless, as Śruti has shown simultaneous assumption of several bodies by one and the same diety.

For the refutation vide reference in the Bṛhadāraṇyaka, Chap. III, 9, 1-9.

शब्द इति चेन्नातः प्रभवात् प्रत्यक्षानुमानाभ्याम्॥२८॥

[Another objection, against Sūtra 26, is raised and refuted].

शब्दे (in word, regarding Vedic words), **इति** (this way), **चेत्** (if), **न** (no; that cannot stand), **अतः** (from this; from these words), **प्रभवात्** (from the origin), **प्रत्यक्षानुमानाभ्यां** (**प्रत्यक्षं**—the direct knowledge, *i.e.,* Śruti; **अनुमानं**—the inferential knowledge, *i.e.,* Smṛti; hence both from Śruti and Smṛti).

[The Sūtra consists of two parts—an objection and its reply. The objection-portion is:—**शब्द इति चेत्**; and the reply-portion is:—**न अतः प्रभवात् प्रत्यक्षानुमानाभ्याम्**].

Explanation—The Vedic words have been proved, in the Pūrva-Mīmāṁsā philosophy, to be permanent, *i.e.,* without any beginning or end. Now if gods are said to have bodies they must have births and deaths, which all embodied beings are subject to; and therefore the Vedic words for individual deities cannot exist before their birth, nor can those words signify any dieties, when they have ceased to exist at dissolution. So the permanency of Vedic words fails. To such an objection the reply is that there cannot be any such incongruity in respect of Vedic words; for both Śruti and Smṛti hold that inidividual gods owe their origin to Vedic words.

The Vedic words exist from eternity and have got fixed significance. The Vedic names for gods signify their *types* and not the individuals; and therefore the births or deaths of individual gods cannot affect the types, far less the permanent Character of Vedic words.

Vide the Śruti:—

"एते इति वै प्रजापतिर्देवानसृजत"

(With the word 'these' Prajāpati called the gods into existence).

Vide the Smṛti—

"सर्व्वेषाञ्च स नामानि कर्म्माणि च पृथक् पृथक्।
वेदशब्देभ्य एवादौ पृथक् संस्थाश्च निर्म्ममे॥"

(He, the Creator, in the beginning created, from Vedic words, different names, deeds and forms of all).

Manusaṁhitā, Chap. I, 21.

अतएव च नित्यत्वम्॥२९॥

[A side issue is deduced from Sūtra 28].

अतएव (from the same reasons), च (also), नित्यत्वम् (eternal nature).

Explanation—The eternal nature of Vedic words is also established from the same reasons (adduced in Sūtra 28), *i.e.*, because those words signify permanent *types*.

समाननामरूपत्वाच्चावृत्तावप्यविरोधो दर्शनात् स्मृतेश्च॥३०॥

[An argument, in favour of Sūtra 29, is adduced].

समान (equal, similar); समाननामरूपत्वात् (because of equality or similarity of names and forms), च (also), आवृत्तौ (in repetition; in rotation; in the cycles of creation), अपि (even),

अविरोधः (no inconsistency), **दर्शनात्** (from Śruti), **स्मृतेः** (from Smṛti), **च** (as well as).

Explanation—Names and forms of one cycle of creation being similar to those of another, as is understood from Śruti as well as from Smṛti, there is no incongruity in the permanence of Vedic words, although creation and destruction are coming by rotation.

Vide the Śruti—

"सूर्य्याचन्द्रमसौ धाता यथापूर्व्वमकल्पयत्"

(The Creator designed and brought forth the sun and the moon as He did before *in previous Kalpas, i.e., cycles of creation)*:

Ṛgveda X, 190, 3.

Also vide the Smṛti:—

"यथर्त्तावृतुलिङ्गानि नानारूपाणि पर्य्यये।
दृश्यन्ते तानि तान्येव तथा भावा युगादिषु॥"

(As the same signs of seasons appear again and again in their due course, so do beings appear and re-appear in successive cycles).

मध्वादिष्वसम्भवादनधिकारं जैमिनिः॥३१॥

[Another objection, to Sūtra 26, is raised].

मध्वादिषु (in Madhu-Vidyā and like), **असम्भवात्** (because of impossibility), **अनधिकारं** (no privilege), **जैमिनिः** (the sage Jaimini, the author of the Pūrva-Mīmāṁsā).

Explanation—The sage Jaimini says that the sun and the other gods being the deities to be worshipped in Madhu-Vidyā and the like (which are different forms of divine meditation), it is impossible that they should also be the worshippers; so they have not the privilege of divine meditation prescribed in Śruti; for obviously they cannot worship themselves.

For Madhu-Vidyā vide parts I-XI, Chap. III of the Chāndogya-Upaniṣad.

[This Sūtra has been refuted by Sūtra 33].

ज्योतिषि भावाच्च॥३२॥

[An argument, in support of the objection raised in Sūtra 31, is adduced].

ज्योतिषि (as luminaries), भावात् (for existence), च (also).

Explanation—And because the deities exist as luminaries of heaven (such as the sun etc)., and for the matter of that the necessary qualifications for Brahma-worship (*viz*. body, desire etc). are wanting in them, the gods cannot have the right of divine meditation.

भावंतु वादारायणोऽस्ति हि॥३३॥

[This Sūtra refutes the arguments in the previous two Sūtras two Sūtras two Sūtras and concludes the discussion].

भावं (possession of right), तु (but), वादारयणः (the sage, Bādrāyaṇa), अस्ति (is exists), हि (because).

Explanation—But Bādarāyaṇa holds that the gods too have the right of meditation on Brahma, because there are indications in Śruti to that effect. A particular god (say the sun) may be disqualified for a particular form of divine meditation (say Madhu-Vidyā); but that is no reason why he should be disqualified for other forms.

The luminaries of heaven are external manifestations of heavenly deities endowed with all the necessary qualifications of divine meditation; and they can assume any form at will, as is evident from Śruti and Smṛti.

Vide the Śruti:—

"तं वा एतं देवा आत्मानमुपासते॥"

(The gods indeed do worship Him—the Universal Soul).

Chāndogya, Chap. VIII, 12, 6.

शुगस्य तदनादरश्रवणात् तदाद्रवणात् सूच्यते हि॥३४॥

[The discussion on the privilege of divine meditation, begun in Sūtra 25, is continued].

शुक् (**शोकः**, sorrow, grief), **अस्य** (of him, referring to King Jānaśruti noted below), **तत्** (**तस्य**, his, referring to a sage in the appearance of a swan), **अनादरश्रवणात्** (from hearing some contemptuous terms), **तदा** (then), **आद्रवणत्** (from the hurrying on to), **सूच्यते** (is indicated), **हि** (**यतः**, as, because).

Explanation—King Jānaśruti was in grief on hearing some contemptuous terms used about him by a sage in the appearance of a swan; and then he hastened to the sage Raikka who addressed him as Śūdra (**शूद्र**), because in a sorrowful mood he had hurried to the sage. So the Śūdra origin of Jānaśruti cannot be suggested by the speaker's rebuke. [Besides there is no evidence on record to show that the Śūdras ever wielded the sceptre in Vedic times].

It is to be noted here that the syllable '**शु**' of the word '**शुक्**' joined with the first syllable '**द्र**' of the word '**द्रवणं**', forms the word '**शुद्र**' (**शूद्र**).

The reference is to the story of the King Jānaśruti and the sage Raikka (Chāndogyopaniṣad, Chap. IV. 1—3). A certain King named Jānaśruti used to make frequent gifts to the deserving. On one night some sages appeard before the King in the shape of swans. One of them praised the King, and another blamed him, saying that he was quite unworthy of so much praise, as he, being unacquainted with the knowledge of Brahma, could by no means compare with the sage Raikka who was versed in that knowledge. The King was much mortified to hear the swan speak of him so contemptuously, and on the following morning he sought out the sage Raikka and begged him for the favour of imparting him the knowledge of Brahma. The sage at first sent him away by adderessing him as 'Śūdra', but, seeing his earnestness, at last yielded.

From the story related above, it is not at all evident that Jānaśruti, though addressed as Śūdra, was really a Śūdra by birth, as is indicated by the special meaning in which the sage used the word. (How the special meaning is arrived at, has already been shown—शु+द). Thus, from the example of Jānaśruti, receiving Brahma-Vidyā from his preceptor Raikka, it does not follow that Śūdras by birth are qualified for Brahma-Vidyā.

क्षत्रियत्वावगतेश्चोत्तरत्र चैत्ररथेन लिंगात्॥३५॥

[An argument, in support of Sūtra 34, is adduced].

क्षत्रियत्वावगतेः (because of his Kṣatriyahood being ascertained), च (also), उत्तरत्र (later on; in a subsequent part of the text; in the latter part of the story of the King Jānaśruti and the sage Raikka, in the Chāndogya); चैत्ररथः (a descendant of Chitraratha, whose name was Abhipratāri); चैत्ररथेन (with Abhipratāri; who was descendant of the Kṣatriya king Citraratha), लिङ्गात् (from the suggestion).

Explanation—The Kṣatriyhood of Jānaśruti is inferred from the fact as suggested in a subsequent part of the text, of Jānaśruti interdining with Abhipratāri of Citraratha family, who was known to be a Kṣatriya by birth; and so Jānaśruti was not a Śūdra.

For the reference vide Chāndogya, Chap. IV, parts I-3.

संस्कारपरामर्शात् तदभावाभिलापाच्च॥३६॥

[The discussion, on the privilege of Brahma-Vidyā on the part of the Śūdras, is continued].

संस्कारः (a purificatory rite); संस्कारपरामर्शात् (from the injunction of receiving instruction in Brahma-Vidyā after having undergone the purificatory rite of investiture with the Sacred Thread), तदभाव (तस्य अभाव, want of that, want of the purificatory rite), अभिलापत् (from the statement), च (also).

Explanation—From the injunction of receiving instruction in Brahma-Vidyā after having undergone the purificatory rite of investiture with the Sacred Thread, and also from the prohibition of the Śūdras from such purificatory rite, it is proved that the Śūdras are not entitled to Brahma-Vidyā.

Vide:—

"तं होपनिन्ये" (*Before initiation, he* invested him with the sacred thread).

Śatapatha Brāhmaṇa, Chap. XI, 5, 3, 13.

Also vide—

"शूद्रश्चतुर्थवर्णं एकजातिर्नच संस्कारमर्हति।"

(The Śūdra is the fourth caste, once born; and he is not eligible for any purificatory rite).

Manusaṁhitā, Chap. X, 4 and 126.

तदभावनिर्द्धारणे च प्रवृत्तेः॥३७॥

[The same discussion, on the Śūdras' right is continued].

तदभाव (non-existence of that; not being a Śūdra), **निर्द्धारणे** (in the decision; on deciding), **च** (also), **प्रवृत्तेः** (from inclination; from preference).

Explanation—That the Śūdras are not entitled to Brahma-Vidyā, is also proved by the fact that Gautama preferred to invest Satyakāma with the Sacred Thread and accept him as a disciple for imparting Brahma-Vidyā after feeling satisfied that the boy was not born a Śūdra.

The reference is to the story of the sage Gautama and Satyakāma, the son of a widow named Jawālā. Satyakāma enquired of his mother about his lineage, as he wanted to practise Brahmacarya residing in the preceptor's house. His mother replied that she was constantly busy with household duties in the life-time of her husband, and she did not find any opportunity to enquire of her husband for his lineage, she only knew that her son's name was Satyakāma and her own name was Jawālā. The boy then went to the sage Gautama and prayed for Brahma-Vidyā. On being asked by Gautama about his lineage, he spoke everything candidly as he had been told by his mother. Then Gautama said to Satyakāma 'My boy, I understand that you are certainly Brāhmin by birth, as none other than a

Brāhmin speaks the truth with such simplicity. So I will invest you with the Thread'. The sage performed his purifying rite and initiated him. (For reference vide the Chāndogyopaniṣad, Chap. IV, 4).

श्रवणाध्ययनार्थप्रतिषेधात्॥३८॥

[The same discussion, on the Śūdras right, is continued].

श्रवण (hearing), **अध्ययन** (reading), **अर्थ** (appreciating the meaning), **प्रतिषेधात्** (because of prohibition; because of prohibitory injunctions in the scripture).

Explanation—Because of prohibitory injunctions in the scripture about hearing, reading and understanding the Vedas, by the Śūdras, they are not entitled to the knowledge of Brahma in the way prescribed by the Vedas.

For prohibitory injunction vide—

"शूद्रसमीपे नाध्येतव्यम्" (*The Veda* is not to be read in the presence of a Śūdra).

स्मृतेश्च॥३९॥

[The discussion, on the right of the Śūdras, is concluded here].

स्मृतेः (from Smṛti; from prohibition in Smṛti), **च** (also).

Explanation—There is such prohibition (as stated in Sūtra 38) in Smṛti also.

Vide the Smṛti:—**"न शूद्राय मतिं दद्यात्"** (He is not to impart instruction in Brahma-Vidyā to a Śūdra).

In Sūtras 34-39 it has been discussed and proved that the Śūdras are not entitled to Brahma-Vidyā in the way prescribed in the Vedas; and there is no demurring to this conclusion of the Ācārya Bādarāyaṇa. But one's heart aches to think that the all-embracing Śrutis, the most liberal scriptures in the world, should be unkind to any earnest seeker after Brahma simply on the ground of his birth. We are inclined to think, however, that Śūdras, as a caste, are not interdicted. A person's caste is known only from his conduct, as is evident from the case of Satyakāma, stated in Sūtra 37, where, by his truthfulness and simplicity, he was decided by the sage Gautama to belong to the Brāhmin caste. There are instances on record, of promotion of men from one class to another, judging by their conduct. The story of the sage Vaiśvāmitra is a case in point; he being born a Kṣatriya, became a Brāhmin by his practising religious austerities and leading a life of abstinence. The word 'Śūdra' literally means 'one stricken with grief', as traced from **'शुगस्य.....सूच्यते'** (Sūtra 34) in connection with the story of the King Jānaśruti and the sage Raikka, where Jānaśruti is stated to have been at first refused Brahma-Vidyā by the sage, on the plea of his being a Śūdra (meaning sorrow-stricken, and not of the Śūdra caste), which was a disqualification for his admission as a student of Brahma-Vidyā. But he was at last admitted to discipleship, when he was found earnest for Brahma-Vidyā.

The scripture has therefore indicated, by the word 'Śūdra', the class of men to whom the loss of material possession is felt painful, and in whom there has not arisen a genuine desire for the priceless treasure of Brahma-Vidyā. The imparting of Brahma-Vidyā to unworthy persons would be casting pearls before swine.

कम्पनात् ॥४०॥

[After discussing the side issues in Sūtras 25-39, the framer of the Sūtras resumes the examination of the main issue].

[An argument, in support of Sūtra 24, is adduced here].

कम्पनात् (from shaking or vibrating).

Explanation—The Spirit, referred to in the Kaṭha-Śruti as having the size of the thumb and being indicated by the word 'Prāṇa', is Brahma, as can be understood from the description of the universe moving in Him and trembling in fear of Him, and of the people obtaining immortality by knowing Him.

For the description vide the Śruti:—

"यदिदं किञ्च जगत् सर्व्वं प्राण एजति निःसृतम्।
महद्भयं वज्रमुद्यतं य एतद्विदुरमृतास्ते भवन्ति॥"

(This universe emanates from and pulsates through Prāṇa and trembles in fear of Him, as if in terror of a great thunder uplifted about to be hurled; and people worshipping Him obtain immortality).

Kaṭhopaniṣad, Chap. II, 3, 2.

ज्योतिर्दर्शनात्॥४१॥

[The argument, in support of Sūtra 24, is continued].

ज्योतिः (Light; the Self-luminous and All-illumining One), दर्शनात् (from seeing; as it is found in Śruti).

Explanation—The Spirit, referred to in Sūtra 24, is Brahma, because in the latter part of the same Śruti. He is found to be designated as the Self-luminous and All-illumining One (these attributes being applicable to Brahma only).

For reference vide the Śruti—

"तमेव भान्तमनुभाति सर्व्वं तस्य भासा सर्व्वमिदं विभाति॥"

(Fully quoted and translated under Sūtra 22).

आकाशोऽर्थान्तरत्वादिव्यपदेशात्॥४२॥

[Another expression, of the Chāndogya Śruti, is taken up for discussion].

आकाशः (Ākāśa), अर्थान्तरत्वादि (use in a different sense and so on), व्यपदेशात् (from statement).

Explanation—The term 'Ākāśa', used in the Chāndogya Śruti, does not bear its ordinary signification, the Sky, but signifies the Infinite Spirit, Brahma; as it is stated to be the source of all names and forms, and also because It is qulaified by such words as Infinite, Immortal, Self.

For reference vide the Śruti—

"आकाशो ह वै नामरूपयोर्निवहिता ते यदन्तरा तद ब्रह्म तदमृतं स आत्मा।"

(Ākāśa is the Revealer of all names and forms. Within Him are they—the names and forms; He is Brahma, He is the Imperishable One, He is Self).

Chāndogya, Chap. VIII, 14, 1.

सुषुप्त्युत्क्रान्त्योर्भेदेन॥४३॥

[The 3rd Brāhmaṇa, of the 4th Chapter of the Bṛhadāraṇyakopaniṣad is taken up for discussion].

सुषुप्त्युत्क्रान्त्योः (in सुषप्ति, *i.e.,* sound sleep, and in उत् क्रान्ति, *i.e.,* death), भेदेन (as different).

Explanation—A doubt may arise as to the identity of the Being, spoken of in the Bṛhadāraṇyaka Śruti, Chap. IV, 3—whether He is the Universal Soul or the individual soul. In this Sūtra it is established that He is Brahma (the Universal Soul), as, in the same Śruti, this Being has been clearly shown as different from the individual soul, who, unlike the Supreme Being, passes through the stages of sound sleep and death.

Vide the Śruti (for the state of sound sleep)—

"अयं पुरुषः प्राज्ञेनात्मना सम्परिष्वक्तो न बाह्यं किञ्चन वेद नान्तरम्॥"

(This individual soul, being embraced by Supreme Consciousness, *i.e., Brahma,* knows not anything external or internal).

Bṛhadāraṇyaka, Chap. IV, 3, 21.

Also vide (for death).

"अयं शारीर आत्मा प्राज्ञेनात्मनान्वारूढ़ उत्सर्ज्जन् याति।"

(This embodied soul being presided over by Supreme Consciousness, shuffles off the body and moves on).

Ibid, Chap. IV, 3, 35.

पत्यादिशब्देभ्यः॥४४॥

[An argument, in support of Sūtra 43, is adduced].

पत्यादि ('Lord' etc)., **शब्देभ्यः** (from the words).

Explanation—The Being; referred to in Sūtra 43, is Brahma, because of the words 'Lord' etc. being applied to Him.

Vide the Śruti:—

"स सर्व्वस्य वशी सर्व्वस्येशानः सर्व्वस्याधिपतिः।"

(He is the Controller, the Ruler, the Lord of all).

Bṛhadāraṇyaka, Chap. IV, 4, 22.

SECTION—IV

This section examines some passages from Śruti, where terms occur, which may be mistaken for the names of the inanimate matter of Sāṅkhya, and authoritatively declares that Śrutis lend no support whatsoever to the Sāṅkhya theory of creation. It moreover proves that Brahma is the mate·ial as well as the efficient cause of the universe.

Sūtras 1-6 examine different expressions in the Kaṭha Śruti, which may apparently lead to a contrary conclusion; and thus establish that the inanimate matter of Sāṅkhya is not recognised by Śruti to be the cause of the universe.

Sūtra 3 makes a distinction between the Pradhāna of the Sāṅkhya philosophy and the Prakṛti of Śruti. The Sāṅkhya philosophy also admits both nature (its Pradhāna) and Spirit (its Puruṣa) but its Pradhāna (the primordial Matter) is inanimate and perfectly distinct and separate from its Puruṣa (the inactive Spirit). Śruti, on the other hand, postulates its Prakṛti (the causal nature) as co-existing with, and being part and parcel of, Brahma (the Universal Spirit) for eternity.

Sūtra 7 shows, that in the Sāṅkhya philosophy the word 'Mahat' means Intellect or the prolific nature; but in Śruti it means the conscious and animated Universal Ego, *i.e.,* the sum total of the individual egoes beyond Intellect. Similarly the word 'Abyakta' (the Unmanifested) means, in Sāṅkhya, the insentient primordial Matter; while in Śruti it means the undeveloped causal body of the universe, yet homogeneous and undifferentiated.

Sūtra 8-10 examine an expression of the Śvetāśvatara Śruti and prove by reference to the Bṛhadāraṇyaka and the Chāndogya Śrutis that the matter of Sāṅkhya is not the subject-matter of the Śvetāśvatara Śruti.

Sūtras 11-13 show that the number twenty-five of the principles recognised by Sāṅkhya can, by no means, be the meaning of the expression "पञ्च पञ्च जना" which is interpreted as such by the Sāṅkhyas.

Sūtra 14 states, that all the expressions, such as Ākāśa, Āditya (the sun), Prāṇa and others used in the sense of Brahma, indicate that Brahma is their ultimate cause but they are only manifestations of His different aspects.

Sūtras 15-22 show, from the Taittirīya, the Kauṣītaki, the Bṛhadāraṇyaka and the Chāndogya Śrutis, as well as by references to the views of the sages Jaimini, Āśmarathya, Audulomi and Kāśakṛtsna, that the Universal Self and none else is meant by the words 'Asat' (Unmanifested), Kartā (the Lord and Maker) and Ātmā (the Self), used in those Śrutis.

Sūtras 23-28 show, that Brahma is the material as well as the efficient cause of the universe.

There is a school of thought which teaches the universe to be an illusion without any real existence. Sūtra 26 alludes to the theory and lays down that the universe is not strictly unreal, but is a manifestation of Brahma; it may be said to be unreal in the sense that the present state of its existence, is not permanent: It may be said to be an illusion in the sense that it has no separate existence apart from Brahma. It is further inferred from this Sūtra, that the Spirit (Brahma) of Śruti is both active and inactive (vide notes at the end of Sūtra 26). Sāṅkhya is an uncompromising advocate of dualism and splits up the composite nature of the Supreme Being into two distinct entities—Puruṣa (the inactive principle) and Prakṛti (the active principle). Śruti, on the other hand, would not tolerate this distinction, but would endow its Puruṣa with all the properties of Sāṅkhya's Prakṛti, necessary for cosmic evolution and involution. Besides Sāṅkhya's Puruṣas are many, while Śruti's Puruṣa is one without a second.

आनुमानिकमप्येकेषामिति चेन्न शरीररूपकविन्यस्तगृहीतेर्दर्शयति च॥१॥

[By the Sūtras 5-12, section I, Chap. I it has been shown that Brahma, and not Pradhāna (the matter) of the Sāṅkhya philosophy, is the cause of the universe. Here a discussion begins, whether that Pradhāna, claimed to be the cause of the universe, is supported or not by Śruti itself.

This Sūtra states that 'Abyakta' (the unmanifested) of Śruti does not mean Pradhāna of Sāṅkhya].

आनुमानिकम् (the inanimate matter founded upon inference, the Pradhāna of the Sāṅkhya philosophy, which is reasoned out there to be the original cause of the universe), **अपि** (also), **एकेषाम्** (of some branches or schools of Śruti, **इति** (this), **चेत्** (if); **न** (no), **शरीररूपकविन्यस्तगृहीतेः** (from acceptance of body arranged in a figurative speech; to mean the *causal* body which is figuratively represented in Śruti), **दर्शयति** (Śruti shows), **च** (also).

[The Sūtra consists of an objection to Sūtra 2, section I, Chap. I, and its reply. The objection-portion is—'**आनुमानिकमप्येकेषामिति चेत्**'; and the reply-portion is—**न, शरीररूपकविन्यस्तगृहीतेः, दर्शयति च**].

Explanation—It may be argued that the insentient Matter of the Sāṅkhya philosophy, too, is mentioned, by some Śruti, to be the Supreme Cause of the universe, for instance, in the passage of the Kaṭha-Śruti quoted below; where, it is contended, the Śruti mentions the primordial Matter ('**अव्यक्त**'—the unmanifested) to be superior to, (and so the original cause of), the prolific nature ('**महत्**'—the primal evolution of Matter) But this argument cannot hold, because the word '**अव्यक्त**' (the unmanifested) is indeed used in the Śruti to mean the (causal) body (assumed by the soul) which still waits to be evolved and differentiated, and not Pradhāna (the matter) of Sāṅkhya. This causal body is figuratively represented in the Śruti, only a few lines before, in an allegory; and the same Śruti later on enjoins that a wise person consigns 'Mahat' (the prolific nature) to the Universal Soul, showing, thereby, that in Śruti, Pradhāna (the primordial Matter) of Śankhya has no place in the order of evolution from the Universal Soul down to the mind. So by 'Abyakta' (the unmanifested) in the passage under discussion, is not meant the Pradhāna of Sāṅkhya.

Vide the passage under discussion:—

"महतः परमव्यक्तमव्यक्तात् पुरुषः परः।"

(Abyakta—the unmanifested—is superior to 'Mahat,'—the prolific nature, and Puruṣa—the Spirit—to Abyakta).

Kaṭhopaniṣad, Chap. I, 3, 11.

[The Sāṅkhya philosophy postulates two existences—'Puruṣa' (spirit) and 'Pradhāna' (matter), the former being entirely passive and the latter endowed with all energy; while Śruti makes matter, *i.e.,* nature, part and parcel of the One Energising Supreme Spirit].

For the figurative representation of the Body unmanifested, vide—

"आत्मानं रथिनं विद्धि शरीरं रथमेव तु।
बुद्धिन्तु सारथिं विद्धि मनः प्रग्रहमेव च ॥"

(Know the Body to be a car, the Soul its rider, the Intellect the driver and the mind to be the reins).

Kaṭha-Śruti, Chap. I, 3, 3.

For the consigning of 'Mahat' (the prolific nature) to the Universal Soul, vide:—

"यच्छेद् वाङ्मनसि प्राज्ञ स्तद्यच्छेद् ज्ञान-आत्मनि।
ज्ञानमात्मनि महति तद् यच्छेद् शान्त आत्मनि॥"

(A wise man restrains his speech in thought, thought in

individual ego, individual ego in 'Mahat', *i.e., the prolific nature—the Universal Ego,* and that again in the Tranquil Supreme Spirit).

Kaṭha-Śruti, Chap. I, 3, 13.

सूक्ष्मन्तु तदर्हत्वात्॥२॥

[An objection to Sūtra 1, is refuted].

सूक्ष्मं (subtle), **तु,** (but), **तदर्हत्वात्** (from its propriety, because of its propriety to be termed so).

Explanation—An objection may be raised that the body (as stated in Sūtra 1), which is apparently a gross one and as such fully manifested, cannot be meant by the word 'Abyakta' (unmanifested). But this objection cannot stand because the 'body' may justly and properly be termed so; as the 'body' here does not mean the fully developed gross body, but the causal body, that yet remains to be manifested, and so deservedly termed 'Abyakta' (the unmanifested), being extremely subtle and beyond any sense-perception.

This 'Abyakta' (the causal body) is, no doubt, the subtlest form of all the three bodies—the gross body (**स्थूलदेह**), the subtle body (**सूक्ष्मदेह**) and the causal body (**कारणदेह**).

तदधीनत्वादर्थवत्॥३॥

[The argument, in support of Sūtra 1 is continued].

तदधीनत्वात् (because of its subordination to Him; as it is subordinate to Him), **अर्थवत्** (full of meaning, operative).

Explanation—It may be argued, that if 'Abyakta' is the subtlest form of the body, then it is no other than 'Pradhāna' (of the Sāṅkhya philosophy), which, according to Sāṅkhya, is the cause of the universe. But the argument cannot stand, because the 'Abyakta' here is not an independent principle , as Sāṅkhya would like to have it, but is subordinate to the Univerasal Spirit, being His inherent creative will, and becomes operative in being evolved as the universe under His guidance. So the 'Abyakta' here is not the independent 'Pradhāna' of Sāṅkhya.

ज्ञेयत्वावचनाच्च॥४॥

[The argument, in support of Sūtra 1, is continued].

ज्ञेयत्व (that it is the object to be known), **अवचनात्** (for want of prescription; as it is not prescribed to be worth knowing).

Explanation—The Sāṅkhya philosophy calls matter the First Cause. But the First Cause has been stated in Śruti as the object to be known. In the following Śruti 'Abyakta' (the unmanifested) is not stated to be an object of pursuit. So it is not the First Cause, and consequently cannot be mistaken for the matter of Sāṅkhya.

Vide the Śruti—

"यच्छेद् वाङ्मनसि प्राज्ञः.....शान्त आत्मनि।"

(quoted and translated under Sūtra 1).

Here there is a blank between '**महत्**' and '**शान्त आत्मा**', proving that Abyakta need not be known.

वदतीतिचेन्न प्राज्ञो हि प्रकरणात्॥५॥

[As objection to Sūtra 4 is raised and refuted].

बदति (says, states), **इति** (this), **चेत्** (if), **न** (no), **प्राज्ञः** (the Intelligent Spirit, the Lord of the causal body), **हि** (because) **प्रकरणात्** (because of the general subject-matter of the chapter).

[This Sūtra consists of two parts, namely an objection and its reply. The objection-portion is:—**वदतीति चेत्**; and the reply-portion is:—**न, प्राज्ञो हि प्रकरणात्**]।

Explanation—It may be argued by way of objection to Sūtra 4, that the Śruti describes 'Abyaktat' (the unmanifested) to be the object to be known, as can be traced in the passage (quoted below) of the Kaṭha Śruti. But the argument cannot stand, as the Intelligent Universal Spirit is meant there; because He is the general subject-matter of the Chapter.

For the reference vide:—

"अशब्दमस्पर्शमरूपमव्ययं तथारसं नित्यमगन्धवच्च यत्।
अनाद्यनन्तं महतः परं ध्रुवं निचाय्य तं मृत्युमुखात् प्रमुच्यते ॥"

(One becomes released from the grip of Death by knowing Him, Who is beyond the reach of the ear, the touch, the eye, the taste and the smell; Who is eternal, without change, without beginning and without end; and Who is the permanent Reality and, at the same time, superior to the Prolific Nature).

Kaṭha Śruti, Chap. I, 3, 15.

Here the question may arise, "Who is it that is 'superior to the Prolific Nature'? Is it the Pradhāna of Sāṅkhya or the Brahma of Vedānta?" The answer is, it must of Brahma or the Highest Spirit, Who is the subject-matter of the discourse in the chapter.

For expression to the effect, vide:—

"पुरुषान्न पर किञ्चित् सा काष्ठा सा परागतिः"

(Nothing can transcend the Spirit, Who is the highest limit and the final goal).

Kaṭha Śruti, Chap. I, 3, 11.

In this passage the 'Spirit' is said to be the Final Goal, the First Cause; and in the following passage He is represented as the most difficult to be known, and, as such, the fittest object of enquiry.

"एष सर्व्वेषु भूतेषू गुढ़ोत्मा न प्रकाशते।"

(In all the individual beings, He is the Inmost Soul, Who does not reveal Himself to *everybody*).

Kaṭha Śruti, Chap. I, 3, 12.

त्रयाणामेव चैवमुपन्यासः प्रश्नश्च॥६॥

[The objection raised in Sūtra 5, is further refuted].

त्रयाणाम् (of the three), एव (only), च (also) एवं (in this way), उपन्यासः (presentation by way of answer) प्रश्नः (question) च (also).

Explanation—In this Kaṭha Śruti, referred to in the preceding Sūtras (1-5), there are questions and answers regarding three subjects only; namely, the firesacrifice, the individual soul and the Universal Soul. There being no question about Pradhāna (Matter), there is no reply about the same; and so Pradhāna has no place in the discourse.

महद्वच्च॥७॥

[An argument, in support of Sūtra 1 is adduced].

महत् (the Great; the Prolific Nature; the Universal Ego), वत् (similar to, like), च (also).

Explanation—According to the Sāṅkhya philosophy, 'Mahat' (the earliest evolution of 'Pradhāna', the unmanifested Primordial Matter) is Intellect, which itself is inanimate (जड़); while the Śruti uses the word to mean the Universal Ego, conscious and animate, which is the Great Ātmā, technically called Hiraṇyagarbha, beyond Intellect. Like this 'Mahat', the term 'Abyakta' (literally the unmanifested) is also used to mean, not 'Pradhāna' (the insentient Primordial Matter) of Sāṅkhya, but the causal body of the Universe, yet undifferentiated (as has been stated before).

For the use of the word 'Mahat', vide the Śruti:—

"बुद्धेरात्मा महान् परः।"

('Mahān Ātmā'—*The Great Universal Ego,* is superior to Intellect).

Kaṭha Śruti, Chap. I, 3, 10.

चमसवदविशेषात्॥८॥

[An expression, from the Śwetāśwatara Śruti, is taken up for discussion in support of Sūtra 1].

चमसः (A ladle, a kind of big spoon), वत् (like, just as), अविशेषात् (for want of any specification).

Explanation—By the term 'Ajā' (the unborn one), as it is expressed in the verse, quoted below, of the Śwetāśwatara Śruti, the theory of the 'Pradhāna' of Sāṅkhya cannot be established for want of any specific adjunct used to qualify the word to mean 'Pradhāna', just as the passage 3, of Brāhmaṇa 2, Chap. II of the Bṛhadāraṇyaka Śruti, does not clearly show, by the word 'Chamasa', the specific kind of ladle intended, in the absence of any specification therein.

Vide the verse referred to—

"अजामेकां लोहितशुक्लकृष्णां वह्वीः प्रजाः सृजमानां सरूपाः।

अजो ह्येको जुषमाणोऽनुशेते जहात्येनां भुक्तभोगामजोऽन्यः"॥

(One tricoloured she-goat, white, red and black *in parts,* is begetting a litter of progeny, similarly variegated. One kid lies by her side and sucks her milk, while some other, when filled, gives her up).

Śvetāśvatara Śruti, Chap. IV, 5.

Here the terms 'Ajā' and 'Aja' are used metaphorically in a double sense, they are understood by the Sāṅkhyas to mean, on one hand, a she-goat and her young ones, and, on the other, Matter Eternal and the individual souls feeding on it and at last getting rid of it. The three colours are said to be indicative of the three 'Guṇas'[3] of Sāṅkhya, and the offspring to be indicative of the Jīvas, who are, according to them, infinite in number. But the contention is groundless, because there is no such specific adjunct in the Śruti as could justify us in putting such a meaning to the colours and the offspring, even as by the simple statement 'अर्वाग्बिलश्चमस ऊर्ध्व बुध्नः' (a Chamasa, concave on the lower side and convex on the upper),[4] we do not clearly understand what particular kind of Chamasa is meant; what it is, can only be known by explanatory statements, if any, in its connection. So by fixing our attention only on the detached text 'अजामेकां.....', quoted above we are not justified in identifying the 'Ajā' with 'Pradhāna' of Sāṅkhya.

What is really meant by the Śruti, by the term 'Ajā', is told in the next Sūtra.

ज्योतिरूपक्रमा तु तथा ह्यधीयत एके॥९॥

[This is explanatory to Sūtra 8].

ज्योतिः (light , fire), **उपक्रमा** (beginning with), **तु** (indeed), **तथा** (in that, way, so), **हि** (because), **अधीयते** (read, indicate), **एके** (some Śrutis).

Explanation—The Ajā (unborn female one), referred to in the previous Sūtra, is that which consists of the essence of the three subtle elements beginning with fire, *i.e.,* the Creative Potency, at first evolving as fire, water and earth; because it is so indicated by some Śruti (Chāndogya), where the three above mentioned colours are shown to belong essentially to fire, water and earth respectively, called by Brahma into existence, one after another.

It must be noted that the Creative Potency is Brahma's inherent energy, which emanates from Him at the time fo creation.

For reference vide the Chāndogya
Śruti, part 2-4, Chapter VI.

कल्पनोपदेशाच्च मध्वादिवदविरोधः॥१०॥

[The argument, in support of Sūtra 8, is continued].

कल्पना (**संकलन; रचना; सृष्टि;** design; creation), **उपदेशात्** (from the teaching, because the Śruti teaches), **मध्वादिवत्** (as in the case where, among others, the main thing, the sun, has been described as 'Madhu', *i.e.,* honey, in the Madhu-Vidyā), **अविरोधः** (no incongruity).

Explanation—The 'Aja', of the quoted Śruti, meaning the Trio—fire, water and earth—is a group of the three elements, which are discribed by the Śrutis as things *created*; so it may be contested here, that the term 'Ajā' (uncreated) is a misnomer. This apparent contradiction is reconciled by remembering that the Trio—the group of the three elements—being one and the same with the Creative Potency (देवात्मशक्ति), is co-eternal with the self-existing Brahma, and so may share the designation 'Ajā' (without birth) with the Lord Himself; just as in Madhu-Vidyā and some other Vidyās the sun and other objects are prescribed as symbols of worship, only because the Self-Existing Brahma resides in them and manifests Himself in and through them.

The three phases of one and the same 'Ajā'—white, red and black, though co-existing, only unfold themselves, in succession, in the three elements—fire, water and earth.

For Madhu-Vidyā vide parts 1-10, Chapter III of the Chāndogya Śruti.

For the fact that 'Ajā' (the unborn one) of Sūtra 8 indicates the energy (the Creative Potency) of Brahma, vide the expression 'देवात्मशक्ति' (God's own inherent Energy) in the passage of the Śvetāśvatara Śruti, quoted and translated under Sūtra 12, Section I, Chapter I.

न संख्योपसंग्रहादपि नानाभावादतिरेकाच्च॥११॥

[This Sūtra discusses whether the twenty-five principles of the Sāṅkhya philosophy are admitted by Śruti].

न (not; the principles of the Sāṅkhya philosophy are not admitted by Śruti), संख्या (number), उपसंग्रहात् (from statement), अपि (even though), नानाभावात् (because of different meanings), अतिरेकात् (because of excess), च (also).

Explanation—The twenty-five principles of the Sāṅkhya philosophy are not admitted by Śruti, even though the number appear to be twenty-five; because the agreement in number is only apparent, the principles so enumerated bearing a different meaning from those of Sāṅkhya; and also because the number appears to exceed twenty-five on the basis of calculation.

The principles of the Sāṅkhya philosophy are propounded as independent of Spirit (or 'Puruṣa' in the language of Sāṅkhya), but here, in the controversial passage, the objects, mentioned in number, are known to be entirely dependent on Spirit (or Brahma of Śruti), Who is said here to be the stay of them all. So they cannot be accepted as the independent principles of Sāṅkhya. Moreover, even if the numerical expression mentioned in the Śruti under discussion is admitted to mean the number twenty-five, it cannot mean exactly the same twenty-five principles of Sāṅkhya, since there are found two additional items in the text (1) Ākāśa and (2) Soul or Spirit (Brahma, in Which the rest are said to be established)—in excess of the number twenty-five, while the twenty-five principles occurring in Sāṅkhya's list of enumeration, include Ākāśa and Spirit.

Vide the Śruti—

"यस्मिन् पञ्च पञ्चजना आकाशश्च प्रतिष्ठितः।
तमेव मन्य आत्मानं विद्वान् ब्रह्मामृतोऽमृतम्॥"

(I, who know Him and so am beyond the reach of death, believe Him to be Brahma, the Immortal Self, the support of Ākāśa and the five persons of the five—the five deities controlling the five).

Bṛhadāraṇyaka, Chap. IV, 4, 17.

प्राणादयो वाक्यशेषात्॥१२॥

[This is explanatory to Sūtra 11].

प्राणादयः (the vital functions, etc)., **वाक्यशेषात्** (from the subsequent passage).

Explanation—From the passage subsequent to that quoted in the preceding Sūtra, it appears that the numerical expression in the passage does not indicate twenty-five, but indicates the five ones beginning with the vital function.

For the subsequent passage, vide—

"प्राणस्य प्राणमुत चक्षुषश्चक्षुरुत श्रोत्रस्य श्रोत्रमन्न. स्यान्नं मनसो ये मनो विदुः।"

(Those who know the controller of the force that governs the vital function, of the power of vision in the eye, of the power of hearing in the ear, of the power of assimilating the food and of the power that regulates the thought).

Bṛhadāraṇyaka, Chap IV, 4, 18.

ज्योतिषैकेषामसत्यन्ने॥१३॥

[The argument, in support of Sūtra 11 is continued].

ज्योतिषा (by light) **एकेषाम्** (of some; of the followers of the Kāṇva school; according to the Kāṇvas), **असति** (not existing; not being mentioned; not being included), **अन्ने** (of food).

Explanation—The food not being included among the five in the passage as the Kāṇvas read it, the defect may be remedied by inclusion of 'Jyoti' (light) occurring in the beginning of the passage.

The beginning of the passage stands thus—

"तद्देवा ज्योतिषां ज्योतिः"।

(It the Devās *worship* as Light that illuminates all lights).

Bṛhadāraṇyaka, Chap. IV, 4, 16.

कारणत्वेन चाकाशादिषु यथा व्यपदिष्टोक्तेः॥१४॥

[The doubts, that may arise from Sūtra 13, that different Śrutis may draw different conclusions as to the cause of the universe, is removed by this Sūtra].

कारणत्वेन (**कारणत्वप्रयोगेन**; by attributing the quality of being the cause), **च** (and), **आकाशादिषु** (to Ākāśa and other symbols), **यथा** (as), **व्यपदिष्ट** (taught in different Śrutis), **उक्तेः** (because of the statement).

Explanation—All the Śrutis are unanimous in finding that Brahma is the cause (both efficient and material) of the universe, because they all teach that Ākāśa and others are causes of the universe, meaning thereby that it is Brahma that energises through them.

समाकर्षात्॥१५॥

[Some expressions, from the Taittrīya, the Chāndogya and the Bṛhadāraṇyaka Śrutis are taken up for discussion].

समाकर्षात् (from connection with a distant expression).

Explanation—The doubt about the meaning of a word or passage can be removed by reference to its connection with a distant passage in the same text; because such connection is found to exist in the different passages of Śruti. The exact meaning of such words as 'Asat' (apparently meaning non-entity), 'Abyākṛta' (apparently non-manifest Pradhāna of Sāṅkhya), is thus ascertained to be Brahma.

Compare the Śrutis:—

"सोऽकामयत बहुस्यां प्रजायेयेति।"

(He desired, I will be many—I will manifest myself).

Taittirīya Śruti, Chap. II, 6, 2.

"असद्वा इदमग्र आसीत्।"

(This was at first 'Asat'—*apparently a non-entity)*.

Taittirīya, Chap. II, 7, I.

"असदेवेदमग्र आसीत्तत् सदासीत्।"

(This universe was at first unmanifested, it was then in the Self-existent *Brahma)*.

Chāndogya, Chap. III, 19, 1.

The meaning of the word 'Asat' of the second passage, is ascertained to be Brahma by reference to the first passage where the same question (namely, the state of the universe before creation) is answered in a clearer way.

Similarly, the meaning of the word 'Abyākṛta', in the Bhṛadāraṇyaka Śruti; Chap. I, 4, 7, in the passage **"तद्धेदं तर्ह्य व्याकृतमासीत्"** (thus, therefore, that was the 'Unmanifested'), is ascertained to be Brahma as still undeveloped, by a reference to the passage **"स एष इह प्रविष्ट आनखाग्रेभ्यः"** (the same is pervading all through and through, down to the tips of the nails of the fingers and toes), 'Abyākṛta' being recognised in the last passage more clearly by the words 'स एष' (the selfsame One).

It is to be noted here that nowhere in the passages, dealing with the Cause of the universe, does the Pradhāna of Sāṅkhya find a place.

जगद्वाचित्वात्॥१६॥

[A passage, from the Kauṣītaki Śruti, is taken up for discussion].

जगत् (the universe), वाचित्वात् (because it means).

Explanation—The expression 'Kartā' (Lord and Maker) of the Kauṣītaki Śruti, quoted below, indicates Brahma, and not the individual soul, nor the Universal Life-Force; because the word 'एतत्' (this) means the universe which is stated to be the work (*i.e.* creation) of the said Maker, and also because the Śruti under discussion is in explanation of Brahma.

For the expression vide—

"यो वै वालाके एतेषां पुरुषाणां कर्त्ता, यस्य वैतत् कर्म्म स वै वेदितव्यः।"

(O, Bālāki, He is to be known, Who is the Lord of all these individual souls and Whose work is all this visible universe).

Kauṣītaki Śruti, Chap. IV, 18.

(Dialogue between Ajātaśatru and Bālāki).

जीवमुख्यप्राणलिङ्गान्नेतिचेत्तद्व्याख्यातम्॥१७॥

[An objection to Sūtra 16, is raised and refuted].

जीव (the individual soul), मुख्यप्राण (the chief vital force), लिङ्गात् (because of the discriminating marks), न (not), इति (this), चेत् (if); तत् (that), व्याख्यातम् (is answered).

[The Sūtra consists of an objection and its reply. The objection-portion is:—**जीवमुख्यप्राणलिङ्गान्नेतिचेत्**; and the reply-portion is:—**तद्व्याख्यातम्**].

Explanation—It may be argued, that because of the discriminating marks of the individual soul and of the chief vital force used in the teaching of the king Ajātaśatru to Bālāki in the Kauṣītakyupaniṣad, Brahma is not intended by the term "Kartā" referred to in Sūtra 16. The objection has already been met in Sūtra 32, Sec. 1, Chap. 1 (to be explained in the same way, as in the instruction of Indra to Pratardana).

अन्यार्थं तु जैमिनिः प्रश्नव्याख्यानाभ्यामपिचैवमेके॥१८॥

[An argument, in support of Sūtra 16, is adduced].

अन्यार्थं (for another purpose), **तु** (but), **जैमिनिः** (the sage Jaimini), **प्रश्नव्याख्यानाभ्याम्** (from the question and the reply), **अपि** (also), **च** (and), **एवं** (in this way), **एके** (others, other Śrutis).

Explanation—But the sage Jaimini thinks that in this chapter of the Kauṣītaki Śruti, referred to in Sūtras 16 and 17, the mention of the individual soul, has a different purpose, namely to show that he is distinct from Brahma, as is evident from the question and the answer (quoted below) in the same Śruti as well as in other Śrutis (as for instance, the Bṛhadā-raṇyaka).

For the question and the answer in the Kauṣītaki, vide—

प्रश्नः—। "क्वैष एतद्बालाके पुरुषोऽशयिष्ट क्वैतदभूत्। कुत एतदागात्।

उत्तरः—। यदा सुप्तः स्वप्नं न कंचन पश्यत्यथास्मिन् प्राणे एवैकधा-भवति।"

(Question:—O, Bālāki, where did this individual soul lie down *in sound sleep*? Where was he? Whence did he return to *consciousness*?

Answer—When the individual soul in sound sleep does not dream at all, he becomes united with this very Life-Energy.—*Which has been proved to be Brahma in Sūtra 24,*

Sec. 1, Chap I).

Kauṣītaki, Chap. IV, 19 D and G.

Vide in the Bṛhadāraṇyaka—

प्रश्नः—"एष विज्ञानमयः पुरुषः क्वैष तदाभूत् कुत एतदागात्"—

उत्तरः—"य एषोऽन्तर्हृदय आकाश स्तस्मिन् शेते।"

(Question—Wherein did this intelligent soul remain then, *i.e. during sound sleep*? Whence did he return *to the waking state*?

Answer:—This individual soul lies in *the Universal Soul represented by* Ākāśa within the heart).

Bṛhadāraṇyaka, Chap. II, 1, 16 and 17.

वाक्यान्वयात्॥१९॥

[A passage, from the Bṛhadāraṇyaka Śruti, is taken up for discussion].

वाक्यान्वयात् (from the construction and connection of expression with one another).

Explanation—The word 'Ātmā' (originally meaning the individual self) in the passage, of the Bṛhadāraṇyaka Śruti, quoted below, indicates the Universal Self, as can be understood from the construction of the sentence and the connection of the preceding and following expressions with one another.

Vide the passage referred to—

"आत्मा वा अरे द्रष्टव्यः श्रोतव्यो मन्तव्यो निदिध्यासितव्यो, मैत्रेय्यात्मनो वा अरे दर्शनेन श्रवणेन मत्या विज्ञानेनेदं सर्व्वं विदितम्।"

(Verily the Self is to be seen *i.e.,* intuited, to be heard, to be thought of and continually to be concentrated upon. O, Maitreyi, by the seeing, hearing, meditating and concentrating of self, everything of this universe becomes known).

Bṛhadāraṇyaka, Chap. II, 4, 5.

प्रतिज्ञा-सिद्धेर्लिङ्गमाश्मरथ्यः॥२०॥

[An argument, in support of Sūtra 19, is adduced].

प्रतिज्ञासिद्धेः (because of a proof of the proposition; as it helps to prove the proposition). **लिङ्गम्** (an indicatory mark; an indication), **आश्मरथ्यः** (the sage Āśmarathya).

Explanation—The sage Āśmarathya thinks that to designate Brahma, by the term Ātmā, *i.e.*, the individual soul (as is done in the Śruti quoted in the previous Sūtra), is an indication of proof of the proposition.

The indication is that the individual souls are not different from Brahma, the Ultimate Cause, of which all the individuals are phases; and therefore to know Brahma, the cause, is to know all—that being the proposition sought to be established.

[Compare Sūtra 9, Sec. I, Chap. I].

उतक्रमिष्यत एवम्भावादित्यौडुलोमिः।

[The argument, in support of Sūtra 19, is continued].

उत्क्रमिष्यतः (of him who would pass away from the body), **एवम्भावात्** (because of this condition; because of attaining the status of Brahma), **इति** (this), **औडुलोमिः** (the sage Auḍulomi).

Explanation—The sage Auḍulomi holds, that as the emancipated individual soul, after passing away from the body, attains the status of Brahma, the name 'Ātmā' primarily expressive of the individual self, is given to Brahma.

अवस्थितेरिति काशकृत्स्नः॥२२॥

[The argument, in support of Sūtra 19, is continued].

अवस्थितेः (because of the existence, because of abiding in), **इति** (this) **काशकृत्स्नः** (the sage Kāśakṛtsna).

Explanation—The sage Kāśakṛtsna holds the view, that because the Universal Self is abiding in the individual self, as the controller, the word 'Ātmā' may be accepted in the sense of the Universal Self.

For the existence of the Universal Self in everything, vide Sūtra 19, Sec. II, Chap. 1.

प्रकृतिश्च प्रतिज्ञादृष्टान्तानुपरोधात्॥२३॥

[This Sūtra states that the Universal Soul is the material cause as well as the efficient cause of the universe].

प्रकृतिः (the material cause), च (also, *i.e.*, as well as the efficient cause) प्रतिज्ञा (the proposition) दृष्टान्त (example), अनुपरोधात् (for want of conflict).

Explanation—The Universal Soul is also the material cause (as well as the efficient cause) of the universe; as viewed from this stand-point, the proposition sought to be proved by the sage Uddālaka to his son Śvetaketu (in the Chāndogya Śruti), and the instance cited to prove it do not meet with any conflict.

For, if the material cause be different from the efficient cause, then the knowledge of one cannot make known the other, and consequently the proposition fails; and the instance clearly illustrates the material cause.

For the proposition vide:—

"उत त्वमादेशमप्राक्ष्य येनाश्रुतं श्रुतं भवत्यमतं मतं भवत्यविज्ञातं विज्ञातं भवति।"

(Didst thou inquire after that truth, whereby the unheard becomes heard, the unconceived becomes conceived and the unknown becomes known?)

Chāndogya, Chap. VI, 1,3.

For the example vide:—

"यथा सौम्यैकेन मृत्पिण्डेन सर्व्वं मृण्मयं विज्ञातं स्यात्।"

(As *for instance*, my son, by the knowledge of one lump of earth, all things made of earth are known).

Chāndogya, Chap IV, 1, 4.

अभिध्योपदेशात्॥२४॥

[An argument, in support of Sūtra 23, is adduced].

अभिध्या (the will), उपदेशात् (from the instruction).

Explanation—From the instruction in Śruti, that Brahma willed to manifest Himself as many, *i.e.*, as the universe, it follows that He willed to evolve the universe out of Himself, showing that He is at once the material and the efficient cause of creation.

For the instruction, vide the quotation from the Chāndogya Śruti and its translation under Sūtra 5, section I, Chapter I.

साक्षाच्चोभयाम्नानात्॥२५॥

[The argument, in support of Sūtra 23, is continued].

साक्षात् (direct), च (also), उभय (both, *i.e.,* the efficient as well as the material cause), अम्नानात् (from the statement).

Explanation—The Śruti has direct statements that Brahma is the efficient as well as the material cause of the universe.

Vide the Śruti—

"ब्रह्म वनं ब्रह्म स वृक्ष आसीत्।"

(The forest was Brahma, the tree was Brahma).

From this Śruti it is evident that Brahma is the material cause.

Also vide:—"एतद्यदध्यतिष्ठदभु वनानि धारयन्"

(Upholding all these worlds, presided over them).

This Śruti shows Brahma as the efficient cause as well.

आत्मकृतेः परिणामात्॥२६॥

[The argument, in support of Sūtra 23, is continued].

आत्मकृतेः (because He Himself created) परिणामात् (by way of evolution).

Explanation—As Brahma is said to have created this universe by Himself and out of Himself by way of evolution, He is the material as well as the efficient cause of this universe.

For reference vide—

"तदात्मानं स्वयमकुरुत" (He Himself created His own self).

Taittirīyopaniṣad, Chap. II, 7, 1.

There is a school of thought wherein the whole universe is taught to be an illusion without any reality in the background. This Sūtra refutes that theory and lays down that the universe is not strictly unreal, but is a manifestation of Brahma; if may be said to be unreal in the sense, that the present state of its existence is not permanent; it may be said to be an illusion in the sense, that it has only a phenomenal existence—that is, has no existence separate from Brahma—it is not an illusion, but it is in a state of flux. Another school of thought represented by Ācārya Rāmānuja considers Brahma as always active and possessing the six attributes, omnipotence etc., (षड़ैश्वर्य), that find their employment in dealing with the afffairs of the universe.

Another school of thought, represented by Ācārya Śaṅkara, considers Brahma as essentially inactive, immutable, without sound, without touch, without form, without taste, without odour and free from death and decay, that is, no quality is predicable of Him; and this, the school maintains, is known from the fact that the greater portion of Brahma remains so, only a fourth part being manifested as the visible universe. This manifestation is, according to the school, apparent and illusory.

a fourth school, represented by Ācārya Nimbārka admits Brahma as both active and inactive,—active in respect of the phenomenal world, and inactive in respect of the noumenal world, which is by far the greater portion of Him, (the manifested portion being also admitted as real and not illusory).

योनिश्च हि गीयते॥२७॥

[The argument, in support of Sūtra, 23, is continued].

योनिः (source, parent), **च** (also), **हि** (**यतः**, as, because), **गीयते** (is recited; is stated).

Explanation—Brahma is the material cause of the uni-

verse, also because He is stated in Śruti to be the source of the universe.

For reference vide:—

"अचिन्त्यमव्यक्तमनन्तरूपं शिवं प्रशान्तममृतं ब्रह्मयोनिम्।
तथादिमध्यान्तविहीनमेकं विभुं चिदानन्दरूपमद्भुतम्॥"

(Him, Who is incomprehensible, unspeakable, infinite in form, all good, all peace, immortal, *the parent of the universe,* without beginning, middle and end, without rival, all pervading, all consciousness, all bliss, and inscrutable).

Kaivalyopaniṣad, Part I, 6.

एतेन सर्व्वे व्याख्याताः व्याख्याताः॥२८॥

[The argument is concluded].

एतेन (by this, by what has been said), सर्व्वे (all), व्याख्याताः (explained), व्याख्याताः (the repetition indicates the termination of the chapter).

Explanation—By what has been said in the foregoing Sūtras, it is to be understood, that the teachings of all the Śrutis (even those that have not been discussed) point to the Supreme Being Brahma, as the only cause of the universe.

CHAPTER II

SECTION—I

Previously it has been proved on the authority of Śruti; that the Matter is not the cause of the universe; this section proves, by arguments, that Brahma is the cause of the universe, and removes all the plausible objection that may arise against such conclusion.

In the fourth section of the first chapter, it was established that the Pradhāna and the Mahat of Sāṅkhya were not identical with the Abyakta and Mahān Ātmā of Vedānta. Now it may be argued that if the Sāṅkhya theory be discarded on that ground, there is no room left for Sāṅkhya; inasmuch as being itself a Smṛti, its main object is to support the findings of Śruti. Sūtra 1 and 2 of this section give a reply to this contention by saying that accepting the Sāṅkhya theory of dead Matter as the cause of the creation, there is the like difficulty of discarding other orthodox Smṛtis, which support the Vedantic theory of an Intelligent Creator.

Sūtra 3 discards the theory of the Yoga philosophy of Patañjali regarding the cause of the universe.

Sūtra 4 and 5 raise an objection that as Brahma and the universe are dissimilar in nature and properties, one being sentient etc., and the other insentient etc., one cannot be the cause of the other.

Sūtras 6 and 7 refuted the objection by stating that there are instances, even in the world, of generation of the inanimate from the animate, (as for instance, the production of hair from the living body), as well as, of the animate from the inanimate, (as for instance, the birth of scorpions and other insects from cowdung); and they prove that it is not necessary that the cause and the caused should be similar in all respects.

Sūtra 8 raises an objection that at the time of general dissolution, when the effect (the universe) is merged in the Cause (Brahma), the latter must be contaminated by the former.

Sūtra 9 refutes the objection by showing that there are direct instances to the contrary, just as the products of earth, such as, pots, pitchers etc., at the time of dissolution, do not transform earth into their own nature; but on the contrary they are themselves transformed into the substance of earth.

Sūtras 10 to 12 and Sūtra 28 show that arguments, directed against the view, that Brahma is the cause of the universe, may be urged against the opponents as well, such as the Sāṅkhyas—and the Vaiśeṣikas (in the Sāṅkhya philosophy, the nameless and formless Pradhāna is said to produce all names and forms; and in the Vaiśeṣika system invisible and formless atoms are said to unite and form a visible universe). The Sūtras further show, that arguments in this way, like those of quarrelling sophists, may be followed out for ever without any conclusion being arrived at; and that under such circumstances, the conclusion of the Vedas is to be respected. In this way all the views, antagonistic to the Vedas, are refuted.

Sūtra 13 states that there is a distinction between Brahma, the Universal Soul and Jīva, the individual soul, just as is found between the ocean and its waves, between the sun and its rays. While Sūtras, 4 and 6 state that the inanimate universe is distinct from Brahma, on the other hand, Sūtras 14 to 19 show that the animate and inanimate creation has no separate existence from Brahma, and that it existed as unmanifested in Brahma before its evolution in the manifested form. From all these Sūtras taken together it is concluded that the universe, consisting of both the animate and the inanimate, is identical with, as well as different from, Brahma, just as a wave or a bubble is identical with, and at the same time different from, water; and that Brahma, in spite of His manifestation in the universe, remains mostly beyond it.

Sūtras 20 to 22 remove an apprehension that Brahma, in the shape of the individual soul, is subject to pleasure and pain, by showing that though Brahma assumes the form of the individual soul, yet He also transcends the latter, and remains uncontaminated by any property of Jīva, whom He controls from within. Though the individual soul is none but Brahma Himself, yet Brahma remains the absolute Lord, and as such, above pleasure and pain.

Sūtras 23 and 24—An objection is raised that as a potter requires some materials, such as clay, for the construction of a pot, so Brahma must be dependent upon some raw materials, out of which the universe is to be evolved. This objection is met by showing that in all cases materials are not necessary; as for instance, milk itself is transformed into curd; and that it is also known that a saint by the exercise of mere volution can create particular things; so it is perfectly reasonable to conclude that Brahma has created this universe simply by the fiat of His will.

Sūtras 25-29—Another objection is raised that as Brahma is without parts, it is reasonable to say that Brahma becomes entirely transformed into the universe, if He be the material cause of universe, but this would make Brahma limited to the extent of the universe. Again to avoid the difficulty, if He be described as having parts, the attribute 'without parts', predicated of Brahma in Śruti becomes incongruous. This objection is refuted by showing that, as Śruti declares that Brahma is the material, as well as the efficient cause of the universe, like the spider building its web out of its own material; at the same time, Śruti authoritatively declares that Brahma is not exhausted in the creation, but retains by far the greater portion of Him aloof from the creation. Brahma being shown in Śruti as all-powerful, it is perfectly within His power to be so exhibited, and at the same time to remain mostly beyond such exhibition.

Sūtra 30 states by argument, as well as on the authority of Śruti, that Brahma requires no organs or instruments for creation.

Sūtras 31-32.—Another objection is raised that as Brahma has been described in Śruti as having no desires, He cannot have any necessity for the creation of the universe. This is refuted by showing that creation is, on the part of Brahma, a mere *pastime* (proceeding out of the nature, inherent in, and inseparable from, Him).

Sūtras 33-34.—Another objection that Brahma is partial to some and unkind to others in the creation, is refuted by showing that actions of a man, in his previous birth are the determining factors of his suffering and enjoyment in this life, and so the creator is not responsible for this. A further objection is raised that as there was no distinction of work before the creation of the universe, the difference made at the beginning of the creation between the rich and the poor, or between the happy and the unhappy cannot be said to depend on previous good or bad actions.This objection is refuted by saying, that creation of the universe is described by Śruti as without a beginning, and that it comes again and again by cycles; so there have been previous creations, through time eternal, before this present cycle began; that births, of animal sousl at the beginning of the present cycle of creation, depend on the consequences of their good or bad actions during the previous cycle; and that it is also not reasonable to suggest that the creation of the universe is accidental.

Sūtra 35 states that all the attributes, assigned to the cause of the universe, are found appropriate in Brahma alone, and in none else. Brahma is, therefore, the cause of the universe.

स्मृत्यनवकाशदोषप्रसङ्ग इति
चेन्नान्यस्मृत्यनवकाशदोषप्रसङ्गात्॥१॥

[The conclusion, arrived at in section IV, chapter I, that Brahma is the cause of the universe, is being corroborated by

Smṛtis other than Sāṅkhya; the earliest and the most orthodox of these Smṛtis being the Laws of Manu].

स्मृतिः (*here* the Sāṅkhya Smṛti, the Sāṅkhya philosophy), **अनवकाश;** (no room), **दोषः** (defect), **प्रसङ्गः** (chance), **इति** (this), **चेत्** (if); **न** (no; *i.e.,* that argument cannot stand), **अन्यस्मृतिः** (other Smṛtis), **अनवकाशदोषप्रसंगात्** (because of the similar risk of a defect of having no room).

[This Sūtra consists of two parts, namely an objection and its reply. The objection-portion is:—**स्मृत्यनवकाश-दोषप्रसङ्ग इति चेत्**; and the reply-portion is:—**न, अन्यस्मृत्यनवकाशदोषप्रसङ्गात्**].

Explanation—It may be argued that if Brahma is admitted to be the cause of the universe, no room is left for the Sāṅkhya philosophy, which propounds that inanimate Matter is the cause of the universe. But the argument cannot stand, because the Sāṅkhya theory, if accepted, would give rise to the same defect of rejecting the Smṛtis, other than Sāṅkhya, that advocate Brahma as the cause.

इतरेषाञ्चानुपलब्धेः॥२॥

[An argument, in support of Sūtra 1, is adduced].

इतरेषां (of other Smṛtis; of Smṛtis other than Sāṅkhya), **च** (also), **अनुपलब्धेः** (because of non-cognisance).

Explanation—Sāṅkhya is to be discarded, because of non-cognisance, by other Smṛtis, of its theory of Matter being the cause of the universe.

It should be noted here that of two systems running the same risk of being rejected, preference is to be given to that one which follows Śruti more closely. The Sāṅkhya system, having no authority of Śruti, as shown in the first chapter, must be rejected in preference of other systems, that propound Brahma as the cause of the universe and, as such, are based on Śruti.

एतेन योगः प्रत्युक्तः॥३॥

[The Yoga philosophy of Patañjali is refuted here].

एतेन (by this), **योगः** (the Yoga philosophy), **प्रत्युक्तः** (is refuted).

Explanation—For the same reason as adduced against the Sāṅkhya philosophy, the Yoga philosophy, by Patañjali is also rejected in as much as it also accepts the theory, that Matter is the cause of the universe.

न विलक्षणत्वादस्य तथात्वञ्च शब्दात्॥४॥

[Some plausible objections, against Brahma being the cause of the universe are raised in this Sūtra and in the subsequent one].

न (not, *i.e.,* Brahma is not the cause of the universe), **विलक्षणत्वात्** (because of difference in nature), **अस्य** (its, *i.e.*, of the universe), **तथात्वं** (the same thing, *i.e.*, the said difference), **च** (also), **शब्दात्** (from the corroboration of Śruti).

Explanation—Brahma is not the cause of the universe, because of the apparent difference, in nature, of the universe from Brahma; and the difference is also corroborated by Śruti.

An objection may be raised in the following way—It is reasonable that the effect must be of the same nature or essence with the cause. Now if Brahma is taken to be the cause of the universe, the nature of the two must be similar. But as they appear to be quite different in essence, one being sentient and the other insentient, Brahma cannot be the cause of the universe. This difference in nature is also known from statements of Śruti, where the effect—the universe—is said to be an amalgam of sentient and insentient things, and Brahma as purely sentient (This objection is refuted by Sūtra 6).

For a statement of Śruti vide—

"विज्ञानं चाविज्ञानं च .....अभवत्।"

(He became the sentient as well as the insentient).

Taittirīya Śruti, Brahmaballi, Chap. II, 6, 2.

अभिमानिव्यपदेशस्तु विशेषानुगतिभ्याम्॥५॥

[This Sūtra meets an apprehended objection to Sūtra 4].

अभिमानी (the presiding deity), **व्यपदेशः** (an expression, an indication), **तु** (indeed), **विशेषः** (specific adjunct), **अनुगतिः** (the act of pervading), **विशेषानुगतिभ्याम्** (from the specific adjunct, as well as from the fact of pervading).

Explanation—It may be objected that the division of things into sentient and insentient, as is indicated by the Śruti quoted in the previous Sūtra, is only apparent; but, in reality, there is no such thing as insentient, as the same authority, *viz.*, Śruti, speaks of the so called insentient objects, as fire, water etc., as behaving exactly like sentient beings, indicating thereby, that there is no fundamental difference in nature amongst objects. To this, this Sūtra replies that whenever an inanimate object is described in Śruti as behaving like animate beings, we are to understand that it is an indication of a deity, presiding over and identifying himself with the object, as is evident from the specific adjunct applied to it and from the express statement of a presiding deity pervading it.

Vide the Śruti—

"हन्ताहमिमास्तिस्रो देवता अनेन जीवेनात्मनानुप्रविश्य नामरूपे व्याकरवाणि।"

(I will evolve names and forms by penetrating, as individual souls, these three deities, namely, fire, water and earth).

Chāndogya, Chap. VI, 3, 2.

Here the three objects mentioned are specified by the appositional adjunct, 'these three deities', indicating thereby that the inanimate objects may be called gods, having reference to their presiding deities. From this Śruti we also learn that a sentient self pervades each insentient object. This proves that the world, without the deities, is virtually inanimate as taken by itself.

दृश्यते तु॥६॥

[Objections, raised in Sūtras 4 and 5, are now refuted].

दृश्यते (is seen), **तु** (but).

Explanation—But generation of the inanimate from the animate, (as for instance, the production of hair from the living body), as well as, of the animate from the inanimate, (as for instance, the birth of scorpions and other insects from cow-dung), is frequently met with. So the objections, raised in Sūtras 4 and 5, are not valid, *i.e.,* origination of insentient creation from the sentient Creator is not unreasonable.

असदितिचेन्न प्रतिषेधमात्रत्वात्॥७॥

[An objection, to Sūtra 6, is raised and refuted].

असत् (non-existent), **इति** (this), **चेत्** (if), **न** (no), **प्रतिषेध मात्रत्वात्** (because of denial; as it simply denies).

[The Sūtra consists of two parts, an objection and its reply. This objection-portion is:—**असदितिचेत्**; and the reply is:—**न प्रतिषेधमात्रत्वात्**].

Explanation—An objection, to Sūtra 6, may be raised, that if the nature of the effect be admitted not to be derived from the nature of the cause, the nature of the former, and for the matter of that, the former itself, must also be admitted to have been non-existent before causation; and consequently it must also be admitted that 'something' is produced out of 'nothing'. To this objection the reply is that Sūtra 6 does not lay down a general condition of causation, namely that the cause and its effect must be different in nature; but it simply denies the contention that the cause and the effect should be similar *in all respects*.

अपीतौ तद्वत्प्रसङ्गादसमञ्जसम्॥८॥

[A plausible objection, against Brahma being the cause of the universe, is raised here].

अपीतौ (at the time of the general dissolution of the universe; महाप्रलये), तद्वत् (like that, like the effect). प्रसङ्गात् (from consequent following), असमञ्जसम् (incosistent, absurd).

Explanation—At the time of dissolution the effect is absorbed in the cause; and consequently it follows that the cause becomes like the effect; *i.e.,* the cause is affected by the nature of the effect. Now if Brahma be accepted as the cause of the universe, then at the time of the general dissolution Brahma must be affected by the nature of the universe; *i.e.,* He must be insentient like the universe; which is absurd. Brahma, therefore, cannot be the cause of the universe.

न तु दृष्टान्तभावात्॥९॥

[The objection raised in Sūtra 8, is refuted].

न (not), तु (but), दृष्टान्तभावात् (because of existence of examples, as there are direct instances).

Explanation—There is no such universal rule, that the cause, at re-absorption, attains the nature of the effect; as there are instances to the contrary; for example, the effects of earth, such as pots and pitchers, when re-absorbed in earth, do not turn the earth into pots and pitchers, but they themselves are transformed as earth. This rather shows, that instead of Brahma being transformed into the universe, the universe is transformed into Brahma, being merged in Him, at the time of its dissolution. So there cannot be any objection to Brahma being accepted as the cause of the universe on the ground suggested in Sūtra 8.

स्वपक्षे दोषाच्च॥१०॥

[The objections, raised in Sūtras 4 and 8, are levelled against the opponents].

स्वपक्षे (on the side of the first party; on the objection-side), दोषात् (out of defect), च (also).

Explanation—The objections, raised about **Brahma** being the cause of the universe in Sūtras 4 and 8, may **also** be counted on the objection-side, *i.e.*, are similarly applicable against Sāṅkhya also; as the primordial Matter, admitted in Sāṅkhya to be the cause of the universe, is void of all sound, touch, appearance etc.; and from this Matter the universe, full of sound, touch and appearances, is stated to have originated.

That Brahma is the cause of the universe, which is admitted by Śruti, cannot be thrown out by this sort of reasoning.

तर्काप्रतिष्ठानादप्यन्यथानुमेयमिति चेदेवमप्यनिर्मोक्षप्रसङ्गः॥११॥

[Objections, raised in Sūtras 4 and 8, are further, refuted].

तर्क (argument), अप्रतिष्ठानात् (having no firm footing, being unable to stand), अपि (even though), अन्यथा (in another way), अनुमेयम् (to be inferred, to be as certained by arguing), इति (this), चेत् (if), एवम् (in this way; admitting the possibility of further argumentations), अपि (even), अनिर्मोक्ष (non-deliverance, absence of a way out), प्रसङ्गः (consequence).

[This Sūtra consists of two parts; namely, an objection and its reply. The objection-portion is:—तर्काप्रतिष्ठानादप्यन्यथानुमेयमिति चेत्; and the reply-portion is:—एवमप्यनिर्मोक्षप्रसङ्गः।]

Explanation—It may be argued that though the argument, advanced in Sūtra 4 and 8, cannot stand, yet the cause of the universe can be ascertained by arguing in a way different from that of Śruti (*i.e.*, in the way of Sāṅkhya). To this the reply is that even if the possibility of further argumentation be admitted, the consequence would be non-deliverence out of the dificulty; *i.e.*, the difficulty of arguments having no firm stand would remain the same.

Conclusions, arrived at by mere, argumentation, however well-reasoned, and not based on any authoritative statement, cannot be accepted as final; as there still remains the chance of their being refuted by more expert sophists. So the conclusion of Śruti must be accepted.

एतेन शिष्टापरिग्रहा अपि व्याख्याताः॥१२॥

[Other views, not accepted by the Vedas, are refuted].

एतेन (by this, by what has been said against Sāṅkhya), **शिष्टः** (trained; *i.e.*, trained in the Vedas), **अपरिग्रहः** (non-acceptance), **शिष्टापरिग्रहाः** (all other views not accepted by those who are well-in-structed in the Vedas; all the different views contrary to the Vedas), **अपि** (also), **व्याख्याताः** (explained off *i.e.*, refuted).

Explanation—All the different views, contrary to the Vedas, are explained off, (i.e., refuted) by what is said against Sāṅkhya.

भोक्त्रापत्तेरविभागश्चेत् स्याल्लोकवत्॥१३॥

[An objection is raised and refuted].

भोक्तृ (one who enjoys and suffers; one subject to pleasure and pain), **आपत्तेः** (from the objection; if it be objected; as an objection may arise), **अविभागः** (no distinction), **चेत्** (if); **स्यात्** (exists), **लोकवत्** (as in the world; as it appears in the world).

[The Sūtra consists of two parts; namely an objection and its reply. The objection portion is:—**भोक्तृपत्तेरविभागश्चेत्**; and the reply-portion is:—(**अविभागेऽपि विभागः**) **स्यात् लोकवत्**।]

Explanation—Acceptance of Brahma as the material cause of the universe, may be objected to, on the ground that Brahma, in the shape of an individual soul, becomes subject to pleasure and pain, and there remains no distinction between the Creator and the created. To this objection the reply is, that in spite of the disappearance of distinction, there still exists some distinction; as instances are found in this world in the case of the ocean and its waves, and of the sun and its light.

It is deduced from this Sūtra, consistently with Śruti, (vide the passage referred to in Sūtra 25, Sec. I, Chap. I), that although Brahma passes into the universe (immanent aspect), by far the greator portion of Him remains unaffected (transcendent aspect).

तदनन्यत्वमारम्भणशब्दादिभ्यः॥१४॥

[That the effect is not separate from the cause, is shown here].

तत् (तस्य, its, of the universe), अनन्यत्वम् (no difference); आरम्भणम् (origin); आरम्भणशब्दादिभ्यः (from the word *origin* and the like).

Explanation—There is no difference between the universe and Brahma, as is understood from the passage, containing the words *origin* and the like, in the Chāndogya Śruti, to the effect that everything is Brahma. As for instance, there is no separate existence, from earth, of anything made of earth; so there is no separate existence, from Brahma, of anything of this universe.

For the passage containning the word *origin* vide—

"वाचारम्भणं विकारो नामधेयं मृत्तिकेत्येव सत्यम्।"

(For the full expression, its translation and reference vide at the end of Sūtra 9, Sec. I, Chap. I).

For a similar passage vide—

"सर्व्वं खल्विदं ब्रह्म तज्जलानिति शान्त उपासीत"

(For its translation and reference vide Sūtra 2, Sec 1, Chap. I).

It is deduced from this Sūtra that the universe, consisting as it does, of both animate and inanimate objects, has no separate existence from Brahma. Sūtra 13 shows that there is distinction between Jīva, the individual soul and Brahma, the Universal Soul. Sūtra 4, jointly with Sūtra 6, shows that the inanimate universe is distinct from Brahma. From all these

Sūtras taken together, it is concluded that the universe, consisting of both the animate and the inanimate, is identical with, as well as different from, Brahma; just as a bubble is from water.

भावे चोपलब्धेः॥१५॥

[The argument, begun in Sūtra 14 as to how it follows that the effect (the universe) is inseparable from its material cause, Brahma, is continued].

भावे (in case of presence or existence), **च** (also), **उपलब्धेः** (from perception).

Explanation—The effect is perceived only when the cause is present in it; otherwise not. This also proves that the effect is not different from the cause.

For the presence of the cause in the effect vide—

"सन्मूलाः सौम्येमाः सर्व्वा प्रजाः सदायतनाः सत्प्रतिष्ठाः"

(All these created things, O my son, originate from *Sat i.e.*, Brahma, rest in Him and resort to Him).

Chāndogya, Chap. VI, 8, 4.

सत्त्वाच्चावरस्य॥१६॥

[The argument, begun in Sūtra 14, is continued].

सत्वात् (from the existence), **च** (also), **अवरस्य** (of the posterior; *i.e.* of the effect as it comes after the cause; *i.e.*, of the universe).

Explanation—Also from the pre-existence of the universe in Brahma before its evolution in the manifested form, it is understood that the effect is not a separate entity from the cause.

For the existence of the universe in Brahma vide—

"ब्रह्म वा इदमग्र आसीत्"

(Before creation, this *universe* existed as Brahma).

Bṛhadāraṇyaka, Chap. I, 4, 10.

असद्व्यपदेशान्नेति चेन्न धर्म्मान्तरेण वाक्यशेषात् युक्तेः शब्दान्तराच्च॥१७॥

[The argument, that the universe had no existence before creation, is refuted].

असत् (non-existent), व्यपदेशात् (being stated as), न (not, *i.e.* the universe had no existence), इति (this), चेत् (if), न (no, *i.e.*, that is not so), धर्म्मान्तरेण (by other attributes; *i.e.*, by epithets other than 'non-existent'), वाक्यशेषात् (from the latter part of the passage), युक्तेः (from reasoning), शब्दान्तरात् (from another expression), च (also).

[The Sūtra consists of two parts; namely, an objection and its reply. The objection-portion is:—असद्व्यपदेशान्नेतिचेत्; and the reply-portion is:—न धर्म्मान्तरेण वाक्यशेषात्, युक्तेः, शब्दान्तराच्च।]

Explanation—From the word 'असत्' (literally meaning 'non-existent') in the Śruti, it may be argued, that before causation, the universe had no existence. But that argument cannot stand; as the latter part of the same passage uses epithets, other than 'non-existent', to describe the state of the universe before causation; from which we learn that the universe was existent before creation. That the universe existed before creation is also established by the reasoning, that some thing cannot come out of nothing and also by clear statements in other passages of Śruti.

From the reasons adduced above, the word 'असत्', used in the beginning of the passage, must be understood to mean, not *absolutely non-existent,* but *existent in an extremely subtle form*; and as such, not existing in its present gross form.

The beginning of the passage is:—

"असदेवेदमग्र आसीत्"

(This *universe* was at first but *non-existent).*

Chāndogya, Chap. III. 19, 1.

The latter part of the passage is—

"तत् सदासीत्"

(That was existent).

Ibid.

For clear statements in other passages of the Śruti vide the quotation under Sūtra 5, Sec. I, Chap. I.

पटवच्च॥१८॥

[An example, in support of Sūtra 17, is presented].

पटवत् (like a screen; as a screen), **च** (also)

Explanation—As a rolled screen is subsequently unrolled; so the universe, which rested unmanifested before causation, became afterwards manifested.

यथा च प्राणादिः॥१९॥

[Another illustration, in support of Sūtra 17, is presented].

यथा (as), **च** (also), **प्राणादिः** (the Prāṇa and other vital functions; the five vital functions; the Life-Energy and other vital forces).

Explanation—As in the suspension of our mental operation, caused by stopping of respiration, accessory to meditation, all the five vital functions or forces become inoperative by being merged in the principal force (the Life-Energy); but when that suspension of mental operation is released by relaxing the tension those vital forces become again operative; so the universe also, remaining merged in the Universal Soul, Brahma, becomes manifested in creation.

इतरव्यपदेशाद्धिताकरणादिदोषप्रसक्तिः॥२०॥

[The discussions on the relation of the universe to Brahma having been finished, the question of the relation of the individual soul to Brahma is being raised by way of an objection in this Sūtra].

इतरः (other *than Brahma, i.e.,* the individual soul), **व्यपदेशात्** (from the expression, by expressing), **हिताकरणादिदोषः** (**हितअकरण-आदि दोषः**—the defect of not doing good), **प्रसक्तिः** (**प्रसङ्गः** occasion).

Explanation—By stating the individual soul to be one with Brahma, there arises the occasion for apprehending a defect in the wisdom and intelligence of Brahma that He is not doing good to Himself by creating sorrows in consequence of repeated births and deaths, for Himself. (This objection is refuted later on).

अधिकं तु भेदनिर्देशात्॥२१॥

[The objection, raised in Sūtra 20, is refuted].

अधिकं (something more), **तु** (but), **भेदनिर्देशात्** (by pointing out the distinction).

Explanation—Though Brahma assumes the form of the individual soul, yet He is not exhausted thereby, but remains as something more, *i.e.,* as the controller of the individual soul; this is evident from the distinction pointed out in Śruti. So there is no occasion for the defect spoken of in Sūtra 20.

For the distinction referred to vide the Śruti—

"आत्मानमन्तरो यमयति।"

(*Who*, being within, controls the soul). (Bṛhadāraṇyaka (Mādhyandina branch), Chap III, 7, 22.

अश्मादिवच्च तदनुपपत्तिः॥२२॥

[The objection, raised in Sūtra 20, is further refuted].

अश्मादिवत् (like stone), **च** (also), **तत्** (**तस्य**, its, of the objection raised in Sūtra 20), **अनुपपत्तिः** (unreasonableness).

Explanation—As the stone is a transformation of earth, and in fact the same as earth, and yet different from it; likewise, the individual soul is essentially the same as the Universal Soul but in his special characteristics he is also different from Him. So, though the individual soul is in reality the same as Brahma, yet he, being a transitory manifestation, is subject to enjoyment and suffering; but the Universal Soul being the real and permanent entity, these transient conditions can never touch Him; just as the transitory form, stone, cannot affect the primary element, earth, with its defects. So the objection raised in Sūtra 20 is unreasonable.

उपसंहारदर्शनान्नेति चेन्न क्षीरवद्धि॥२३॥

[An objection, that materials are necessary for the creation of the universe is refuted].

उपसंहार (collection of materials), **दर्शनात्** (from seeing), **उपसंहारदर्शनात्** (as workmen are found to collect materials to accomplish their works), **न** (not), **इति** (this), **चेत्** (if); **न** (no; *i.e.*, the objection cannot stand), **क्षीरवत्** (like milk), **हि** (**यतः**, as because).

[The Sūtra consists of two parts; namely, an argument against Brahma being the creator of the universe, and its reply. The argument is :—**उपसंहारदर्शनान्नेतिचेत्**; and the reply is:—**न क्षीरवत् हि**].

Explanation—It may be argued that as workmen are found to collect materials to accomplish their works, Brahma also must have required materails where of to create the universe; but because there was, before creation, no other thing than Brahma, He could not have brought about his work of creation for want of any material; just as a potter could not have made his pots if there had been no materials, such as earth and water, before him. This argument is refuted by saying that materials are not required in every case; as for instance, milk itself is transformed into curd. so Brahma, by His inscrutable power, manifests Himself in the form of the phenomenal world.

देवादिवदपि लोके॥२४॥

[An argument, in support of Sūtra 23, is adduced].

देवादिवत् (like the deities and the saints), **अपि** (also), **लोके** (in this world).

Explanation—It is well known that a deity or a saint can create particular things by the exercise of mere volition, without the aid of any constituent materials. Likewise Brahma has brought forth this universe out of Himself, simply by the fiat of His will.

कृत्स्नप्रसक्तिर्निरवयवत्वशब्दकोपो वा॥२५॥

[An objection, that Brahma is not the material cause of the universe, is raised].

कृत्स्न (entire, full, total), **प्रसक्तिः** (exigency), **निरवयवत्व** (being without parts); **शब्द** (word; expressions in Śruti), **कोपः** (**विरोधः**, incongruity), **शब्दकोपः** (incongruity in the expressions of Śruti), **वा** (otherwise).

Explanation—If Brahma be the material cause of the universe, and if He be accepted as having no parts, then the exigency arises that He is transformed into the universe in His entirety. This would mean that He is entirely exhausted in the universe. In order to avoid this defect if He be admitted to be in some part manifested in the universe and in other parts to remain beyond the universe then He must be divisible and therefore finite in form, which is incongruous with the doctrine of Śruti. So Brahma is not the material cause of the universe. (The objection is refuted in the next Sūtra).

श्रुतेस्तु शब्दमूलत्वात्॥२६॥

[The objection, raised in Sūtra 25, is, refuted].

श्रुतेः (from Śruti; as it is stated in Śruti); **तु** (but), **शब्द** (here, Śruti); **मूल** (foundation) **शब्दमूलत्वात्** (as Śruti is the foundation).

Explanation—It is stated in Śruti that Brahma is the material, as well as the efficient, cause of the universe; and it is further stated therein, that He is also beyond the universe. As Śruti is the foundation of all proofs about Brahma, it cannot be rejected by mere argumentation. Therefore, the objection raised in Sūtra 25 is futile.

For statement of the Śruti vide—

"यथोर्णनाभिः सृजते तथा पुरुषाद्भवति विश्वम्।"

(As the spider weaves the cob-web *out of its own substance*, so the universe comes into existence out of the Spirit).

आत्मनि चैवं विचित्राश्च हि॥२७॥

[The objection, raised in Sūtra 25, is further refuted].

आत्मनि (in the individual soul), **च** (also) **एवं** (thus), **विचित्राः** (diverse), **च** (also), **हि** (यतः, because).

Explanation—As even the limited souls can exist thus, *i.e.*, without being entirely transformed into diverse objects created by them by dint of volition, (for instance, when a man creates many things in his dream, or when a god produces many wonderful things by his supernatural power), it is surely possible for the All-powerful Brahma to exist without being entirely transformed into the universe.

(Compare Sūtra 24 of this section).

स्वपक्षे दोषाच्च॥२८॥

[The objection, raised in Sūtra 25, is further refuted].

स्वपक्षे (**पूर्व्वपक्षे**, on the first side of the argument, on the objection-side) **दोषातं** (from defects), **च** (also).

Explanation—The argument, raised in Sūtra 25, cannot stand, also because the same charge can be levelied against the objection-side.

The objections, raised, by way of defects, against the view that formless Brahma is the cause of the universe, are, on the contrary, applicable against the opposite view, such as, those of the Vaiśeṣika and the Sāṅkhya philosophies. In Vaiśeṣika, invisible and formless atoms are admitted to unite to form a visible thing with a shape; but if a formless atom unite with another formless atom, the result cannot but be formless. In Sāṅkhya, the primordial Matter, which is admitted there as the cause of the universe, is also stated to be formless. In both these systems of philosophy the formation of a visible thing out of a formless cause is admitted; so similar objections, are applicable against them as well.

सर्व्वोपेता च सा तद्दर्शनात्॥२९॥

[The objection, raised in Sūtra 25, is further refuted].

सर्व्वोपेता (**सर्व्व-उपेता**, endowed with all powers, all-powerful), **च** (also), **सा** (**सा देवता**, that Deity, *i.e.*, Brahma), **तद्दर्शनात्** (as that is shown in the Śruti).

Explanation—That Brahma is all-powerful, as is shown in the Śruti. So it is perfectly within His powers to be manifested as the universe, and to be, at the same time, beyond it.

विकरणत्वान्नेति चेत्तदुक्तम्॥३०॥

[Another objection, to Brahma being the cause of the universe, is refuted].

करण (an organ of sensation or action), **विकरणत्वात्** (because of want of organs of sensation and voluntary action), **न** (not), **इति** (this), **चेत्** (if), **तदुक्तम्** (that is already replied to).

[The Sūtra consists of an objection and its reply. The objection-portion is:—**विकरणत्वात् न इतिचेत्**; and the reply-portion is:—**तदुक्तम्**.]

Explanation—The Śruti says that Brahma has no organs of sensation and voluntary action; it may, therefore, be objected that, though Brahma is all-powerful, it does not become possible for Him, without organs, to create the universe.

To this objection the reply has already been made in Sūtras 23 and 28, (milk requires no organ to be transformed into curd; and these objections may be urged against the views of Sāṅkhya and Vaiśeṣika as well). Śruti says that He can do everything without the aid of organs.

Vide the Śruti:—

"अपाणिपादो जवनो गृहीता पश्यत्यचक्षुः स शृणोत्यकर्णः।"

(Seizing without hands, running without legs, He sees without eyes and hears without ears).

Śvetāśvatara-Śruti, Chap. III, 19.

न प्रयोजनवत्वात्॥३१॥

[Another objection, to Brahma being the cause of the universe, is raised].

न (not, *i.e.,* Brahma cannot be the creator), प्रयोजनवत्त्वात् (because of necessity).

Explanation—If Brahma be said to be the creator of the universe, He must have some necessity for doing so; but He being described in Śruti as void of all desires, He cannot be said to be the creator of the universe, as He cannot have any motive or necessity for creating. (This objection is refuted by the following Sūtra).

लोकवत्तु लीलाकैवल्यम्॥३२॥

[The objection, raised in Sūtra 31, is replied to].

लोकवत् (as in the world), तु (but), लीलाकैवल्यम् (लीलामात्रम्, mere pastime).

Explanation—Brahma has created the universe, not out of any desire or motive; but it is simply His pastime (proceeding from His own nature, which is inherent in, and inseparable from, Him), as it is seen also in the world, that sometimes a rich man does some action without any necessity, simply for fun.

वैषम्यनैर्घृण्ये न सापेक्षत्वात् तथा हि दर्शयति॥३३॥

[The accusation, that Brahma is partial and unkind in His creation of the universe, is removed].

वैषम्यं (inequality, partiality), **नैर्घृण्यं** (unkindness), **न** (no, *i.e.*, cannot be ascribed to Brahma), **सापेक्षत्वात्** (because of dependence upon, as it is dependent on something else), **तथा** (the same), **हि** (also), **दर्शयति** (shows, *i.e.*, the Śruti shows).

Explanation—Partiality and unkindness on account of the difference, found in the creation, between the rich and the poor, the high and the low, cannot be ascribed to Brahma; as enjoyment and suffering of the individual soul are determined by his own previous good and bad actions. Śruti also shows the same thing.

Vide the Śruti:—

"पुण्यो वै पुण्येन कर्म्मणा भवति पापः पापेन।"

(One becomes virtuous by his virtuous deed and sinful by his sinful act).

Bṛhadāraṇyaka, Chap III, 2, 13

न कर्म्मविभागादिति चेन्नानादित्वादुपपद्यते चाप्युपलभ्यते च॥३४॥

[An objection, against Sūtra 33. is raised and refuted].

न (no; that individual souls reap the consequences of their own deeds of past life, is not true), **कर्म्मविभागात्** (**कर्म्म-अविभागात्**, as there was no distinction of works before creation), **इतिचेत्** (if it be objected in this way), **न** (no, the objection cannot stand), **अनादित्वात्** (as it is without a beginning), **उपपद्यते** (is proved by reasoning), **च** (and), **अपि** (assuredly), **उपलभ्यते** (is found in Śruti), **च** (also).

[The Sūtra consists of two parts; namely, an objection and

its reply. The objection-portion is:—न कर्म्माविभागात् इति चेत् and the reply-portion is:—न, अनादित्वादुपपद्यते चाप्युपलभ्यते च।].

Explanation—An objection may be raised to Sūtra 33, to the effect that as there was no distinction of works before creation of the universe, there being the absolutely one Real Being, (vide the quotation, from the Chāndogya, under Sūtra 5, Sec. 1, Chap I), the creation, at the beginning, of one man as rich and happy, and of another as poor and unhappy cannot depend on his own previous good or bad works. This objection cannot stand; as the creation of the universe is also without a beginning; there was never a time that may be said to be an absolute beginning, creation and destruction of the universe are following each other continually by rotation without any beginning and end; and the condition of individual souls in any particular cycle of creation is predetermined by their actions in the previous cycle[5]. By reasoning also it can be deduced that the universe could not be created suddenly. It is also found in Śruti that creation is but an infinite chain of interminable links without a beginning and without an end.

Vide the Śruti—

"सूर्य्याचन्द्रमसौ धाता यथापूर्व्वमकल्पयत्"

(The creator designed and brought forth the sun and the moon just as He did before *in previous Kalpas*, *i.e.* cycles).

Ṛgveda, X, 190, 3.

सर्व्वधर्म्मोपपत्तेश्च॥३५॥

[Another reason, to prove that Brahma is the cause of the universe, is adduced].

सर्व्वधर्म्म (all the attributes) उपपत्तेः (from the reasonableness), च (also).

Explanation—As all the attributes, belonging to the cause of the universe, are reasonably found in Brahma, He must be admitted to be the cause.

SECTION—II

In the first section of the Second Chapter, Brahma's authorship of the universe has been established on the authority of the scriptures supported by logic. In this section, the framer of the Sūtras proceeds to examine the theories of creation advanced by other schools of thought in vogue in his time. Here he refutes by reasoning the matter-theory of Sāṅkhya philosophy, the Atom-theory of the Vaiśeṣika philosophy, the momentary and the Nihilistic view of the Buddhists, the Jaina-theory of simultaneous existence and non-existence, the Pāśupata theory of co-ordinate duality and the theory of Energy unaided by Intelligence.

In Sūtras 1-10, the principle of the Sāṅkhya philosophy is further refuted by reasoning. From the methodical arrangement, seen in the causation of the universe, it is not reasonable to suppose that blind Matter, without the aid of intelligence, can have any inclination for the creation of the universe. The argument, that as the cloud spontaneously melts into rain, and as the cow's milk does of itself ooze out of the udder into the mouth of the calf, so Matter may spontaneously pass into the state of the universe, cannot stand, because in both the cases an intelligent power works on the back-ground. Sāṅkhya professes that Pradhāna (Matter) has no external cause to put it into activity—it can work quite independently—his Puruṣa (Spirit) being always inactive and indifferent; so the contention, that Matter, in *presence* of Spirit, acquires a tendency towards action, is groundless. The argument, that as grass eaten by a cow is itself turned into milk, so Matter is of itself turned into the visible universe, cannot also stand; as no such transformation is found on the part of the grass eaten by a bull; so, without admitting an additional cause, Matter by itself cannot be said to be the cause of the universe. Again it may be argued, that as a cripple, sitting on the shoulders of a blind man, shows the way and the blind man walks, so the independent and blind Matter, in conjunction with the passive but intelligent Spirit, originates the universe; this argument also cannot stand; as in that case, the perfect inactivity and indifference of Puruṣa on the one hand, and the absolute independence of Pradhāna on the other, cannot be reconciled with each other. Transformation of Pradhāna into the universe is explaned in Sāṅkhya by assuming successive predominance of one of the three Guṇas (the constituents of Pradhāna) over the rest. But Sāṅkhya assumes that on the eye of creation there was perfect equilibrium among the three constituents of Matter, namely Satva (intelligence), Rajas (activity) and Tamas (inertia), and so there was nothing to start Pradhāna into activity. Thus, there being, in the beginning of creation, no cause for the disturbance of the state of equilibrium and for the desired subordination of two constituents to the preponderating third, it was not possible for Pradhāna to be transformed into the universe. This view of the sage Kapila, as it is found in the Sāṅkhya philosophy, is also contrary to the views of the Vedas.

Sūtras 11-17 refute the Atom-theory of the Vaiśeṣika philosophy, where the indivisible minute atoms are stated to be the cause of the universe. If an atom be admitted to be divisible and thus have some magnitude, it ceases to be an atom; as in that case *it may be conceived to be further divisible,* however infinitesimally small it may be; on the other hand, if an atom be said to be without any magnitude, it is not possible for any number of such partless atom to produce by their union a substance with form. Moreover the inanimate atoms can have no tendency, of themselves, to unite together and cohere, so as to form compounds. Adṛṣta, the sum total of previous deeds waiting, as a latent force, to bear fruit in future, is admitted in

Vaiśeṣika as the cause of cohesion of atoms at the time of creation. But if the latent force be an inherent property of atoms, they will always remain united; so there will be no dissolution, and no chance for fresh creation; if the force, being an inherent property of atoms, happens to act but unexpectedly, another cause for such unexpected happening is required to be assumed. If the latent force, on the other hand, be not an inherent property of atoms, it cannot urge them towards mutual cohesion. So there cannot be creation of the universe by cohesion of atoms. It is admitted in the Vaiśeṣika system, that the atoms of earth, water, fire and air are perceptible to the senses, being possessed of smell, taste, appearance, and touch; they also, therefore, become perishable, as is the case with every perceptible thing; and this is contrary to the Vaiśeṣika theory itself. If all classes of atoms be admitted to posses the same common attributes, then the atoms of earth, water, fire and air, lose all their distinctness; if, on the contrary, each class of atoms be admitted to possess any particular attribute, and not any other, such as smell, taste, colour or touch, then every substance, such as earth made of the atoms of earth, or water made of the atoms of water should have only the particular attribute of the causal atoms of which it is made; but, in fact, each of the substances, earth, water etc., is found to possess more attributes than one, such as smell, taste, colour and touch. Thus, whether all the atoms are admitted to possess the same common attributes, or a different particular attribute for each of them, the case on either hypothesis becomes defective. So the atom-theory of Vaiśeṣika on the causation of the universe does not stand to reason in any way. This atom-theory is also not accepted by the Vedas.

Sūtra 18-32 refute the Buddhistic theory of momentarism and nihilism. According to them things are of two kinds, namely external (things visible, tangible, etc). and internal (thinking, feeling etc).; external things are produced by the union of atoms, and internal things are produced by uninterrupted and continuous flow of momentary and broken consciousnesses.

Atoms and consciousnesses are, according to them, both inanimate. But there is nothing animate to guide them to unite into an external thing or to form a continuous mental phenomenon. The union of atoms and the continuous flow of mental phenomena are, according to them, caused by relation of interdependence; but this mutual interdependence cannot produce cohesion. They think every thing as momentary; things of the previous moment do not exist in the next moment. At the time of the appearance of the consequent, the antecedent has already disappeared; so it is not possible for the antecedent to be the cause of the consequent. Even the Buddhists admit the existence of a cause for an effect; for instance, senses, light, mental activity and objects perceptible by the senses are, in their view, the causes for the generation of consciousness. So if a cause be required to be admitted for the production of an effect, the antecedent event (*i.e.*, the cause) must exist simultaneously also with the subsequent event (*i.e.*, the effect). Consequently the theory of momentary existence of things, itself, falls to the ground. Destruction due to a cause, and destruction without any cause, which the Buddhists contrive, are also impossible; because even in their view, the continuous flow of cause and effect goes on without interruption. Again, had destruction been a reality, this continuous flow of cause and effect would have been impossible. Moreover the cause cannot be said to be totally destroyed, as it gives rise to the consciousness of identity, that is, it reminds one that a particular thing was previously perceived.Everything, in their view, is momentary; to consider it permanent is ignorance; destruction of this ignorance is salvation. Destruction of ignorance again, is effected by the adoption of some means (penance etc)., or it takes place spontane ously of itself; but it becomes defective in both ways; because, on the one hand, this destruction of ignorance cannot be attained by any means, which itself, like every other thing, is also momentary according to the Buddhistic view; on the other hand, it does not occur spontaneously, as in that case there would have been no necessity for their scriptural precepts for the attainment of salvation. Ākāśa is regarded by the Buddhists as a non-entity, which is not reasonable; because Ākāśa is the receptacle of sound, just as earth, air etc., are the receptacles of smell, touch etc.; and therefore why should Ākāśa alone be singled out as a non-entity to the exclusion of earth, air etc.? The things we perceive at the present moment are recognised to have been perceived previously; from this consciousness of identity also, it may be concluded that the Buddhistic theory of every thing being momentary is irrational. The universe, which is a reality, is stated by them to have arisen out of non-entity; this is an absurd supposition. If an existing thing can arise out of nothing, then an indifferent man also can attain salvation without efforts; *i.e.*, salvation may be gained like a windfall. The external things are stated by them to have no objective reality; but this is not true, as they are actually perceived to exist. It cannot be held, that as the scene in a dream is a fantasm, so the scene in a wakeful state is also a fantasm; because dreaming consciousness is of a different kind from waking consciousness: the consciousness in a dream depends on the previous knowledge acquired in the wakeful state; while consciousness in a wakeful state does not depend on anything else, but on the actual perception by the senses. The Buddhists hold that though external things do not actually exist, impressions (वामना) exist; and from these impressions diversities of consciousness arise. This is also not possible; as, in their view, there can be no perception of an external thing which is itself non-existent; and if there has been no previous perception, there is nothing to leave an impression on the mind. To follow their theory of nihilism, impression cannot be an existing thing, on the additional ground, that self (अहं, ego), which receives the impression. is itself in their view momentary. So the nihilism of the Buddhists, purporting that nothing exists, is fallacious, being cotrary to all proofs, such as perception, inference, analogy and scripture.

Sūtras 33-36 refute the Jaina theory, according to which, everything is at once existing and non-existing; and the soul is of the size of the body; but the body, attained at the final emancipation, is unchangeable and everlasting; and the final emancipation is the existence in a state of permanent bliss in space beyond the worlds. This theory is untenable; as two contradictory attributes, namely existence and non-existence, are predicated of one and the same thing at the same time—which is inconceivable. The view that the soul is commensurate with the body, also cannot be entertained; because an animal soul living in a small body, such as the body of an ant, at the termination of its body, may attain, from the consequences of its actions, a larger body, such as the body of an elephant; and consequently the soul must either retain its smaller bulk when it has transmigrated into the body of the elephant, or it must increase its bulk to the full dimensions of the elephant. In the former case, the theory, that the soul is commensurate with the body, fails; and in the latter case the stability of the dimensions of the soul is impaired, and as a consequence, the soul becomes changeable and perishable like the body of flesh and blood; and this is absurd. By admitting the size of the body, attained at the final emancipation, to be everlasting, its size at the initial and the intervening stages must also be admitted to be everlasting, must be always everlasting; thus there remains no distinction between the states of emancipation and bondage. So the theory, that the body at the final emancipation is everlasting and that the soul is co-existent and of the same size with the body, and that only the aggregate of the two conjointly constitutes the universe, is not a sound one.

Sūtra 37-41 refute the theory, of the followers of Paśupati (the Lord of animals), which holds Paśupati, their God, as the efficient cause of the universe, and the inanimate primordial Matter as its material cause. This view is contrary to the Vedas, which hold Brahma both as the efficient and the material cause of the universe. God, in their view, is ever pure, without attributes and activity; so no relation can be established between Him and the inanimate primordia Matter; consequently He cannot urge and regulate matter to work. That by assuming a body, like a potter, God becomes the efficient cause of the universe, is also a fallacious conclusion; as all bodies are perishable. It is untenable that God, Who is according to the Pāśupats, eternal, should inhabit in a perishable body and so become dependent on another additional instrument. God cannot have bodily form. It cannot be argued, that as the bodiless individual soul functions through a body by means of organs of senses, so God functions through the universe by means of similar organs; as in that case God also like the individual soul, becomes subject to enjoyment and suffering, terminable by births and deaths and destitute of omniscience; for, nothing, with organs of senses and subject to enjoyment and suffering, is found to be omniscient and imperishable; and thus God loses all His supremacy. This sort of God is not admitted by the Pāśupats even.

Sūtras 42-45 refute the theory that the universe is caused out of the inanimate Energy without the help of a wise and intelligent Spirit. As energy is never found to exist without a support, Energy cannot, without the support of Spirit, be the cause of the universe. It is seen in the world that a female, after sexual union with a male, becomes the cause of progeny without further help from the male; so it may be argued that Energy, in union with Spirit at the beginning, itself becomes the cause of universe without further help from Spirit. This analogy also cannot hold good, as before creation Spirit had no organs of generation by which He could unite with Energy. This theory is also contrary to the views of Śruti and Smṛti. If it be admitted that Energy has intelligence for its essential attribute, and is the cause Energy and Brahma become identical. Vedānta also admits that Brahma is possessed of inherent energy, and that the universe is originated from the energy of Brahma. By such admission, the theory of the supremacy of Energy without Spirit, in the causation of the universe loses its force; and thus Brahma is proved to be the Supreme Cause.

To put all things concisely in a nutshell, Ācārya Vyāsa refutes, in this section, all the theories prevalent in his time and inconsistent with the Vedānta theory: the theories refuted are (1) the theory of Blind Matter, (2) the Cohesion of Atoms, (3) the Idea and the Impression, (4), the Union of the Co-eternal Body and Soul, (5) the Conjunction of the inactive Spirit with the inanimate Matter and (6) Energy independent of Spirit, as the supreme cause of the universe.

रचनानुपपत्तेश्च नानुमानम्॥१॥

[An argument is adduced to the effect that Sāṅkhya's Matter is not the cause of the universe].

रचना (the method of arrangement in the creation; the design in creation), **अनुपपत्तेः** (from want of reason; as it is unreasonable), **च** (also), **न** (not), **अनुमानम्** (what is arrived at by inference, *i.e.*, the Matter of Sāṅkhya).

Explanation—From the intelligent, elaborate and methodical design in creation, it is not reasonable to infer that blind Matter can be credited with the authorship of the multifarious causation.

प्रवृत्तेश्च॥२॥

[This is an argument in support of Sūtra 1].

प्रवृत्तिः (inclination); **प्रवृत्तेश्च** (**प्रवृत्तयनुपपत्तेश्च**, because inclination also is impossible).

Explanation—Blind Matter cannot be the cause of the universe, because it is also impossible for it to have an inclination for creation.

पयोऽम्बुवच्चेत् तत्रापि॥३॥

[The argument, in support of Sūtra 1, is continued].

पयोऽम्बुवत् (like milk and water), **चेत्** (if), **तत्र** (in those cases), **अपि** (too).

Explanation—It may be argued that as the cow's milk does, of itself, ooze out of the udder into the mouth of the calf, and as the cloud spontaneously melts into rain, so matter may spontaneously pass into the state of the universe. This argument cannot stand, seeing that in both cases there are such design and arrangement as require an intelligent power to work in the back-ground, (as is also stated in Śruti).

For the Intelligent Power, working in the back-ground, vide the Śruti:—

"योऽप्सु तिष्ठन्नद्भ्योऽन्तरो योऽपोऽन्तरो यमयति।"

(Who, dwelling in the water, is the Internal Spirit of the water and rules the water from within).

Bṛhadāraṇyaka, Chap. III, 7, 4.

व्यतिरेकानवस्थितेश्चानपेक्षत्वात्॥४॥

[The argument, in support of Sūtra 1, is continued].

व्यतिरेक (an external agent), **अनवस्थितेः** (from non-existence, as it does not exist), **च** (also), **अनपेक्षत्वात्** (because of indifference).

Explanation—According to the Sāṅkhyas there is no external agent to urge Pradhāna into activity, their Puruṣa being supposed to be always indifferent and unresponsive to the first stimulus for starting the process of creation. So there is no agency to disturb the primordial equilibrium, and Sāṅkhya's Pradhāna cannot, therefore, be the efficient cause of the universe.

अन्यत्राभावाच्च न तृणादिवत्॥५॥

[The argument, in support of Sūttra 1, is continued].

अन्यत्र (in the other case), **अभावात्** (for want), **च** (also), **न** (not), **तृणादिवत्** (like the grass etc).

Explanation—It may be argued, that as the inanimate grass, eaten by a cow, is of itself turned into milk; so Matter is of itself turned into the visible universe. But this argument cannot stand, because the grass eaten by the male of the bovine species never turns into milk. So without admitting an additional cause, matter, by itself, cannot be said to be the cause of the universe.

अभ्युपगमेऽप्यर्थाभावात्॥६॥

[The argument, in support of Sūtra 1, is continued].

अभ्युपगमे (admitting, taking for granted), **अपि** (even), **अर्थाभावात्** (for want of any purpose).

Explanation—Even admitting, for the sake of argument, that blind Matter is capable of an inherent tendency for a change, its action cannot be purposive, so as to account for the design in creation.

It is difficult to understand how insentient Pradhāna can intelligently and voluntarily present, before the sentient Puruṣa (spirit), enjoyment (**भोग**) and release (**मोक्ष**) one after the other, and how it can produce things with purpose and design.

पुरुषाश्मवदितिचेत् तथापि॥७॥

[The argument, in support of Sūtra 1, is continued].

पुरुष (a person), **अश्म** (a stone; a loadstone; a magnet), **वत्** (like); **पुरुषाश्मवत्** (like a cripple and a blind man, and also like a magnet and a piece of iron), **इति** (this), **चेत्** (if), **तथापि** (still).

Explanation—It may be argued, that as a cripple sitting on the shoulder of a blind man, shows the way and the blind man follows his lead, and as a magnet leads a piece of iron; so the transformable Matter (though actually separate and insentient, as admitted by Sāṅkhya), in conjunction with the intelligent (though unchangeable and inactive) Spirit, originates the universe. But the argument cannot stand; as, in that case, the perfect inactivity and indifference of Puruṣa on one hand, and the absolute independence of Pradhāna on the other, cannot be reconciled with each other.

अंगित्वानुपपत्तेश्च॥८॥

[The argument, in support of Sūtra 1, is continued].

अङ्गित्व (being preponderant), **अनुपपत्तेः** (because of impossibility; as it is impossible), **च** (also).

Explanation—According to the Sāṅkhyas Matter is propounded to be composed of three 'Guṇas' (like the strands of a rope), namely, Satva (intelligence), Rajas (activity) and Tamas (inertia). These three Guṇas being the constituents of all objects. matter, which is composed of them, is inferred to be the cause of the universe. Again Sāṅkhya holds, that before creation the three Guṇas remain in a state of equilibrium, and creation begins when the equilibrium is disturbed by the preponderance of one, the Satva, over the two others.

This Sūtra says that such preponderance is impossible. Why should one Guṇa preponderate over the other two, Sāṅkhya cannot explain. So, for this impossibility of such preponderance of one over the others, Matter cannot be accepted to be the cause of the universe.

अन्यथानुमितौ च ज्ञशक्तिवियोगात्॥९॥

[The argument, in support of Sūtra 1, is continued].

अन्यथा (in other ways), **अनुमितौ** (in the inference; if it be inferred), **च** (even), **ज्ञ-शक्ति** (facutly of consciousness) **वियोगात्** (because of dissociation).

Explanation—Even if we suppose that the said preponderance can be accounted for in one way or another, and thus the transformation of the primordial Matter into the universe be somehow explained; yet it can, on no account, be concluded that matter can be held to be the cause of the universe, as it is held to be destitute of the faculty of consciousness.

विप्रतिषेधाच्चासमञ्जसम्॥१०॥

[The argument, in support of Sūtra 1, is concluded].

विप्रतिषेधात् (because of contradiction), **च** (also), **असमञ्जसम्** (inconsistent).

Explanation—The view of the sage Kapila, as stated in

the Sāṅkhya philosophy, holding matter as the cause of the universe, is inconsistent, because it conflicts with the view of the Vedānta, and is, at the same time, self-contradictory.

महद्दीर्घवद्वा ह्रस्वपरिमण्डलाभ्याम् ॥११॥

[The theory of the Vaiśeṣika philosophy, that formless indivisible atoms enter into the composition of the universe, is now refuted].

The theory of the Vaiśeṣika philosophy is stated below: The Vaiśeṣika philosophy of the sage Kaṇāda, holds that all things having any shape or form are perishable, and they are all made of minute, indivisible, formless and immutable particles known as atoms. These indivisible and formless atoms are stated to be the cause of the universe. They are of four kinds—the atoms of earth, the atoms of water, the atoms of fire and the atoms of air. Prior to the dawn of creation, only these atoms exist distinct from one another; and nothing with any shape or form exists. At the beginning of creation, one atom (a monad) unites with another, forming a *diad* (an aggregate of two atoms), which in turn unites with another, forming a *triad* (an aggregate of three atoms), and so on. In this way a visible world is brought into existence].

महत् (the size of an aggregate of three atoms; the size of a *triad*), दीर्घ (the size of an aggregate of four atoms), वत् (like), वा (again); ह्रस्व (the size of a diad), परिमण्डल (the size of a monad—the minutest single atom); ह्रस्वपरिमण्डलाभ्याम (by the union of monads and of diads).

Explanation—Again, the inconsistency in the origination of an aggregate of three and of four atoms from the union of monads and of diads of Vaiśeṣika, is like the inconsistency in the origination of the universe from the insentient Matter of Sāṅkhya. The former inconsistency is thus exposed—

If the atom be admitted as having any parts of any appreciable magnitude then it cannot be an atom, as in that case it may be conceived to be further divisible. On the other hand, if atoms be said to be without parts of any appreciable magnitude, as they are so said in Vaiśeṣika, it does not become possible for such two partless atoms to produce, by their union, a substance having any magnitude; similarly for three atoms and so on. Consequently, composite bodies can never be formed by the union of atoms. The Vaiśeṣika theory of origination of the universe from indivisible atoms is, therefore, untenable.

उभयथापि न कर्म्मातस्तदभावः॥१२॥

[The argument, against the Vaiśeṣika philosophy, commenced in Sūtra 11, is continued].

उभयथा (on both hypotheses), अपि (also), न (not), कर्म्म (action); अतः (therefore) तदभावः (negation of that, *i.e.*, negation of the creation of the universe by cohesion of atoms).

Explanation—All actions bear fruit; but some may wait as latent force to bear fruit in future. This latent force or 'Adṛṣṭa' (अदृष्ट) is said to be the cause of cohesion of atoms in the Vaiśeṣika philosophy. Now, if the possession of the latent force be an inherent property of the atoms, they will always remain united; and there being nothing to break up the bond, there will be no general dissolution, and no necessity of any action on the part of atoms for cohesion in view of fresh creation; moreover if that force act only unexpectedly, another cause for that unexpected action is to be postulated. If the possession of the latent force, on the other hand, be an inherent property of the doer of actions (*i.e.*, the individual soul), and as such in no way connected with the atoms, it cannot urge atoms to unite. On both these hypotheses there is, therefore, negation of creation of the universe by cohesion of atoms.

समवायाभ्युपगमाच्च साम्यादनवस्थितेः॥१३॥

[The argument against the Vaiśeṣika philosophy, commenced in Sūtra 11, is continued].

समवाय (relation of inherence, one of the seven categories of the Vaiśeṣika philosophy, supposed to be inherent in a monad and a diad, by which they stand to each other in the intimate relation of cause and effect), **अभ्युपगमात्** (from admission, admitting), **च** (also), **साम्यात्** (because of parity of reasoning), **अनवस्थितेः** (for want of decision; as the argument may be continued *ad infinitum* without coming to a conclusion).

Explanation—Even admitting the existence of an intimate relation inherent in a monad, as well as in a diad, for their cohesion, as stated in the Vaiśeṣika, its atom-theory cannot stand. As a diad is perfectly different in structure, from its cause (combination of two monads), the Vaiśeṣika system contrives an intimate relation inherent in a monad as well as in a diad for bringing about their cohesion; but as this relation itself is a thing equally perfectly different from a monad and also from a diad, a second relation is to be assumed for putting the first relation into operation, and so on; the argument may thus be continued *ad infinitum* without coming to a decision. So the contrivance of an intimate relation inherent in a monad and a diad, is useless.

नित्यमेव च भावात्॥१४॥

[The argument, against Vaiśeṣika, commenced in Sūtra 11, is continued].

नित्यम् (permanent), **एव** (certainly), **च** (also), **भावात्** (from the possibility).

Explanation—If the tendency of action, towards cohesion be their inherent nature, they cannot but act always, and as a result the universe will continue for ever, and no dissolution will take place. If, again, the tendency be not in their nature, they can never act, and as a result the universe will never be created and only the state of Chaos will continue for ever. So whether the tendency for action be inherent in atoms or not, the possibility of a permanent Cosmos or a permanent Chaos would arise.

रूपादिमत्वाच्च विपर्य्ययो दर्शनात्॥१५॥

[The argument, against Vaiśeṣika, commenced in Sūtra 11, is continued].

रूपादिमत्वात् (having the qualities of colour, smell, taste and touch), च (also), विपर्य्ययः (contrariety), दर्शनात् (as is seen; from common experience).

Explanation—The atoms must be admitted as having the qualities of colour, taste, smell and touch, because their effects are found to possess these as their inherent qualities. Now, if atoms have these qualities, they must be perishable, as all objects having these qulaities, are found, in common experience to be so. But to say that atoms are perishable would belie the Vaiśeṣika view. Moreover, the attributes, which do not exist in the constituent atoms, cannot exist in the constituted aggregate. The atomic theory, being thus self-contradictory, cannot be accepted.

उभयथा दोषात्॥१६॥

[The argument, against Vaiśeṣika, is continued].

उभयथा (in both ways, on either side), च (also), दोषात् (because of defect; as it is defective).

Explanation—If the four kinds of atoms be admitted to possess common attributes, then they cease to be distinct kinds of atoms. If, on the contrary, each class of atoms be admitted to possess a, specific attribute only, such as smell taste, colour or touch, then earth made of the atoms of earth, or water made of the atoms of water, should have only the particular attribute of the causal atoms, of which it is made; but earth, or water, as it is, is found to possess more attributes than one, such as smell, taste, colour and touch. So whether all the four classes of atoms are admitted to possess the same common attributes, or each of them possesses only a specific attribute of its own, the case on either supposition becomes faulty. Therefore the atom-theory of Vaiśeṣika cannot be logically maintained.

अपरिग्रहाच्चात्यन्तमनपेक्षा॥१७॥

[The argument, against Vaiśeṣika, is concluded].

अपरिग्रहात् (because of non-acceptance), च (also), अत्यन्तम् (very much, altogether; *in toto*), अनपेक्षा (disregard; rejection).

Explanation—The atom-theory of the Vaiśeṣika philosophy, being also not accepted by the teachers of the Vedas and the legilators like Manu, should be rejected *in toto*.

समुदाये उभयहेतुकेऽपि तदप्राप्ति : ॥१८॥

[After refuting the atomic theory of Vaiśeṣika, the framer of the Sūtras is now refuting the Buddhistic theories.

The Buddhistic theories are stated below:—

Amongst the Buddhists there are three schools of thought; one school admits the objective reality of everything within the mind and without it; the second school admits the existence of consciousness or idea only; and the third school does not admit the existence of anything internal or external:—this is extreme nihilism (शून्यवाद).

According to the first school mentioned above, all the external things have existence, so also all the internal things, such as consciousness, feelings etc. There are four classes of atoms, such as those of earth, water, fire and air; they are respectively hard, oily, hot and mobile. By mutual union of these atoms all external things are produced. As seedlings are produced from seeds, so from the elements of earth, water, fire, air, Ākāśa and consciousness the animal is produced, without any necessity, in their opinion, of the superintendence of any sentient being. The successive and continuous stream of consciousness as 'I' is termed soul, and there is no permanent soul existing behind the stream.

According to the second school there is no existence of any external thing, everything is simply consciousness or idea. This is pure idealism. According to them the perception of external things is a peculiar trait or flux of consciousness and the perception of internal things is also another trait or flux of consciousness. Internal feelings as well as external things are produced by uninterrupted and continuous flow of momentary and broken consciousnesses (क्षणिकवाद).

According to the third school, there is no real existence of any internal or external thing. Non-existence of everything, in their view, is the only truth.

According to the first and the second school the visible universe is momentary; things of the previous moment do not exist in the next moment, one disappears and the next moment it is replaced by another, there is no connection between the one and the other; everything is like a scene in bioscope, which is produced by the successive appearance and disappearance of several isolated pictures].

समुदायः (the totality of a thing, the aggregate of things), उभयहेतुकः (produced by the two causes), समुदाये उभयहेतुके (even to assume the composition of the aggregates by the two causes), अपि (even), तद् (तस्य its), अप्राप्तिः (non-establishment); तद प्राप्तिः (it cannot be established).

Explanation—According to the Buddhistic theory, things are of two kinds, namely, external objects and internal feelings and ideas. An external object is an aggregate composed, by the union of atoms; and an internal feeling or idea is an aggregate composed, by the uninterrupted and continuous flow, of momentary and broken consciousneses. Atoms and consciousnesses are, according to them, both inanimate; and there is no intelligent power to guide them to unite as an external object (a successive series of perception), or to form an internal state of conciousness (successive series of sensation). Now, even by assuming the formation of the aggregates by the two kinds of causes as stated above the combination itself is not possible for these external atoms and internal sensations, without the intervention of a sentient guide. So the Buddhistic theory cannot be established.

इतरेतरप्रत्ययत्वादुपपन्नमिति चेन्न सङ्घातभावानिमित्तत्वात्॥१९॥

[An objection, against Sūtra 18, is raised and refuted].

इतरेतर-प्रत्ययत्वात् (by reason of their mutual action and reaction), **उपपन्नम्** (proved), **इति** (this), **चेत्** (if), **न** (no, the argument cannot stand), **सङ्घातभाव** (existence of cohesion; cohesion), **अनिमित्तत्वात्** (because of its being no cause; as it is an insufficient cause).

[This Sūtra consists of two parts, an argument for the Buddhistic theory and its reply. The argument is:—**इतरेतरप्रत्ययत्वादुपपन्नमितिचेत्**; the reply is:—**न सङ्घातभावानिमित्तत्वात्.**]

Explanation—It may be argued that the union of atoms and the continuous flow of sensations stated in Sūtra 18, are proved by the mutual interdependence existing among them. But the argument cannot stand, as this mutual interdependence cannot be the cause of their cohesion. Of two things one may produce the other, but that is no reason why they should unite together.

उत्तरोत्पादे च पूर्व्वनिरोधात्॥२०॥

[The argument against the Buddhistic theory, commenced in Sūtra 18, is continued].

उत्तरोत्पादे (at the time of the production of the subsequent thing), **च** (and), **पूर्व्वनिरोधात्** (because of destruction of the previous thing).

Explanation—As according to the Buddhistic theory everything is momentary, a thing of the present moment disappears in the next moment, when its successor appears, *i.e.*, at the time of the appearance of a subsequent thing, the previous thing already disappears; so it is not possible for the previous thing to be the cause of the subsequent thing. Therefore this theory does not stand to reason.

असति प्रतिज्ञोपरोधो यौगपद्यमन्यथा॥२१॥

[The argument, against the Buddhistic theory, is continued].

असति (in the case of non-existence of any cause; if it be admitted that an effect is produced without a cause), प्रतिज्ञा (the proposition that senses, light, mental activity and objects perceptible by the senses, are causes for the generation of consciousness), उपरोधः (contradiction denial), यौगपद्यम् (simultaneous existence), अन्यथा (on the other hand; otherwise).

Explanation—If it be admitted that an effect is produced without a cause, then the theory of causation is altogether ignored; and so the proposition admitted by the Buddhists, that senses, light, mentality and objects of perception together give rise to consciousness, is contradicted. On the other hand, if a cause be required to be admitted for the production of an effect, then it must also be admitted that the cause exists simultaneously with the effect in the next moment, or in other words it must also be admitted that the thing of the previous moment exists in the next moment, otherwise it cannot be the cause of the thing that is to exist in the next moment, (vide the previous Sūtra). But to admit that a thing exists for two moments is to go against their own theory of momentary existence.

प्रतिसंख्याऽप्रतिसंख्यानिरोधा प्राप्तिरविच्छेदात्॥२२॥

[The argument, against the Buddhistic theory, is continued].

प्रतिसंख्यानिरोधः (conscious destruction; destruction due to some cause or agency; causal destruction,) अप्रतिसंख्यानिरोधः (unconscious destruction; destruction by itself without any cause; casual destruction), अप्राप्तिः (non-attainment; impossibility), अविच्छेदात् (because of non-interruption; becasue it goes on without interruption).

Explanation—The destruction of the flow of cause and effect, due to some agency, or destruction without any agency, which the Buddhists assume, are also impossible, because even in their view the flow of cause and effect goes on without interruption, and therefore cannot be subject to either kind of destruction causal or casual. Nor can any individual antecedent of a series be said to be totally destroyed, as it is recognised in its immediate consequent.

उभयथा च दोषात्॥२३॥

[The argument, against the Buddhistic theory, is continued].

उभयथा (in both ways), **च** (also), **दोषात्** (because of defect).

Explanation—Salvation, in the Buddhistic view, is the destruction of *ignorance* (this ignorance is to consider a thing, as permanent, which is, in their opinion, momentary). This ignorance can be destroyed by the adoption of some means, such as penance etc.; or it may destroy itself. But both the alternatives are defective. Because, on the one hand, this destruction of ignorance cannot be attained by the adoption of a penance or the like; for, like every other thing, the means is also momentary according to the Buddhistic view, and is therefore not likely to produce such destruction; on the other hand, destruction cannot take place of its own accord, for in that case all Buddhistic instructions for the attainment of salvation will be useless.

Thus, if we believe in the Buddhistic theory, there can be no voluntary effort on the part of the Sādhaka (the person devoted to religious practices), for the disruption of his continued worldly experiences (**अविद्या**), nor is there any hope of their ever coming to a stand-still by mere exhaustion; for the causes continue to produce their effects, which again continue to produce their own effects and so on, and there is no room left for Sādhanā (practices for salvation).

आकाशे चाविशेषात्॥२४॥

[The argument, against the Buddhistic theory, is continued].

आकाशे (with regard to Ākāśa), **च** (also), **अविशेषात्** (because there is no speciality).

Explanation—The Buddhists do not recognise the existence of Ākāśa *i.e.*, they regard Ākāśa as a non-entity. But this is unreasonable; for being the receptacle of a quality it is a distinct entity like earth, air etc. Ākāśa is the receptacle of sound, earth of smell, and so on, so there is no reason, why Ākāśa alone should be rejected as being a non-entity, while earth, air etc., are recognised as being entities.

अनुस्मृतेश्च॥२५॥

[The argument, against the Buddhistic theory, is continued].

अनुस्मृतेः (from recollection; from the recognition of previously perceived things), च (also).

Explanation—The things previously perceived are recognised to be perceived at the present moment. From this consciousness of identity also, it is concluded that the Buddhistic theory, of everything being momentary, is false.

नासतोऽदृष्टत्वात्॥२६॥

[The argument, against the Buddhistic theory, is continued].

न (not), असतः (of the unreal; of a non-entity), अदृष्टत्वात् (because it is not seen).

Explanation—According to the Buddhistic view, a real thing, *i.e.*, the world, is stated to have sprung into existence out of nothing; but experience belies the theory: an earthenware, for instance, is never found to be produced without clay. Such a hypothetical production can only exist in the imagination, for instance, the child of a barren woman, So this Buddhistic view is untenable.

उदासीनानामपि चैवं सिद्धिः॥२७॥

[The argument, against the Buddhistic theory, is continued].

उदासीनानाम् (of the indifferent), अपि (even), च (also), एवं (in this way), सिद्धिः (success).

Explanation—If something can arise out of nothing, then a man who is indifferent to success, can also attain success in anything (such as gaining salvation) without making any efforts at all; *i.e.*, a real thing (success) may arise out of nothing (inaction). Such a theory will only establish the reign of chance and chaos in place of the reign of law and order.

नाभाव उपलब्धेः।।२८।।

[The argument, against the Buddhistic theory, is continued].

न (not), अभावः (non-existence), उपलब्धेः (because of perception; because they are perceived).

Explanation—The view, of that section of Buddhists which holds that every phenomenon resolves itself into consciousness and idea, without any reality corresponding to it, cannot also be accepted. The external phenomena are not non-existent, as they are actually witnessed by out senses of perception, and reported as such to us and direct us to take action on a firm faith in their objective reality.

वैधर्म्याच्च न स्वप्नादिवत्।।२९।।

[The argument, against the Buddhistic theory, is continued].

वैधर्म्यात् (because of dissimilarity), च (also), न (not), स्वप्नादिवत् (like dreams etc).

Explanation—It is futile to argue, that as the scene in a dream is non-existent, though perceived, so the scene in a wakeful state is also non-existent; because the consciousness in a dream and that in a wakeful state are dissimilar: the consciousness in a dream depends on the previous consciousness in the wakeful state; but the consciousness in the wakeful state does not depend on anything else, but on actual perception by the senses; moreover, the falsity of a dream-perception is established by the succeeding waking state, but the perception of the waking state ever stands unchallenged and uncontradicted.

न भावोऽनुपलब्धेः॥३०॥

[The argument, against the Buddhistic theory, is continued].

न (not), भावः (existence; existence of impressions), अनुपलब्धे (because of want of perception; as there is no perception of an external thing).

Explanation—A class of Buddhists, referred to in Sūtra 28, says that though an external thing does not actually exist, yet its impressions do exist; and from these impressions, diversities of perception arise. This also is not possible, as in their view, there can be no perception of an external thing (which is itself non-existent); and if there be no perception of an external thing, how can it leave an impresssion?

क्षणिकत्वात्॥३१॥

[The argument, against the Buddhistic theory, is continued].

क्षणिकत्त्वात् (because it is momentary).

Explanation—The impression also cannot be said to be abiding, when self (अहं, ego) which is the receptacle of impressions, is according to the Buddhistic view, itself momentary.

सर्व्वथानुपपत्तेश्च॥३२॥

[The argument, against the Buddhistic theory, is concluded here].

सर्व्वथा (in every way), अनुपपत्तेः (it being illogical), च (also).

Explanation—The philosophical Nihilsm of Buddhists, purporting that nothing exists, is fallacious; because it runs counter to every method of proof, (1) perception, (2) inference, (3) testimony of revealed words, and (4) analogy.

[As Śākya Sinha, known as Gautama Buddha, the last and greatest exponent of Buddhism, flourished according to the Hindus, long after the compilation of the Vedānta Sūtras by Ācārya Vyāsa; the latter probably criticises, in his philosophy, the Buddhistic theories than in vogue, but does not say anything against the doctrine preached by Gautama Buddha, who is regarded by the Hindus as the ninth incarnation of Viṣṇu].

नैकस्मिन्नसम्भवात्॥३३॥

[Ācārya Vyāsa, after refuting the 'Nihilistic' views of the Buddhists, now proceeds to refute the Jaina theory; according to which everything is existing as well as non-existing, and the soul is of the size of the body which is apparently subject to constant change; but the body, attained at the final emancipation is unchangeable and ever-lasting. The body which as soul attains on the eve of the final emancipation, represents the size of the soul. Final emancipation, in their view, is the existence in a state of permanent bliss in the space beyond all the worlds].

न (not), **एकस्मिन्** (in one), **असम्भवात्** (as it is absurd).

Explanation—The Jainas admit two contradictory attributes, namely existence and non-existence, to be predicable of everything; which is absurd, just like simultaneous existence of light and darkness in one place.

१२एवं चात्माऽकार्त्स्न्यम्॥३४॥

[Other defects, of the Jaina theory, are shown].

एवं (in this way; as it is suggested by the Jaina theory), **च** (also), **आत्मा** (soul), **अकार्त्स्न्यम्** (**अपूर्णता** instability of dimensions).

Explanation—It is also impossible for us to accept the view of want of integrity on the part of the soul, as suggested by the Jaina theory, which holds, that the soul is of the size of the body. This is absurd, because the soul dwelling in a small body, such as that of an ant, may, at the termination of its body, attain larger dimensions, such as those of an elephant, from the consequences of its actions. Then the soul, which was of the dimensions of an ant, will have either to expand to the size of an elephant, or to remain contracted as before though in the huge body of the elephant. In the former case the stability of the dimensions of the soul is impaired and in the latter case the Jaina theory itself falls to the ground.

न च पर्य्यायादप्यविरोधो विकारादिभ्यः ॥३५॥

[Defects, of the Jaina theory, are being shown].

न (not), च (also), पर्य्यायात् (from succession; because of assuming by succession), अपि (even), अविरोधः (no inconsistency), विकारादिभ्यः (from change etc.; as it then becomes subject to change etc)..

Explanation—It cannot also be said that there is no inconsistency in the theory of the soul being commensurate with bodies; it assumes in successive stages; because, on the assumption of the hypothesis, the soul would be subject to change etc., in eonsequence of the change in the bodies it inhabits.

There is inconsistency even in holding that the soul has a form, and that in the body of an elephant it increases and in the body of an ant it diminishes alternately according to the dimensions of the body assumed; because in the case of the soul having any form, it becomes changeable and perishable like the body of flesh and blood.

अन्त्यावस्थितेश्चोभयनित्यत्वादविशेषः ॥३६॥

[Discussion, on the defects of the Jaina theory, is concluded].

अन्त्य (the size at the final stage or emancipation), अवस्थितेः (because of permanent existence), च (also), उभयनित्यत्त्वात् (as both are permanent), अविशेषः (no distinction).

Explanation—The Jainas say that the size of the body, and consequently that of the soul, attained at the time of the final emancipation, is unchangeable and everlasting. If so, the size of the body and also that of the soul at the initial and the intermediate stages must also be supposed to be permanent; a thing, once admitted to be unchangeable, must continue to be so. So the size being permanent in all the stages—the state of final emancipation, the state of bondage and so on—the distinction between the emancipated and the unemancipated states becomes illusory. So the theory that the soul is commensurated with the body is untenable.

पत्युरसामञ्जस्यात्॥३७॥

[The framer of the Sūtras is now refuting the doctrine of the followers of Paśupati. They are divided into four classes, namely Kāpāla, Kālāmukha, Pāśupata and Śaiva. Their scripture describes five categories; namely, cause, effect, union (by the practice of meditation), ritual and cessation of sorrow, *i.e.* final emancipation. Cause indicates God and primordial matter (Pradhāna). Effect indicates prolific nature and everything produced. Union means union with Paśupati, their God, through abstract meditation. Their rituals consists of (1) bathing thrice a day, (2) smearing the forehead with ashes, (3) intertwining the fingers in religious worship (Mudrā), (4) putting on the hand a rosary of the berries called *Rudrākṣas,* (5) taking food off a human skull, (6) smearing the body with the ashes of a burnt human body, (7) worshipping the deity immersed in a wine-vessel and similar other rules of conduct. At the final emancipation, the soul attains, according to some of their sects, a state of cessation of all desires, insensible to others, the soul still retains its intelligence and sensibility].

पत्युः (of Paśupati, of the Lord of animals), **असामञ्जस्यात्** (because of discordance; as it is inconsistent).

Explanation—The followers of Paśupati recognise God as the efficient cause, and also recognise the primordial Matter as the material cause of the universe. So this theory being contrary to the view of Śruti, where Brahma is stated to be both the efficient and the material cause of the universe, cannot be accepted.

सम्बन्धानुपपत्तेश्च॥३८॥

[The argument, against the Pāśupata view, is continued]

सम्बन्ध (relation), **अनुपपत्तेः** (because it cannot be established), **च** (also).

Explanation—Paśupati, the Lord of animals, cannot be the ruler of nature, and, for the matter of that, the cause of the universe; because no relationship of Regulator and Regulated, can be established between the Lord, Who is, according to the Pāśupata view, perpetually absolute and inactive, and the primordial matter which is intert and inanimate. So Paśupati cannot be the cause of the universe.

अधिष्ठानानुपपत्तेश्च॥३९॥

[The argument, against the Pāśupata view, is continued].

अधिष्ठानं (assumption of a body), **अनुपपत्तेः** (because it cannot be established), **च** (also).

Explanation—Because His assumption of a body also cannot be established, so the Lord of animals cannot be the ruler of Matter.

That by assuming a body the Lord becomes the efficient cause of the universe, is also a fallacious conclusion. It is seen in the world that a potter, having a bodily form, constructs a pot with the matter, earth; if from this analogy the Lord is inferred to be the efficient cause of the universe, He is to be admitted to have a bodily form; but all bodies are perishable. Even the Pāśupats admit their Lord as eternal. It is untenable that Eternal God resides in a perishable body, and so becomes dependent on another additional cause. So it cannot be inferred that God has any bodily form.

करणवच्चेन्न भोगादिभ्यः॥४०॥

[An objection, against Sūtra 38, is raised and refuted].

करणवत् (having organs of sensation and action), चेत् (if *it be conceived*); न (no, it cannot be accepted), भोगादिभ्यः (because of enjoyment etc.; as in that case He becomes subject to enjoyment and suffering).

[This Sūtra consists of two parts, namely, an argument and its reply. The argument is:—करणवच्चेत्; and the reply is:—न भोगादिभ्यः].

Explanation—If it be conceived by way of argument, that as an animal soul though bodiless, has organs of senses through which he is related to the body, so God also has organs of senses through which He is related to the universe; the reply is that the conception cannot stand to reason, as in that case God also, like the animal soul, becomes subject to enjoyment and suffering, and hence forfeits His Godhead.

अन्तवत्त्वमसर्व्वज्ञता वा॥४१॥

[The argument, raised in Sūtra 40, is further refuted, and thus the Pāśupata view is rejected].

अन्तवत्त्वम् (terminableness), असर्व्वज्ञता (absence of omniscience), वा (or; and also).

Explanation—If God be admitted to have organs of senses, and so to be subject to enjoyment and suffering, as stated in Sūtra 40, He, like an ordinary animal becomes terminable by births and deaths, and also destitute of omniscience; as nothing, with organs of senses and subject to enjoyment and suffering, can be conceived to be omniscient and without births and deaths. And this sort of God is not admitted by the Pāśupats even. So, the theory of the Pāśupats, that God is not the material cause of the universe, cannot be maintained,

उत्पत्त्यसम्भवात्॥४२॥

[The theory, that the universe is originated out of insentient Energy without the help of Intelligence, is now being refuted].

उत्पत्ति (causation), **असम्भवात्** (because of impossibility; as it is absurd).

Explanation—The theory that Energy is supreme in the causation of the universe, is unsound, as it is absurd.

The spirit, representing the animal soul, is always found to be a receptacle of energy—energy cannot remain without a support. Therefore Energy without the support of Spirit, cannot, by itself, be the cause of the universe.

न च कर्त्तुः करणम्॥४३॥

[The argument, against the theory that Energy is the supreme cause, is continued].

न (no), **च** (also), **कर्त्तुः** (of the Lord; of the intelligent Progenitor), **करणम्** (organs).

Explanation—It is seen in the world that a female, after sexual union with a male, is capable of propagating the species without further intercourse with the male; so it may be argued that Energy, in union with Spirit at the beginning, has itself brought forth this universe without further association with the Progenitor. This argument also cannot hold good, as before creation, Spirit—the Intelligent Progenitor—possessed no organs of generation, by which He could unite with Energy.

विज्ञानादिभावे वा तदप्रतिषेधः॥४४॥

[The argument, against the theory of Energy being the supreme cause, is continued].

विज्ञानादिभावे (on the admission of possession of intelligence etc)., **वा** (if *on the other hand*), **तत्** (तस्य its), **अप्रतिषेधः** (no denial).

Explanation—If, on the other hand, it be admitted that Energy, as possessed of intelligence etc., is the cause of the universe, then there is no denial of such theory; as in that case Energy and Brahma become identical. Vedānta also admits that Brahma is possessed of inherent energy, and that the universe is originated by the energy of Brahma. By such admission, Brahma is admitted to be the supreme cause, and the theory of the supremacy of Energy without Spirit, in the causation of the universe, falls to the ground.

विप्रतिषेधाच्च।।४५।।

[The argument, against the theory of Energy without Spirit to be supreme cause of the universe, is concluded here].

विप्रतिषेधात् (because of contradiction; because it contradicts), **च** (also).

Explanation—The theory of Energy, without Spirit, to be the supreme cause of the universe, is not acceptable, also because it is not countenanced by Śruti and Smṛti.

SECTION—III

This section deals with the order of creation, as it is taught in Śruti, of the five primal elements, namely Ākāśa, air, fire, water and earth, and ascertains the essential characteristics of the individual soul.

Sūtras 1-6 discuss the creation of Ākāśa, and arrive at the conclusion, that Ākāśa was created from, and by Brahma; vide (1) the Chāndogyopaniṣad, where, though there is no mention made of Ākāśa itself, everything manifested (implying thereby the inclusion of Ākāśa also) is admitted to be, in reality, caused from Brahma, and (2) the Taittirīyopaniṣad, where the creation of Ākāśa is clearly stated.

Sūtras 7-13 consult several Śrutis and arrive at the conclusion that the Taittirīya Śruti, by describing that air has been created from Ākāśa, so fire from air, water from fire, and earth from water, means that Brahma, as their indwelling Spirit, has actually evolved these successive elements.

Sūtras 14-15 state that the order of dissolution of the elements is just the reverse of the order of creation, and that Prāṇa (*i.e.*, the Life energy), mind and all the senses, in addition to the five primary elements, are the creations of Brahma.

The rest of this section is devoted to the special characteristics of the individual soul, by comparing different Śrutis bearing on this point.

Sūtras 16-30 show, that it is the body only which is subject to birth and death, but the soul in the body is a parmenent and intelligent being undergoing no change or decay; that he is minute (limited), but not all-pervading, as can be understood from his movements at deaths and births of his bodies; such movements are impossible for an all-pervading entity; that the minuteness of the individual soul is not incongruous with the perception of sensation throughout the whole body, just as the smell of a flower spreads throughout a greatly larger space than that occupied by the flower; and as a light emanating from a very small source, illuminates the whole house. As the individual soul possesses, on a small scale, the immense powers of the Universal Soul, the expression 'all-pervading', applicable to the latter alone is sometimes applied to the former. Though the individual soul is not by nature all-pervading, yet he is said to be so in respect of his potentialities which are co-eternal with the soul himself—though the attributes belong to a minute being (the individual soul), they are far-reaching in their action, and resemble the attributes of the All-pervading Brahma. In short the individual soul and the Supreme Soul agree in their essential attributes, but differ only in this, that the former being minute has his limitations and the latter being Vast transcends all bounds.

Sūtras 31 and 48-52 show the defects of Sāṅkhya's assumption that the emancipated individual souls are all of them equally pervading through time and space like Brahma. By accepting the individual soul to be naturally all-pervading, both knowledge and ignorance, two contrary qualities, become his permanent characteristics; that is to say, if the individual soul be all-pervading and not limited, his permanent omniscience has to be admitted; on the other hand, there is no denying the fact of his worldly bondage due to ignorance, which, being permanent, will never open a way out for salvation. The recognition of all-pervasiveness of the individual souls would be open to the further objection that there would be intermixture of works done by each, and consequent confusion in the award of rewards and punishments; even by having recourse to Adṛṣṭa (pre-determination) such confusion of works and their consequences cannot be avoided; because if all the souls be all-pervading, their actions will overlap or coincide. The view of all-pervasiveness of the individual soul, by nature, is therefore an unfair conclusion.

Ācārya Śaṅkara explains Sūtras 19-28 by holding that the individual soul, by nature, is not minute, but all-pervading; and that according to the extent of knowledge, the individual soul expands. Sūtra 31 is explained by Śaṅkara in such a way that if the mind, the inner agent of the senses, be ignored, there remains no difference between the individual soul and the Universal Soul.

Sūtras 32-41 show, by referring to different Śrutis that the individual soul and not his intellect (बुद्धि) is the primary agent in the performance of actions; but the source of this agentship of the individual soul is the Universal Soul, Who governs the individual soul from within.

Here Ācārya Śaṅkara holds that it is not possible for the individual soul to be the agent of actions, because the individual soul is stated by the Ācārya to be, by nature, the same as the Universal Soul. He further holds that Bijñāna or Buddhi (intellect) of the individual soul is the actual agent and not the instrument of action, and, as such, receives all rewards and punishments. His absolute monism cannot tolerate any distinction between the individual soul and the Universal Soul, Who, according to him, is unchangeable and inactive. The responsibility of all actions, therefore, is fixed upon intellect, which makes all the difference between man and man.

Sūtras 42-44 establish that the individual soul is a part of, as well as the same with, Brahma, as admitted by both, Śruti and Smṛti.

Sūtras 45 and 46 show that though the individual soul is a part and parcel of the Universal Soul, yet the latter is not affected by the enjoyments and sufferings of the former; just as a source of light, as for instance the sun does not become contaminated by its touch, through its parts (the rays), with the impurities of the earth.

Sūtra 47 teaches, that the individual souls are required to follow the different directory and prohibitory rules laid down in the scripture for them, according to their different capacities, differing only because of their connection with material bodies, high and low: for instance, fire ought to be procured from the house of a learned Brāhmaṇa, but not from the burning pyre of a cremation ground; water poured from a clean vessel or offered by a clean person is to be preferred to what can be had from a defiled vessel or polluted hands.

न वियदश्रुतेः॥१॥

[This Sūtra raises a contention that Ākāśa is uncreated, and as such, not produced out of Brahma].

न (not *created*), वियत् (Ākāśa), अश्रुतेः (as Śruti does not say so).

Explanation—Ākāśa is not a created thing (it is eternal), as the Śruti (Chāndogya) does not mention the creation of Ākāśa.

Here the reference is to the Chāndogya Śruti.

Vide the Śruti:—

"तदैक्षत वहु स्यां प्रजायेयेति तत्तेजोऽसृजत"

(For translation and reference, vide Sūtra 5, Sec. 1, Chap. I).

अस्ति तु॥२॥

[The contention, raised in Sūtra 1, is partially met here].

अस्ति (*there* is *Śruti*), तु (but).

Explanation—But there is Śruti which expressly says so: Though there is no statement in the Chāndogya Upaniṣad regarding the causation of Ākāśa, yet there is a passage in the Taittirīya Śruti, on its causation.

For reference vide the Śruti:—

"तस्माद्वा एतस्मादात्मन आकाशः सम्भूतः। आकाशाद्वायुः। वायोरग्निः। अग्नेरापः। अद्‌भ्यः पृथिवी"

(From this *Universal* Soul, originated Ākāśa; from Ākāśa the air; from the air the fire; from the fire the water; from the water the earth).

Taittirīya (Brahma-Valli), Chap. II, 1, 3.

गौण्यसम्भवाच्छब्दाच्च॥३॥

[Here is an objection attempting to explain away Sūtra 2].

गौणी (having a metaphorical sense), **असम्भवात्** (as it is impossible), **शब्दात्** (from Śruti; because Śruti says so), **च** (also).

Explanation—The origination of Ākāśa stated in the Taittirīya Śruti, should be taken in a metaphorical sense and not in its literal sense; because the causation of the formless and all-pervading Ākāśa is inconceivable and because Śruti also says that Ākāśa is immutable.

For reference vide the Śruti:—

"वायुश्चान्तरिक्षं चैतदमृतम्।"

(The air and the Ākāśa are immutable).

Bṛhadāraṇyaka, Chap. II, 3, 3.

स्याच्चैकस्य ब्रह्मशब्दवत्॥४॥

[An argument, in support of the above objection is now advanced].

स्यात् (is *possible*), **च** (also), **एकस्य** (of the one and the same word), **ब्रह्मशब्दवत्** (like the word 'Brahma').

Explanation—The acceptation is all lowable, of one and the same word '**सम्भूत**' (originated), in the Taittirīya Śruti quoted under Sūtra 2 above, in a secondary sense in the case of Ākāśa, and in the primary sense in the case of the subsequently stated elements, namely air, fire, water and earth; as the same word is found, in the same sentence in Śruti, used in different meanings; as for instance, the word 'Brahma' in the following quotation, used in one place, in its primary sense and in another place in a secondary sense.

For reference vide the Śruti—

"तपसा ब्रह्म विजिज्ञासस्व तपो ब्रह्म।"

(Desire to know Brahma by meditation; meditation is Brahma).

Taittirīya, Chap. III, 5, 1.

प्रतिज्ञाहानिरव्यतिरेकाच्छब्देभ्यः॥५॥

[The objection raised in Sūtra 1, and continued in 3 and 4, is now replied to].

प्रतिज्ञाहानिः (prejudice to the original proposition), **अव्यतिरेकात्** (because of absence of exclusion), **शब्देभ्यः** (from Śrutis; as there are expressions in Śruti).

Explanation—The contention, that Ākāśa is an eternal substance without any origin, is prejudical to the knowledge of only One (the cause, Brahma), everything else (all effects) becomes known; for the proposition presupposes that there is but One Eternal Substance, of which the rest are mere manifestations. If Ākāśa be taken to be an uncreated entity like Brahma, then it must be an additional substance required to be known, being quite distinct from and independent of Brahma; and this is detrimental to the proposition stated above. The proposition remains intact, only if all things including Ākāśa be admitted to have sprung into existence out of the One Only Cause, Brahma. That nothing has an independent existence apart from Brahma, is corroborated by statements in Śruti as well.

For the proposition, referred to, vide:—

"येनाश्रुतं श्रुतं भवत्यमतं मतमविज्ञातं विज्ञातम्"

(By knowing Whom the unheard is heard, the unconceived is conceived and the unknown is known).

Chāndogya, Chap. VI, 1, 3.

For statement in Śruti that nothing has an independent existence from Brahma, vide—

"सर्व्वं खल्विदं ब्रह्म" (quoted and translated under Sūtra 2, Sec. I, Ch. I).

"ऐतदात्मामिदं सर्व्वं" (quoted and translated under Sūtra 6, Sec. I, Chap. I).

"इदं सर्व्वं यदयमात्मा" (that Self is all that is).

Bṛhadāraynaka, Chap. II, 4, 6.

यावब्दिकारं तु विभागो लोकवत्॥६॥

[The argument, begun in Sūtra 5, is concluded here].

यावत् (wherever), विकारं (transformation), तु (certainly), विभागः (distinction, specification), लोकवत् (as in the world).

Explanation—Whatever is a transformation, must be regarded as originated. That Ākāśa, too, is a transformation, is clear from the passages quoted above (such as 'ऐतदात्म्यमिदं सर्व्वं'—the essence of all this is Brahma). It is to be noted here, that though all the elements originate from Brahma, yet Ākāśa and air are not mentioned by name in the Śruti (the Chāndogya Upaniṣad); whereas fire, water and earth are distinctly stated therein to have originated from Him (vide the Śruti quoted under Sūtra 1 of this section) The specification is like that found in similar cases of ordinary experience in the world; for instance, to mean all the sons of a particular person, Devadatta, only a few of them are named.[6]

Again, there is another thing to be considered. It is admitted by all, that the individual soul, the intellect etc., are different from and at the same time independent of, Ākāśa. Now, if Ākāśa were uncreated and therfore all-pervading, it would certainly comprehend the individual soul, the intellect and the like, a position which militates against common sense.

एतेन मातरिश्वा व्याख्यातः॥७॥

[This Sūtra states that air also, like Ākāśa, has been created by, and from, Brahma].

एतेन (by this *parity of reasoning*), मातरिश्वा (air), व्याख्यातः (*is* explained).

Explanation—By the explanation of the causation of Ākāśa (as given above), the causation of air also is explained.

The causation of Ākāśa and that of air are both to be explained in the very same way; for there may be the same objection against the causation of air as that raised above against the causation of Ākāśa.

असम्भवस्तु सतोऽनुपपत्तेः॥८॥

[This Sūtra states that Brahma has no origin, as it is neither proved by reasoning nor directly stated by Śruti].

असम्भवः (no origination; no creation), तु (but), सतः (of the true One eternally existing, referred to in the Chāndogya Śruti quoted under Sūtra 5, Sec. I, Chap. I; of the really Eternal Being; of Brahama), अनुपपत्तेः (since it defies any method of proof).

Explanation—But there is not origination of Brahma, Who is the True One existing eternally; since such origination cannot be established by any method of proof.

Brahma is without any origin, as according to Śruti, He is alone the True One, Who exists eternally. On the supposition of the origin of Brahma, He cannot be said to be eternal; so such a supposition is against Śruti. It is also against reasoning; for by admitting such an origin, the question of a source of that origin arises; then again another source of that source and so on; and thus an argument may be pursued *ad infinitum* without coming to a conclusion.

तेजोऽतस्तथाहि आह॥९॥

[This and the following three Sūtras take up the position that the three elements—fire, water and earth, were not created directly from Brahma; and Sūtra 13 refutes the argument].

तेजः (the heat; the fire), अतः (from this; from air, which

has been just spoken or in Sūtra 7), तथा (thus, so) हि (as; because): आह (says).

Explanation—It may be argued that fire was produced from air, as Śruti says just the same thing.

Though the Chāndogya Śruti says that fire was created by, and from, Brahma (vide the quotation from the Chāndogya under Sūtra 5, Sec. I, Ch. I) yet the Taittirīya Śruti says that it was caused from air (vide the quotation under Sūtra 2 of this section). [This consistency of the two Śrutis is shown in Sūtra 13 next].

आपः॥१०॥

[The same thing may be said of water].

आपः (water)

Explanation—Similarly, in course of succession, water was caused from fire.

For reference, vide the statement in the Taittirīya Śruti "**अग्नेरापः**" in the passage quoted and translated under Sūtra 2 above, of this section.

Also vide—

"**तत्तेज ऐक्षत बहु स्यां प्रजायेयेति तदपोऽसृजत।**"

(That fire willed 'Let me be many, let me unfold myself'; so He created water).

Chāndogya, Chap. VI, 2, 3.

पृथिवी॥११॥

[The same thing may be said of earth].

पृथिवी (the element earth).

Explanation—Similarly, in course of succession, earth was caused from water.

For reference vide the statement in the Taittirīya Śruti

"अद्भ्यः पृथिवी" in the passage quoted and translated under Sūtra 2 above, of this section.

Also vide—

"ता आप ऐक्षन्त वह्व्यः स्याम प्रजायेमहीति ता अन्नमसृजन्त"

(That Water willed 'Let me be many, let me unfold myself', so He created food—*meaning the element earth*).

Chāndogya, Chap. VI, 2, 3.

पृथिव्यधिकाररूपशब्दान्तरेभ्यः॥१२॥

[An argument, in support of the contention raised in Sūtra 11, is adduced].

पृथिवी (earth), **अधिकाररूपशब्दान्तरेभ्यः** (**अधिकारात्**—as it is the subject of discourse in the chapter; **रूपात्**—as the description of the colour indicates; **शब्दान्तरात्**—as another Śruti states so).

Explanation—In the passage of the Chāndogya Śruti quoted under the preceding Sūtra (Sūtra 11), the word **'अन्न'** (food) has been used in the sense of the primary element earth; because (1) the subject-matter of discourse in that chapter is the creation of the primary elements (and not that of any secondary element or compound, such as food), (2) the description of the black colour of 'Anna' (food) given there, indicates that it means earth, (3) and a different Śruti (the Taittirīya) clearly states that earth was created from water (vide the quotation from the Taittirīya and its translation under Sūtra 2 above).

For the description of the colour of earth which is represented by the word 'Anna,' vide the Śruti:—

"यदग्ने रोहितं रूपं तेजसस्तद्रूपं यच्छुक्लं तदपां यत् कृष्णं तदन्नस्य।"

(The red colour of fire is that of the *primal element* fire, the white is that of the primal water and the black is that of food, *meaning the primal earth)*.

Chāndogya, Chap. VI, 4, 1.

तदभिध्यानात्तु तल्लिङ्गात् सः॥१३॥

[The contention raised in Sūtra 9 is now refuted].

तत् (तस्य, His, of Brahma), अभिध्यानात् (संकल्पात्, from determination; from volition or will); तदभिध्यानात् (because of the exercise of His will), तु (but), तल्लिङ्गात् (from His discriminating mark; from expression distinctly indicative of Brahma), सः (He, the Supreme Ruler; Brahma).

Explanation—Though it is stated in the Chāndogya Śruti; that the elements have created, each one, the other next to it (vide the quotations from the Chāndogya Śruti under Sūtras 10 and 11), yet the Supreme Ruler, the Universal Soul, is indeed the Creator of everything because Śruti says, that by the exercise of His will Brahma has created this universe; and because there are passages in Śruti to show that Brahma Himself acting from within them, has turned them into the desired for object and has employed no secondary agent to serve His end.

The elements, being inert, have no power to create; the Chāndogya Śruti, by describing the elements as creating those subsequent to each of them, means that Brahma Himself, acting from within them, was the real Creator of all those elements, as will be understood from the following quotation from the Bṛhadāraṇyaka.

For the exercise of His will, vide the Śruti—

"सोऽकामयत बहु स्यां प्रजायेयेति।"

(quoted and translated under Sūtra 17, Sec. I, Chap. I).

For the expressions that Brahma, acting from within, is the guide of the element (for instance, fire) vide:—

"योऽग्नौतिष्ठन्नग्नेरन्तरो यमग्निर्न वेद यस्याग्निः शरीरं योऽग्निमन्तरो यमयत्येष त आत्मान्तर्य्याम्यमृतः।"

(Who, existing in fire, is different from fire; Whom fire does not know; Whose body is fire; Who being within guides fire; He is your asked-for Everlasting Ātmā, *the Universal Soul,* the Regulator within).

Bṛhadāraṇyaka, Chap. III, 7, 5.

So also for similar expressions about the other elements, vide passages 3, 4, 7 and 12 of the same part of the same chapter of the same Śruti.

विपर्य्ययेण तु क्रमोऽत उपपद्यते च॥१४॥

[The process of dissolution of the elements is described].

विपर्य्ययेण (in an inverse order), **तु** (indeed), **क्रमः** (the process of *dissolution*), **अतः** (from that of *creation*), **उपपद्यते** (is proved by reasoning; stands to reason), **च** (also).

Explanation—The order of dissolution of the elements is just the reverse of that of their causation; and it also stands to reason that all compounds dissolve into their constituents.

For authority vide the Smṛti—

"जगत् प्रतिष्ठा देवर्षिं पृथिव्यप्सु प्रलीयते।

ज्योतिष्यापः प्रलीयन्ते ज्योतिर्वायौ प्रलीयते।"

(O divine Ṛṣi, earth, the basis of the universe, is dissolved into water, water into fire, fire into air).

अन्तरा विज्ञानमनसी क्रमेण तल्लिङ्गादिति चेन्नाविशेषात्॥१५॥

[A further objection, to the causation of the primary elements from Brahma, is raised and refuted].

अन्तरा (intervening between), **विज्ञानमनसी** (the senses and the mind), **क्रमेण** (according to the successive order), **तल्लिङ्गात्** (as there is indication in Śruti to that effect), **इति** (this), **चेत्** (if); **न** (no, the objection cannot stand), **अविशेषात्** (because of no speciality; as there is no speciality mentioned in Śruti about the causation of the elements).

[The Sūtra consists of two parts, namely an objection and

its refutation. The objection-portion is:—**अन्तरा विज्ञानमनसी क्रमेण तल्लिङ्गादिति चेत्**; and the refutation-portion is:—**न, अविशेषात्**].

Explanation—It may be argued, that between This (Universal Soul) and the elements there is mention in Śruti, of the mind and the senses; and so Ākāśa and the other elements should not be considered to be created out of, and to disappear in, Brahma, but to be created out of, and to disappear in, the mind and the senses according to the order of succession; as there is indication in Śruti to that effect. This argument is not reasonable, as there is no speciality mentioned in Śruti, about the creation of the elements; the mind, the senses and the elements have all, without any exception, been stated therein as created out of Brahma.

For the description of the Śruti referred to, vide—

"एतस्माज्जायते प्राणो मनः सर्व्वेन्द्रियाणि च।
खं वायुर्ज्योतिरापश्च पृथिवी विश्वधारिणी॥"

(From This, *i.e., the Universal Soul,* Prāna (the Life-energy), the mind and all the organs of senses and actions Ākāśa, air, fire, water and earth which is the support of all beings have been created).

Muṇḍakopaniṣad, Chap. II, 1, 3.

This is only a serial mention of the organs and the elements, and not a statement as to the order of their origination.

चराचरव्यपाश्रयस्तु स्यात्तद्व्यपदेशो भाक्तस्तद्भावभावित्वात्॥१६॥

[The essential character of the animal soul (the individual soul) is introduced for discussion].

चराचरव्यपाश्रयः (in connection with the bodies fixed and mobile), **तु** (indeed), **स्यात्** (becomes), **तद्व्यपदेशः** (that expression, *i.e.*, the popular expressions of births and deaths of the animal soul), **भाक्तः** (secondary; metaphorical; not literal), **तद्भावभावित्वात्** (**तद्भावे**—on the existence of that *i.e.,* the body; **भावित्वात्**—depending).

Explanation—The popular expressions of birth, growth, decay and death of the animal soul, are indeed metaphorical and refer to the fixed and mobile bodies assumed by it; births and deaths are not of the soul, but appear to be so owing only to its union with the body. In other words, it is only the body, and not the soul, which undergoes births and deaths.

नात्माऽश्रुतेर्नित्यत्वाच्च ताभ्यः॥१७॥

[The discussion, on the essential characteristics of the animal soul (the individual soul) is being continued].

न (not), **आत्मा** (the self, the soul), **अश्रुतेः** (because of no mention in Śruti; as it is not found in Śruti), **नित्यत्वात्** (because of its permanence; as it is eternal), **च** (also) **ताभ्यः** (from them; according to the Śrutis).

Explanation—The soul has no birth, as there is no mention made of it in Śruti; and also because the soul is eternal according to Śruti.

For the permanence of the individual soul according to Śruti, vide:—

"जीवापेतं वाव किलेदं म्रियते न जीवो म्रियते।"

(*It is* this *body which* dies, when left by the soul; but the individual soul does not die).

Chāndogya, Chap. VI, 11, 3.

Also vide—

"न जायते म्रियते वा विपश्चित्।"

(The intelligent one, *i.e., the soul*, is not born, nor does it die).

Kaṭhopaniṣad, Chap. I, 2, 18.

ज्ञोऽतएव॥१८॥

[The discussion, on the true character of the individual soul, is continued].

ज्ञः (intelligent), अतएव (therefore; for this very reason).

Explanation—The individual soul (the ego) has self-consciousness and is therefore, intelligent.

Jīva (the individual soul) is of the nature of Caitanya (consciousness), and he does, in fact, undergo no birth or death.

उत्क्रान्तिगत्यागतीनाम्॥१९॥

[The discussion, on the character of the individual soul, is continued].

उत्क्रान्तिः coming out; passing out; उत् क्रान्तिगत्यागतीनाम् (उत्क्रान्तिः, गतिः, आगतिः तासाम् श्रवणात्—from the description in Śruti, of the passing out, going and returning.)

Explanation—The individual soul is minute and not all-pervading, as is understood from the description, in Śruti, of its movements, of its passing out from the body and its going away from, and coming back to, this world.

For the passing out of the individual soul, vide—

"तेन प्रद्योतनेन एष आत्मा निष्क्रामति चक्षुषो वा मूर्ध्नो वा अन्येभ्यो वा शरीरदेशेभ्यः।"

(By that illuminated passage this soul passes away through the eye or the head or through other parts of the body).

Bṛhādaraṇyaka, Chap. IV, 4, 2.

"स यदास्माच्छरीरादुत्क्रामति स हैवैतैः सर्व्वैरुत्क्रामति।"

(When he passes away from this body, he does this, attended by all of those *Indriyas)*.

Kauṣītaki, Chap. III, 4.

For going away from this world, vide—

"ये वै केचनास्माल्लोकात् प्रयन्ति चन्द्रमसमेव ते सर्व्वे गच्छन्ति"

(All those, who go away from this world, go to the moon).

Kauṣītaki, Chap. I, 2.

For return, vide—

"तस्माल्लोकात् पुनरेत्यस्मै लोकाय कर्म्मणे।"

(From the other world *the soul* comes again to this world for doing works).

Bṛhadāraṇyaka, Chap. IV, 4, 6.

स्वात्मना चोत्तरयोः॥२०॥

[An argument, in support of Sūtra 19 is adduced].

स्वात्मना (directly with the agent—the soul), **च** (also), **उत्तरयोः** (of the latter two; of the going away and coming back, as stated in the previous Sūtra).

Explanation—The individual soul is minute and not all-pervading, as the exercise of the last two movements, referred to in Sūtra 19 (going to the moon and returning from it), is directly connected with the agent, the soul, though the first movement (the passing away from the body) may mean only cessation of the exercise of a definite function just as in the case of a person no longer retained in office.

नाणुरतच्छ्रुतेरिति चेन्नेतराधिकारात्॥२१॥

[An objection, to Sūtra 19, is raised and refuted].

न (not), **अणुः** (minute), **अतत्** (not that, otherwise), **श्रुतेः** (as it is stated in Śruti), **इति** (this), **चेत्** (if), **न** (no, the argument cannot stand), **इतर** (**जीवेतर**—other than the individual soul; the Universal Soul), **अधिकारात्** (from the subject-matter of the portion in the chapter).

[The Sūtra consists of an objection and its reply. The objection portion is:—**न अणुः, अतच्छ्रुतेः इति चेत्**; and the reply portion is:—**न, इतराधिकारात्**].

Explanation—If it be argued that the individual soul is not minute, as it is stated in a certain Śruti to be otherwise; then the reply is, that the argument cannot stand, as the statement in the Śruti refers not to the individual soul, but to the Universal Soul, Who is the subject-matter of the portion in the chapter of the Śruti.

The reference is to the Bṛhadāraṇyaka (chapter IV). In chapter IV, 3, 7, the Śruti, begins the discourse regarding the individual soul with the words **"योऽय विज्ञानमयः प्राणेषु हृद्यन्तर्ज्योतिः पुरुषः"** (Which is that self? It is the spirit, this intelligent inner light within the heart, operating through the senses); then the topic is changed from the individual soul to the Universal Soul (in Chap. IV, 4, 13) with the words **"यस्यानुवित्तः प्रतिबुद्ध आत्मा"** (By whom the Universal Soul has been known and realised); and in the course of the latter discourse, occurs, the statement on which the objection is based, in chapter IV, 4, 25, with the words **"महान् अज आत्माऽजरोऽमरोऽमृतोऽभयो ब्रह्म"**. (This is the Great Unborn Self, undecaying, immortal, eternal Brahma immune from fear). So the Śruti speaks of the Universal Soul as the Great One, and not of the individual soul with its limitations; and there is nothing stated in the Śruti against the fact, that the individual soul is minute.

स्व-शब्दोन्मानाभ्याञ्च॥२२॥

[The argument, in support of Sūtra 19, is continued].

स्व-शब्द (the word itself; the word directly denoting 'minute'), **उन्मान** (**उत्**—subtle, **मान**—measure; *hence* subtle division; *hence* smaller even than the small); **स्वशब्दोन्मानाभ्याभ्** (as there are the word directly denoting 'minute' and the expression denoting 'smaller even than the small as measured by division'), **च** (also).

Explanation—The individual soul is small, and not great and all-pervading also because there are, in Śruti, the words, directly denoting 'minute' and the expression denoting smaller even than, the small as measured by division.

For reference vide the Śruti—

"एषोऽणुरात्मा चेतसा वेदितव्यः।"

(This minute self is to be known by the mind).

Muṇḍaka Śruti, Chap. III, 1, 9.

Also vide:—"**बालाग्रशतभागस्य शतधा कल्पितस्य च भागो जीवः।**"

(The individual soul is of the size of the hundredth part of a part, which itself is one hundredth part of the point of a hair).

Śvetāśvatara, Chap. 5, 9.

अविरोधश्चन्दनवत्॥२३॥

[The argument, in support of Sūtra 19, is continued].

अविरोधः (no incongruity; it is not incongruous), **चन्दनवत्** (like the sandalwood paste).

Explanation—The minute character of the individual soul is not incongruous with the existence of sensation throughout the whole body, as in the case of a drop of sandal-wood paste.

As one drop of sandal-wood paste, smeared on one part of the body, makes the whole body thrill with joy; so the individual soul, though naturally minute, manifests itself throughout the whole body, and experiences all the sensations of pleasure and pain.

अवस्थितिवैशेष्यादिति चेन्नाभ्युपगमाद्धृदि हि॥२४॥

[An objection to Sūtra 23, is raised and refuted].

अवस्थिति (existence), **वैशेष्यात्** (because of the speciality), **इति** (this), **चेत्** (if it be argued); **न** (no, the argument cannot stand), **अभ्युपगमात्** (because of consent or voucher), **हृदि** (in the heart), **हि** (certainly).

[The Sūtra consists of two parts namely an objection and its reply. The objection-portion is:—**अवस्थितिवैशेष्यादिति चेत्** and the reply portion is:—**न, अभ्युपगमात् हृदि हि**].

Explanation—If it be argued that the similarity, as shown in the preceding Sūtra, is not quite exact because of the peculiarity, that the drop of sandal-wood paste covers only a part of the body; then the reply is, that the argument cannot stand, the analogy is quite appropriate, as Śruti vouches for the localisation of the soul in a particular part of the body, the heart.

It may be said, that, in the case of the sandal-wood paste, it is in contact with only a limited surface of the body from which it refreshes the whole body; while in the case of the soul, it does not exist in any particular locality, but is percipient of all sensations throughout the whole body; so the similarity shown in the previous Sūtra is not quite appropriate. To refute the argument, the latter part of this Sūtra means to say that the soul also has a particular place to abide in, the heart in the body, from which place it perceives pleasure or pain all over the body. So the analogy is not faulty.

For reference vide the Śruti—

"हृदि ह्येष आत्मा" (This soul is in the heart).

Praśnopaniṣad, Chap. III, 6.

"कतम आत्मेति योऽयं विज्ञानमयः प्राणेषु हृद्यन्तर्ज्योतिःपुरुषः"

(translated under Sūtra 21 of this section).

गुणाद्वालोकवत्॥२५॥

[The argument, in support of Sūtra 23, is continued].

गुणात् (by its virtue), वा (or; a further example is given), आलोकवत् (like a light).

Explanation—Or it is like a small light which, by its own virtue, illuminates the whole house.

A further example is given here by way of comparison. Just as a small light within a house, by its own virtue, illuminates the whole house, so the individual soul, though minute, renders the whole body percipient, by its own inherent attribute.

व्यतिरेको गन्धवत्तथाहि दर्शयति॥२६॥

[Sūtra 23 is further elucidated by this Sūtra].

व्यतिरेकः (expansion), **गन्धवत्** (like a smell), **तथा** (thus; in the same way), **हि** (as), **दर्शयति** (Śruti shows).

Explanation—The soul's expansion is like that of a smell, as Śruti also shows such expansion of the virtue of the soul.

As the smell of a flower, situated within the space of the flower, diffuses throughout a larger space, similarly consciousness, which is the virtue of the individual soul situated within the space of the heart, expands throughout the whole body; Śruti also states so.

For reference vide the Śruti:—

"एष प्रज्ञ आत्मेदं शरीरमात्मानमनुप्रविष्टः आलोभ्यम आनखेभ्यः।"

(The intelligent *individual* soul has entered, into this body, with which he identifies himself, down to the tips of the hairs and the nails).

Kauṣītaki, Chap. IV, 20.

पृथगुपदेशात्॥२७॥

[This Sūtra is a defence in favour of the preceding one where knowing is used as an attribute of the individual soul, and so separate from it].

पृथक् (different), **उपदेशात्** (from the statement; as Śruti states).

Explanation—Though, there is no fundamental difference between the individual soul and his knowing, they are different in the sense that knowing is the attribute (of the individual soul), which is the substance; and the individual soul is the possessor of that attribute, because Śruti states a difference between the two.

For reference vide the Śruti:—

"प्रज्ञया शरीरमारुह्य"

(Taking possession of his body by the faculty of knowing).

तद्गुणसारत्त्वात्तु तद्व्यपदेशः प्राज्ञवत्॥२८॥

[The discussion on the true character of the individual soul, commenced in Sūtra 16, is continued].

तदगुणसारत्त्वात् (by virtue of the possession of that attribute), **तु** (but), **तद्व्यपदेश** (that appellation), **प्राज्ञवत्** (as in the case of the 'Omniscient').

Explanation—The appellation 'all-pervading', is given to the individual soul, because the special feature of his property is to function through the whole body and also at distant places, and thus it becomes all-pervading like the Omniscient Lord.

By virtue of his functioning, he may be pervading, though he is not essentially pervading in himself.

In other words, he is all-pervading only in respect of his property, and not in respect of his size or magnitude, which is minute as shown in the previous Sūtras. The size or magnitude of the individual soul really implies his limitations.

For reference vide:—

"महान्तं विभुमात्मानं मत्वा धीरो न शोचति।"

(The wise do not grieve, thinking the soul to be grand and all-pervading).

Kaṭhopaniṣad, Chap. I, 2, 22.

Ācārya Śaṅkara has explained the Sūtras 19-27 as objections, which, in his view, have been refuted by this Sūtra. This Sūtra is explained by him in a different way, and his explanation runs thus—According to the extent of intellect, the size of the individual soul has been fixed. In the Chāndogya Śruti (Chap. III, 14, 3) the Universal Soul has been described to be smaller than a corn of paddy or barley, though infact He is all-pervading; similarly, the individual soul, too, has been described to be extremely small (vide the Śruti, quoted under Sūtra 22 of this section), though, in fact, he is all-pervading.

यावदात्मभावित्वाच्च न दोषस्तद्दर्शनात्॥२९॥

[An additional reason is adduced in support of Sūtra 28].

यावत् (as long as), **आत्मभावित्वात्** (because they exist); **यावदात्मभावित्वात्** (because they *i, e.*, the attributes exist as long as the self *i, e.*, the possessor of the attributes exists), **च** (also), **न** (no), **दोषः** (harm), **तद्दर्शनात्** (as Śruti also shows that).

Explanation—There is no harm in describing the individual soul as all-pervading in respect of his attributes alone, for the additional reason that his attributes exist as long as the self does. Now, the self is, as admitted on all hands, existing through time eternal, and so are also his attributes: Śruti. also shows that.

For the Śruti vide:—

'नहि विज्ञातुर्विज्ञातेर्विपरिलोपो विद्यते अविनाशित्वात्।'

(The knowing faculty of the knower—Self—never ceases to exist as both are imperishable *and* therefore co-eternal).

Ācārya Śaṅkara explains this Sūtra in a different way; he takes the word **'आत्मभावित्व'** to mean existence, and his explanation is as follows—It may be said by way of objection that owing to his conjunction with intellect, the soul attains secular state; but as the soul and the intellect are separate things, this conjunction between them must sometimes cease to exist, and final emancipation will then come of itself. Against this supposed objection the framer of the Sūtras says that there is no fear of such defect; because, as long as this intellect, in conjunction with the soul, succeeds in keeping up the idea of ego, *i.e.*, as long as the *clear vision* does not arise as to the actual state of the world, this conjuction is not removed.

पुंस्त्वादिवत्त्वस्य सतोऽभिव्यक्तियोगात्॥३०॥

[A proof is now given in support of Sūtra 28, by showing

the perpetual connection between the individual soul and this intellect].

पुंस्त्व (virility; power of procreation); पुंस्त्वादिवत् (like the virility, etc)., तु (but), अस्य (its; of knowledge), सतः (existing perpetually), अभिव्यक्तियोगात् (because of appropriateness of manifestation; as manifestation is appropriate).

Explanation—That the intellect (a property) of the individual soul exists along with it perpetually, is reasonable; during deep sleep and general dissolution it remains in a dormant fine state and becomes manifest again along with the soul during his wakeful state or the new creation as the case may be, and thus never ceases its connection with the soul; this is appropriate, just as the power of procreation etc., which remains in a dormant or fine state in the child, becomes operative in puberty.

नित्योपलब्ध्यनुपलब्धिप्रसङ्गोऽन्यतरनियमो वाऽन्यथा॥३१॥

[The defects of the supposition, that the individual soul is by nature all-pervading, are being shown].

नित्य (perpetual), उपलब्धिः (perception), अनुपलब्धिः (want of perception; ignorance); नित्योपलब्ध्यनुपलब्धि (perpetuity of both, knowledge and ignorance), प्रसङ्गः (दोषः, fault; defect), अन्यतर (either of the two), नियमः (rule), वा (or), अन्यथा (otherwise *than being minute*; on the supposition that the individual soul is all-pervading and not minute).

Explanation—The theory of the omnipresence of the individual soul makes it open to either of the two objections, namely, continuous perception or emancipation, and continuous imperception or perpetual bondage.

If the individual soul be all-pervading and not minute, he is present in all hearts and is consequently omniscient; and on the other hand, as his worldly bondage also appears to exist, ignorance also becomes permanent; *i.e.*, he becomes, as a rule, always bound or always emancipated. But neither of these altternatives can be consistent with the everyday fact, that he being previously in a state of bondage, becomes emancipated afterwards by virtue of his actions.

Ācārya Śaṅkara has explained this Sūtra in the following way—It is to be admitted that the individual soul has the internal organ, called the mind, as an incidental condition of his; otherwise permanent consciousness or permanent ignorance has to be accepted. This internal organ, the mind, constitutes the sole difference between the individual soul and the Universal Soul; and but for this distinctive medium, there is nothing to stand in the way of both being identified as one and the same entity. This view of Ācārya Śaṅkara however, does, no doubt, produce a very salutary effect in practising divine meditation by suspending the operation of the mind.

कर्त्ता शास्त्रार्थवत्वात्॥३२॥

[Another characteristic of the individual soul is being stated].

कर्त्ता (the agent who is to perform works), **शास्त्रार्थवत्त्वात्** (so that the Śāstric injunctions may have a meaning).

Explanation—The individual soul is to be admitted as the agent who is to perform works, so that the Śāstric injunctions may have a meaning.

The individual soul (the human being) has been enjoined upon to perform such works as would bear fruit in the next life, and in order to attain release from the bondage of those works he has also to do some work in the form of worship of the Universal Soul. Now, had he not been the agent of such works, those injunctions in Śurti would have been quite useless and meaningless.

For such a precept in Śruti, vide—

"स्वर्गकामो यजेत, मुमुक्षुर्ब्रह्मोपासीत।"

(He, who desires to attain heaven, has to perform sacrifices; and he, who desires to attain salvation, has to worship Brahma *in meditation).*

विहारोपदेशात्॥३३॥

[An argument, in support of Sūtra 32, is adduced].

विहार (wandering at will), **उपदेशात्** (from declarations; as Śruti declares).

Explanation—The individual soul is to be admitted as the agent, as Śruti declares him to be freely moving about.

For reference vide the Śruti—

"स इयतेऽमृतो यत्रकामम्"।

(He, the immortal one, goes about wherever he likes).

Bṛhadāraṇyaka, Chap, IV, 3, 12.

'एवमेवैष एतान् प्राणान् गृहीत्वा स्वे शरीरे यथाकामं परिवर्त्तते'।

(Thus he, taking the senses along with him, moves about within his own body just as he pleases).

Bṛhadāraṇyaka, Chap. II, 1, 18.

उपादानात्॥३४॥

[Another argument, in support of Sūtra 32, is adduced].

उपादानात् (because, of taking as *instruments*).

Explanation—The individual soul is to be admitted as the agent, because he is described in Śruti to take the senses along with him as instruments of his work, while roaming within his own body during sleep.

For reference vide the Śruti—

"एवमेवैष एतात् प्राणान् गृहीत्वा–"

(For translation vide the same under Sūtra 33).

व्यपदेशाच्च क्रियायां न चेन्निर्द्देशविपर्य्ययः॥३५॥

[The argument, in support of Sūtra 32, is continued].

व्यपदेशात् (from a statement in Śruti), **च** (also), **क्रियायां** (in respect of performance of rites), **न चेत्** (or else, otherwise), **निर्द्देशविपर्य्ययः** (reversal of the statement).

Explanation—Also from a statement in Śruti in respect of performance of rites, it is understood that the individual soul is the agent; or else there would be the reversal of the statement.

In the passage quoted below it is found that 'intelligence'—meaning the intelligent person—performs all actions both sacred and secular. If intelligence were taken in the literal sense, then it should have been used in the instrumental case instead of in the nominative case as it has been used here; because it is quite meaningless to speak of the inert intelligence as the performer of the actions.

Vide the passage referred to above—

"विज्ञानं यज्ञं तनुते। कर्म्माणि तनुतेऽपि च॥"

(Intelligence, *i.e. the intelligent person* performs sacrifices and also performs all other actions).

Taittirīya (Brahmaballi) Chap. II, 5.

उपलब्धिवदनियमः॥३६॥

[The argument, in support of Sūtra 32. is continued].

उपलब्धिवत् (like perception), **अनियमः** (no rule).

Explanation—The rule is not similar to that which holds good in perception, *i.e.,* there is no hard and fast rule as to the class of actions to be chosen by the agent, while there is a fixed relation between the perceived object and its perceiver.

An objection may arise that if the individual soul be the agent, why should he do any act productive of harmful effects? The framer of the Sūtras says here, by way of reply, that, though the individual soul perceives the good or bad effects of his actions, there is no binding rule that he will do only those works which are productive of good results; because the individual soul is not all-powerful and all-knowing; so, being conditioned and influenced by external circumstances he becomes inclined to do sometimes a good thing, and sometimes a bad thing.

In the presence of an object of perception before us, there is no bar to its being perceived by us; but, on the other hand, the clearest perception of a right thing or duty is necessarily no incentive to its performance.

शक्ति-विपर्य्ययात्॥३७॥

[The argument, in support of Sūtra 32, is continued].

शक्ति-विपर्य्ययात् (because of overturning of agentship *i.e.*, of **कर्त्तृत्व**).

Explanation—If, on the other hand, the intellect, which is but an instrument of action, is made to usurp the place of the agent, there becomes a transference of authorship and responsibility; since the intellect (Vijñāna) is elevated to the rank of the doer, while the doer himself has no status in the performance of the rites prescribed by the Śāstras. The result is, the credit and responsibility of actions are fathered upon the instrument, while the actual performer is altogether left out of account. The individual soul, and not the intellect, is therefore the agent.

समाध्यभावाच्च॥३८॥

[The argument, in support of Sūtra 32, is continued].

समाधि (religious abstraction; the state of deep meditation in divine worship, which amounts to the absorption of self in pure consciousness), **अभावात्** (for want; for impossibility; as it becomes an impossible thing).

Explanation—The individual soul must be taken to be the agent, as otherwise religious abstraction becomes an impossible thing.

There is instruction, in the scripture of a kind of deep meditation in divine worship, that amounts to the absorption of the self in the consciousness of himself, which is not possible for the inert intellect to attain; and so, the instruction in the scripture about deep divine meditation becomes useless and meaningless, if intellect be taken to be the agent instead of the individual soul.

यथा च तक्षोभयथा॥३९॥

[The argument, in support of Sūtra 32, is continued].

यथा (as), **च** (also), **तक्ष** (a carpenter), **उभयथा** (both ways—sometimes on duty and at other times off duty).

Explanation—A carpenter, being possessed of a volition, in spite of having the instruments at hand, is seen with his tools in his hand while at work, but he lays them aside while he chooses to be off duty. If the intellect of the performer be substituted for the performer himself, it does not matter whether the performer is a willing or unwilling partner to the action.

Ācārya Śaṅkara has explained this Sūtra in a different way: A carpenter, working with his tools, feels tired with hard work and gives up his work; now he leaves aside his tools, gets refreshed and feels quite at ease. Similarly the individual soul, possessed with dualistic ideas, deludes himself into the belief that he is a responsible agent and is the builder of his fortune; but when he succeeds in shaking off his dualistic ideas, he awakens from his delusion and finds that he is Brahma.

परात्तु तच्छ्रुतेः॥४०॥

[A limitation to Sūtra 32 is stated].

परात् (from the Supreme Soul; dependent on the Universal Soul), **तु** (indeed), **तत्** (that; agentship), **श्रुतेः** (from Śruti).

Explanation—It can be understood from Śruti, that the agentship of the individual soul is, indeed, subordinate to, and controlled by, the Supreme Being.

For reference vide the Śruti:—

"अन्तः प्रविष्टः शास्ता जनानां"

(*The Universal Soul*, entering within, governs the individual souls).

कृतप्रयत्नापेक्षस्तु विहितप्रतिषिद्धावैयर्थ्यादिभ्यः॥४१॥

[This Sūtra proceeds to narrow the scope of Sūtra 40 within certain limits].

कृतप्रयत्नापेक्षः (having regard to the works done), **तु** (but; however); **विहितप्रतिषिद्धौ** (injunctions and prohibitions), **वैयर्थ्य** (futility; meaninglessness), **अवैयर्थ्य** (no futility); **विहितप्रतिषिद्धा-वैयर्थादिभ्यः** (so that the Śāstric injunctions and prohibitions may not be meaningless, and so on).

Explanation—It may be argued, on the strength of the previous Sūtra, that if the individual soul be under the control of the Universal Soul *i.e.,* if his actions are pre-determined by the Supreme Will, then the latter, and not the individual soul, must be primarily held responsible for all actions good or evil performed by the agent; but the charge cannot be laid at the door of Brahma, for the reason (as stated in the present Sūtra), among others, that Brahma awards reward and punishment, judging by the merit and demerit of the work done by Jīva in his previous births; otherwise the injunctions and prohibitions of Śāstra would be meaningless. The Śāstras are the final authority for distinguishing the right conduct from the wrong one. The injunctions in the Śāstras are based on the dualistic conception of Jīva and Brahma, and consequently the former is conceived to be subordinate to and controlled by the latter.

अंशो नानाव्यपदेशा दन्यथ चापि दाशकितवादित्वमधीयत एके॥४२॥

[The framer of the Sūtras now shows that the individual soul is different from, as well as the same with, Brahma].

अंशः (a part), **नानाव्यपदेशात्** (from the statement of 'variety' of 'difference', in Śruti), **अन्यथा** (otherwise), **च** (also), **अपि** (even), **दाशकितवादित्वम्** (the status of a fisherman, a knave, etc.; **दाश**-a fisherman, **कितव**—a knave), **अधीयते** (read; indicate), **एके** (some Śrutis).

Explanation—The individual soul is a *part* of the Universal Soul, as can be understood from the expression of 'difference' between them in Śruti; on the other hand Śruti has expressed otherwise also, namely, that the individual soul is identical with (*i.e.*, the same as) the Universal Soul; and some Śrutis read that even a fisherman and knave are no other than Brahma.

For reference, that the individual soul is different from, and a part of, the Universal Soul, vide—

"ज्ञाज्ञौ द्वावजावीशानीशौ"

(There are two unborn,—the Ruler, the Omniscient *Universal Soul*, and the ruled, the ignorant *individual soul)*.

Śvetāśvatara Śruti, Chap. I, 9.

For reference that the individual soul is the same as the Universal Soul, vide—

"तत्त्वमसि श्वेतकेतो" (That thou art, O Śvetaketu).

Chāndogya, Chap. VI, 8, 7.

For reference that even a fisherman and knave are Brahma, vide—

"ब्रह्मदाशा ब्रह्मदासा ब्रह्मकितवाः"

(The fishermen, the serfs and the knaves are all Brahma).

मन्त्रवर्णात्॥४३॥

[An argument in support of Sūtra 42, that the individual soul is a part of Brahma, is adduced].

मन्त्र (a hymn, a sacred verse); **मन्त्रवर्णात्** (from the letters in sacred verses).

Explanation—That the individual soul is a part of the Universal Soul, can be understood from the very letters in a hymn in the Chāndogya Śruti.

For reference vide the Śruti—

"पादोऽस्य सर्व्वा भूतानि" (One foot, *i, e*, the *fourth part* of

Him are all beings—*the whole creation covers only a fraction of Him*).

Chāndogya, Chap. III, 12. 6.

अपिच स्मर्य्यते॥४४॥

[The argument, that the individual soul is a part of Brahma, is concluded here].

अपि (also), **च** (and), **स्मर्य्यते** (is said by Smṛti; Smṛti says so).

Explanation—And Smṛti also says so—that the individual soul is a part of the Universal Soul.

For reference vide—

"ममैवांशो जीवलोके जीवभूतः सनातनः।"

(A part of mine, in the animal world, is the individual soul, who is existing eternally).

Bhagavad Gītā, Chap. XV, 7.

प्रकाशादिवत्तु नैवं परः॥४५॥

[The speciality of the Universal Soul is shown].

प्रकाशादिवत् (like a luminary; like the sun etc)., **तु** (indeed), **न** (not), **एवं** (like this; like the individual soul), **परः** (the Supreme Soul).

Explanation—Though the individual soul is a part and parcel of the Universal Soul, yet the latter does not become affected by the enjoyment and suffering of the former; just as a luminary, like the sun, does not become contaminated by its touch, through its parts—the rays—with the impurities of the earth.

स्मरन्ति च ॥४६॥

स्मरन्ति (Smṛtis state), **च** (also).

Explanation—Smṛtis also state that the Universal Soul

does not undergo the consequences of the actions of the individual soul.

For reference vide:—

"तत्र यः परमात्माऽसौ स नित्यो निर्गुणः स्मृतः।
न लिप्यते फलैश्चापि पद्मपत्रमिवाम्भसा॥"

(Of these He, Who is the Supreme Soul, is known as eternal and unaffected by the properties of Matter [निर्गुणः]. Moreover, He is not affected by the consequences of actions, even as a lotus leaf is not wetted by contact with water).

अनुज्ञापरिहारौ देहसम्बन्धाज्ज्योतिरादिवत्॥४७॥

[The necessity, for observance of directory and prohibitory rules, is explained].

अनुज्ञापरिहारौ (direction and prohibition), **देहसम्बन्धात्** (because of connection with body), **ज्योतिरादिवत्** (like fire and so on).

Explanation—Though the individual souls are parts of the Universal Soul, yet they are required to follow the different directory and prohibitory rules laid down in scripture for them, according to their different capacities owing to their connection with material bodies, high and low. For instance, fire ought to be procured from the house of a learned Brāhmaṇa, but not from the burning pyre of a cremation ground; water poured from a clean vessel or offered by a clean person is to be preferred to what can be had from an unclean vessel or an unclean person.

असन्ततेश्चाव्यतिकरः॥४८॥

[The discussion, on the special characteristic of the individual soul, is continued].

सन्ततिः (**व्याप्तिः**, extension); **असन्ततेः** (**अव्याप्तेः** as it is not extended all over; as it is not all-pervading), **च** (also), **अव्यतिकरः** (no confusion).

Explanation—As the individual soul is not all-pervading there is no confusion of actions or of their fruits.

The individual soul, not being all-pervading, has no connection with all the bodies at the same time; but as a seperate soul animating the particular body of his own, he is affected by the peculiar properties of that one alone. Therefore the effects of works done by the soul in one body, belong to him in respect of that body only, and not of any other body; *i. e.*, all the individuals are not affected by the works performed by a particular individual. But if the individual soul be admitted to be all-pervading, he becomes connected with all the bodies simu-ltaneously, and so there becomes confusion of works and their effects.

आभासा एव च॥४९॥

[The defect, of admitting the individual soul as all-pervading, is being shown].

आभासा (unfair conclusions), **एव** (certainly), **च** (also).

Explanation—The view, that the individual soul is all-pervading, is certainly an unfair conclusion.

In the Sāṅkhya philosophy of Kapila the individual soul (Puruṣa) has been stated to be all-pervading; if this view be accepted, there would ensue confusion of works and their effects, as shown in the preceding Sūtra, this view of Sāṅkhya is therefore an unfair conclusion.

There is a different reading of this Sūtra in the commentary of Ācārya Śaṅkara, where it runs as "**आभास एव च**" (**आभासः** —a semblance; a reflected image), which is explained by the Ācārya in the following way—The individual soul is a reflection of the Supreme Soul in the world, just like a reflection of the sun in water; if the reflected image of the sun, in the water of a particular vessel trembles, that in the water of any other vessel does not move on that account; just so, when the individual soul in one body is undergoing the effects of his actions, the soul in any other body is not affected on that account.

अदृष्टानियमात्॥५०॥

[The discussion, begun in Sūtra 49, is continued].

अदृष्ट (the accumulated stock of previous actions waiting as a latent force to bring forth fruits in future), अनियमात् (for want of any binding rule).

Explanation—If we admit the individual soul to be all-pervading, the confusion arising from intermixture of works and their consequences, as shown in Sūtra 48, cannot be avoided, even by having recourse to Adṛṣṭa (the latent force); because if all the souls equally are all-pervading, there cannot be any binding rule as to upon which of them the force will act.

अभिसन्ध्यादिष्वपि चैवम् ॥५१॥

[The discussion, begun in Sūtra 49, is continued].

अभिसन्ध्यादिषु (in matter of personal determination etc.), अपि (also), च (and), एवम् (in the like manner).

Explanation—And there is want of order, also in matters of personal determination etc., if the individual soul be admitted to be all-pervading.

If the individual soul be all-pervading, there cannot be any order in motives or matters of personal determination, such as 'I will do a certain thing', or 'I will not do a certain thing', for in such a case, every one becomes conscious of the determination of every other, and thus no order of determination and its rendering into action can be maintained; and further, collisions between wills cannot be avoided; but as, in the world, there is order found everywhere, so the individual soul is concluded not all-pervading.

प्रदेशादिति चेन्न अन्तर्भावात्॥५२॥

[An objection to Sūtra 51 is raised and refuted].

प्रदेशात् (because of particular locality; on account of his belonging to a particular locality), इति (this), चेत् (if), न (no the argument cannot stand), **अन्तर्भावात्** (as he exists equally within every body—as all the souls interpenetrate one another).

[This Sūtra consists of two parts; namely, an objection and its reply. The objection-portion is:—**प्रदेशात् इति चेत्**; and the reply-portion is:—**न, अन्तर्भावात्**]

Explanation—It may be argued that the order of determination and work is maintained on the supposition that each individual soul is restricted to a particular dwelling place—his body; the argument cannot stand, because every soul being considered as all-pervading, exists equally within every body and becomes aware of the determinations of all other souls, owing to their interpenetration with one another. The conclusion, that the individual soul is all-pervading, is, therefore, unworthy of acceptance.

SECTION—IV

This section is devoted to the discussion of the creation of the Indriyas (the senses and the centres of action), the chief vital energy, the body and other material things, and establishes that they derive their origin from Brahma.

Sūtras 1-4 establish, by discussing different Śrutis and by refuting all plausible objections, that the Indriyas (the senses of perception and the centres of action) spring from Brahma.

Sūtras 5-7 show that the Indriyas are eleven in number, and are minute and not all-pervading.

Sūtras 8-13 and 17-18 state that Prāṇa, the chief vital energy, is also created out of Brahma; that it stands superior to all the Indriyas possessed by the self; that it is different from air in general, as well as from the five vital forces, and it is also not the resultant of combined functions of all the (eleven) Indriyas: that though it is different from the Indriyas and hence not included in their number of eleven, yet it is, like them, an instrument of action, since it has a specific and extraordinary function, namely, to sustain life and support the body and the Indriyas; and that it is minute and not all-pervading.

Sūtras 14-16 show that the Indriyas are guided in their activities by Fire and other divinities; but as they are connected permanently with, and are subservient to, the embodied soul, the latter, and not the guiding deities, is their master.

Sūtra 19 states that though the Indriyas are subservient to the embodied soul, their names and forms have been contrived and fashioned by Brahma.

Sūtras 20-21 show that all material bodies have been produced by the interfusion of the five minute primary elements, namely, earth, water, fire, air and Ākāśa (though the last mentioned two are omitted from the Chāndogya Śruti for facility of understanding); and that a material object is named after that particular primary element whose share preponderates in the composition. As for instance, the material water is produced from the mixture of all the five primary elements; but as the share, contributed by the element water, preponderates in the composition of the material water, the latter is named after, and is said to be produced from, the former.

तथा प्राण॥१॥

[The creation of the Indriyas (the senses of perception and the instruments of action) is now described].

तथा (similarly; like the creation of the five primal elements, as stated in the previous section), **प्राणाः** (Indriyas; the senses of perception and the instruments of action).

Explanation—Like the five primary elements, the Indriyas (the senses of perception and the instruments of action) have also originated from Brahma.

For reference vide the Śruti—

"एतस्माज्जायते प्राणो मनः सर्व्वेन्द्रियाणि च।
खं वायुर्ज्योतिरापश्च पृथिवी विश्वधारिणी॥"

(For translation vide Sūtra 15, Section III, Chapter II).

गौण्यसम्भवात्॥२॥

[A plausible objection to Sūtra 1 is refuted].

गौणी (a secondary sense), **असम्भवात्** (as it is impossible); **गौण्यसम्भवात्** (from the absurdity of its being taken in a secondary sense).

Explanation—The Indriyas (the senses and the instruments of action) originate directly and immediately from

Brahma; and the statement in Śruti about their creation cannot be taken in an indirect and secondary sense, which is misconception.

In the chapter dealing with creation in the Taittirīya Śruti there is no statement regarding their creation. Now, it may be argued by way of objection, that in the Śruti quoted under Sūtra 1, the creation of the Indriyas has been stated not in a literal but in a secondary sense. The objection is thus refuted by Sūtra 2—

The creation of everything from Brahma has been reiterated in Śruti, and there is no Śruti contradicting it.

For reference to the chapter of creation in the Taittirīya Śruti, vide—

"तस्माद् वा एतस्मादात्मन आकाशः सम्भूतः। आकाशाद्वायुः। वायोरग्निः। अग्नेरापः। अद्भ्यः पृथिवी।"

(For translation and reference, vide Sūtra 2, Sec. III, Chap. II).

For the creation of everything from Brahma, vide:—

"यतो वा इतानि भूतानि जायन्ते।"

(From Whom originate all these things).

Taittirīya Bhṛguballi, I, 1.

In the face of the clear statement in Śrutis that all things are created from Brahma, it is idle to suppose that the senses of perception and the instruments of action are the sole exceptions.

तत्प्राक् श्रुतेश्च ॥३॥

[An argument, in support of Sūtra 2, is adduced].

तत्प्राक् (before them; prior to them), श्रुतेः (from Śruti), च (also).

Explanation—The secondary sense is unacceptable, also because the Śruti (quoted under Sūtra 1 above) places the

Indriyas prior to Ākāśa etc. The finite verb 'originate' occurs first, then the words signifying prāṇa and the Indriyas, and last of all come Ākāśa, air etc. Now that the finite verb is accepted in its primary sense in connection with Ākāśa etc., why should it be taken in a secondary sense in connection with the Indriyas which the Śruti has placed prior to Ākāśa etc.?

तत्पूर्व्वकत्वाद्वाचः॥४॥

[Another argument, in support of Sūtra 2, is adduced].

तत्पूर्व्वकत्वात् (because preceded by them, *i. e.*, the elements; being constituted by the elements), वाचः (speeches; the speech and others with it; speech, Prāṇa and mind, meaning the instruments of actions and the senses); तत्पूर्व्वकत्वाद्वचः (the speech etc. being constituted by the elements—fire, water and earth).

Explanation—Because in the Chāndogya Śruti (quoted below), the Indriyas (the instruments of senses and actions), represented by the three terms वाक्, प्राण and मनः (speech, life-energy and mind) are stated to be constituted by the elements, fire, water and earth respectively; therefore, by the statement in the Śruti of the direct causation of the elements, it is suggested that the Indriyas have Brahma for their immediate cause.

For the statement that the Indriyas are constituted by the elements, vide the Śruti—

"अन्नमयं हि सोम्य मन आपोमयः प्राणस्तेजोमयी वाक्।"

[O my boy, the mind is the subtlest elaborated form of food (*i. e.*, earth), the Prāṇa is the subtlest elaborated form of water, and Vāk (the speech) is the subtlest elaborated form of Tejas (fire)].

Chāndogya, Chap. VI, 5, 4.

For the direct causation of the elements by, and from, Brahma, vide the discussion in Sūtras 1-13, Sec. III. Chap. II.

सप्त गतेर्विशेषितत्वाच्च॥५॥

[The number of the Indriyas is now discussed].

सप्त (seven) **गतेः** (from the movement), **विशेषितत्वात्** (from the specification), **च** (also).

Explanation—The Indriyas are seven in number, which can be understood from the fact that they are seven only that follow in the wake of Prāṇa at death, and also from the fact that those very seven are specially enumerated in that same text. [This is said by way of objection, which is replied to in the next Sūtra].

For the senses etc., following Prāṇa vide the Śruti—

"प्राणमुत्क्रामन्तं सर्व्वे प्राणा अनूत्क्रामन्ति।"

(Prāṇa following *in the wake of the self* all the Indriyas [senses and instruments of actions] accompany Prāṇa).

Bṛhadāraṇyaka, Chap. IV, 4, 2.

For the specification of the senses etc., vide—

"न पश्यति.....न जिघ्रति.....न रसयते.....न वदति...न शृणोति.....न मनुते....न स्पृशते"

(He does not seen nor smell, nor taste, nor speak, nor hear, nor think, nor touch).

Bṛhadāraṇyaka, Chap. IV, 4, 2.

From this quotation, it is understood that seven, and only seven, are the Indriyas specified as follows—(1) sight, (2) smell, (3) taste, (4) speech, (5) hearing, (6) mind and (7) touch.

हस्तादयस्तु स्थितेऽतो नैवम्॥६॥

[Sūtra 5 is refuted and the actual number of the Indriyas is ascertained].

हस्तादयः (the hands and other organs of actions), **तु** (but), **स्थितेः** (being determined), **अतः** (therefore), **न** (not), **एवम्** (so; the same as stated in the preceding Sūtra).

Explanation—But there remaining unnoticed the hands and other organs the number of Indriyas is not exactly seven, as stated in Sūtra 5. (The number of Indriyas is eleven in all).

for reference vide the Śruti—

"हस्तो वै ग्रहः" (The hand is also an Indriya).

Bṛhadāraṇyaka, Chap. III, 2, 8.

"दशे मे पुरुषे प्राणा आत्मैकादश"

(Ten are these Indriyas in a person and mind with these completes the number eleven).

Bṛhadāraṇyaka, Ch. III, 9, 4.

In addition to the seven Indriyas mentioned in the previous Sūtra, there are four others, that complete the number:—There are the five organs of senses, namely (1) of sight, (2) of hearing, (3) of smell, (4) of taste and (5) of touch; again there are five organs of action, namely (1) of speech, (2) of taking, (3) of going, (4) of evacuating and (5) of begetting; and over and above these ten, there is the mind, the internal organ, which guides them all; thus there are altogether eleven organs or Indriyas.

अणवश्च ॥७॥

[The nature of the Indriyas is now ascertained].

अणवः (minute), **च** (also).

Explanation—The Indriyas are also minute, and not all-pervading, as can be understood from their coming out of the body. Had they been all-pervading like the sky, there would have been no movement possible on their part.

For reference vide the Bṛhadāraṇyaka Śruti—

"प्राणमुत्क्रामन्तं सर्व्वे प्राणा अनुत्क्रामन्ति।"

(Quoted and translated under Sūtra 5 of this section).

श्रेष्ठश्च॥८॥

[This chief vital energy is being characterised now].

श्रेष्ठः (the highest of them, meaning the Life-Energy; the vital element), च (also),

Explanation—The highest of them, meaning मुख्यप्राणः (the chief vital energy), is also created out of Brahma like the five elements.

For reference as to the expression 'The highest', meaning the Life-Energy, *i. e.*, the chief vital energy, vide—

"प्राणो वाव ज्येष्ठश्च श्रेष्ठश्च।"

(The Life-Energy is indeed the foremost and the highest).

Chāndogya, Chap. V, 1, 1.

For reference as to the Life-Energy being created out of Brahma, vide—

"एतस्माज्जायते प्राणो मनः सर्व्वेन्द्रियाणि च।"

(For translation and reference, vide Sūtra 15, Sec. III, Chap. II).

न वायुक्रिये पृथगुपदेशात् ॥९॥

[The characteristics of the chief vital energy are continued].

न (not), वायुक्रिये (the air and the function), पृथगुपदेशात् (because of separate mention).

Explanation—Prāṇa, the Life-Energy, is neither the air, nor the combined function of all the Indriyas, since Śruti has mentioned it separately in addition to the air, the other primary elements and all the Indriyas.

Prāṇa—the Life-Energy—is the force operating through, and sustaining, the whole universe collectively and each individual part of it separately, as the chief vital power; and thus it has some direct connection with the air and the Indriyas for which 'Prāṇa' is sometimes termed, in the scripture, as air and sometimes it is used as a synonym for Indriya. As to its connection with the air, it principally expresses itself in the regulation of the respiratory functions, which, if duly regulated, turn into a spiritual force at the time of meditation; and as to its connection with the Indriyas it is their guide and fountain of energy, from which each of them receives the necessary impulse for action.

For the separate mention of Prāṇa, vide the Śruti:—

"एतस्माज्जायते प्राणो मनः सर्व्वेन्द्रियाणि च।
खं वायुर्ज्योतिरापश्च पृथिवी विश्वधारिणी॥"

(Quoted and translated under Sūtra 15, Sec. III, Chap. II,)

चक्षुरादिवत्तु तत्सह शिष्ट्यादिभ्यः॥१०॥

[The characteristics of Prāṇa, the chief vital energy, are continued].

चक्षुरादिवत् (like the eye and others), तु (but), तत्सह (together with them); शिष्टि. (शासनम्, instruction); शिष्ट्यादिभ्यः (because of scriptural instruction and other reasons).

Explanation—Prāṇa, the chief vital energy, is like the eye etc., one of the tools of the individual soul (though it stands foremost among them); because it is placed in the same category with the eye and the other Indriyas in a colloquy amongst them, described in the Bṛhadāraṇyaka Śruti (Chap. VI, 1, 7-14); and there are also other reasons shown subsequently.

अकरणत्वाच्च न दोष स्तथाहि दर्शयति॥११॥

[An objection, against Sūtra 10, is refuted].

अकरणत्वात् (on the plea of want of some special function), च (also), न (no), दोषः (defect; objection), तथा (thus, so), हि (as; because), दर्शयति (scripture shows).

Explanation—There can reasonably be no objection to the view that Prāṇa is an instrument of function like the Indriyas, the eye etc., on the plea of want of some specified function on its part. Because Śruti points out that it has also some specific function to perform, namely, to support the body and energise it with all the Indriyas.

Having no function like the ordinary Indriyas it cannot be, however, styled an Indriya and hence is excluded from their list of eleven (vide Sūtra 6).

For reference vide the Śruti—

"तान् वरिष्ठः प्राण उवाच—मा मोहमापद्यथाह. मवैतत् पञ्चधात्मानं प्रविभज्यैतद्बाणमवष्टभ्य विधारयामि।"

(The chief vital energy, the highest, said to them: "Be not deceived, I alone dividing myself five-fold, enter this body and support it.")

Praśnopaniṣad, Chap. II, 3.

पञ्चवृत्तिर्मनोवद्व्यपदिश्यते॥१२॥

[The characteristics of the chief vital energy are continued].

पञ्चवृत्तिः (one having five functions), **मनोवत्** (like the mind), **व्यपदिश्यते** (is described).

Explanation—As the mind, being endowed with several functions, such as desire, contemplation etc., serves the individual soul; similarly the chief vital energy is described in Śruti as doing good to the individual soul, being vested with the five functions called the five vital forces. [The five functions are Prāṇa (respiration), Apāna (evacuation), Samāna (assimilation), Vyāna (circulation) and Udāna (celebration)].

For reference vide the quotation and its translation under the preceding Sūtra.

अणुश्च॥१३॥

[The characteristics of the chief vital energy are continued].

अणुः (minute), **च** (also).

Explanation—The chief vital energy is also minute, like

the Indriyas (as stated in Sūtra 7), and not all-pervading as can be understood from its coming out of the body. Had it been all-pervading, there could have been no movement on its part.

For the movement of the chief vital energy, vide the quotation from the Bṛhadāraṇyaka Śruti under Sūtra 7 of this section.

ज्योतिराद्यधिष्ठानं तु तदामननात् ॥१४॥

[Now follows a discussion, on the dependence of Prāṇa, the senses and other organs].

ज्योतिरादि (the fire and others), **अधिष्ठानं** (guidance by the deities presiding over them), **तु** (indeed), **तदामननात्** (because of such statement *in Śruti*).

Explanation—Prāṇa, the senses and the organs are under the guidance of the deities, such as fire and others presiding over them; as Śruti also states so.

For reference vide the Śruti—

"अग्निर्वाग् भूत्वा मुखं प्राविशत्।"

(Fire, in the form of speech, entered the mouth).

Aitareyopaniṣad, Chap. I, 2, 3.

प्राणवता शब्दात् ॥१५॥

[From the preceding Sūtra a doubt may arise, that the divinities, guiding the senses etc., may be their lords; the doubt is removed by this Sūtra].

प्राणवता (with one possessing the Indriyas, *i. e.,* with the individual soul. '**प्राण**' here is a synonym for Indriya), **शब्दात्** (from Śruti).

Explanation—Although the Indriyas are guided by the dieties, as stated in the preceding Sūtra, it is known from Śruti that they are related to the embodied soul, as servants are to their master, for subserving his interest.

For reference vide the Śruti—

"अथ यत्रैतदाकाशमनुविषण्णं चाक्षुषः पुरुषो दर्शनाय चक्षुः।"

(Then where there is the eye, entering this opening—*the cavity of the eye,—it is there* to serve the spirit, the ego of sight, for the purpose of seeing).

'The spirit, the ego of sight' is the embodied soul who claims and feels the eye to be his own, and the eye is to serve him by presenting him with the objects of vision. In the like manner, it is described in Śruti, that the other Indriyas also are servants of the same master, the embodied soul; so the individual soul, and not the presiding deities, is the master of the Indriyas.

तस्य नित्यत्वात् ॥१६॥

[An argument, in support of Sūtra 15, is adduced].

तस्य (its, *i.e.*, of the connection of Karaṇas, the instruments, with the individual soul), **नित्यत्वात्** (as it is permanent).

Explanation—As the connection of Karaṇas (the instruments) with Jīva (the individual soul) is permanent, Jīva and not the guiding deities, is their master; seeing that the deities are not permanently connected with them.

For permanent connection of the senses etc., with the embodied soul, vide the Śruti—

"तमुत्क्रामन्तं प्राणोऽनूत्क्रामति, प्राणमनूत्क्रामन्तं सर्व्वे प्राणा अनूत्-क्रामन्ति"।

(When it—*the embodied soul*— leaves the body Prāṇa, the chief vital energy, follows and when Prāṇa passes away all the Prāṇas—the Indriyas—accompany it).

Bṛhadāraṇyaka, Chap. IV, 4, 2.

त इन्द्रियाणि तद्व्यपदेशादन्यत्र श्रेष्ठात् ॥१७॥

[The distinction between Prāṇa (the chief vital energy) and Prāṇas (the Indriyas), is now pointed out].

ते (those), इन्द्रियाणि (the senses of perception and the organs of action), तद्व्यपदेशात् (as they are so differentiated in Śruti), अन्यत्र श्रेष्ठात् (श्रेष्ठात् अन्यत्र, other than *the chief vital energy which is* the highest).

Explanation—Those Indriyas, the senses and instruments of action, other than the chief vital energy which is the highest—are distinct independent principles, and are not the functions of the latter, as they are so differentiated by Śruti.

For reference vide the Śruti—

"एतस्माज्जायते प्राणो मनः सर्व्वेन्द्रियाणि च।"

(For translation and reference, vide Sūtra 15, Sec. III, Chap. II).

भेदश्रुतेर्वैलक्षण्याच्च ॥१८॥

[An argument, in favour of Sūtra 17, is adduced].

भेद (the difference between the chief vital energy and the Indriyas), श्रुतेः (from Śruti), वैलक्षण्यात् (because of difference in respect of function), च (also). भेदश्रुतेर्व्वैलक्षण्याच्च (also because Śruti points out a distinction between Prāṇa and the Indriyas).

Explanation—The Indriyas are independent principles and not functions of the chief vital energy, as is evident from the distinction pointed out by Śruti as well as from their distinctive functions: the Indriyas serve the purpose of perceptions and acts of volition, whereas the chief vital energy sustains the body and vitalises the Indriyas.

Reference:—In the Bṛhadāraṇyaka Śruti (Chap. I, 3), it is stated, that the gods in their struggle with the 'Asuras' *i. e.*, the powers of evil, found that the Indriyas, such as the speech, the nose, the eye, the ear and the mind were vitiated by the 'Asuras'; so they took the help of the chief vital energy, which the 'Asuras' could not vitiate; and thus the gods became victorious over the 'Asuras'. Here the chief vital energy is spoken of, as different from and superior to all the Indriyas etc.

For reference, vide:—"**अथ हेममासन्यं प्राणमुचुः**"

(Then they—*the gods*—appealed to Prāṇa, *the chief vital energy,* which is superior to the Indriyas).

Bṛhadāraṇyaka, Chap. I, 3, 7.

In Śaṅkara's commentary this Sūtra is divided into two parts; the one is numbered 18, as '**भेदश्रुतेः**' and the other 19, as '**वैलक्षण्याच्च।**'

संज्ञामूर्त्तिक्लृप्तिस्तु त्रिवृत्. कुर्व्वत उपदेशात् ॥१९॥

[After describing the chief vital energy and the Indriyas, the framer of the Sūtras shows that they have all been named and shaped by the Universal Soul].

संज्ञा (name), **मूर्त्ति** (form), **क्लृप्तिः** (conception; contrivance); **संज्ञामूर्त्तिक्लृप्तिः** (contrivance of names and forms), **तु** (too), **त्रिवृत्कुर्व्वतः** (of Him Who made the elements tripple), **उपदेशात्** (as Śruti has stated so).

Explanation—Names and forms have been contrived by Him (the Universal Soul), Who made each one of the three elements, fire, water and earth, triple; as Śruti has stated so.

For reference vide the Śruti:—

"**सेयं देवतैक्षत हन्ताहमिमास्तिस्त्रो देवता अनेन जीवेनात्मनानुप्रविश्य नामरूपे व्याकरवाणीति। तासां त्रिवृतं त्रिवृतमेकैकां करवाणि।**"

(He, this Divinity,—*the Supreme Soul*—reflected 'Ah! I, entering into these three deities—Fire, Water and Earth, as their individual souls, will manifest names and forms; I will divide each of these three into three parts, and intermix them').

Chāndogya, Chap. VI, 3, 2-3.

मांसादि भौमं यथाशब्दमितरयोश्च ॥२०॥

[Creation of the animal body and other visible things is now stated].

मांसादि (flesh with other constituents of the body; hence the body consisting of flesh etc). **भौमं** (**भूमेःकार्य्यं**, made of earth), **यथाशब्दम्** (as Śruti has said so), **इतरयोः** (of the other two, *i. e.*, of water and fire), **च** (also).

Explanation—Flesh etc. are made of earth; and also the other two elements, water and fire, enter into the composition of the animal body (the three elements, by their intermixture form the animal body); as Śruti says so.

[Air and Ākāśa, which are not ordinarily visible, also participate in the formation of the animal body, so they are implied to be included amongst the primary elements; only the visible elements are mentioned here for facility of understanding. Thus the Tribṛtkaraṇa (triplication, *i. e.*, formation of bodies by the intermixture of the three visible elements fire water and earth) is practically no other than Pañcīkaraṇa (quintuplication *i. e.,* formation of bodies by the intermixture of the five primary elements—Ākāśa, air, fire, water and earth)].

For reference, vide the Śruti—

"अन्नमशितं त्रेधा विधीयते तस्य यः स्थविष्ठो धातुस्तत् पुरीषं भवति यो मध्यमस्तन्मांसं, योऽणिष्टस्तन्मनः।"

(The food consumed is separated, *by metabolism,* into three parts, its grossest ingredient becomes the stool, the finer ingredient becomes the flesh and the subtlest ingredient becomes the mind).

Chāndogyopaniṣad, Chap. VI, 5, 1.

Also vide Chāndogya, Chap. VI, 5, 2 and 3.

वैशेष्यात्तु तद्वादस्तद्वादः॥२१॥

[Sūtra 20 is amplified here].

वैशेष्यात् (from the special preponderance of one element), **तु** (but), **तद्वादः** (that special designation); **तद्वादः**—(the repetition of the phrase indicates the termination of the chapter).

Explanation—A material thing derives its special

designation from the preponderance of a particular element in its composition, though it has been produced by the intermixture of all the five primary elements.

All material things are constituted by the five primary elements intermixed together; but a material thing is named after, and is said to be produced from that particular primary element whose share predominates in the composition. As for instance, the material earth, like other material things, is made by the intermixture of all the five minute primary elements, namely earth, water, fire-air and Ākāśa; but as the share of the particular primary element 'earth' preponderates in the composition, it is named 'earth' after the name of the preponderating element.

CHAPTER III

SECTION—I

After discussing different passages of Śruti and refuting all plausible objections that may arise in course of the argument, this section deals with the journey of the animal-soul, after death, to the region of the moon, and his return to this world after enjoying there the fruit of his actions. Shortly speaking, it accounts for the death and re-birth of the animal-soul, and thus states the relation between this world and the next.

Sūtras 1-6 state that the animal soul, at the dissolution of the body, departs, attended by the subtle essences of the five primary elements, as well as by the Indriyas.

Sūtra 7 discusses a passage of the Chāndogya Śruti, where persons, having no knowledge of Self, but doing sacrifices as well as works of public utility, have been described to become, in the region of the moon, the food of the gods, meaning thereby that they contribute to the enjoyment of the gods by their presence and service in that world.

Sūtras 8-11 show that the souls, on enjoying the fruits of that portion of their works which is enjoyable in the other world, descend with the fruit of the remaining works, which can have their fruition only in this world; and this unenjoyed portion (Anuśaya) determines the character of this new life.

Sūtras 12-16 raise an objection asking if we are to assume, from the passages of Śruti, that evil-doers also go to the world of the moon and return to this world, by suffering at first tortures in the abode of Yama and then by ascending to the moon and descending there-from to the earth again; as both Śruti and Smṛti have described frequent wanderings of the soul to the abode of Yama, which consists of seven hells.

Sūtras 17-21 refute the objection raised above, by proving, on the authority of Śruti, that the souls of evil-doers are precluded from going to the moon, but they frequently undergo the cycles of births and deaths. The Chāndogya Śruti, in the course of explaining the Pañcāgni Vidyā (for details vide the note to Sūtra 1 of this section), has described two paths for the departed soul on leaving the body, namely, the path of the gods and the path of the fathers; the former leads to the world of Brahma and is attainable by Self-knowledge alone and the latter leads to the sphere of the moon and is attainable by religious sacrifices and works of public utility. For the evil-doers who are not fit for attaining either of the two paths mentioned above, the same Śruti has described a third course, which consists of frequent undergoing of the process of births and deaths in this world (with periods of residence in hell for purging away their sins of a heinous nature, if necessary); and to their case the rule of the five oblations, as described in the Chāndogya Śruti (vide the note to Sūtra 1 of this section), does not apply; there are also traditions, that some exalted personages, such as Dhṛṣṭadyumna, were not born in ordinary course from a mother's womb; it is also observed that of the four classes of organic beings namely viviparous animals, oviparous animals, vegetables, and animals springing from heat and moisture—the latter two are produced without sexual conjunction.

Sūtras 22-27 describe, by a right interpretation of different passages of the Chāndogya Śruti, the process of descent back to the world, of the soul, from the sphere of the moon. From the moon the soul passes into a state of similarity to, and not of identity with, Ākāśa, air, vapour, mist, cloud and rain gradually, and then falling on the earth as rain is sucked up by a corn or a plant or the like; these stages are accomplished in a short time. On entering into a corn or a plant, the soul remains merely in conjunction with it which is already animated by another soul; after having entered into a corn or a plant, the soul enters into conjunction with him—who, after eating the corn or the fruit, performs the act of copulation—and ultimately, entering the mother's womb, is brought forth as a child.

तदन्तरप्रतिपत्तौ रंहति सम्परिष्वक्तः प्रश्ननिरूपणाभ्याम्॥१॥

[This Sūtra states that the soul, while leaving the body, takes with it the subtle essences of the elements.]

तदन्तरप्रतिपत्तौ (**देहान्तरग्रहणार्थं**, for the purpose of transmigration or translation of the soul from one body to another), **रहति** (goes, *i. e.*, the soul goes), **सम्परिष्वक्तः** (encased or enclosed in the subtle essences of the elements), **पश्ननिरूपणाभ्याम्** (as is evident from the question and its decision.)

Explanation—The soul, for the purpose of transmigration, goes out, enclosed within the subtle essences of the elements; as can be understood from the question and its decision in the description of the Upāsanā (worship), known as Pañcāgni-Vidyā (the offering to the five-fold fire) of the Chāndogya-Upaniṣad (Chapter V, parts 3-10.)

In the explanation of the Pañcāgni-Vidyā in the Chāndogya Śruti there is, at the outset, a question, among others, asking:—

"वेत्थ यथा पञ्चम्यामाहुतावापः पुरुषवचसो भवन्ति।"

(Dost thou know how, in the fifth offering, water is so transformed as to be called an embodied soul?.)

Chāndogya, Chap. V, 3, 3.

And for the solution of this question it is said—

"इति तु पञ्चम्यामाहुतावापः पुरुषवचसो भवन्ति।",

(In this manner water, in its fifth stage of offering, is so transformed as to be called an embodied soul.)

Chāndogya, Chap. V, 9, 1.

The Pañcāgni Vidyā is explained in the Chāndogya Śruti in the story of a king named Pravāhana, and an ascetic named

Gautama, where the former explained the Vidyā (the mode of meditation) to the latter—Agnihotra is a Vedic rite to be performed at sun-rise and sun-set by every Dvija or twice-born. This rite can be turned into a mode of worship of Brahma if a wider and more spiritual meaning can be given to it. Now, in every Vedic sacrifice there are—(1) the sacrificer, (2) the oblation or the thing sacrificed, and (3) the fire to which the oblation is offered. The deities, presiding over the sacrificer's senses and centres of action, may be collectively conceived to be the sacrificer, thus eliminating the sacrificer's own personality; his morning and evening prayers may be conceived as the offerings; and Div (Heaven) may be conceived to be the fire to whom the offering is made. The Chāndogya Śruti says that gods offer to Heaven the libation of subtle water, which is a transformation of the Soma-juice or milk offered to the fire in the sacrifices in this world; and by the offering the moon-beam is produced; then to the god of rains, the gods offer the moon-beam as libation; by which rains and dews are produced; rains and dews, in their turn, are offered to the earth, by which grains are produced; grains are offered to the embodied human being, by which semen is produced; this semen is again offered to the woman as libation, by which a man is produced. Thus heaven, the god of rains, the earth, the embodied being and the woman are conceived as five consecutive fires; and as a result of the fifth libation related above, a man is brought forth; *i. e.*, the watery offering, presented at first to Heaven, becomes, by the process of five successive oblations, transformed into a man. These five consecutive Agnihotras are spoken of in Chāndogya as Pañcāgni-Vidyā.

At the dissolution of the body, the individual soul, enveloped in fine particles of water, goes through the well-known southern route marked by smoke (Pitṛyāna), to the region of the manes, and presently reaches the sphere of the moon, and there at the termination of enjoyment of the fruits of his pious deeds, he again resumes a body of subtle water and falls back upon the sky, then he assumes an aerial form, then a form of vapour, next a form of cloud, which, dissolved in rain water, descends upon the earth. Having entered into a grain of paddy or barley corn, He may be eaten by any animal; then entrance into the womb of a female and is brought forth as a child in the fullness of time. The framer of the Sūtras means to say that the word 'water' mentioned here, does not indicate simply water, but all the five subtle elements; and water being the preponderating element in the mixture, it is named after water. The Śruti means to say that the departed individual soul, being enveloped in the subtle elements, ascends through the passage of the smoke, and goes towards the south to the region of the moon. On the other hand the Śruti points out at the same time, that those, who worship Brahma with a view to enlightenment, offer to the Lord the reverence of their heart, as tribute, in lieu of the watery libation. The latter worshippers—the worshippers of Brahma, at the dissolution of their body, take the northern route of the rays (Deva-yāna) and attain salvation. Those who renounce the world and take to forest-life for facility of divine meditation, attain salvation through the northern route of the rays. The Śruti concludes with the remark that the route to salvation is the same for both the classes of worshippers—the worshippers of Brahma through the medium of the five fires and the ascetics who have renounced the world. This Pañcāgni-Vidyā is also related at length in Bṛhadāraṇyaka.

त्र्यात्मकत्वात्तु भूयस्त्वात् ॥२॥

[The previous Sūtra is amplified here.]

त्र्यात्मकत्त्वात् (because of its consisting of the essences of the three), तु (but); भूयस्त्वात् (because of preponderance.)

Explanation—By the *water* enveloping the departing soul, all the three subtle elements, namely—fire, water and earth are implied. The water, spoken of in the Chāndogya Śruti, is indeed a compound consisting of the three subtle elements, of which the share contributed by water happens to be the largest.

For the intermixture of the three subtle elements, vide the Śruti—

"त्रिवृतमेकैकां करवाणि" (quoted at length and translated under Sūtra 19, Sec. IV, Chap. II.)

प्राणगतेश्च॥३॥

[A further reason is adduced to show that the subtle essences of the elements accompany the soul at the dissolution of the body.]

प्राणगते: (because of the departure of the senses and the centres of action), **च** (also.)

Explanation—As Śruti has stated the departure of the senses etc., with the individual soul at the dissolution of the body, and as they cannot stay without the support of the elements, it follows that the individual soul, at the dissolution of the body, departs attended by the subtle essences of the elements.

For reference vide the Śruti—

"तमुत्क्रामन्तं सर्व्वे प्राणा अनुत्क्रामन्ति।"

(quoted at length and translated under Sūtra 16, Sec. IV, Chap. II.)

अग्न्यादिगतिश्रुतेरिति चेन्न भाक्तत्वात् ॥4॥

[An objection to Sūtra 3, is raised and refuted.]

अग्न्यादिगति: (movement into Fire and so on; that they enter the fire-god and the other guiding deities), **श्रुते:** (as Śruti says), **इति** (this), **चेत्** (if), **न** (no; it cannot be accepted), **भाक्तत्वात्** (because it is secondary.)

[The Sūtra consists of two parts, namely, an objection and its reply. The objection-portion is:—**अग्न्यादिगतिश्रुतेरिति चेत्**; and the reply-portion is:—**न भाक्तत्वात्।**]

Explanation—If it be objected that the Indriyas do not go with the soul, at the time of death, seeing that, according to Śruti, they enter Fire and the other guiding deities; the reply is, that the objection cannot stand, because Śruti has said so only in a secondary sense, as can be understood from the subsequent passage in the same Śruti.

Fire and other deities, who act as the guides of the Indriyas and co-operate with them, stop their co-operation on the eve of death; *i. e.*, at the time of death the deities having ceased to guide the Indriyas any longer, the latter consequently lose their respective functions, and are supposed to be immersed in the guiding deities. But such is not the fact. The Indriyas remain at that time quite inoperative, waiting for accompanying the departing soul. The statement in Śruti, that the Indriyas enter into the deities, is only to be interpreted in a secondary sense; meaning, they seem as if they have entered into their respective guiding deities; just as is the case with the hairs of the head and the body, which are stated subsequently in the same Śruti to enter into the trees and shrubs, since they cannot actually lose themselves in the trees and shrubs.

For reference as to the entering of the indriyas into the deities vide the Śruti—

"यत्रास्य पुरुषस्य मृतस्याग्निं वागप्येति वातं प्राणश्चक्षुरादित्यम्।"

(When the speech of the dead person loses itself in Fire, the vital breath in Air, and the eye-sight in Sun.)

Bṛhadāraṇyaka, Chap. III, 2, 13.

For the subsequent expression referred to vide—

"औषधीर्लोमानि वनस्पतीन् केशाः।"

(The hairs of the body disappear in the shrubs, and the hairs on the head in the trees.)

Bṛhadāraṇyaka, Chap. III, 2, 13.

But this is not endorsed by experience; the statement is nothing but a figure of speech.

प्रथमेऽश्रवणादितिचेन्न ता एव ह्युपपत्तेः॥५॥

[An objection to the Śruti, referred to in Sūtra 1, that water, in the fifth libation, is transformed into a man, is raised and refuted.]

प्रथमे (in the first *of the five oblations described in the Chāndogya Śruti*), **अश्रवणात्** (because it is not stated to be so in the Śruti), **इति** (this), **चेत्** (if); **न** (no; this objection cannot stand), **ताः** (they, the water), **एव** (only), **हि** (certainly, indeed), **उपपत्तेः** (as it is proved by reasoning.)

[The Sūtra consists of two parts, namely, an objection and its reply. The objection-portion is:—**प्रथमेऽश्रवणादिति चेत्**; and the reply-portion is:—**न ता एव ह्युपपत्तेः**]

Explanation—If the decision in Sūtra 1 (namely, that the water, in the fifth libation, is transformed into a man) be objected to on the ground that there is no mention of water in the first of the five oblations described in the Śruti; then the reply is that the objection cannot stand, because, though in place of water we find mention of 'faith' or 'reverence' yet it is reasonable to interpret 'faith' or 'reverence' to mean water.

In the Pañcāgni Vidyā described in the Śruti, the thing offered as oblation in the first sacrifice is said to be 'faith'; and there is no mention made of water so it may be objected that transformation of the water into a human being by the courses of libation is not in accordance with Śruti; but this objection cannot stand, as it is reasonable to accept 'faith' in the sense of water, for then and then only, the whole description of the Pañcāgni Vidyā becomes consistent; and a statement in the Śruti corroborates our interpretation.

For reference to show that faith (Śraddhā) is offered as oblation, Vide—

"तस्मिन्नेतस्मिन्नग्नौ देवाः श्रद्धां जुह्वति।"

(In this *sacrificial* fire, *in the first of the five sacrifices,* the gods offer faith or reverence as oblation.)

Chāndogya, Chap. V, 4, 2.

For reference to show that 'Śraddhā' actualy means water, according to Śruti vide—

"श्रद्धा वा आपः" (Śraddhā, indeed, is water.)

Taittirīya Saṁhitā, I, 6, 8, 1.

अश्रुतत्वादिति चेन्नेष्टादिकारिणां प्रतीतेः॥६॥

[An objection to Sūtra 3, that the soul departs attended by the subtle particles of the elements, is raised and refuted.]

अश्रुतत्त्वात् (as there is no mention in Śruti), इति (this), चेत् (if); न (no; the objection cannot stand), इष्टादिकारिणां (of the persons doing works of sacrifice and of public utility), प्रतीतेः (as it appears.)

[The Sūtra consists of two parts, namely, an objection and its reply. The objection-portion is:—अश्रुतत्वादिति चेत्; and the reply-portion is:—न, इष्टादिकारिण प्रतीतेः।]

Explanation—If, on the plea that there is no mention made in the Śruti of the soul moving away, though the Śruti is explicit on the movement of watery particles and other elements, an objection be raised against the assertion that on death the soul departs clothed in the subtle essences of the elements; then the reply is, that this objection cannot stand; as migration on the part of the soul on death is understood from Śruti, where persons, doing sacrifices and works of public utility in this life, are stated to be rewarded with admittance into the world of the moon through the route of smoke.

For reference vide the Śruti—

"अथ य इमे ग्राम इष्टापूर्त्ते दत्तमित्युपासते तेधूममभिसम्भवन्ति।"

(Again those, who, living in a village, practise sacrifices, works of public utility, and give away alms, find the route of smoke.)

Chāndogya, Chap. V, 10, 3.

"पितृलोकादाकाशमाकाशाच्चन्द्रमसमेषः सोमो राजा तद्देवानामन्नं तं देवा भक्षयन्ति।"

(From the region of the manes they reach Ākāśa, and from Ākāśa they go to the moon *and are turned into its substance;* this *moon is called* Soma, the king, who is the food of the gods, whom the gods enjoy.)

Chāndogya, Chap. V, 10, 4.

भाक्तं वाऽनात्मवित्त्वात् तथाहि दर्शयति॥७॥

[The passage of the Chāndogya Śruti, quoted last in the preceding Sūtra, namely that the performers of good deeds become the food of the gods, is explained in this Sūtra to remove the apprehension that they become food in its actual sense.]

भाक्तं (metaphorical), **वा** (but), **अनात्मवित्वात्** (because of want of the knowledge of Self), **तथा** (thus), **हि** (because), **दर्शयति** (shows; Śruti shows.)

performers of mere good works without the knowledge of Self, being serviceable companions to the gods, are said to be the food of the gods in a metaphorical sense; Śruti also shows this.

For reference vide the Śruti—

"अथ योऽन्यां देवतामुपास्तेऽन्योऽसावन्योऽहमस्मीति न स वेद यथा पशुरेवं स देवानाम्।"

(Now if a man worships a deity other than Brahma, thinking the deity as one, and himself as another, he remains ignorant of *Self*. He is like a beast *subservient* to the gods.)

Bṛhadāraṇyaka, Chap. I, 4, 10.

कृतात्ययेऽनुशयवान् दृष्टस्मृतिभ्यां यथेतमनेवं च ॥८॥

[The return of the individual soul to this world is now described.]

कृत्यात्यये (on the exhaustion of the rewards of works, which are enjoyable in the other world), **अनुशयवान्** (the individual soul possessing the remnant or unenjoyed portion of his rewards), **दृष्टस्मृतिभ्यां** (as can be understood from direct statement in Śruti and Smṛti), **यथा इतं** (by the way he went), **अनेवं** (in the inverse order), **च** (also.)

Explanation—On the exhaustion, by enjoyment in the other world, of the rewards of the works which are capable of being enjoyed there, the individual soul, being possessed of the remnant of the works which, by their nature, cannot be enjoyed there and so waits to be enjoyed in this world, returns here, in the inverse order, by the same route through which he ascended after death; this is proved by Śruti and Smṛti as well.

For the Śruti vide—

"तद् य इह रमणीयचरणा अभ्याशो ह यत्ते रमणीयां योनिमापद्येरन् ब्राह्मणयोनिं वा क्षत्रिययोनिं वा वैश्ययोनिं वाथ य इह कपूयचरणा अभ्याशो ह यत्ते कपूयां योनिमापद्येरन् श्वयोनिं वा शूकरयोनिं वा।"

(Those, whose conduct, *during the previous life,* has been good, presently obtain some good birth, such as the birth of a Brahmin, a Kṣatriya or a Vaiśya; those whose conduct has been evil, presently obtain some evil birth, such as that of a dog or a pig.)

Chāndogya, Chap. V, 10, 7.

For the Smṛti vide—

"वर्णाः आश्रमाश्च स्वकर्म्मनिष्ठाः प्रेत्य कर्म्मफलमनुभूय ततः शेषेण विशिष्टजातिकुलरुपायुः श्रुतवृत्तवित्तसुखमेधसो जन्म प्रतिपद्यन्ते।"

(The members of the different castes and of the different orders of life who are engaged in the works prescribed for them, after leaving this world and enjoying the fruits of their works in the other world, take rebirths, owing to the unenjoyed portion of their rewards, in distinguished castes and families, with special appearance, longevity, knowledge, conduct, property, comfort and intelligence.)

चरणादिति चेन्नोपलक्षणार्थेति कार्ष्णाजिनिः॥९॥

[An objection is raised, with respect to the remaining works (अनुशयः) stated in the preceding Sūtra, and is refuted.]

चरणात् (from the conduct; as there is the word meaning conduct; as Śruti shows that the conditions of the new birth depend on the conduct in the previous birth), **इति** (this), **चेत्** (if), **न** (no; the objection is without force), **उपलक्षणार्था** (meaning by ellipsis; *here* meant to signify secondarily the real intention of Śruti; *hence* meant to connote the remainder of the works after enjoyment in the other world), **इति** (this), **कार्ष्णाजिनिः** (the sage named Kārṣṇājini.)

[The Sūtra consists of two parts, namely, an objection and its reply. The objection-portion is:—**चरणादितिचेत्**; and the reply-portion is:—**न, उपलक्षणार्थेति कार्ष्णाजिनिः।**.]

Explanation—If an objection be raised in the way that there is no necessity of assuming the effects of the remaining works for causing re-birth, (as the passage of the Śruti, quoted in the previous Sūtra, shows that the conditions of the new birth depend on the conduct [**चरणं**] in the previous birth); then the reply is, that the objection is without force, because the scriptural term, meaning conduct, is meant here to connote the remainder of the works after enjoyment in the other world, by a secondary implication of the term; this is the opinion of the sage, Kārṣṇājini, quoted by the framer of the Sūtras meaning his full concurrence in it.

आनर्थ्यक्यमिति चेन्न तदपेक्षत्वात् ॥१०॥

[A further objection, to the reply-portion of the preceding Sūtra regarding the word '**चरणं**' (conduct), is raised and refuted.]

आनर्थ्यक्यम् (uselessness, purposelessness), इति (this), चेत् (if); न (no; the objection cannot stand), तदपेक्षत्त्वात् (because of dependence on that; as they depend on conduct.)

[The Sūtra consists of two parts, namely, an objection and its reply. The objection-portion is:—आनर्थ्यक्यमितिचेत्; and the reply-portion is:—न, तदपेक्षत्त्वात्।]

Explanation—In case the word 'चरणं' be taken in its secondary sense (*i. e.*, remainder of the works), a further question arises as to whether it should be thought purposeless in its direct sense (*i. e.*, conduct.) The reply is:—No; such works as sacrifices and the like must be accompanied with right conduct; as he, whose conduct is not good, does not attain religious merit by mere performance of sacrifices; so the direct meaning (conduct) of the word 'चरणं' has also been kept in view, and is therefore not without any use.

For reference vide the Smṛti—

"आचारहीनं न पुनन्ति वेदाः"

(The Vedas do not cleanse him, who is wanting in good conduct.)

सुकृतदुष्कृते एवेति तु वादरिः॥११॥

[Further discussion on the meaning of the word 'चरणं' is made here.]

सुकृतदुष्कृते (good and evil works), एव (nothing but), इति (this), तु (however), वादरिः (the sage named Bādari.)

Explanation—The sage Bādari, however, thinks that the word 'Caraṇa' denotes nothing but good and evil works.

अनिष्टादिकारिणामपि च श्रुतम्॥१२॥

[The movement of persons doing evil works is now described. In this connection this Sūtra is adduced by way of objection, and is refuted by Sūtra 17 below.]

अनिष्टादिकारिणाम् (*to speak* to the persons doing evil works and the like), **अपिच** (also), **श्रुतम्** (as stated in Śruti.)

Explanation—To speak of the persons doing evil works, they also go to the world of the moon; as Śruti says that all persons, righteous or iniquitous, are equally entitled to the world of the moon.

For reference vide the Śruti—

"ये वै के चास्माल्लोकात् प्रयन्ति चन्द्रमसमेव ते सर्व्वे गच्छन्ति।"

(Whoever depart from this world, all of them go to the moon.)

Kauṣītaki-Upaniṣad, Chap. I, 2.

संयमने त्वनुभूयेतरेषामारोहावरोहौ तद्गतिदर्शनात्॥१३॥

[Description of the movement of persons doing evil works is continued.]

संयमने (in the abode of Yama), **तु** (but), **अनुभूय** (after suffering), **इतरेषाम्** (of persons other than the good; *i. e.,* of evil-doers), **आरोहावरोहौ** (ascending and descending), **तद्गतिः** (movement there; journey to the abode of Yama), **दर्शनात्** (as can be understood from Śruti; because Śruti speaks so.)

Explanation—Persons doing evi-works, at first suffer torture in the abode of Yama, and then they ascend to the sphere of the moon, whence they again descend; because Śruti speaks of their frequent journeying to the abode of Yama.

[This is also said by way of objection and is refuted by Sūtra 17.]

For reference vide the Śruti—

"न साम्परायः प्रतिभाति बालं
प्रमाद्यन्तं वित्तमोहेन मूढ़म्।
अयं लोको नास्ति पर इति मानी
पुनः पुनर्वशमापद्यते मे॥"

(The thought of the next world is never welcome to the fool blinded by the delusion of wealth; 'this is the *only* world', he thinks, 'and there is none beyond'; thus he comes, birth after birth, under my sway.)

Kaṭhopaniṣad, Chap. I, 2, 6.

[This passage occurs in a colloquy between Naciketā and his Guru, Yama.]

स्मरन्ति च॥१४॥

[Description of the journey of persons doing evil works is continued.]

स्मरन्ति (Smṛtis declare), च (also.)

Explanation—The Smṛtis also declare this, (that persons doing evil works come within the clutches of Yama.)

Vide the Smṛti—

"सर्व्वे चैते वशं यान्ति यमस्य भगवन् किल।"

(O revered Sir, it is said that they all come under the sway of Yama.)

अपि सप्त ॥१५॥

[Particulars of the abode of Yama are given.]

अपि (also), सप्त (seven.)

Explanation—Moreover, there are seven hells.

Smṛti mentions seven hells, Raurava, etc., by name, which serve as places of torture for the evil-doers.

तत्रापि च तद्व्यापारादविरोधः॥१६॥

[The same topic continues.]

तत्र (there; over the seven hells stated in the preceding Sūtra), अपि (even), च (also), तद्व्यापारात् (from his authority; *i. e.*, from the authority of Yama), अविरोधः (no bar.)

Explanation—There is no bar to the jurisdiction and authority of Yama over those seven hells superintended by Citragupta and others, for in those hells too Yama exercises his power.

This Sūtra shows that there is no inconsistency in calling these hells as the abode of Yama, as they are all under his government, though supervised by his lieutenants, Citragupta and others.

विद्याकर्म्मणोरिति तु प्रकृतत्वात्॥१७॥

[The view, expressed in Sūtras 12-16, is now refuted.]

विद्याकर्म्मणो: (of knowledge and works), **इति** (this), **तु** (but), **प्रकृतत्वात्** (these being the subject of discourse in Śruti.)

Explanation—The different journeys of the departed souls to the other world through the two paths described in the Pañcāgni Vidyā of Śruti, are the results of divine meditation and religious sacrifices, according as they were practised in life; because these two are the subjects of discourse in Śruti.

The Śruti, on the occasion of explaining the Pañcāgni Vidyā, has at the outset described, for the departed soul, two paths, namely, the path of the gods and the path of the fathers; the former is attainable by divine meditation and the latter by religious sacrifices and works of public utility; but the said Śruti subsequently points out a third course for the evil-doers, who are not fit for attaining either of the above-mentioned two paths; the third course is an interminable cycle of births and deaths in this world without ascending to the sphere of the moon and descending therefrom. So the evil-doers are, according to Śruti, precluded from going to the region of the moon; and the quotation from the Kauṣītaki-Śruti, noted under Sūtra 12 of this section, is to be understood with the limitation that all those who have practised divine meditation, and also those who have performed religious sacrifices or works of public utility, and not the evil-doers, go to the moon on departure from this world.

For reference vide the Śruti—

"अथैतयो: पथोर्न कतरेण च तानीमानि क्षुद्राण्यसकृदावतीनि भूतानि भवन्ति जायस्व म्रियस्वेत्येतत्तृतीयं स्थानं तेनासौ लोको न सम्पूर्य्यते"।

[By neither of these two paths (*i. e.,* the paths of the gods and of the fathers) do those small ephemeral creatures travel, while undergoing the interminable series of births and deaths; this is a third course; and therefore that world *of the moon* never becomes overcrowded.]

Chāndogya, Chap. V, 10, 8.

न तृतीये, तथोपलब्धेः ॥१८॥

[The preceding Sūtra is made clearer by this Sūtra.]

न (not; need not be attended to), तृतीये (in the third; with regard to the third course), तथा (thus), उपलब्धेः (because of perception; as it is understood from the expression in Śruti.)

Explanation—With regard to the third course, stated in Sūtra 17, the rule of the five oblations, described in the Chāndogya Śruti (quoted and translated under Sūtra 1 of this section), need not be attended to for the purpose of obtaining a new body; as it is so understood from the same Śruti.

From the same Śruti, (quoted and translated under the preceding Sūtra), it is understood that rebirth by the third course as described there, is reached without having recourse to oblations.

स्मर्य्यतेऽपि च लोके ॥१९॥

[The argument commenced in Sūtra 17, to refute the objections raised in Sūtras 12-16 is continued.]

स्मर्य्यते (is stated in Smṛti), अपि च (also), लोके (in this world.)

Explanation—It is also understood in this world from statements in Smṛti, that some persons were not born in the ordinary way from mothers, by following the course of five oblations.

There are instances of Droṇa, Dhṛṣṭadyumna, Sītā and Draupadī, who took extraordinary processes of births. In their cases there was wanting the fifth oblation which is made to the woman. Hence in many other cases also, procreation may be supposed to take place independently of oblations. So every body does not require to have recourse to the five oblations, and to come from the moon, to take his birth in this world.

दर्शनाच्च ॥२०॥

[The argument, commenced in Sūtra 17, is continued.]

दर्शनात् (from observation), च (also.)

Explanation—It is also observed that of the four classes of organic beings—namely, oviparous animals, viviparous animals, animals springing from a seed or from the ground, and animals springing from heat and moisture—the last two classes are produced without sexual conjunction, so that in their case the number of oblations is of no consequence.

तृतीयशब्दावरोधः संशोकजस्य॥२१॥

[This Sūtra refutes the objection that may arise regarding the number of classes of organic beings, as the Chāndogya Śruti mentions only three of them.]

तृतीयशब्दः (the third term), अवरोधः (inclusion), संशोकजस्य (of that which springs from heat and moisture.)

Explanation—The third term (creatures springing from the ground) includes those that are produced from heat and moisture.

So there are in fact, four classes of organic beings according to the sources of their origin.

For the third term vide the Śruti—

"अण्डजं जीवजमुद्भिज्जमिति।"

(That which springs from an egg, that which springs from a living being, and that which springs from ground.)

Chāndogya, Chap. VI, 3, 1.

तत्स्वाभाव्यापत्तिरुपपत्तेः॥२२॥

[The way of descent of the individual soul from the sphere of the moon is now discussed.]

तत् (**तेषां**, their), **स्वाभाव्य** (similarity of nature), **आपत्तिः** (attainment), **उपपत्तेः** (from reasoning; as this is reasonable.)

Explanation—In course of descent of the individual soul from the moon, he attains a similarity of nature with Ākāśa, air, and vapour and so on, and not identity with them; as this is reasonable.

Śruti states that in descending from the moon the individual soul returns to Ākāśa, and thence to the air, then becoming air it becomes vapour and so on. Now a question arises whether the soul becomes identical with Ākāśa, air, etc., or simply resembles them. This Sūtra clears up the doubt by saying that the soul simply resembles Ākāśa, air, vapour and so on; as that is only reasonable.

For reference vide the Śruti—

"अथैतमेवाध्वानं पुनर्निवर्त्तते" यथेतमाकाशमाकाशाद्वायुं वायुर्भूत्वा धूमो भवति धूमो भूत्वाभ्र भवति अभ्रं भूत्वा मेघो भवति मेघो भूत्वा प्रवर्षति।"

(He returns again through the very way he went, to the Ākāśa, from the Ākāśa to the air; then after becoming air he passes into the state of vapour, from vapour into mist, from mist into cloud; and from cloud he precipitates as rain.)

Chāndogya, Chap. V. 10, 5 and 6.

नातिचिरेण विशेषात् ॥२३॥

[The discussion on the soul's way of descent is continued.]

न (not), **अतिचिरेण** (in a very long time), **विशेषात्** (because of special statement; as can be understood from the special statement of Śruti.)

Explanation—These stages of passing, on the part of the individual soul, are accomplished not in a very long time; as can be understood from the special statement of Śruti.

The soul's journey, through the stages of the Ākāśa, the air, the vapour, the mist, the cloud and the rain, takes a shorter time than its passing through the stages of corn, semen and fœtus, which take a much longer time of hard suffering, as there is the special statement in Śruti, that after its entrance into a corn the escape is beset with much greater difficulty.

For the special statement referred to, vide—

"अतो वै खलु दुर्निष्प्रपतरम्" ।

(From thence the escape is beset with much greater difficulty.)

Chāndogya, Chap. V, 10, 6.

This passage throws out a hint that the path of the gods should be preferred by all means, if only to escape the interminable sufferings of births and deaths preceded by ascents and descents.

अन्याधिष्ठिते पूर्व्वदभिलापात् ॥ २४ ॥

[The discussion on the way of descent of the individual soul is continued.]

अन्याधिष्ठिते (into what is possessed by another; into the corn or plant which is already animated and occupied by another soul), **पूर्व्ववत्** (like the previous ones), **अभिलापात्** (because of statement), **पूर्व्ववदभिलापात्** (as it is expressly stated in Śruti to be a passing stage like the previous stages of Ākāśa, air, etc.)

Explanation—The animal soul, while descending, enters into the corn or plant, which is already animated and occupied by another soul; and so he has to use it only as his halting station, without being identified with it; as it is expressly stated in śruti to be a passing stage like the previous stages of Ākāśa, air, etc.

The animal soul, while passing through the stage of corn or plant, does not become the soul of that corn or plant, which is already occupied by another soul to which the corn or the plant really belongs; the animal soul, by entering into the corn or the plant, has to use it, like the previous stages of Ākāśa, etc., as his vehicle, through which he is to proceed until he reaches the stage of consummation—his birth as an animal being. Śruti says that the soul, descending from the moon and after passing through Ākāśa, the air, the vapour, the cloud and the rain, obtains the appearance of paddy or barely corn, herbs or trees, or sesamums or beans. The present Sūtra draws the conclusion from the latter part of the said Śruti that the animal soul simply enters into the corn or the plant, already animated and possessed by another soul, without losing its distinctive identity.

For reference as to the animal soul obtaining the appearance of paddy, barley corn, etc., vide—

"ते इह व्रीहि यवा ओषधि वनस्पतयस्तिलमाषा इति जायन्ते"।

(Then they are born as paddy or barley corn, herbs or trees, sesamums or beans.)

Chāndogya. Chap. V, 10, 6.

अशुद्धमिति चेन्न शब्दात्॥२५॥

[An objection, to Sūtra 24, is raised and refuted.]

अशुद्धम् (unholy), इति (this), चेत् (if); न (no; the objection cannot stand), शब्दात् (from the scripture; as the scripture says.)

[The Sūtra consists of two parts, namely, an objection and its reply. The objection-portion is:—अशुद्धमिति चेत्; and reply portion is:—न, शब्दात् ।]

Explanation—An objection may be raised that the sacrificial work, such as the Jyotiṣṭoma sacrifice and the like, where animal-life is injured, is unholy, and as such, its result may cause the sacrificer to be actually born as a corn or a plant as penalty for his cruel deed; so to become a corn or a plant is really to be born as such, and not simply to be mixed with it; then the reply is that such objection is groundless, as the scripture says that there is no demerit arising from slaughter for sacrificial purposes.

रेतःसिग्योगोऽथ ॥२६॥

[The discussion on the way of descent of the animal-soul is continued.]

रेतःसिक् (one who ejects the seminal fluid; one who performs the act of copulation), **योगः** (assimilation), **अथ** (afterwards; after the animal-soul enters into a corn or a plant.)

Exaplanation:— The animal-soul, after having entered into a corn or a plant, becomes assimilated to him who (on eating the corn or the fruit) performs the act of coition. In every stage of its passage it retains its distinctive identity from the bodies with which it may happen to be conjoined.

For reference vide the Śruti —

"यो यो ह्यन्नमत्ति यो रेतः सिञ्चति तद्भूय एव भवति ।"

(Whenever one eats the food, whenever one performs the act of copulation, he—*the descending soul* becomes again that *food and that semen i.e.,* he becomes part and parcel of the individual into whom he enters.)

Chāndogya, Chap. V, 10, 6.

Here 'He becomes' cannot reasonably mean that he (the animal-soul on descent) becomes the very same individual whom he enters in; but the meaning is that he remains in him in conjunction only, until he enters into the mother's womb, with the seminal fluid injected.

योनेः शरीरम् ॥२७॥

[The discussion, on the nature of descent of the animal-soul, is concluded here.]

योनेः (from the uterus), **शरीरम्** (the body.)

Explanation—From the uterus the body is developed.

After having passed through the various preceding stages, the animal-soul at last enters into the mother's womb, where he receives a fully developed human body.

SECTION—II

This section starts with the explanation of the states of dream, sound sleep and swoon; then it discusses the two-fold nature of Brahma, one immanent, and the other transcendent; and lastly it deals with the relation of Brahma to the individual soul as well as to the universe.

Sūtras 1-6 discuss the state of dreams. The vision in dreams, as it is of a wonderful character, being not entirely true nor entirely false—is the creation, not of the individual soul, but of the Universal Soul, the Lord of the universe, acting through the individual soul. As some dreams are indicative of future good or bad fortunes, it is impossible for the individual to dream a good or a bad dream according to his own choice, he being, in his present state of bondage, ignorant of the future. The individual soul, in his emancipated state, can certainly exercise his will for the creation of vision in dreams; but the power, in the stage of his bondage, remains eclipsed by the superior will of the Universal Soul, who directs his actions according to the merits and demerits of his past conduct; and the suppression of his power is due to his being encaged in the body.

Ācārya Śaṅkara gives his opinion in course of his explanation of Sūtra 3, that dream is a mere illusion, as it is wanting in the reality of the waking state.

Sūtras 7-9 treat of the state of sound sleep, when the individual soul enters through several veinules into the pericardium or Medulla oblongata (?), and there reposes in the Universal Soul; and state that waking takes place when the individual soul returns from the Universal Soul to the world of the senses. A doubt may arise whether it is the same individual who is sound sleep is absorbed in the Universal Soul, that returns in awaking; or whether like a drop of water lost in the ocean, it loses all its identity; this doubt is removed by showing that the same soul returns in awaking, as can be understood from the reason of its subsequent works, and his remembrance of the past, as well as from the passages in Śruti to that effect, and also from religious injunctions.

Sūtra 10 says that a swoon is half death;

Sūtras 11-21 show, by refuting all plausible objections and by reference to passages of Śruti and Smṛti, that the Universal Soul does not contract any blemish from His union with the individual soul; because He has two-fold characteristics; namely, (1) transcendent, always pure and absolute, and (2) immanent, all-powerful and related to the universe; that though the Universal Soul and the individual soul reside together in the same body in close association with each other, the latter enjoys the fruit of his previous actions, while the former remains simply as a disinterested spectator without participating in the enjoyment; that the Universal Soul, the One without a second, though abiding in every individual being, remains unstained like the sun reflected in a thousand vessels of water; that due to the ripples in the water the reflected images of the sun are broken and scattered and they tremble when the water is stirred while the real sun remains, all the time, the same; so is the Universal Soul, abiding in the animal body, Who remains intact, although His reflected rays—the individual souls—are seen disturbed by the vicissitudes of life.

For the views of Ācārya Śaṅkara, vide the last para of the explanation of Sūtra II.

In Sūtras 22-30, after discussing the purity of the Universal Soul, in spite of His closest association with individual soul, the framer of the Sūtras goes on to examine His essential attributes. In His cosmic nature Brahma has two forms: visible and invisible; but He is not exhausted in these two cosmic forms; He has a superior nature, which is beyond the universe, unrevealed, and so beyond perception by the senses, only to be realised in the heart purified by staunch devotion. As fire is brought out by strokes of the hammer so the universal soul is revealed by the practice of deep meditation. The two-fold character of Brahma is completely established in Sūtras 11, 22 and 27, by showing that He is active *in* relation to the universe, but calm and tranquil *out of* relation to it; and that He is the same with, as well as different from, the universe and the individual soul (vide also Sūtras 42-44 of Section III, Chapter II, where the individual soul has been shown to be the part of, as well as the same with, the Universal Soul.) Brahma is but partially revealed through the animate and the inanimate world, but remains unrevealed beyond the creation. The whole universe disappears in Him during the general dissolution, and re-appears at the dawn of creation; just as some parts of a snake become closed when it twists into coils, and become again disclosed when it uncoils itself.

Sūtras 31-41 show, by reasoning as well as by references to the scripture, that there is no entity other than the Universal Soul. He is compared to a *cause-way*, not to show that He connects the universe with something else beyond Him, but to indicate that He is the protector of the worlds within the universe, and is also, like a cause-way, the support of the individuals while crossing over this ocean of life. He is conceived to be symbolised and located in a limited space, for facility of meditation on the part of the comparatively weak in intelligence. He is proved to be all-pervading and the giver of fruit of works, according to their merits.

सन्ध्ये सृष्टि राह हि ॥१॥

[The state of dream is now considered.]

सन्ध्ये (in the intermediate stage; in the state where this world and the next world meet; in the state intermediate between waking and sound sleep; *hence* in the state of dream), सृष्टिः (creation), आह (says; *i.e.*, Śruti says), हि (because, as.)

Explanation—In the intermediate stage, namely, in the state of dream, there is another creation, as Śruti says so.

Now a question arises whether the objects of dreams are created by the Universal Soul or by the individual soul. the framer of the Sūtras adduces at first, as a thesis, that the individual soul is himself the author of dream-percepts, as Śruti says 'He (*i.e.*, the individual soul) indeed is the creator.'

For reference vide the Śruti—

"तस्मिन् सन्ध्ये स्थाने तिष्ठन्..... न तत्र रथा न रथयोगा न पन्थानो भवन्त्यथ रथान् रथयोगान् पथः सृजते.....सहि कर्त्ता।"

(When he remains in the intermediate stage, *i.e.*, in dream.... There are no chariots, no horses, no road; but he creates chariots, horses and roads;.... he indeed is the creator.)

Bṛhadāraṇyaka, Chap. IV, 3, 9-10.

निर्म्मातारं चैके पुत्रादयश्च॥२॥

[The thesis, adduced in Sūtra 1 by way of first argument, that the individual soul creates the objects in dreams, is amplified here.]

निर्म्मातारं (the shaper, the builder), च (moreover), एके (some), पुत्रादयः (sons and others); च (also.)

Explanation—Moreover, some Śrutis say that in the state of dream, the individual soul is the builder of objects of desire, such as sons and the like.

For reference vide the Śruti—

"य एष सुप्तेषु जागर्त्ति कामं कामं पुरुषो निर्म्मिमाणः।"

(It is he, the individual soul, as the objector understands the term—who is awake, while the senses sleep, shaping one thing after another according to his liking.)

Kaṭha-Śruti, Chap. II, 2, 8.

मायामात्रं तु कार्त्स्न्येनानभिव्यक्तस्वरूपत्वात् ॥३॥

[The thesis, adduced in Sūtras 1 and 2, is now criticised.]

मायामात्रं (Simply a Māyā—an illusion; a strange thing), **तु** (but), **कार्त्स्न्येन** (in entirety; entirely), **अनभिव्यक्तस्वरूपत्वात्** (because of the real nature being unmanifested.)

Explanation— The creation in dreams is all the doing of the Universal Soul; as it is of a strange and illusive character, being not entirely true, nor entirely untrue; and as such, it cannot be done by the individual soul, for his essential characteristics including creative powers, in the present state of bondage are as yet unrealised; limited and conditioned as he is, his inherent powers cannot have full play; and therefore it is not possible for him to create the strange things of dream.

The above is the explanation given by Ācārya Nimbārka. Ācārya Śaṅkara explains this Sūtra in another way, saying that dreams are mere illusions, and that they do not possess the essentials of objective reality, as perceived in the wakeful state.

सूचकश्च हि श्रुतेराचक्षते च तद्विदः॥४॥

[An argument, in support of Sūtra 3, is adduced.]

सूचकः (indicative), **च** (moreover), **हि** (as), **श्रुतेः** (from Śruti), **आचक्षते** (declare), **च** (also), **तद्विदः** (experts in that; dream-experts; those who know the secrets of dream.)

Explanation—Moreover the dream is indicative of the future, as is known from Śruti; and those, who are experts in the secrets of dream, also declare it to be so.

It is said in Śruti that some dreams are indicative of future good, and some are of bad fortunes; and also those,. who are expert interpreters of dreams, hold the same view. So the Universal Soul is the creator of dreams and not the individual soul; for had it been possible for him to shape his dreams, he would never have dreamt a bad dream, but would always have dreamt only propitious ones.

For reference vide Scripture—

"यदा कर्म्मसु काम्येषु स्त्रियं स्वप्नेषु पश्यति ।
समृद्धिं तत्र जानीयात्तस्मिन् स्वप्न-निदर्शने ॥

(When a man, engaged in some works upon which he has set his heart, sees in his dream a woman, he may infer success from that sign in the dream.)

Also vide —

"अथ यदा स्वप्नेषु पुरुषं कृष्णं कृष्णादन्तं पश्यति स एनं हन्ति।"

(If he sees in dreams a blackman with black teeth, that man kills him.)

N.B.—Dreams, though of a strange and illusory nature, are a good index of the high or low spiritual and moral condition of the dreamer.

पराभिध्यानात्तु तिरोहितं ततो ह्यस्य बन्धविपर्य्ययौ॥५॥

[Sūtra 3 is amplified here.]

पराभिध्यानात् (from the will of the Highest, the Universal Soul), **तु** (but), **तिरोहितं** (hidden, eclipsed), **ततः** (from Him; due to Him), **हि** (certainly), **अस्य** (his, of the individual soul), **बन्ध विपर्य्ययौ** (bondage and its reverse, *i.e.,* release.)

Explanation—The natural will-power of the individual soul is eclipsed by the superior will of the Universal Soul, who guides the individual soul in all matters according to the latter's past deeds. In the same way his bondage and release also explained, as being due to the will of the Supreme Being.

For reference vide the Śruti—

"संसारबन्ध-स्थिति-मोक्षहेतुः।"

(*The universal soul is* the cause of bondage, sustenance and release of the individual soul.)

देहयोगाद्वा सोऽपि ॥६॥

[Sūtra 5 is amplified.]

देहयोगात् (from conjunction with the body; due to his being embodied), वा (and), सः (that *i.e.*, इच्छाशक्तितिरोभावः, the concealment or disappearance of the will-power of the individual soul), अपि (also.)

Explanation—And the concealment of the will-power of the individual soul for the creation of visions in dreams, referred to in the preceding Sūtra, is due to his being embodied.

तदभावो नीड़ीषु तच्छ्रुतेरात्मनि च ॥७॥

[The state of dreamless deep sleep is now discussed.]

तदभावः (absence of that, *i.e.*, of dreams; sound sleep), नाड़ीषु (in the veinules; in the capillaries, तच्छ्रुतेः (that from Śruti; that is known from Śruti), आत्मनि (in Self; in the Universal Soul), च (also.)

Explanation—Sound sleep rests in the tubular organs of the body, and also in the Universal Soul; this is known from Śruti.

Śruti describes that in the state of sound sleep the individual soul enters into several capillaries, named Hitās leading from the heart, and the enters into Purītat (the Pericardium or the Medulla oblongata [?]), and there reposes in the Universal Soul.

For reference vide the Śruti—

"य एषऽन्तर्हृदय आकाशस्तस्मिंश्छेते।"

(He reposes in Ākāśa, *i.e., the Universal Soul,* Who resides within the heart.)

Bṛhadāraṇyaka, Chap. II, I, 17.

"यदा सुषुप्तो भवति तदा न कस्यचन वेद हिता नाम नाड्यो द्वासप्तति सहस्त्राणि हृदयात् पुरीततमभिप्रतिष्ठन्ते ताभि प्रत्यवसृप्य पुरीतति शेते।"

(When the soul goes to sound sleep, when he does not know anything, he enters into the seventy-two thousand veinules, names Hitās, running from the heart to the Pericardium [Medula-oblongata ?] and passing through them, he reposes in the Pericardium.)

Bṛhadāraṇyaka, Chap. II, I, 19.

"सता सौम्य तदा सम्पन्नो भवति स्वमपीतो भवति।"

(O, my son, he becomes united with the True One—he attains the status of Self.)

Chāndogya, Chap. VI, 8, I.

अतः प्रबोधोऽस्मात्॥८॥

[The mode of waking from deep sleep is now described.]

अतः (therefore), **प्रबोधः** (awaking), **अस्मात्** (from that; from the Universal Soul.)

Explanation—Therefore the waking takes place from the Universal Soul.

The Universal Soul only is the place of the repose of deep sleep; on that account the scriptural chapters dwelling on sleep, invariably teach that in the waking state, the individual soul returns to consciousness from the Universal Soul.

For reference vide the Śruti—

"इमा सर्व्वाः सत आगत्य न विदुः सत आगच्छामहे।"

(*On awaking,* all these individuals, coming from Sat [the True One], do not know that they have come from Sat.)

Chāndogya, Chap. VI, 10, 2.

स एव तु कर्म्मानुस्मृति-शब्दविधिभ्यः॥९॥

[A doubt may arise that the individual who in sound sleep, is absorbed in the Universal Soul, is not the same individual in the waking state; as in the case of a drop of water, which being mixed with the vast sheet of water of the ocean, loses its identity. This Sūtra removes that doubt.]

स (he), **एव** (and no other), **तु** (buy), **कर्म्मानुस्मृतिशब्दविधिभ्यः** (because of work, remembrance, scriptural text and precept.)

Explanation—But he, and no other returns in awaking, because of work, remembrance, scriptural text and precept.

The very individual soul who, in sound sleep, is absorbed, in the Universal Soul, returns on awaking; as can be understood from his subsequent works, his remembrance of past things, the scriptural text (*i.e.,* Śruti), as well as injunctions for acquiring knowledge or for doing good works, which become useless if the soul becomes emancipated in the state of sound sleep and so does not return, or returns a different individual.

For reference vide the Śruti—

"ते इह व्याघ्रो वा सिंहो वा वृको वा वराहो वा कीटो वा पतङ्गो वा दंशो वा मशको वा यद् यद् भवन्ति तदा भवन्ति।"

(Whatever these *creatures* are here, whether a tiget, or a lion, or a wolf, or a boar, or a worm, of a winged insect, or a gnat, or a mosquito, that they become again.)

Chāndogya, Chap. VI, 10, 2.

मुग्धेऽर्द्धसम्पत्तिः परिशेषात् ॥१०॥

[The state of a swoon is discussed.]

मुग्धे (in a senseless state; in a swoon), **अर्द्धसम्पत्तिः** (attainment of half the state *of death*), **परिशेषात्** (because of excess; as it is a state in addition to all others.)

Explanation—In a swoon there is attainment of half the state of death; and it is a state in addition to all other states.

A swoon is more akin to death than to dream, sound sleep or wakeful state; hence it is called half-death—a state almost bordering upon death. The state of swoon is not the same with any one the four states, *viz.*, wakefulness, dream, sleep and death.

न स्थानतोऽपि परस्योभयलिङ्गं सर्व्वत्र हि॥११॥

[This Sūtra states that the Universal Soul is not

contaminated; even though He regulates, by His presence, the different states of the individual soul.]

न (not), **स्थानतः अपि** (in spite of His location), **परस्य** (of the Highest; of the Supreme Soul), **उभयलिङ्गे** (two-fold characteristics), **सर्व्वत्र** (everywhere), **हि** (यतः, for, as.)

Explanation—The Supreme Soul is not contaminated by the defilements, imperfections and limitations of the individual soul; even though He regulates by His presence the different states of the latter's consciousness, namely his waking, his dream, his sleep; since everywhere in Śruti He is said to have two-fold characteristics.

It has already been shown (in Sūtra 8, section II, Chapter I) that the Universal Soul, though all-pervading and existing in every individual soul, does not become affected by the pleasure and pain of the latter. In this Sūtra it is said that he is not the least infected by His existence in the states of dream, sound sleep etc; because all the scriptures have described Him as having two-fold characteristics, namely, (1) All-pervading, All-powerful and Relative (जगदनुग) and (2) Transcendent, All-peace and Absolute.

For reference that the Universal Soul is not at all affected by the properties of mater, vide the Śruti—

"अशब्दमस्पर्शमरूपमव्ययं
तथारसं नित्यमगन्धवच्च यत्।"

(For translation, vide under Sūtra 5, section IV, Chap. I.)

Kaṭha-Śruti, Chap. I, 3, 15.

For reference that Universal Soul is possessed of properties, vide the Śruti—

"सर्व्वकर्म्मा सर्व्वकामः सर्व्वगन्धः सर्व्वरसः।"

(For full quotation and translation, vide under Sūtra 2, section II, Chapter I.)

Ācārya Śaṅkara explains this Sūtra in the following way: An attempt is made to ascertain, on the ground of Śruti, the nature of the Universal Soul, with Whom the individual soul becomes united in the state of deep sleep, in consequence of the cessation of the limiting adjuncts. The scriptural passages about the Universal Soul are of a double character; some indicate that He is with properties (सगुण.) others state that He is without properties (निर्गुण.) But He cannot by Himself possess contradictory characteristics; as it is absurd to admit that one and the same thing should, by itself, possess certain qualities, such as colour, taste, etc. and at the same time should not possess them. It is also not reasonable to suppose that He possesses double characteristics on account of conjunction with limiting adjuncts (उपाधिः) such as a human body; the essential character of a thing must always remain the same, whatever may be the conditions imposed on it. If, however, it appears to be altered, it is surely due to ignorance. So Brahma is not of double *nature*; nay, not so, even if He be looked at through the perspective of limiting conditions.

The difference between the views of the two great Ācāryas (Śaṅkara and Nimbārka) would be brought out, if the wording of the Sūtra is punctuated as follows —

Nimbārka:—न स्थानतोऽपि परस्य, उभयलिङ्गं सर्व्वत्र हि (Here the nominative is supposed to be understood in the Sūtra, and उभयलिङ्ग is taken to be reason.)

Śaṅkara.—न स्थानतोऽपि परस्य, उभयलिङ्गं सर्व्वत्र हि (Here उभयलिङ्गं) is taken to be the nominative, and सर्वत्र हि to be the reason.) What is sought to be proved by the Sūtra, according to Nimbārka, is Brahma's absolute purity in spite of the connection with the impurities: whereas Śaṅkara interprets the Sūtra to show that in no way can Brahma be said to possess double (and contradictory) attributes. Both take their stand on the authority of Śruti.

भेदादिति चेन्न प्रत्येकम् तद्वचनात्॥१२॥

[An objection to the preceding Sūtra is raised and refuted.]

भेदात् (because of difference of conditions), **इति** (this), **चेत्** (if) **न** (no; that objection cannot stand), **प्रत्येकम्** (each), **अतत्** (not that; to the contrary), **वचनं** (declaration), **प्रत्येकमतद्वचनात्** (because of each Śruti declaring to the contrary.)

[The Sūtra consists of two parts, namely, an objection and its reply. the objection-portion is:—**भेदादिति चेत्**; and the reply-portion is:—**न, प्रत्येकमतद्वचनात् ।**]

Explanation—It may be objected that because of the changes admitted to exist in the Universal Soul by His connection with the individual soul through different states, such as, dream, sound sleep etc., He also is open to the limitations of the latter; the reply is, that the objection cannot stand, because all the Śrutis declare to the contrary.

The individual soul, though pure and sinless in reality, yet contracts limitations from contact with the body. Similarly the Universal Soul, Who is naturally pure, free and spotless, may, it may be apperhended, incur limitations by connection with the different states of the individual soul. But such apprehension has been set aside by Śruti, which declares everywhere, that though the Universal Soul is the 'regulator within' of all, yet He does not undergo any limitation.

For reference vide the Śruti—

"एष ते आत्मान्तर्याम्यमृतः"

(For full quotation and translation see under Sūtra 19, section II, Chap. I1)

Bṛhadāraṇyaka, Chap. III, 7, 3.

अपिचैवमेके ॥१३॥

[A further argument is adduced in support of Sūtra II.]

अपि (also), **च** (moreover, and), **एवम्** (thus), **एके** (some Śrutis.)

Explanation—And some Śrutis also teach, that the individual soul and the Universal Soul reside together in the same body; of the two, the former enjoys the consequences of previous actions, but the latter remains simply as a witness or a looker-on without partaking of them.

For reference, vide the quotation, with its translation, from the Muṇḍaka Śruti, under Sūtra 7, Sec. III, Chap. I.

अरूपवदेव हि तत् प्रधानत्वात् ॥१४॥

[A further argument is adduced in support of Sūtra II.]

अरूपवत् (without form; formless), एव (decidedly), हि (certainly), तत्प्रधानत्वात् (as He is paramount.)

Explanation—The Universal Soul is decidedly formless, as He is paramount over all names and forms.

Śruti says that the Universal Soul is the creator of names and forms; so He is undoubtedly paramount over them. Therefore, the limitations, attached to names and forms, cannot touch Him.

For reference vide the Śruti—

"नामरूपे व्याकरवाणीति।"

(Let me evolve names and forms.)

Chāndogya, Chap. VI, 3, 2.

प्रकाशवच्चावैयर्थ्यात् ॥१५॥

[A further argument is adduced in support of Sūtra 11.]

प्रकाशवत (having the property of revealing; revealer), च (moreover), अवैयर्थ्यात् (because of not being meaningless; so that the expressions in Śruti to that effect may not be meaningless.)

Explanation—Moreover, the Universal Soul should be accepted as the revealer of the manifested world, so that the expressions in Śruti to that effect may not be meaningless.

The Universal Soul is possessed of the virtue of illuminating (displaying every thing); or else the expressions of the scripture to that effect become meaningless. Even as a light reveals an object covered in darkness, but is not affected by the darkness, similarly the Universal Soul reveals every thing, but is not affected by it. So the Universal Soul is of a double character.

For the scripture vide—

"आदित्यवर्णं तमसः परस्तात्।"

(*Who*, like the sun, is possessed of the property of illuminating every thing, *having the virtue of revealing every thing,* and resting far beyond the reach of darkness, *i.e., above ignorance.*)

Bhagvat Gītā, Chap. VIII, 9.

आह च तन्मात्रम् ॥१६॥

[An argument, in explanation of Sūtra 15 regarding the authority of the scripture, is adduced.]

आह (says, declares), **च** (moreover), **तन्मात्रम्** (only that much; only that which is the subject-matter of its discussion.)

Explanation—Moreover, as the scripture declares only that which is the subject-matter of its discussion and no more, no passage of the scripture is to be considered as meaningless.

दर्शयति चाथो अपि स्मर्य्यते ॥१७॥

[The argument, in support of Sūtra 11, is continued.]

दर्शयति (Śruti shows), **च** (also), **अथो** (moreover), **अपि** (likewise, similarly), **स्मर्य्यते** (Smṛti states.)

Explanation—Śruti shows the two-fold characteristics of Brahma, and Smṛti also corroborates it.

For the Śruti vide—

"एष आत्मापहतपाप्मा विजरो विमृत्युर्विशोकोविजिघत्सोऽपिपासः सत्यकामः सत्यसंकल्पः ।"

(For translation vide Sūtra 14. Sec. III, Chap. I.)

For the Smṛti vide—

"यस्मात्क्षरमतीतोऽहमक्षरादपि चोत्तमः ।
अतोऽस्मि लोके वेदे च प्रथितः पुरुषोत्तमः ॥"

(As I am beyond the inanimate world, and also superior to the animate world, I am, therefore, known, in the world as well as in the Vedas, as the Puruṣa *par excellence*.)

Bhagavat Gītā, Chap. XV, 18.

Also Vide—

"अहं सर्व्वस्य प्रभवो मत्तः सर्व्वं प्रवर्त्तते ।"

(I am the fountain-head of all; and all motives are regulated from me, *i.e.*, I hold the key to all men's motives and propensities.)

Ibid, Chap. X, 8.

अतएव चोपमा सूर्य्यकादिवत्॥१८॥

[The argument in support of Sūtra 11, is continued.]

अतएव (therefore, for this reason), **च** (also), **उपमा** (resemblance), **सूर्य्यकादिवत्** (to the little suns, etc., *i.e.,* the images of the sun and the like.)

Explanation—For this reason, there is the resemblance to the reflected images of the sun and the like.

The Universal Soul, though all-pervading, does not incur the limitations of the individual soul owing to His two-fold characteristics, as stated in Sūtra II. The scripture, with a view to indicate the absolute purity of the Universal Soul, has stated the relation between Him and the individual soul as that between the sun or the moon and its reflected images in water.

For reference vide—

"यथात्मैको ह्यनेकस्थो जलाधारेष्विवांशुमान् ।"

(As the sun is *reflected* in different vessels of water, so the One Self, *the Universal Soul*, is present in many *individuals*.)

Also vide—

"एक एव तु भूतात्मा भूते भूते व्यवस्थितः ।
एकधा बहुधा चैव दृश्यते जलचन्द्रवत् ॥"

(The only One Self, *the Universal Soul,* abides as the Soul of all individual souls; He appears one and many, *at the same time*, like the moon in the sky and its images in the water, *i.e., as the one moon is multiplied by its reflections in different vessels of water.*)

अम्बुवदग्रहणात्तु न तथात्वम्॥१९॥

[An objection, to the preceding Sūtra, is raised.]

अम्बुवत् (like water), **अग्रहणात्** (because of non-acceptance; because it cannot be accepted), **तु** (but), **न** (not appropriate), **तथात्वम्** (that nature.)

Explanation—It is not of that nature *i.e.,* the similarity, spoken of in the preceding Sūtra, is not appropriate; because the case is not on all fours with the reflected image in the water.

Water receives the reflectin of the sun from a distant source and is a separate thing from the sun; on the other hand the Universal Soul is not at a distance from the states of the individual soul, and is not different in essence from him. So the similitude is inappropriate. Even supposing the parallelism to be true, the reflected image of the sun is found to be disturbed and broken by the agitated water. May we not similarly except the reflection of the Universal Soul to be equally agitated and affected by the limitations of the individual soul ?

वृद्धिह्रासभाक्त्वमन्तर्भावादुभयसामञ्जस्यादेवम् ॥२०॥

[The objection raised in the preceding Sūtra is refuted.]

वृद्धिह्रासभाक् (participating in the increase and decrease); **वृद्धिह्रासभाकत्वम्** (the status of participation in increment and decrement; undergoing distortion and contortion), **अन्तर्भावात्** (because of the state of existence within), **उभयसामञ्जस्यात्** (so that both the cases may be consistent), **एवम्** (this much.)

Explanation—The similarlity is only in point of the participation in the distortion and contortion due to penetration within. This much is accepted so that both the cases may be consistent.

The instance of the sun and its reflection is given only to point out that the Universal Soul, though abiding in the individual soul, is not affected by his changes; even as the sun in the sky though seen in water, is not at all affected, like its image, by the agitations of water. So far there is similarity between the two cases; and so the comparison cannot be considered to be inapt, as it is suggested in the preceding Sūtra. Moreover, whenver two things are compared, they are made so only in respect of some particular point or points they have in common; but exact similitude in all points would mean absolute identity.

दर्शनाच्च ॥२१॥

[A further reason is adduced to refute the objection raised in Sūtra 19.]

दर्शनात् (as it is found *to be so*), **च** (also.)

Explanation—In common parlance, we say that, likeness, between two individual things in certain important point or points, is a sufficient ground for describing the one as the other, for the comparison of one with the other. As for instance. This youth is a lion; the expression does not mean that the youth resembles lion in all respects, but only in respect of the lion's strength and courage.

प्रकृतैतावत्त्वं हि प्रतिषेधति ततो ब्रवीति च भूयः॥२२॥

प्रकृतं (**कथित**, mentioned *first*), **एतावत्त्वं** (this much); **प्रकृतैतावत्त्वं** (only the characteristics mentioned first), **हि** (for), **प्रतिषेधति** (prohibits, denies), **ततः** (over and above that), **ब्रवीति** (says, declares), **च** (also), **भूयः** (something more.)

Explanation—By the prohibitory expression not this, not this the Śruti denies the two characters, (the visible and the invisible forms of Brahma) spoken of at the outset, to be the only characters of Brahma as reflected in creation; for the same Śruti declares later on that He is something more—over and above the two forms.

The Bṛhadāraṇyaka Śruti (Chap. II, 3) speaks of Brahma as having two forms—visible and invisible; The visible form consists of earth, water and fire; and the invisble form consists of Ākāśa and air. Then again the same Śruti says No, no He is not this, He is not this. Now a doubt arises as to whether this denial amounts to an absolute negation of all forms with regard to Brahma. This Sūtra clears up the doubt, and says that the denial is not an absolute negation of all forms, but is only to point out that Brahma is not exhausted in those two forms only; He is something more. That this is the real intention of the denial is ascertained from the latter part of the same Śruti, where Brahma is ascertained to be possessed of these two forms and also to be something beyond these forms.

For reference as to the two forms vide—

"द्वे वाव ब्रह्मणो रूपे मूर्त्तं चैवामूर्त्तं च ।"

(Two forms of Brahma there are indeed, the visible and the invisible.)

Bṛhadāraṇyaka, Chap. II, 3, 1.

To see that Brahma is not only possessed of those two forms, but also transcending those forms, compare:—

"नह्येतस्मादिति नेत्यन्यत् परमस्ति ।"

(It is not that Brahm has no other form than these two, seeing that He has another form, subtler and finer than either.)

Bṛhadāraṇyaka, Chap. II, 3, 6.

तदव्यक्तमाह हि ॥२३॥

[The character of Brahma is discussed.]

तत् (that, *i.e.* Brahma), अव्यक्तम् (unrevealed), आह (Śruti says), हि (surely.)

Explanation—Brahma is unrevealed, *i.e.*, incomprehensible, and beyond perception by the senses; as Śruti says so. (Brahma is never fully comprehended, though He may be partially apprehended.)

For the Śruti vide—

"न चक्षुषा गृह्यते नापि वाचा नान्यैर्देवैस्तपसा कर्म्मणा वा ।"

(He is not apprehended by the eye, nor by the speech, nor by the other senses, nor by penance, nor by *good* works.)

Muṇḍaka-Śruti, Chap. III, 1, 8.

अपि संराधने प्रत्यक्षानुमानाभ्याम्॥२४॥

[The discussion on the character of Brahma is continued.]

अपि (only, certainly), **संराधने** (**आराधने,** in devout meditation], **प्रत्यक्षानुमानाभ्याम्** (from Śruti as well as Smṛti.)

Explanation—Brahma becomes apprehended only through devout meditation; as is understood both from Śruti and Smṛti.

For the Śruti vide—

"ज्ञानप्रसादेन विशुद्धसत्त्वस्ततस्तु तं पश्यते निष्कलं ध्यायमानः ।"

(When a man's heart becomes cleansed by pure knowledge, then he, through meditation, realises Him, the Perfect One.)

Muṇḍaka-Śruti, Chap. III. I, 8.

For the Smṛti vide:—

"भक्त्या त्वनन्यया शक्यः अहमेवंविधोऽर्ज्जुन।

ज्ञातं द्रष्टुञ्च तत्त्वेन प्रवेष्टुञ्च परन्तप॥"

(But by exclusive devotion, O Arjuna I, being revealed in this form, am capable of being rightly known, seen and entered into.)

Bhagavat Gītā, Chap. XI, 54.

प्रकाशादिवच्चावैशेष्यं, प्रकाशश्च कर्म्मण्यभ्यासात् ॥२५॥

[The discussion on the character of Brahma is continued.]

प्रकाशः (that which illumines; the sun); **प्रकाशादिवत्** (like the sun and the like), **च** (also), **अवैशेष्यं** (similarity), **प्रकाशः** (appearance, revelation, manifestation), **च** (also), **कर्म्मणि** (in work), **अभ्यासात्** (from practice), **कर्म्मण्यभ्यासात्** (from practice in necessary work; by having recourse to practical means adapted to the particular purpose.)

Explanation—There is also similarity between Brahma and the sun and the like; as in both the cases, the manifestation is due to practical means adapted to the purpose in view.

As the image of the sun is revealed by catching its reflection in a mirror, or the sparks of fire are revealed by strokes of the hammer, similarly Brahma is realised by practice of devotion.

अतोऽनन्तेन तथा हि लिङ्गम् ॥२६॥

[The result of realisation of Brahma is incidentally stated here.]

अतः (from this revelation or realisation of Brahma, as stated in the preceding Sūtra, as stated in the preceding Sūtra), **अनन्तेन** (with the Infinite Being, *i.e.*, with Brahma), **तथा** (such), **हि** (यतः, as, for), **लिङ्गम्** (indication *in Śruti*.)

Explanation—By the realisation of Brahma, the mediator attains equality with Him, the Infinite Being; as there is indication to that effect, in Śruti.

For reference vide the quotation, and its translation, under Sūtra 2, section III chapter I.

उभयव्यपदेशात्त्वहिकुण्डलवत् ॥२७॥

[The discussion on the characteristic of Brahma is resumed.]

उभयव्यपदेशात् (as Śruti expresses the two-fold character of Brahma), **तु** (indeed), **अहिकुण्डलवत्** (like the snake and its coils; as the snake is related to its coils.)

Explanation :—According to Śruti, Brahma stands in two-fold character in His relation the creation, just as the snake stands in its relation to its coils.

In Sūtra 22 it is established that Brahma is partially revealed in the form of the universe, and partially remains unrevealed beyond the creation. The creation remains concealed in Him during the general dissolution, and emerges out of Him again at the dawn of creation; just as some parts of a snake's body become closed when it twists itself into coils, and become again disclosed when it stretches its length.

प्रकाशाश्रयवद्वा तेजस्त्वात् ॥२८॥

[The relation between Brahma and the individual soul also is discussed.]

प्रकाशः (the sun's rays), **आश्रयः** (the support, *i.e.*, the source), **प्रकाशाश्रयौ** (the rays and their source; the sun and its rays); **प्रकाशाश्रयवत्** (like the relation between the sun and its rays), **वा** (or other), **तेजस्वात्** (by virtue of their light; as in respect of light they are the same.)

Explanation—The relation between the Universal Soul and the individual soul also may be compared in addition to what is stated in the preceding Sūtra, with that between the sun and its rays, to use a better illustration. The sun is different from its rays, yet at the same time, is the same with its rays; for the sun and its rays are both light. Similarly, the Universal Soul is both different from and yet the same with the individual soul.

Sūtra 26 has shown that the individual soul attains equality with Brahma by meditation; this may lead us to think that the two are different entities; but this Sūtra removes such apprehension by declaring that the two are also fundamentally the same entity.

पूर्व्ववद्वा ॥२९॥

[An apprehended objection is refuted.]

पूर्व्ववत् (as before), **वा** (or.)

Explanation—If an objection be raised before (as in Sūtra 25, section I, chapter II), it is refuted exactly in the same way as done there, that is, Brahma is not completely exhausted in His transformation into the universe.

प्रतिषेधाच्च ॥३०॥

[Sūtra 29 is substantiated.]

प्रतिषेधात् (from the denial; because of denial), **च** (moreover.)

Explanation—Moreover, the Universal Soul is not infected by the imperfections of the individual soul; because Śruti denies such infection.

For reference vide the Śruti—

"सूर्य्यो यथा सर्व्वलोकस्य चक्षु

र्न लिप्यते चाक्षुषैर्वाह्यदोषैः॥

एकस्तथा सर्व्वभूतान्तरात्मा

न लिप्यते लोकदुःखेन वाह्यः॥"

(As the sun, the eye of all individuals, does not become affected by visible impurities of external things *though touching them by its rays*; similarly the One Universal Soul, Who is the inner self of all beings, does not become affected by the sorrows *and sufferings* of individuals. as he is beyond them.)

Kaṭha Śruti, Chap. II, 2, II.

परमतः सेतून्मान-सम्बन्धभेदव्यपदेशेभ्यः ॥३१॥

[An objection is raised that some entity must be admitted superior to Brahma.]

परम् (superior), **अतः** (from this; from Brahma), **सेतून्मान-सम्बधभेदव्यपदेशेभ्यः** (from the expressions of causeway, dimensions, relation and difference); **सेतू** (a causeway), **उन्मानं** (dimensions, a limitation), **सम्बन्धः** (relation), **भेदः** (difference), **व्यपदेशाः** (expressions.)

Explanation—There must be an entity superior to Brahma Who is under discussion; because Śruti says, (1) that He is a causeway (to lead to something else), (2) that He has dimensions (and as such, is limited; indicating thereby, that there is something beyond that limit); (3) that He has a relation (indicating that He must be related to some one still higher), and (4) that He is different (from some one still higher.)

For the causeway vide:—

"स सेतुर्विधृतिरेषां लोकानामसंभेदाय"

(He is the causeway, the bulwark against chaotic confusion.)

Chāndogya, Chap. VIII, 4, 1.

For the dimensions vide the description of "चतुष्पाद् ब्रह्म षोड़शकलम" ।

(Brahma has four aspects, each to be studied under a four-fold division, thus making up the number of His aspects to be sixteen.)

Chāndogya (Chap. IV, parts 5-8.)

For the relation vide:—

"अथ य आत्मा स सेतुः.... एवं सेतुं तीर्त्वाऽन्धः सन्नन्धो भवति.... "

(Now the Universal Soul is the causeway... reaching this causeway, the blind get back their eye-sight.)

Chāndogya, Chap. VIII, 4, 1-2.

[Brahma, as the causeway, forms a sort of connection between the individual soul and the highest good, sought by him through the causeway.]

For difference vide—

"तेनेदं पूर्णं पुरुषेण सर्व्वं ततो यदुत्तरतरं तदरूप-मनामयम् ।"

(All this is filled with the Spirit; and that, which is superior to this, is without form—without imperfection.)

Śvetāśwatara, Chap. III, 9.

सामान्यात्तु॥३२॥

[The objection, raised in the preceding Sūtra, is refuted here.]

सामान्यात् (because of the resemblance; because He resembles it), **तु** (but.)

Explanation—There is nothing superior to Brahma. But he is called the causeway, because He resembles it in a certain respect. He is the support of all while crossing over this ocean of the world; even as a causeway is a great protection (help) in crossing a canal.

बुद्ध्यर्थः पादवत् ॥३३॥

[The second ground, of the objection raised in Sūtra 31, is refuted.]

बुद्ध्यर्थः (for the purpose of easy conception), **पादवत्** (with the legs.)

Explanation—Brahma is assumed to have dimensions for facility of meditation. As for instance, He is said to have four legs (aspects), as successive steps in meditation.

For reference vide the Śruti—

"मनो ब्रह्मेत्युपासीतेत्यध्यात्मं..... तदेतच्चतुष्पाद् ब्रह्म वाक्पादः प्राण पादश्चक्षुःपाद श्रोत्रंपादः।"

(Practise meditation, taking the mind as Brahma—this is the form of worship with the aid of the constituents of the individual soul—This Brahma is of four feet, *namely*, the spech *as* a foot, the chief vital energy *as* a foot the eye *as* a foot, and the ear *as* a foot.)

Chāndogya, Chap. III, 18, 1-2.

स्थानविशेषात् प्रकाशादिवत् ॥३४॥

[Sutra 33 is further substantiated.]

स्थानविशेषात् (because of special place or locality), **प्रकाशादिवत्** (like the light and the like.)

Explanation—As the light, the sky, the air, and the like, through their special relation, become specialised; so Brahma, limitless in Himself, is taken to be of a limited size, used as symbol, for the purpose of meditation.

Such symbolical conception or localisation of all-pervading Brahma, for the purpose of meditation, cannot affect His infinity which is His essential character.

उपपत्तेश्च॥३५॥

[The third ground of the objection raised in Sūtra 31 is refuted.]

उपपत्तेः (as it becomes reasonable), **च** (also)

Explanation—That Brahma forms a sort of link between the seeker and the goal sought for, is also reasonable, and does not indicate that the goal is a different entity from Him; for He Himself leads the seeker to Himself.

तथान्यप्रतिषेधात्॥३६॥

[The last ground of the objection raised in Sūtra 31 is refuted.]

तथा (similarly, moreover), **अन्य** (any other), **प्रतिषेधः** (prohibition, negation), **अन्धप्रतिषेधात्** (as there is the negation of any other entity than Brahma.)

Explanation—Moreover, there is no entity other than Brahma; for Śruti would not admit the existence of any entity other than, and superior to Brahma.

The text "**तेनेदं पूर्णं पुरुषेण स्र्वं ततो यदुत्तरतरं तदरूपमनामयम्**" quoted by the objector under Sūtra 31 of this section, should therefore be understood to mean, that all this universe is filled with the Supreme Spirit Who is without any form and without any imperfection, and transcends the creation; so there is no room for the supposition that there is any other Being higher than the Highest.

For reference vide the Śruti—

"यस्मात् परं नापरमस्ति किञ्चित् ।"

[To Whom there is none superior (परं), to whom there is none equal (अपरम्.)]

Śvetāśvatara, Chap. III, 9.

अनेन सर्व्वगतत्वमायामशब्दादिभ्यः॥३७॥

[The Brahma is all-prevading is firmly established here.]

अनेन (by this), **सर्व्वगतत्वम्** (all embracing character); **आयामः** (extent); **आयामशब्दादिभ्यः** (from the statements of Śruti regarding His extent, etc.)

Explanation— By the conclusion arrived at in the preceding Sūtras, that there is none superior or equal to Brahma, His all-embracing character is conclusively established. This is known from the expressions of Śruti regarding extent, etc.

For reference regarding the extent of Brahma vide:—

"तेनेदं पूर्णं पुरुषेण सर्व्वं ।"

(All this is filled with that Spirit.)

"ब्रह्मैवेदं सर्वं" (All this is Brahma.)

फलमत उपपत्तेः॥३८॥

[Another characteristic of Brahma is established.]

फलम् (fruit, effect, result),**अतः** (from Him), **उपपत्तेः** (because of reasonableness, as it is reasonable.)

Explanation— From Brahma individual souls receive the reward of their actions according to their merit. This is quite reasonable; for Brahma is the Lord of all, All-powerful and All-knowing.

श्रुतत्वाच्च ।३९॥

[The preceding Sūtra is strengthened on the support of Śruti.]

श्रुतत्वात् (from the declaration of Śruti to that effect), च (also.)

Explanation— That Brahma is the Giver of the reward of works is also proved from the declarations of Śruti to that effect.

For reference vide the Śruti—

"स वा एष महानज आत्माऽन्नादो वसुदानः।"

(This indeed is the Great Ever-living Self, the Provider of food, Giver of wealth.)

Bṛhadāraṇyaka, Chap. IV, 4, 24.

"एष हि एव आनन्दयति" (It is He alone, Who is the Giver of bliss.)

धर्म्मं जैमिनिरतएव॥४०॥

[An objection is raised to Sūtra 38.]

धर्म्मं (practice of religious duties; pious act; merit produced from pious actions; *hence* religious merit), जैमिनिः (the sage Jaimini, the author of the Pūrva Mīmāṁsā philosophy), अतएव (therefore; *i.e.,* on the same grounds as stated in Sūtras 38 and 39; *i.e.,* on the logical and scriptural ground.)

Explanation— The sage Jaimini thinks that on the same grounds as stated in Sūtras 38 and 39, *i.e.,* on the logical and scriptural ground, religious merit is the sole giver of the fruits of works.

Just as cultivation and other incidental labour are the giver of the harvest, so the religious merit, arising from sacred rites, is the dispenser of the fruit of actions, without any interference from Brahma. Śruti also instructs to practise sacrifices for the purpose of attaining heaven.

For reference vide—

"यजेत स्वर्गकामः"

(He, who is desirous of the heavenly world, has to perform sacrifices.)

पूर्व्वं तु वादारायणो हेतुव्यपदेशात् ॥४१॥

[The view expressed in Sūtra 40 is refuted by citing a contrary one.]

पूर्व्वं (the former; *i.e.*, the Lord *as the Giver of the fruit of actions*), **तु** (but), **वादरायणः** (the sage Bādarāyaṇa, the framer of the Sūtras), **हेतुव्यपदेशात्** (as he assigns a reason for it.)

Explanation— But the sage Bādarāyaṇa, the framer of the Sūtras, holds, that the former, *i.e.,* the Lord, is the Dispenser of the fruit of actions; as Śruti clearly states that all rewards—whether heaven or union with Himself—come from Him.

For reference vide—

"पुण्येन पुण्यं लोकं नयति।"

(He takes one to a purer world by virtue of one's piety.)

Also vide—

"यमवेष वृणुते तेन लभ्यः"

(He gives Himself away to whomsoever He chooses.)

Kaṭha-Śruti, Chap. I, 2, 23.

SECTION—III

The framer of the Sūtras now sets himself to ascertain the end and aim of the Vidyās (meditations) as prescribed in Śruti.

In this section Ācārya Bādarāyaṇa concludes that most of the meditations prescribed in the Upaniṣads, have for their object the knowledge of Brahma; they differ only in form but not in substance, their final goal is the attainment of eternal bliss; and one meditation is as good as another for achieving beatitude. Śruti teaches us to meditate on Brahma, either directly or through the medium of some Pratīka (symbol), such as sun, Ākāśa, mind, Prāṇa, the spirit dwelling in the eye, the empty space within the heart, the Praṇava, (the word 'Om') or the like; we are taught to search for and worship Brahma in and through them, yet taking care at the same time, that they must not usurp His place; with this end kept in view we must, while fixing the mind upon them, hold fast to the divine atributes, His omnipotence, His omniscience, His omnipresence, His bliss fulness, His moral government of the universe and so on. The Vidyās appear to be different only for the difference of the symbols, but the goal everywhere is the same. There are attributes of Brahma found in common in some of the Vidyās; and that the meditator should not look upon himself as a distinct entity from Brahma, is also a *sine qua non*. So in a process of meditation on Brahma the three things found common in all the Vidyās, are to be borne in mind; namely (1) the ultimate aim is to be the attainment of the highest bliss, by the realisation of Brahma with or without the aid of the symbols; (2) the attributes commonly taught in all the Vidyās such as immutability, blissfulness, purity, omnipotence, omniscience, omnipresence and the like, invariably are to be associated with the conception of Brahma; (3) the meditator is to think himself as one with Brahma and must worship Brahma as his own Higher-self (अहंग्रह उपासना.)

Sūtras 1-5 show, by refuting the plausible objections which may arise from some passages of Śruti; that all the different processes of meditation, prescribed by the Upaniṣads aim at the realisation of one and the same Lord of the universe, and therefore in every form of meditation all His essential attributes are to be included in the meditator's conception of Brahma.

Sūtras 6-9 show, that though the same Supreme Being is presented before the meditator, the attributes, under which He is to be conceived may differ in different meditations, even when the meditations bear the same name in the Śrutis. As for instance, the Udgītha Vidyā of the Chāndogya is quite a different thing from the Udgītha Vidyā of the Bṛahadāraṇyaka.

Sūtra 10 states that there should be no mistake in the identity of the Parā Vidyā as taught in Chāndogya, Bṛhadāraṇyaka and Kauṣītaki.

Sūtras 11-17 teach that all the essential attributes of Brahma, freed from all limitations, should be conjoined together and used as a whole, in the conception of Brahma in every Vidyā, even where the attributes are not expressly mentioned. Figurative expressions such as the possession, by Brahma, of the head, the wings and the like, recommended for facility of concentration should not form part of the conception everywhere.

Sūtras 18-23 discuss the interpretation of a few passages dwelling upon some forms of meditation and point out what details are to be associated with and what details to be dissociated from particular meditations.

Sūtras 24 points out that the Puruṣa Vidyā of Chāndogya is quite different from the Puruṣa-Vidyā of Taittirīya, though they pass by the same name.

Sūtra 25 says that any specific prayer for the fulfilment of a wordly desire is to be dissociated from the process of meditation on Brahma.

Sūtras 26-31 prove that after perceiving the Lord, the meditator gets rid of his virtues and vices, attains an excellent state of oneness with Him, and does not return to this world again.

Sūtra 32 shows, that though generally a man, after attaining Brahma, does not return to this world, yet persons as Vasiṣṭha and others, who are commissioned with some particular duty, such as the promulgation of the Vedas and the like, continue to live in, or return to this world, until that duty is accomplished.

Sūtras 33 and 34 deal with the Akṣara Vidyā, *i.e.*, the process of meditation on Brahma in His transcendent aspect (vide Sūtra 24, Sec. IV, Chap. I) where all His negative attributes, such as immortality, sinlessness and absence of imperfections, death, sorrow, taste, odour, etc., are to be cumulated as a whole; and to these negative attributes, the positive qualities, such as consciousness, blissfulness, omniscience, etc., are also to be added, as belonging to the Lord.

Sūtras 35-39 discuss different Vidyās from different Śrutis, such as the Satya-Vidyā, the Dahara-Vidyā, etc.—and show that their common object is the attainment of the Universal Soul.

Sūtra 41 says that a meditation, which is prescribed in connection with a sacrifice, is not a compulsory concomitant of that sacrifice.

Sūtra 42 states that the attributes of Brahma, abstracted from Him, are not to be meditated on, as apart from Brahma.

Sūtras 43-50 show that the fires mentioned in the Bṛhadāraṇyaka Śruti are not for sacrifical rites, but are for meditation.

Sūtras 51-52 say that at the time of meditation the

individual self of the meditator is to be contemplated, as in a state of perfect emancipation, without any difference from the Universal Soul.

Sūtras 53-56 show that the meditations are not fundamentally different, seeing that the common object is the attainment of Brahmahood; the difference in some cases, is verbal and in others nominal or formal; as each of them teaches different sets of the Lord's attributes. In the Vaiśvānara-Vidyā preference is to be given to the meditation on the Universal Soul in His entire form (in the Vaiśvānara-Vidyā, heaven, sun, space, earth, etc., figuratively representing the different limbs of the Lord, should be taken in their aggregate, while meditating on the Universal form of Vaiśvānara, the Lord Universal form of Vaiśvānara, the Lord in His entirety.)

Sūtras 57 and 58 teach that one has to select, at his option, any one of the Vidyās for practice and to hold on to it until the realisation of the Universal Soul is completed. But in cases of aiming at ulterior objects, such as worldly aims, a person may follow one form of prayer of that kind, or more, according to his desires.

Sūtras 59-64 show that the Karmāṅga-Vidyās are meditations connected with sacrificial rites, and that though they are taught to be performed, in some places, along with the sacrifices themselves, they are not essential parts of the latter; but when conjoined with rites, these Karmāṅga-Vidyās material add to their value.

सर्व्ववेदान्तप्रत्ययं चोदनाद्यविशेषात् ॥१॥

[There are many expositions of Brahma in Śruti; as for instance, in some Śruti He is expounded as Vaiśvānara (the Universal Manhood), in another He is shown to be Prāṇa (Life) and so forth. Now a doubt may arise as to whether these exposition are different or they all aim at one and the same thing. This Sūtra clears up the doubt.]

सर्व्ववेदान्तप्रत्ययम् (exposition *of Brahma* in all the Vedānta texts); चोदनादि (injunction etc.), अविशेषात् (as there is no difference); चोदनाद्यविशेषात् (as there is no difference in the injunctions, etc.)

Explanation— The expositions in all the Śrutis are materially the same, and they all point to one and the same purpose of Brahma-worship, though in different shapes adapted to the capacity of the meditator; for there is no difference in the injunctions about meditation, *i.e.*, all the injunctions purport to say that Brahma is to be meditated upon. So the object of those expositions and of meditations is one and the same.

भेदान्नेति चेन्न कस्यामपि ॥२॥

[An objection to the preceding Sūtra is raised and refuted.]

भेदात् (because of different things *to be worshipped in the different forms of meditation prescribed in Śruti*), न (not; the object of meditation is not one and the same), इति (this), चेत् (if); न (no, we contest the objection), कस्याम् (in a certain mode of worship), अपि (even.)

[The Sūtra consists of two parts, namely, an objection and its reply. The object is:—भेदात् न, इति चेत्; the reply is— न, कस्यामपि.]

Explanation— If it be objected that because of the multiplicity of expositions and forms of meditation, and also because of repetition of one and the same exposition and meditation in the same Śruti, the object of those expositions and meditations is not one, but as many as there are expositions and forms of meditation; then the reply is, that the objection is groundless, because sometimes to suit the capacities of different meditators, and sometimes to recapitulate a discourse, different wordings of the same meditation and consequent repetitions in the same Śruti are allowable; and in such cases all the details are not filled in, and some are left out to be understood, and yet they are recognised and admitted to be the same Vidyā (form of worship.)

स्वाध्यायस्य तथात्वे न हि समाचारेऽधिकाराच्च सववच्च तन्नियमः ॥३॥

[An apprehended objection, based on a statement of the Muṇḍaka Śruti, is explained and refuted.]

स्वाध्यायस्य (for the sake of the study of Śruti), तथात्वे (on the same account; that injunction being insisted upon), न (not; there is not a different object of meditation), हि (because), समाचारे (in the book named Samācāra containing the rules for the performance of Vedic rites.) अधिकाराच्च (because of the special qualification for the Ātharvaṇic students), च (also), सववत् (like the rule of the seven libations, namely Saurya etc.), च (also), तन्नियमः (that rule holds good.)

Explanation— From the speciality of the condition prescribed in the Muṇḍaka Śruti for its study, we infer that there is no difference in the object of worship taught in the Śruti; because the same condition is laid down, also in the book of Samācāra, to be fulfilled only by the Atharvaṇik students for the prerogative to acquire the knowledge of Brahma, just like the rule of the seven libations, namely Saurya etc.

The injunction in the Muṇḍaka Śruti (Chap. III, 2, 10) to observe the rite of carrying a fire-vesel on the head as a condition preliminary to the study of the same, does not indicate any difference about the object of worship (which is Brahma), instructed therein, because this practice is also enjoined in the book of Samācāra (which contains rules for the performance of Vedic rites) which it is prescribed to be observed only by the Ātharvaṇic students, and not by any others, and so students other than the Ātharvaṇics (including the Muṇḍaka branch) are not required, by the injunction, to carry a fire-vessel on their heads, as a preliminary to the study or practice of the Brahma-Vidyā taught in the Muṇḍaka Śruti. This is just like the injunction of *Sava* or seven libations to one fire, which is exclusively prescribed for the Ātharvaṇic branch and not for other branches.

For reference of the Muṇḍaka-Śruti vide—

"तेषामेवैतां ब्रह्मविद्यां वदेत शिरोव्रतं विधिवत् यैस्तु चीर्णम्।"

(This form of the worship of Brahma is to be taught to those only, by whom the rite of holding a fire-vessel on the head has been duly performed.)

Muṇḍaka, Chap. III, 2, 10.

Also vide:—"नैतदचीर्णव्रतोऽधीते।"

(A man who has not gone through this rite, is precluded from studying this.)

Muṇḍaka, Chap. III, 2, 11.

This last statement clearly points out that it is a preliminary condition of study and not of worship.

दर्शयति च ॥४॥

[An argument in support of Sūtra 1 is adduced.]

दर्शयति (Śruti shows), **च** (also.)

Explanation— Śruti also directly shows the unanimity of all the different forms of meditation which lead to the knowledge of Brahma.

For reference vide the quotation, with its translation, under Sūtra 4, section I, Chap I.

उपसंहारोऽर्थाभेदाद्विधिशेषवत् समाने च॥५॥

[A deduction is made from the four preceding Sūtras.]

उपसंहारः (combination), **अर्थाभेदात्** (as there is no difference in the purpose, **अर्थ**—purpose; **अभेदः**—no difference), **विधिशेषवत्** (analogous to the subsidiary rites of the main injunction), **समाने** (in the case of equality; the forms of meditation being the same in effect), **च** (also.)

Explanation—The meditation prescribed in all the Śrutis, being the same in effect, a combination of all the attributes of Brahma occurring in the different forms of meditation has to be made in each particular form, as there is no divergence among them about the purpose. The case is analogous to the subsidiary rites of a chief injunction about a particular sacrifice, such as the Agnihotra. [The Agnihotra, mentioned in different texts, is one and the same ceremony, and therefore the different complementary rites prescribed in different texts, have to be combined into one whole and thus to be observed everywhere in the performance of the Agnihotra.]

अन्यथात्वं शब्दादिति चेन्नाविशेषात् ॥६॥

[Now a discussion is introduced on the processes of meditation. Though the object of meditation is the same (Brahma) in every case, the processes even when bearing the same name, may differ. Two distinct processes may go by the same title in different Śrutis. In the present Sūtra the meditations known as the Udgītha Vidyā in the Bṛhadāraṇyaka and the Chāndogya Śrutis are taken up for discussion, and proved in Sūtra 7 to be two distinct processes, although they are styled "Udgītha Vidyā" in both the Śrutis. They are suggested in this Sūtra, to be one and the same by way of objection, which is refuted afterwards from the standpoint of the framer of the Sūtras.]

अन्यथात्वं (*there is* difference between the two), **शब्दात्** (*as is evident* from the wording of the Śrutis), **इति** (this), **चेत** (if); **न** (no. it is not so), **अविशेषात्** (because the opening of the clauses in the two Śrutis is similarly worded.)

[The Sūtra consists of two parts, namely, a supposed objection to the objector's view and its refutation by the objector to strengthen his case. The supposed objection is:—**अन्यथात्वं शब्दात् इति चेत्**; and the reply is:—**न, अविशेषात्**.]

Explanation—If it be argued that the form of meditation (known as the Udgītha Vidyā) in one (Bṛhadāraṇyaka Śruti), is different from that in the other (Chāndogya), as is evident from the wording of the two Śrutis; then the reply is, no, it is not so, the process of meditation is the same in both the Śrutis, for there is no difference in the introduction to the description of that form of meditation in either Śruti.

Regarding the description of the Udgītha form of meditation it is found in the Bṛhadāraṇyaka Śruti that the deities asked Prāṇa to pray for them; while in the Chāndogya Śruti it is found that the deities meditated on Prāṇa itself; so it may be objected that the form of meditation is different in the two Śrutis. By way of reply it may be said from the standpoint of the objector, that the difference in wording is practically nil; as the introduction to the Udgītha Vidyā is the same verbatim in both the Śrutis; the Devas at first contemplated to win victory over the Asuras with the help of the Udgītha (prayer by songs) and the Udgītha meditation was had recourse to.

This Udgītha meditation is described in the Bṛhadāraṇyaka Śruti (Chap. I, 3) and also in the Chāndogya Śruti (Chap. I, 2), as follows—

The nobler and higher propensities of the Indriyas quarrelled with the baser and lower propensenties. The former are termed as Devas and the latter as Asuras. The Devas determined to get the better of the Asuras by singing the Udgītha hymns (a loud sonorours prayer prescribed in the Sāma-Veda.) So they sought the assistance of the various Indriyas to help them with the Udgītha; but the Indriyas were defiled by the Asuras who had soon discovered their weaknesses and vulnerable points. The description so far purports to eb common in both the Śrutis; but henceforth it diverges. The Bṛhadāraṇyaka describes that the Devas at last applied to Prāṇa, who sang the Udgītha and won for them victory over the Asuras; while the Chāndogya says that the deities meditated on Prāṇa itself as the Udgītha, and in consequence were able to defeat the Asuras; but there is no statement in the Chāndogya that Prāṇa sang or was asked to sing the Udgītha for them.

For reference vide:— "उद्गीथेनात्ययाम"

(We shall be victorious by the help of the Udgītha prayer.)

Bṛhadāraṇyaka, Chap. I, 3, 1.

"उद्गीथमाजहुरनेनैनानभिभविष्याम।"

(The—*the deities*—performed the Udgītha; they said 'By this we will defeat them.')

Chāndogya, Chap. I, 2, 1.

"अथ हेममासन्यं प्राणमूचु स्त्वं न उद्गायेति, तथेति तेभ्य एष प्राण उद्गायत्।"

(Then they—the deities—said to Prāṇa, 'Do thou sing for us'; 'so be it' said Prāṇa and sang for them.)

Bṛhadāraṇyaka, Chap. I, 3, 7.

"अथ ह य एवायं मुख्यप्राणस्तमुद्गीथमुपासाञ्चक्रिरे।"

(Then, they—the deities—worshipped, as the Udgītha, that which is Prāṇa.)

Chāndogya, Chap. I, 2, 7.

न वा प्रकरणभेदात् परोवरीयस्त्वादिवत् ॥७॥

[The objection raised in the preceding Sūtra is refuted.]

न (no, the Udgītha meditation is not the same in the two Śrutis), **वा** (it would be more correct to say), **प्रकरणभेदात्** (as the subject-matters [Udgītha) in the two Śrutis are different), **परोवरीयस्त्वादिवत्** (just as the meditation on Brahma in the light of the Highest and Greatest Being is different from other similar forms of meditation in Chāndogya.)

Explanation— It would be more correct to say, that the Udgītha meditation is not the same in the two Śrutis, namely the Bṛhadāraṇyaka and the Chāndogya, because the subject-matters are different, just as there are, in the same Chāndogya Śruti, various forms of meditation, which, in spite of having the Supreme Being for their sole object differ from one another, owing to the difference of attributes assigned to Him; some meditations speak of His highest attributes transcending the universe, while others only mention His immanent aspect, such as is manifested in creation.

In the description of the Udgītha form of meditation in the Chāndogya Śruti, after enunciating the proposition that one should meditate on the word 'Om' as the Udgītha, it is stated that the deities performed the Udgītha; but 'Om' which is only a part of the whole Udgītha is prescribed in the Chāndogya to be worshipped in the light of Prāṇa whereas in the Bṛhadāraṇyaka Śruti, without mentioning any special mark, the Udgītha, as a whole, has been proposed to be worshipped in the light of Prāṇa and owing to this difference of proposition there is consequent difference of process. So, for this difference of proposition and process, the forms of the same Udgītha worship as taught in the two Śrutis, are different. Such difference is also found in various other forms of meditation taught in the same Śruti; as for instance, in the same Chāndogya Śruti, where though the object of meditation is always the same that is, the Universal Soul, yet there is difference mentioning the attributes of Brahma variously described in the different Vidyās.

In short, though the object of meditation taught in all the Upaniṣads is invariably the same, *i.e.,* Brahma, the forms of meditations are various to suit the capacities of likings of the meditators, the attributes predicated being different.

For reference regarding the meditation on the word 'Om' as Udgītha vide the Śruti—

"ओमित्येतदक्षरमुद्गीथमुपासीत।"

(One is to medidate on the word 'Om' as the Udgītha.)

Chāndogya, Chap. I, 1, 1.

संज्ञातश्चेत् तदुक्तमस्ति तु तदपि ॥८॥

[An argument against the preceding Sūtra is refuted.]

संज्ञातः (because of the name; because of the identity of title), **चेत्** (if)[**तत्** (that *objection*), **उक्तम्** (has been replied to), **अस्ति** (is) **तु** (moreover), **तत्** (that), **अपि** (also.)

[This Sūtra consists of two parts, namely, an objection and its reply. The objection is:—**संज्ञातश्चेत्**; and the reply is:— **तत् उक्तम् अस्ति तु तत् अपि** .]

Explanation—If it be said, that because of the identity of the title (Udgītha) the forms prescribed in the two Śrutis, referred to in Sūtra 6, are identical; then the reply is that the argument has already been met in the previous Sūtra by showing that they are not so, because of the difference in the proposition. Moreover, identity of title is also found even in quite separte sacrifical performances; as for instance, the term 'Agnihotra' is indiscriminiately applied to: (1) The daily Agnihotra, (2) Agnihotra and (3) the Solstitia Agnihotra.

व्याप्तेश्च समञ्जसम् ॥९॥

[Sūtra 7 is celebrated here.]

व्याप्तेः (because it extends throughout the whole system of the Udgītha meditation as described in the Chāndogya Śruti) **च** (also), **समञ्जसम्** (consistent.)

Explanation—In Chāndogya the prescription of 'Om' for meditation, with which the Vidyā opens is carried throughout all the forms of the Udgītha meditation, *viz.*, **आध्यात्मिक** (in relation to the meditator's own self), **आधिदैविक** (in relation to the presiding deities) and **आधिभौतिक** (in relation to the world outside) etc.,—as taught therein; so it is but consistent to hold that a part of the Udgītha, namely this 'Om', is to be looked upon as the symbol of Prāṇa in all the Udgītha meditations of the Chāndogya. On the other hand, the Bṛhadāraṇyaka Śruti teaches that the entire Udgītha, from the beginning to the end, should be regarded as the symbol of Prāṇa. this vital point makes a fundamental difference between the two Udgītha Vidyās prescribed in the two Śrutis. So the forms of the Udgītha meditation are different in the two Śrutis, although the name happens to be the same.

सर्व्वाभेदादन्यत्रेमे॥१०॥

[A concrete instance, on the general principle of Sūtra 5, is cited.]

सर्व्वाभेदात् (because of absence of difference in the two Śrutis; because there is no difference anywhere in the two Śrutis *as to Prāṇa being the best and oldest*), अन्यत्र (in another place; in the Kauṣītaki-Upaniṣad), इमे (these qualities of the Indriyas.)

Explanation—In the colloquy among the Indriyas in Bṛhadāraṇyaka and Chāndogya, Prāṇa is held out to be the object of meditation, as it occupies the foremost and highest position among them; and the speech and the other Indriyas have been stated to have their respective powers (of uttering words and so on) borrowed from Prāṇa; but in the description of the Indiryas in the Kauṣītaki-Upaniṣad, their respective powers have not been shown to be borrowed from Prāṇa. This omission need not make any difference between the two expositions; and the defficiency of the Kauṣītaki should be made up by the fuller statement of Chāndogya and Bṛhadāraṇyaka, Prāṇa should be credited with all the respective powers attributed to the special Indriyas, who fail to retain their separate existence in the absence of Prāṇa, which is pre-eminently the foremost and highest among them, the speech and the other Indriyas being all subordinate to, and dependent on it.

For reference as to the superiority of Prāṇa vide—

"प्राणो वाव ज्येष्ठश्च श्रेष्ठश्च"

Chāndogya, Chap. V, 1, 1.

"प्राणो वै ज्येष्ठश्च श्रेष्ठश्च"

Bṛhadāraṇyaka, Chap. VI, 1, 1.

(Prāṇa, *the chief vital energy*, is indeed the foremost and highest.)

For reference as to Prāṇa being the ultimate source of the powers of the Indriyas, vide—

"सा ह वागुवाच यद्वा अहं वसिष्ठास्मि त्वं तद् वसिष्ठोऽसीति यद्वा अहं प्रतिष्ठास्मि त्वं तत् प्रतिष्ठोऽसीति चक्षुः"

Bṛhadāraṇyaka, Chap. VI, 1, 14.

"अथ हैनं वागुवाच यदहं वसिष्ठास्मि त्वं तद् वसिष्ठोऽसीत्यथ हैनं चक्षुरुवाच यदहं प्रतिष्ठास्मित्वं तत् प्रतिष्ठासीति"

Chāndogya, V, I, 13.

(Then the speech said to *Prāṇa*, 'This ability *of uttering words,* to overcome others, which appears to appertain to me, does really belong to thee'; then the eye said, 'This power *of sight* for giving fixity and stability to things in general, which appears to appertain to me, is really thine'.)

For reference in the Kauṣītaki, vide chapter II, 9 A of the same.

आनन्दादयः प्रधानस्य ॥११॥

[The attributes of Brahma, which are acceptable in all form of divine meditation as shown in Sūtra 5, are being clearly stated.]

आनन्दादयः (Blissfulness and other similar attributes), प्रधानस्य (of the Supreme spirit.)

Explanation—Blissfulness and other similar attributes of the Supreme Spirit, such as pure consciousness, omniscience, omnipresence (in the form of the Great Ego residing in every individual) are to be culled together everywhere in the meditation of Brahma.

प्रियशिरस्त्वाद्यप्राप्तिरुपचयापचयौ हि भेदे ॥१२॥

[The discussion commenced in Sūtra 11 is continued, stating here as to which of the atributes are not to be culled together in every form of meditation.]

प्रियशिरस्त्वादि (Joy being His head and so on), अप्राप्तिः (non-acceptance; not acceptable everywhere), उपचयापचयौ (increase and decrease; fluctutations), हि (because), भेदे (in difference; owing to the attribution of different limbs to Brahma.)

Explanation—In the Taittirīya Śruti Joy is stated to be the head of Brahma in the description of a form of meditation; the attribute of having joy for His head and such other attributes are not acceptable in every form of meditation on Brahma; as attributing limbs to Brahma would render Him liable to fluctuations.

For reference vide—

"तस्य प्रियमेव शिरः" (Joy itself is His head.)

Taittirīyopaniṣad, Chap. II, 5, 1.

इतरेत्वर्थसामान्यात् ॥१३॥

[The previous discussion is continued.]

इतरे (the other *attributes mentioned in Sūtra II*), तु (but), अर्थसामान्यात् (because of common purport.)

Explanation—The attributes other than those alluded to in Sūtra 12, *i.e.,* the attributes mentioned in Sūtra 11, are acceptable everywhere, because they have a common purport, they being inherent properties of Brahma.

आध्यानाय प्रयोजनाभावात् ॥१४॥

[The previous discussion is continued.]

आध्यानाय (for the purpose of divine meditation), प्रयोजनाभावात् (as there is no other necessity.)

Explanation—The attributes, such as 'Joy itself is His head,' stated in Sūtra 12, are used for the purpose of setting one's heart upon meditation on Brahma; because they serve no useful purpose other than meditation—they are not the inherent qualities of Brahma.

आत्मशब्दाच्च ॥१५॥

[An argument in support of Sūtra 14, is adduced.]

आत्मशब्दात् (because of the word 'Ātmā,—Self), च (also.)

Explanation—The attributes, spoken of in Sūtra 14, are only for the facility of meditation on Brahma, as also can be understood from the word 'Ātmā' (Self) being inserted there.

From the expression 'But there is another, the Inner Self' in the same passage of the Taittirīya Śruti, where the expression 'Joy itself is His head' referred to in Sūtra 12, occurs, it appears that the head, the wings and the like cannot be the true adjuncts of Self but are attributed to Him, merely for convenience of the meditator.

For reference vide:—

"अन्योऽन्तर आत्मानन्दमयः"

(But there is another Self, in the back ground, Who is 'Ānandamaya'—the Bliss Immense.)

Taittirīya, Chap. II, 5, I.

आत्मगृहीतिरितरवदुत्तरात् ॥१६॥

[It is proved that the word 'Ātmā' of Sūtra 15, stands for the Universal Soul.]

आत्मगृहीतिः (The choice of the word 'Ātmā'; the word 'Ātmā' is chosen to mean the Universal Self), इतरवत् (as in another Śruti, namely the Aitareya Śruti), उत्तरात् (because of a subsequent expression.)

Explanation—The word 'Ātmā' in the Taittirīya Śruti, referred to in Sūtra 15 is chosen there to mean the Universal Soul, as it is used in the Aitareya Śruti; this is also understood from a subsequent expression in the Taittirīya.

The word 'Ātmā', in the passage of the Taittirīya Śruti referred to in Sūtra 15, indicates the Universal Self, as the same word occurs in a passage of the Aitareya Śruti in the same sense.

In the Aitareya Śruti there is the passage:—

"आत्मा वा इदमेक एवाग्र आसीत् नान्यत् किञ्चन मिषत्, स ईक्षत लोकान्नुसृजा इति।"

(At first there existed the only One Self, nothing else stirring; He desired 'Let me create worlds'): and the Taittirīya Śruti also subsequently states: "He desired 'I will by many'" (vide the quotation and its translation under Sūtra 17, Sec. I, Chap. I.) From this subsequent expression about the Universal Soul in the Taittirīya, it is clearly shown that word 'Ātmā' indicates the Universal Soul.

अन्वयादिति चेत् स्यादवधारणात् ॥१७॥

(An objection to Sūtra 16 is raised and refuted.]

अन्वयात् (because of connection), **इति** (this), **चेत्** (if), **स्यात्** (it is so; it does indicate so), **अवधारणात्** (because of ascertainment.)

[The Sūtra consists of two parts, namely an objection and its reply. The objection is:—**अन्वयात् इति चेत्**; the reply is:—**स्यात् अवधारणात्**.)

Explanation—If it be objected that because of its connection with the previously described objects, such as Prāṇa, mind, Anna (food) etc., which are evidently material things the word 'Ātmā used in the Taittirīya does not imply the Universal Self; then the reply is:—The word 'Ātmā' though previously applied to Prāṇa, Anna and other objects quite different from Brahma, is really meant to indicate Brahma, Who is residing in them.

The Śruti begins the teaching with the description of Brahma; and therefore the term 'Self', occurring in the successive statements—that 'Self is all-Prāṇa, and that 'Self is all-Bliss' etc., also, and being used in that connection must indicate Brahma.

For the passage at the beginning of the text vide—

"ब्रह्माविदाप्नोतिपरम् तदेषाभ्युक्ता सत्यंज्ञानमनन्तं ब्रह्म ।"

(One, who knows Brahma, attains the Highest. In this respect it is said 'Brahma is Truth, Knowledge and Infinity'.)

Taittirīya (Brahmavalli), Chap. II, 1, 2.

For reference as to the Self as all-Prāṇa, vide—

"अन्योऽन्तर आत्मा प्राणमयः।" (There is another, the Inner-Self, Who is all-Prāṇa.)

Ibid, Chap. II, 2, 3.

For reference as to the teaching of meditation on the self as all-Prāṇa, in the light of the Universal Soul vide—

"सर्व्वमेव ते आयुर्यन्ति ये प्राणं ब्रह्मोपासते"

(Those, who worship Prāṇa as Brahma, live the fullest term of life.)

Ibid, Chap. II, 3, 1.

For reference as to the self as all-Bliss, vide:—

"अन्योऽन्तर आत्मानन्दमयः" (There is another, the Inner-Self, who is all-Bliss.)

Ibid, Chap. II, 5, 1.

कार्य्याख्यानादपूर्व्वम् ॥१८॥

[The framer of the Sūtras now decides various doubtful questions about different forms of meditation.]

कार्य्याख्यानात् (being enjoined as a preliminary rite), अपूर्व्वम् (*this* new idea; a new character given for the first time.)

Explanation—Sipping water immediately before and after a meal, is to be regarded in Prāṇa-Vidyā (as enjoined in the Bṛhadāraṇyaka Śruti) in the light of a kind of clothing meant for Prāṇa which stands for Brahma in that form of meditation. The prevailing practice of sipping water before and after a meal is in obedience to the teaching of Smṛti which borrows the idea from the Bṛhadāraṇyaka Śruti, and this Śruti gives for the first time a new character to the act of sipping water as preliminary to and a sequel to the act of eating a meal and teaches that the naked Prāṇa is thereby clothed. This new idea is an integral part of Prāṇa Vidyā and must be associated with that form of worship, no matter whether the worshipper actually sips or not; and this sipping of water need not form a part of any other meditation.

In the Bṛhadāraṇyaka Śruti, on the occasion of the discussion of Prāṇa-Vidyā (*i.e.*, the meditation on Prāṇa, the chief vital energy in the light of Brahma), there are instructions, (1) to take a sip of water at the beginning and at end of a meal, and (2) to regard this sip as a covering for Prāṇa. Now the question arises as to which of the two instructions is to be accepted as the special injunction here (whether the very act of taking a sip of water, or to regard the sip as a covering for Prāṇa or both.) The Sūtra says that to conceive the water as a covering for Prāṇa is the special injunction here, as this is enjoined here for the first time, whereas the practice of taking a sip of water, is merely a repetition of what is frequently prescribed in Smṛtis in connection with every act of worship or religious rite and as such requires no special injunction here.

For reference vide:—

"श्रोत्रिया अशिष्यन्त आचामन्त्यशित्वाचामन्त्येतमेव तदनमनग्नं कुर्व्वन्तो मन्यन्ते।"

(The learned take a sip of water when they are about to take a meal, and after the meal also they take another sip of water, and they conceive that they are clothing the naked Prāṇa thereby.)

Bṛhadāraṇyaka, Chap. VI, 1, 14.

समान एवञ्चाभेदात् ॥१९॥

[A corollary to Sūtra 5 is proved.]

समाने (in the same; in the different Śrutis of the same school), एवम् (thus all the attending particulars have to be culled together), च (also) अभेदात (as there is no difference.)

Explanation—In different Śrutis of the same branch the attending particulars of a special form of meditation have to be culled together in each description of that meditation in the different Śrutis; as there is no difference in that form of meditation prescribed in those Śrutis, at least so far as the object of meditation is concerned, the difference being only in respect of minor details. Thus the deficiencies in the adjuncts must be supplemented by adding those adjuncts which are mentioned elsewhere.

In different Śrutis (Agnirahasya and Bṛhadāraṇyaka) of the Vājasaneyi branch there is described the same Śāṇḍilya, Vidyā wherein Self is taught to be meditated as the Universal Mind; in both the descriptions, the object of meditation (Self) being the same; and though there is some difference in minor details, the two descriptions of the Śāṇḍilya Vidyā, in the two Śrutis are practically the same. So a particular point mentioned in one Śrutis in connection with the Śāṇḍilya Vidyā, has to be incorporated with the other, if it be not mentioned in the latter. (Vide Sūtra 5.)

For reference vide—

"आत्मानमुपासीत मनोमयम्।"

(One is to meditate on Self, the Universal Mind.)

Agnirahasya.

"मनोमयोऽयं पुरुषो भाः सत्यस्तस्मिन्नन्तर्हृदये यथा ब्रीहिर्वा यवो वा स एष सर्व्वस्येशानः सर्व्वस्याधिपतिः सर्व्वमिदं प्रशास्ति यदिदं किञ्च"

(This Spirit,—the Universal Mind, the Light, the Truth—is within the heart, like a grain of paddy or barely, He is the Ruler of all, the Lord of all; He governs all whatsoever exists.)

Bṛhadāraṇyaka, Chap. V, 6, 1.

सम्बन्धादेवमन्यत्रापि॥२०॥

(An inference, on the analogy of the preceding Sūtra, is drawn by way of objection.]

सम्बन्धात् (on the ground of intimate relation), **एवम्** (thus), **अन्यत्र** (in other cases), **अपि** (also, too.)

Explanation—One may object, that, on the ground of intimate relation, it ought to hold good in other cases too.

In the Bṛhadāraṇyaka (Chap. V, 5) Brahma as Truth has been taught to be meditated upon in the orb of the sun and in the ball of the eye; and two signifcant names 'Ahah' (day) and 'Ahah' (ego, I) have been given to Him (in each case respectively) as an integral part of the meditation. Now the question arises as to whether both the names have to be used in each meditation or either will do. This Sūtra lays down that as in the previous Sūtra the attending particulars have been proved to be collectively used in every case of the Śāṇḍilya Vidyā on the ground that the object of meditation is the same: similarly here, too, both the names have to be used in the worship of '**सत्यं ब्रह्म**' (Brahma, the Truth) in each case, for the same Brahma is worshipped both in the sun and in the eye.

For reference vide—

"य एष एतस्मिन् मण्डले पुरुषः—तस्योपनिषदहः।"

(The secret name of the Being, Who is in this orb, is 'Ahah'—*Day*.)

Bṛhadāraṇyaka, Chap. V, 5, 4.

"योऽयं दक्षिणोऽक्षन् पुरुषः—तस्योपनिषदहम्।"

(The secret name of the Being, Who is in the right eye, is 'Aham'—*the Ego, i.e., I*)

Bṛhadāraṇyaka, Chap. V, 5, 4.

न वा विशेषात् ॥२१॥

(The conclusion, arrived at in the preceding Sūtra, is set aside.]

न (not *so*), **वा** (but), **विशेषात्** (because of difference in locality.)

Explanation—But the names are not to be used together, because there is difference of localities.

As the solar orb and the eye-ball are too distant and distinct localities for the worship of Brahma, the two significant names, 'Ahah' and 'Aham', referred to in the preceding Sūtra, should not both be employed in the same form of meditation.

दर्शयति च ॥२२॥

[An additional argument is adduced to refute Sūtra 20.]

दर्शयति (*Śruti* shows; Śruti indicates), च (also.)

Explanation—While pointing out the closest resemblance between the two symbols—the solar orb and the human eye-ball, the Śruti at the same time maintains a marked distinction between the two, and advises the meditator not to join the atributes of the one to those of the other; since they are located far from each other. The names Ahah and Aham given to two symbols, also support the conclusion, that the two meditations are not one and the same.

For the close resemblance between the two symbols, vide the Śruti—

"तस्यैतस्य तदेव रूपं यदमुष्य रूपं यावमुष्य गेष्णौ तौ गेष्णौ यन्नाम तन्नाम।"

[The form of this is exactly similar to the form of that; the joints of the one to the joints of the other, and the name of the former (Ahah) to the name of the latter(Aham.)]

Chāndogya, Chap. I, 7, 5.

From the above quoted passage it appears that the Śruti has a special purpose in expressly stating that the attributes of Brahma in the sun are the same in Brahma in the eye, for otherwise according to the principle of Sūtra 5 of this section it would have been quite superfluous for the Śruti to make such an express statement. The special purpose is to indicate, that in this particular form of meditation the principle of Sūtra 5 does not apply. Though the same Being resides both in the eye-ball and the solar ball, the attributes, by which He is to be recognised in each, are quite distinct.

सम्भृति-द्युव्याप्त्यपि चातः॥२३॥

[A restriction of Sūtra 5 is made.]

सम्भृतिः (upholding the universe), **द्युव्याप्तिः** (pervading the heavens), **अपि** (also), **च** (and), **अतः** (on the same grounds.)

Explanation—In the supplementary writings (**खिलवाक्य**)

of the Rāṇāyaṇīya branch of the Taittirīya Śruti, there is mention of certain properties of Brahma, namely, His upholding the universe and His pre-existence from eternity. On the same grounds as stated in Sūtra 21 and 22, these two attributes (mentioned above) are to be kept apart from the properties attributed to Brahma in other forms of meditation; because there, in the Rāṇāyaṇīya branch, Brahma is conceived to be localised in Ākāśa; whereas in other forms of meditation, He is conceived to be localised in the eye or heart etc.

For reference vide—

"ब्रह्मज्येष्ठावीर्य्याः सम्भृतानि ब्रह्माग्रे ज्येष्ठं दिवमाततान॥"

(Upholding the universe and sustaining it are the supreme powers of Brahma; and He it was, that pervaded Ākāśa and was pre-existent before.)

Taittirīya Śruti, Rāṇāyaṇīya branch, Khilas.

पुरुषविद्यायामपि चेतरेषामनाम्नानात् ॥२४॥

[The 'Puruṣa-Vidyā of the Chāndogya Śruti and that of the Taittirīya Śruti, are now examined.]

पुरुषविद्यायाम् (in the form of meditation known as 'Puruṣa-Vidyā'), अपि (also), च (and), इतरेषाम् (of others; of other auxiliary details), अनाम्नानात् (because of not being mentioned; as they are wanting.)

Explanation—And as regards the Puruṣa-Vidyā, it is not the same in both Śrutis (Chāndogya and Taittirīyaka); for, some of the details in connection with this particular form of meditation are with this particular form of meditation are found in one Śruti and are wanting in the other; and this marked discrepancy in the details makes a vital distinction.

In the description of the form of meditation known as the 'Puruṣa-Vidyā', the Chāndogya Śruti represents the sacrificer himself as the sacrifice and the first twenty-four years of his life as the morning libation, and the second and the third periods (of 44 years and 48 years respectively) as the midday and the evening libation; while the 'Puruṣa-Vidyā in the Taittirīyaka Śruti represents the soul of the sacrificer as the sacrificer and his faith as his wife. This vital difference between the two conceptions makes the one quite distinct from the other, though they pass by the same name of 'Puruṣa-Vidyā' in the two Śrutis. So the processes of meditation in them are to be considered as different. Therefore the details of the two meditations are not mutually transferable.

For reference vide—

"पुरुषो वाव यज्ञस्तस्य यानि चतुर्विंशतिवर्षाणि तत् प्रातःसवनम्॥"

(Man is indeed the sacrifice, the first period of twenty-four years of his life is the morning libation.)

Chānodygya, Chap. III, 16, 1.

"तस्यैवं विदुषो यज्ञस्यात्मा यजमानः श्रद्धा पत्नी।"

(The soul of that man, who has such knowledge of the sacrifice, is *to be conceived as* the sacrificer, and his faith as his wife.)

Taittirīyaka Saṁhitā.

वेधाद्यर्थभेदात् ॥२५॥

[Certain expressions, occuring at the beginning of an Upaniṣad of the Atharva-Veda, are taken up for discussion.]

वेधादि (piercing etc.), **अर्थभेदात्** (because of difference in purpose.)

Explanation—At the beginning of an Upaniṣad of the Atharva-Veda, there occurs a prayer for piercing the enemy, piercing his heart and crushing his head, etc. These expressions of piercing and so are not parts of the Vidyās of the Upaniṣad, as they have a different purpose. Similarly, passages like "The Devas (*i.e.,* the deities presiding over the Indriyas) sat down to sacrifice", and other passages, relating to the part taken by the senses etc., should not be regarded as parts of any form of meditation. These passages are clearly unfitted for pious and devout meditation.

For the reference vide:—

"सर्व्वं प्रविध्य हृदयं प्रविध्य धमनीः प्रवृज्य शिरोऽभिप्रवृज्य त्रिधा विपृक्तः।"

(Pierce him—*the enemy*—wholly, pierce his heart, crush his veins, crush his head, thrice crushed.)

Also,—**"देवा ह वै सत्रं निषेवे"** (Devas sat down to sacrifice.)

हानौ तूपायन-शब्दशेषत्वात् कुषाच्छन्दस्तुत्युपगानवत्तदुक्तम् ॥२६॥

[Here is a discussion on the shaking off of virtues and vices by the released soul at death, and their acceptance by his relatives.]

हानौ (in shaking off; in getting rid of the good and the evil), **तु** (indeed), **उपायनशब्दशेषत्वात्** (because the word '**उपायन**', *i.e., acceptance*, is supplementary), **कुशाच्छन्दस्त्युयुपगानवत्** (like Kuśā-sticks, metres, praises and hymns), **तत्** (that, it), **उक्तम्** (is said by the sage Jaimini in his Pūrva-Mīmāṁsā philosophy.)

Explanation—In the Muṇḍaka Śruti of the Ātharvaṇa school it is stated, that a man, on perceiving the Lord of the universe, gets rid of his virtues and vices, the good and evil, and attains an excellent state of oneness with the Lord; so this Śruti shows only that one gets rid of the good and the evil—but is silent on the point as to who accepts his good and evil deeds. In the Śātyāyana branch of Śruti it is said, that after a man has perceived the Lord and consequently has got rid of his good and evil deeds and has thus attained emancipation, his sons inherit his property, and his friends that good and enemies the evil deeds; so the Śrutis shows the acceptance of good and bad deeds of one by others. Now, the Śātyāyana passage, which is indicative of such acceptance, should be regarded as supplementing the Muṇḍaka passage which speaks only of getting rid of the good and evil deeds; as in the cases of Kuśā-sticks, metres, praises and hymns. The principle is also accepted by the sage Jaimini in his Pūrva-Mīmāṁsā philosophy.

The purport is, that though in the Muṇḍaka Śruti it is

only shown that a man gets rid of his good and evil deeds by knowing the Lord, it is to be understood that in the case of the followers of this branch also, the friends and the enemies of the emancipated person inherit his virtues and vices respectively, as stated in the other branch. So the expression 'उपायनं' (acceptance) of the Śātyāyana branch is to be taken as supplementary to the expression indicating 'हानि'(getting rid of the good and the evil) in the Ātharvaṇika branch.

As regards the allusion to Kuśā-sticks etc., it is said in the Kauṣītaki Śruti that the Kuśā-sticks are to be collected from trees, without any specification as to what sort of trees; but in the Śātyāyana branch it is said that the Kuśās are of the Uḍumvara tree; and this latter expression is to be accepted as complementary to the former expression in the Kauṣītaki Śruti. As regards the allusion to metre, that is in Śruti, an injunction to say a prayer composed in metre without any specification of the kind of metre, but in another place there is mention of the Deva-metre to be employed in such a case; therefore the Deva-metre is to be understood in the previous case also. As regards the allusion to praise there is instruction in one Śruti to utter praises for the sacrificial vessel 'Ṣoḍaśi', without specifying the time as to when it should be performed; but in another Śruti it is taught to be performed when the sun has risen; here the latter instruction is to be accepted as supplementary to the former. As regards the allusion to the fourth point, hymn, it is not definitely stated, which of the four priests is to join in the singing of the prayer in a sacrifice; but this doubt has been cleared up by a particular text saying that the Adhvaryu will not join in the singing; putting the two statements together, the conclusion is, that all the priests, except the Adhvaryu, will join.

For reference of 'हानि' (getting rid of), vide—

तदा विद्वान् पुण्यपापे विधूय, निरञ्जनः परमं साम्यमुपैति।"

(For the full passage and translation vide Sūtra 2, Sec. III, Chap. I.)

For reference of 'उपायनम् 'acceptance vide—

"तस्य पुत्रा दायमुपयन्ति, सुहृदः साधुकृत्यां द्विषन्तः पापकृत्याम्।"

(His sons inherit his property, his well-wishers his good deeds and his enemies the evil deeds.)

The Śātyāyana branch.

साम्पराये तर्त्तव्याभावात्तथाह्यन्ये॥२७॥

[This Sūtra decides when the individual soul shakes off his good or bad deeds.]

साम्पराये (at the time of departing from the body), **तर्त्तव्याभावात्** (for want of anything to be reached or enjoyed), **तथा** (thus; in this way, so), **हि** (as, since), **अन्ये** (some other *Śrutis*.)

Explanation—At the time of departing from the body, the individual soul, who has been blessed with the knowledge of the truth, frees himself from his good and evil deeds; as now there remains nothing to be enjoyed by him through his good and evil works; since some other Śrutis also declare so.

The Kauṣītaki Śruti, however, says that such freedom from good and evil deeds occurs after crossing the river Vijarā with the help of the mind, which, of course, takes place not long after death. Now the question arises as to which of these two versions is to be accepted. To clear up this question, this Sūtra positively declares, that the deliverance from works takes place at the time of departing from the body, on the ground that there remains nothing to be reached by him through those works, which are therefore no longer of any use to him and not fit to be retained by him thereafter.

Thus, there being no need of the works being 'retained any longer, the soul shakes them off at the time of leaving the body; and he is said, in the Kauṣītaki Śruti, to do so later, only in a secondary sense.

For reference vide:—

"अशरीरं वाव सन्तं न प्रियाप्रिये स्पृशतः,.... एष सम्प्रसादोऽस्माच्छरीरात् समुत्थाय परं ज्योतिरूपसम्पद्य स्वेन रूपेणाभिनिष्पद्यते।"

(Nothing, desirable or undesirable, can touch the disembodied spirit,.... This blissful soul, on rising from the body, and robed in brightest splendour recovers his pristine form—*the status of the Universal Soul*.)

Chāndogya, Chap. VIII. 12, 1, and 3.

For the crossing of the Vijarā vide—

"स आगच्छति विजरां नदीं तां मनसैवात्येति, तत् सुकृतदुष्कृते विधूनुते, तस्य प्रिया ज्ञातयः सुकृतमुपयन्त्यप्रिया दुष्कृतं।"

(He comes to the river Vijarā and crosses it only by the strength of his mind and there shakes off his good and evil deeds. His friends and relatives inherit his good deeds, and the enemies the evil deeds.)

Kauṣītaki, Chap. I, 4 A and 4 B.

छन्दतः उभयाविरोधात्॥२८॥

[This Sūtra shows that good and evil deeds of the released soul attach to his friends and foes according to their likings.]

छन्दतः (according to their own mind; according to their attitude), उभयाविरोधात् (because of want of difference between the two; as there is no dispute between the two.)

Explanation—The effects of the good and bad works of the person acquiring true knowledge are received by his friends and enemies respectively according to their friendly or hostile attitude towards him; there is no dispute as to who will get the good deed or who the evil—this is clear and decided. We have given above the explanation of the Sūtra after Ācārya Nimbārka.

The Sūtra may, however be explained in another way—In the two Śrutis, quoted in the preceding Sūtra from the Chāndogya and the Kauṣītaki there is no difference in the intention of the passages, as to when a person, acquiring true knowledge, will get rid of his good and bad deeds. It is admitted on all hands, that such a person gets rid of his deeds after death; and the two Śrutis may be easily reconciled, if rising from the body and crossing the Vijarā take place almost simultaneously.

We may explain this Sūtra in a third way—The emancipated soul may shake off his merits and demerits, either at the time of his rising from the body or at the time of crossing the Vijarā at his option (छन्दतः) and thus the two Śrutis may be reconciled (उभयथाविरोधात्) ।

गतेरर्थवत्त्वमुभयथान्यथा हि विरोधः।

[Here is a side issue of Sūtra 27.]

गतेः (of the journey *of the soul that has known Brahma*), **अर्थवत्त्वम्** (significance of the expression; the expression becomes truly significant), **उभयथा** (by both the admissions; by the admission of deliverance from the both—the good as well as the evil deeds; in both cases), **अन्यथा** (otherwise), **हि** (certainly), **विरोधः** (incongruity; inconsistency.)

Explanation—The statement of the journey of the soul who has got Brahma-Jñāna (the knowledge of Brahma), becomes truly significant, by the admission of deliverance from the both—the good as well as the evil deeds; otherwise there becomes inconsistency.

If it be argued that only the evil deeds or vices of the soul are thrown off by his knowledge of Brahma, but the good deeds or virtutes follow him, on his parting from the body, then it is of no good to him to go by the path of the gods and to attain the status of Brahma, which is, according to Śruti, the ultimate goal of the soul who knows Brahma; because, in the latter case, he has to return again and take rebirth in this world after having enjoyed the fruits of his good deeds in heaven; which is quite inconsistent with the statements, of Śruti, on liberation, as they declare that the soul, knowing Brahma, never returns from the next world to take rebirth here.

This Sūtra may be interpreted in another way, thus—The descriptions of the journey of the released soul, as described in the two Śrutis, by the path of the goods, may be consistent with each other if the details of the Kauṣītaki Śruti are inserted in the general account of the other Śruti. There is no difficulty in admitting both the facts to be true—getting rid of the good and bad deeds after death and crossing the river Vijarā. If it be said that the soul gets rid of the good and bad deeds just at the time of parting with the body, without having to cross the Vijarā river, then the passage of the Kauṣītaki Śruti regarding the crossing of the Vijarā, becomes meaningless. This interpretation is unacceptable.

उपपन्नस्तल्लक्षणार्थोपलब्धेर्लोकवत्॥३०॥

[The previous discussion is continued.]

उपपन्नः (proved, justified), **तल्लक्षणार्थोपलब्धेः** (the enjoyment, which is the characteristic feature of a bodily connection, being known; **तत्**—that, the bodily connection; **लक्षण**—characteristic feather; **अर्थ**—**धर्म**, **गुण**, virtue; **उपलब्धेः**—being known), **लोकवत्** (as is seen in the world.)

Explanation—The worshipper of Brahma, after leaving his body, has to proceed by the path of the gods, although all his Karmas have been already consumed. This is quite reasonable; as Śruti clearly states that, even when disembodied the emancipated soul still retains his subtle body with capacities for enjoyments.

Though a person, who knows Brahma, gets rid of all his good and bad deeds at the time of parting with the body, there is justification for his going by the path of the gods, because of the statement in Śruti that he moves about freely enjoying, playing and making merry. Such statements indicate experience of joys in a subtle body, the grosser one now being wanting. This means that the emancipated individual soul partakes of the bliss of the Universal Soul, as it is seen in the world that a servant of the king shares his master's enjoyment.

This subtle body, on the other hand, will also be consumed

and be replaced by another of heavenly light, when the soul receives finally the status of Brahma—his Master.

For reference, vide the Śruti—

"परं ज्योतिरूपसम्पद्य स्वेन रूपेणाभिनिष्पद्यते"।

स उत्तम पुरुषः "स तत्र पर्य्येति जक्षन् क्रीड़न् रममाणः"।

(He, turning into the transcendent light, wins back his own proper status. Then the beatified soul roams about playing and sporting and enjoying himself.)

Chāndogya, Chap. VIII, 12, 3.

अनियमः सर्व्वेषामविरोधः शब्दानुमानाभ्याम् ॥३१॥

[The journey of the soul who knows Brahma, is contineud.]

अनियमः (no restriction), **सर्व्वेषाम्** (of all), **अवरोधः** (no contradiction; agreement), **शब्दानुमानाभ्याम्** (from Śruti as well as Smṛti.)

Explanation—The progress of the released soul by the path of gods is not restricted to those who choose only one particular form of meditation to the exclusion of others, such as the Upakośala Vidyā, the Pañcāgni-Vidyā etc., in which also such a journey is expressly stated; but the progressive path is thrown open to all kinds of meditators of Brahma; for in this view only, the statement of Śruti and Smṛti become consistent.

For reference vide the Śruti—

"य एवमेतद्विदुर्ये चामी अरण्ये श्रद्धां सत्यमुपासते तेऽर्च्चिरभिसम्भवन्ति"

(Those who thus know this, and those who in the forest worship Faith and Truth, attain the passage of Light—*the path of the gods*.)

Bṛhadāraṇyaka, Chap. VI, 2, 15

For Smṛti, vide—

"शुक्लकृष्णे गती ह्येते जगतः शाश्वते मते ।
एकया यात्यनावृत्तिमन्ययावर्त्तते पुनः॥"

(These are the two eternal paths, of light and darkness, for journeying from this world; by the one the soul goes out not return, and by the other he returns again.)

Bhagavat-Gītā, Chap. VIII, 26.

यावदधिकारमवस्थितिराधिकारिकाणाम्॥३२॥

[A plausible objection to Sūtra 31 is refuted.]

यावत् (as long as), **अधिकारम्** (mission; purpose to be fulfilled), **अवस्थितिः** (corporal existence in this world), **अधिकारिकाणाम्** (of those who have a certain mission in life to fulfil.)

Explanation—Those, who are born with a certain mission, remain in this world as long as the mission is not fulfilled.

It may be objected that progress, of persons who know Brahma, by the path of the gods, after their emanicipation from the effects of good and evil Karma does not apply to Vaśisṭha and others like him, who are known, from the Purāṇas (records of pre-historic time), to have been born again, though they had known Brahma. The present Sūtra is a reply to this objection—Corporal existence, for one life or more, of persons like Vaśiṣṭha, who are commissioned from above to fulfil certain purposes, such as the promulgation of the Vedas and the like, continues as long as the mission remains unfulfilled.

अक्षरधियां त्ववरोधः सामान्यतद्भावाभ्यामौपसदवत्तदुक्तम् ॥३३॥

[The negative attributes of the Imperishable are now examined; as the positive attributes were done in Sūtra 11 of this section.]

अक्षरधियां (of the meditation of *negative attributes belonging to* the Imperishable), **तु** (indeed), **अवरोधः** (retention *of the negative attributes of Brahma*), **सामान्यतद्भावाभ्याम्** (because of sameness and of their inclusion among the essential attributes of the Imperishable), औपसदवत् (like the hymn in connection with the Upasada rite); तत् (that), उक्तम् (said *by this sage Jaimini in the Pūrva-Mīmāṁsā.*)

Explanation— The conception of the negative attributes of the Imperishable as stated in the Bṛhadāraṇyaka Śruti, is to be retained in the meditations of the Imperishable everywhere (*i.e.*,, in every Akṣara-Vidyā); because the same Akṣara Puruṣa (the Imperishable One) is recognised in every Akṣara-Vidyā, and also because those negative attributes are presupposed to be included among His essential attributes. This is just like the hymns of the Sāma Veda, chanted in connection with the Upasada oblation: these hymns, though occurring in the Sāma-Veda, yet are recited by the Adhvarvayu after the tune of the Yajurveda. The principle has been established by the sage Jaimini in his Pūrva-Mīmāṁsā.

For reference as to the negative attributes, vide—

एतद्वै तदक्षरं गार्गि ब्राह्मणा अभिवदन्ति अस्थूलमनण्वह्रस्वमदीर्घम्॥"

(O Gārgi, persons who know Brahma, designate Him 'the Imperishable One', Who is neither gross, nor subtle, neither large nor small.)

Bṛhadāraṇyaka, Chap. III, 8, 8.

In the Akṣara-Vidyā, which is discussed in the present Sūtra, Brahma is considered in respect of His character *per se*—apart from the creation (vide the exposition of the views of Śaṅkara under Sūtra 26, Sec. IV, Chap. I.)

इयदामननात् ॥३४॥

(This Sūtra ascertains which of the positive attributes of Brahma have to be adopted for the meditation of the Imperishable One.]

इयत् (this much; only these), आमननात् (because of deep meditation.)

Explanation— The negative attributes (stated in the preceding Sūtra) and the positive attributes, such as consciousness (चित्), joy (आनन्द), omnipresence, omniscience etc., (as stated in Sūtra 11 of this section) only have to be associated together in the Akṣara Vidyā, because the former would be meaningless without the latter; but the attributes 'all-doing'. 'all-smelling', 'all-tasting' and others prescribed for the specific form of meditation, need not be associated with those discussed here.

अन्तरा भूतग्रामवत् स्वात्मनोऽन्यथा भेदानुपपत्तिरिति चेन्नोपदेशान्तरवत्॥३५॥

[Two passages from the Bṛhadāraṇyaka Śruti are taken up for discussion to show that they relate to the same Vidyā.]

अन्तरा (**अन्तरत्त्वं**, the status of being the inmost), **भूतग्रामवत्** (the master of all the constituents of his body and mind), **स्वात्मनः** (of one's own self; of the individual self), **अन्यथा** (otherwise), **भेदानुपपत्तिः** (no justification for the variety in the wording of the two replies), **इति** (this), **चेत्** (if); **न** (no), **उपदेशान्तरवत्** (as in the teaching of another Vidyā [mode of meditation], *namely the Satya-Vidyā in Chāndogya.*)

[The Sūtra consists of two parts, namely, an objection and its reply. The objection-portion is:—**अन्तरा भूतग्राभवत् स्वात्मनो- ऽन्यथा भेदानुपपत्तिः इति चेत्**; the reply portion is:—**न उपदेशान्तरवत्**.]

Explanation—It may be objected, that the entity residing within everything as the innermost being, refers to the individual self, who is the master of the constituents of his mind and body; otherwise there is found no justification for variety in the wording of the two replies given to the same question (vide the dialogue between Uṣasta and Yājñavalkya on one hand, and between Kahola and Yājñavalkya on the other.) The first reply seems to refer to the individual soul, who is unquestionably the master of the constituents of his mind and body, and breathes by respiration; while the second reply clearly refers to the Universal Soul, Who alone can be said to be above hunger and thirst, etc. So it may be apprehended that there are two different Vidyās shown in the two cases, the objects presented for meditation being different—the individual soul in the former and the Universal Soul in the latter. To this objection our reply is, that it is one and the same Vidyā, because in both the cases the subject, matter of question and the answer is Brahma, the Universal Soul, the Inner Regulator of everything, Who is presented for everything, Who is presented for meditation in His two different aspects. This is emphasized by the sage Yājñavalkya himself, when he repeats 'That soul of thine is the innermost soul of all individuals.' The same thing happens in the Satya-Vidyā (सत्य विद्या) explained in the Chāndogya, by the sage Uddālaka to his son Śvetaketu; there the preceptor repeats at the close of each illustration. 'This is the subtlest entity, which is the soul of everything, which permeates all and is the True One, That thou art, O Śvetaketu.' the same Universal Soul is repeatedly illustrated in different ways throughout the chapter for clearer conception. Similarly the different expositions of Yāñjavalkya must refer to the one and the same object of worship—Brahma.

For the question and its reply between Uṣasta and Yājñavalkya vide—

Question:—"यत् साक्षादपरोक्षाद् ब्रह्म य आत्मा सर्व्वान्तरस्तं मे व्याचक्ष्व।"

(Tell me about Him Who is Brahma standing directly revealed to intuition unaided by inference, Who is the Self dwelling within everything.)

Answer:—"एष त आत्मा सर्व्वान्तरः....यः प्राणेन प्राणिति स त आत्मा सर्व्वान्तरः"

(He is thy innermost Soul, Who breathes by respiration, and this thy Soul is also the innermost Soul of all.)

Bṛhadāraṇyaka, Chap. III, 4, 1.

For the question and the answer between Kahola and Yājñavalkya, vide:—

Question:—"**यदेव साक्षादपरोक्षाद् ब्रह्म य आत्मा सर्व्वान्तरस्तन्मे व्याचक्ष्व।**"

(For translation vide above. The question is the same as put by Uṣasta.)

Answer:—"**एष त आत्मा सर्व्वान्तर....योऽग नायापिपासे शोकं मोहं जरां मृत्युमत्येति।**"

(He is thy innermost Soul, Who rests beyond hunger and thirst, sorrow and ignorance, death and decay.)

Bṛhadāraṇyaka, Chap. III. 5, 1.

For reference to the Satya-Vidyā (question and answer between Śvetaketu and his father Uddālaka), vide:—

Question:—"**भूयएवं मां भगवान् विज्ञापयतु।**"

(O revered sire, kindly illustrate this to me further.)

Chāndogya, Chap. VI, 8, 7.

Answer:—"**एषोऽणिमैतदात्म्यमिदं स्र्वं तत् सत्यं स आत्मा तत्त्वमसि श्वेतकेतो।**"

(This is the subtlest entity, the Soul, permeating all this creation, He is the True One, He is Self, *and* He thou art, O Śvetaketu.)

Chāndogya, Chap. VI, 9, 4 ff.

व्यतिहारो विशिंषन्ति हीतरवत्॥३६॥

[The reference in the previous Sūtra are further discussed.]

व्यतिहारः (**विनिमयः**, exchange), **विशिंषन्ति** (explain clearly), **हि** (because), **इतरवत्** (like the other teaching; as has been shown in the Satya-Vidyā.)

Explanation—The special features of both the expositions of Yājñavalkya are to be interchanged between Uṣ asta and Kahola, because in both the expositions (answers) the same Universal Soul (as the innermost Spirit) has been distinctly explained, as has been done in the Satya Vidyā of the Chāndogya.

Both the inquirers asked about the same Universal Soul—the Innermost Spirit. Yājñavalkya answered apparently in different terms to suit the understanding of respective enquirers. But the subject-matter of his expositions is the Universal Soul, Whom he represents to be the Innermost Spirit. In his answer to Uṣasta the innermost Universal Soul is represented as breathing life into every living soul, and in his answer to Kahola He is represented as beyond the reach of hunger, thirst and so on. Being thus specialised in two ways, He is distinctly shown to be different from the individual soul. So in meditation, Uṣasta has to meditate on the special attribute of Brahma, namely existing beyond hunger etc., in addition to His being the inner most Spirit breathing life into every living soul; and similarly Kahola has also to meditate on both the special features of Brahma. This is exactly like the Satya-Vidyā of the Chāndogya, where all the answers explain the same Brahma though apparently in different words and attributes, for the clear conception of the enquirer. The fact, that the Supreme Soul is the True One, is emphatically repeated at the close of Uddālaka's each illustration.

सैव हि सत्यादयः॥३७॥

[This Sūtra shows how in the Satya Vidyā, there is unity in the diversity of the answer.]

सा (that Deity—the Supreme Soul), एव (certainly, हि (because), सत्यादयः (the attribute 'Truth' and the like.)

Explanation—In the Satya-Vidyā, the Deity, *i.e.,* the Supreme Soul, described in the first answer, is described in all the later expositions, because, the attributes 'Truth' and the like of the first exposition are repeated in the subsequent exposition also. Therefore in spite of the repeated questionings and suitable answers thereto, there is a tone of unity running through the whole discourse.

कामादतीरत्र तत्र चायतनादिभ्यः॥३८॥

[Dahara-Vidyā (दहरविद्या) of the Chāndogya and the Bṛhadāraṇyaka Śrutis is now discussed.]

कामादि (**सत्यसंकल्पत्वादि,** effective determination and other attributes like it), **इतरत्र** (in the other; in the Bṛhadārṇyaka Śruti) **तत्र** (there; in the Chāndogya Śruti), **च** (also), **आयतनादिभ्यः** (from the seat and so on; because of the expression 'the seat in the heart' and other attributes applied in common in the two Śrutis.)

Explanation—The Dahara-Vidyā has been described in the Bṛhadāraṇyaka as well as in the Chāndogya Śruti. That these two descriptions are of the same Vidyā, can be understood from the common expression 'the seat of the Supreme Soul in Daharākāśa' (the small empty space, within the heart of the individual, upon which the mediator is taught to fix his mind for realisation of Brahma) as well as from other attributes used in common by both the Śrutis in the exposition of the Dahara-Vidyā. Also the attributes of Brahma—effective determination and the like specially noted by Chānodogya in connection with its Dahara-Vidyā, and at the sametime the attributes of Brahma—the 'Controller of all' and the like—specially noted by Bṛhadāraṇyaka in connection with its Dahara-Vidyā, are to be regarded as supplementary to one another, and are to be conjoined to the Dahara-Vidyā of each Śruti,

For reference to the Dahara-Vidyā vide the Chāndogya:—

"यदिदमस्मिन् ब्रह्मपुरे दहरं पुण्डरीकं वेश्म दहरोऽस्मिन्नन्तराकाशस्तस्मिन् यदन्तस्तदन्वेष्टव्यं तद्वाव विजिज्ञासितव्यमिति।"

"यावान् अयमाकाश स्तावानेषोऽन्तर्हृदय आकाश उमे अस्मिन् द्यावापृथिवी अन्तरेव समाहिते।"

"एष आत्मापहतपाप्मा विजरो विमृत्युर्विशोको विजिघत्सोऽपिपासः सत्यकामः सत्यसंकल्पः।"

(For reference and translation vide Sūtra 14, Sec. III, Chap. I.)

For the same (Dahara-Vidyā), vide the Bṛhadāraṇyaka—

"स वा एष महान् अज आत्मा योऽयं विज्ञानमयः प्राणेषु य एषोऽन्तर्हृदय आकाशस्तस्मिंश्छेते सर्व्वस्य वशी सर्व्वस्येशानः सर्व्वस्याधिपतिः।"

(He is this Great unembodied Self, Who is all-Intelligence, and existing in all the vital centres lies in the empty space within the recess of the heart; He is the Controller of all, the Lord of all and the Ruler of all.)

Bṛhadāraṇyaka, Chap. IV, 4, 22.

आदरादलोपः॥३९॥

[The Sūtra shows that the positive attributes, referred to in the preceding Sūtra, are by no means to be discarded.]

आदरात् (because of careful mention), **अलोपः** (no negation and no omission.)

Explanation—In course of the exposition of the Dahara-Vidyā there are some expressions which apparently amount to a dential of all attributes of Dahara-Brahma. This Sūtra lays down that there is no denial of the attributes, such as 'effective determination' 'supreme control' etc., because the Śruti has carefully mentioned all those attributes in connection with Dahara, *i.e.,* Brahma; and the apparently negative expressions, such as **"नेह नानास्ति किञ्चन"** (Here there is nothing separate from Him) really negate anything that may be supposed to have an existence independent of, and separate from Brahma.

These expressions can by no means be construed into denying of Brahma's attributes such as 'effective control' which Śruti has taken so much pain to affirm of Him (Cf. Sūtra 22, Sec. II, Chap. III.)

उपस्थितेऽतस्तद्वचनात्॥४०॥

[There reward of meditation on the Dahara-Brahma is stated.]

उपस्थिते (on reaching or attaining the status of Brahma by meditation), **अतः** (from that; on that account), **तद्वचनात्** (because there are such statements *in Śruti*.)

Explanation—On attaining the status of Brahma by the Dahara-Vidyā, the emancipated soul acquires, on that account, the power of journeying to any world, of his own free will; because there are corroborative statements in Śruti.

For reference in Śruti, vide the quotation and its translation under Sūtra 30 Sec. III, Chap. III.

तन्निर्द्धारणानियमस्तद्दृष्टेः पृथग्घ्यप्रतिबंधः फलम्॥४१॥

[This Sūtra states that a meditation prescribed in connection with a ceremonial rite, is not compulsory.]

तत् (**तेषाम्** of them; of the Udgīth-meditation and the like), **निर्द्धारण** (compulsory performances), **अनियमः** (no fixed rule), **तद्दुष्टेः** (as it is found in Śruti), **पृथक्** (distinct), **हि** (as, for), **अप्रतिबन्धः** (unobstruction), **फलम्** (reward.)

Explanation—There is no fixed rule for compulsory performance of the Udgītha meditation and the like in ceremonials; because performance of the meditation on 'Om' there, is left optional to the performer, and also because the reward in each case is quite distinct, provided that the performance of the rite be not in any way obstructed; for it is clear that the meditation is sure to produce its own effect independently of the rite, but the rite is liable to interruption and obstruction. If, however, the meditation and the rite be conjoined, reward becomes doubly effective.

The Śruti says:—

"तेनोभौ कुरुते यश्चैतदेवं वेद, यश्च न वेद—यदेव विद्यया करोति श्रद्धयोपनिषदा तदेव वीर्य्यवत्तरं भवति।"

(The ignorant man, as well as the wise man, may both engage in the Udgītha worship; *this shows that the Udgītha worship may be performed, the meditation part being left out.*

That, which is performed with meditatiion, faith and knowledge, becomes, all the more effective.)

Chāndogya, Chap. I, 1, 10.

This Śruti shows that the rite can be performed even without meditation, and that to perform the rite with meditation is to make it more effective. So the Udgītha meditation and all others, done in connection with some ceremonial rite (कर्माङ्ग उपासना), are not compulsory and are to be done by those only who wish to gain greater rewards.

प्रदानवदेव तदुक्तम्॥४२॥

[This Sūtra lays down the principle that the Possessor of attributes is ever to be borne in mind along with the attributes upon which the mind is fixed *i.e.,* while meditating upon the attributes of the Supreme Being, the meditator must not lose sight of the Supreme Being Himself, to Whom the Attributes belong.]

प्रदानवत् (as in the case of the offering of the 'Pradāna-oblation'; as in the case of the cake-offering for Indra), एव (exactly), तत् (that; the principle), उक्तम् (said; established by Jaimini in his Pūrva Mīmāṁsā.)

Explanation—In the Dahara-Vidyā (Chāndogya, Chap. VIII, 1, 6) the attributes, such as 'effective determination' etc., have been taught to be separately meditated upon. But while doing so the Supreme Being, Who possesses those attributes, also has to be meditation upon in each case along with the attributes themselves, just as in the case of the cake-offering to Indra. Indra, though one, is entitled to three oblations in his three capacities; similarly, although the same Supreme Soul is implied by each of these attributes, yet each attribute represents Him in a distinct capacity; so while meditating on the attributes, the Supreme Soul has also to be meditated upon as many times as there are attributes mentioned. The principle has been established by Jaimini in his Pūrva-Mīmāṁsā.

For reference vide—

अथ य इहात्मानमनुविद्य व्रजन्त्येतांश्च सत्यान् कामान्....."

(So those who depart after being acquainted with the Supreme Soul in this world, and also with *the several attributes belonging to Him, such as* 'effective determination', *immunity from evil, freedom from hunger, thirst, etc., etc.*)

Chāndogya, Chap. VIII, 1, 6.

Here the Supreme Soul is to be meditated upon, for as many times and in as many ways, as there are epithets in the quoted text, within the compass of one act of meditation.

लिङ्गभूयस्त्वात् तद्धि बलीयस्तदपि॥४३॥

[A discussion begins as to whether the fires, spoken of in the Vājasaneyakopaniṣad as produced by mind etc. are for ceremonial rites (कर्म्माङ्ग) or are simply imaginary fires for the purpose of meditation (विद्यांग.)]

लिङ्गभूयस्त्वात् (because of an abundance of distinguishing marks), **तत्** (that; the distinguishing mark), **हि** (because), **बलीयः** (stronger); **तदपि** (that also *has been established by Jaimini in his Pūrva Mimāṁsā.*)

Explanation—The fires spoken of in the Vājasaneya Upaniṣad as made of mind, speech, life, etc., are imaginary fires intended for meditation, and not the sacred fires of ceremonials; because there is an abundance of marks distinguish them from ceremonial fires, and because those distinguishing marks are stronger proofs than the context itself which would suggest that the fires are for the actual performance of religious rites. That distinguishing marks are stronger proofs than the context, has been establishing by Jaimini in his Pūrva-Mīmāṁsā.

For reference in the Śruti, vide—

मनश्चितो वाक्चितः प्राणचितश्चक्षुश्चितः कर्म्मचितोऽग्निचितः।"

(*Fires* made of mind, spech, life-energy, eye, works and *ordinary sacrificial* fire.)

Taittirīya, Nārāyaṇa—11.

"यत् किञ्चमानि भूतानि मनसा संकल्पयन्ति तेषामेव सा कृतिः।"

(Whatever these beings conceive in their minds, is the doing of these *fires*.)

For the Pūrva-Mīmāṁsā, vide—

श्रुतिलिङ्गवाक्यप्रकरणस्थानसमाख्यानां समवाये पारदौर्ब्बल्यमर्थविप्रकर्षात्।"

(In the case of occurring together, of a clear statement in Śruti, of distinguishing marks, explanatory texts, subject-matter of the chapter, order of arrangement and derivative meaning, the succeeding ones are of a weaker import than the preceding, because the preceding ones bring out the sense earlier than the suceeding ones.)

पूर्व्वविकल्पः प्रकरणात् स्यात् क्रिया मानसवत् ॥४४॥

[An objection is raised to the preceding Sūtra.]

पूर्व्वविकल्पः (an alternative form of the one already prescribed), **प्रकरणात्** (*as can be understood* from the subject-matter of the chapter), **स्यात्** (may be), **क्रिया** (ceremonial act), **मानसवत्** (like the mental operation; as in the case of the mental operation in the Soma-sacrifice.

Explanation—It may be said by way of objection, that the fires, referred to in the preceding Sūtra, are alternative to the fire already prescribed in a previous passage of the Śruti, and which is ordinarily procured in every sacrifice; as can be understood from the subject-matter of the chapter, which deals with the ordinary sacrificial fire; therefore the fires, referred to in the previous Sūtra, are for the actual performance of ceremonials, and not intended for any special purposes, namely for meditation, as in the case of the mental operation in the Soma sacrifice.

Here it is contended that the distinguishing marks (लिङ्ग) are used merely by way of praise (अर्थवाद) of the ordinary fire that is required for the rite, and therefore have no independent existence such as there would be if they were meant for meditation (उपासना.) Therefore the distinguishing marks are less strong than the leading subject-matter of the chapter, as in the case of the mental operation in the Soma sacrifice, where the earth is considered as the cup and the sea as the contents of the cup (सोमरस); here the act, though mental, is considered as a part of the sacrifice and therefore cannot be a part of meditation. This objection is refuted subsequently by Sūtras 46—50 of this section.]

अतिदेशाच्च ।।४५।।

[Objection to Sūtra 43 is continued by presenting another argument in support of Sūtra 44.]

अतिदेशात् (because of going beyond the local limit; because of the attribution of the virtues of one to another, because of extending the application to other cases), **च** (also.)

Explanation—The fires referred to in Sūtra 43 are intended for the actual performance of the rite, also because, to them have been attributed the virtues of the ordinary fire. [This is also said by way of objection to be refuted in the following Sūtras.]

For reference of the attribution vide—

"तेषामेकैक एव तावान्यावानसौ पूर्व्वः।"

(Each of these *fires* is as important as the one previously mentioned, *i.e., the ordinary sacrificial fire*.)

This statement indicates that the imginary fires are part and parcel of the ordinary sacrificial rite, and have no independent existence for purposes of meditation.

विद्यैव तु निर्द्धारणात् दर्शनाच्च ।।४६।।

[Objections raised in Sūtras 44 and 45 are now refuted.]

विद्या (process of form of meditation), एव (alone), तु (indeed), निर्द्धारणात् (as they are directly ascertained), दर्शनात् (becasue they are clearly stated in Śruti), च (also.)

Explanation—The fires, referred to in Sūtra 43, are for meditation alone and not for a ceremonial performance, because they are directly ascertained to be so, and also because they are clearly stated to be so in Śruti.

For reference as to the ascertainment, vide—

"ते हैते विद्याचित एव"

(They—*the contemplated fires*,—are certainly to be evoked in a particular kind of meditation.)

For the clear statement in the Śruti, vide—

"येषामङ्गिनो विद्यामयक्रतोस्ते मनसाऽधीयन्त मनसा चीयन्त मनसैषु ग्रहा अगृह्यन्त मनसा स्तुवन्त मनसा शंसत् किञ्ज यज्ञे कर्म्म क्रियते।"

(Those, who held these contemplated fires as essentials of the form of divine meditation, mentally contemplated them, mentally piled them up, mentally held offerings for them, mentally adored them, mentally praised them and did everything mentally that is ordinarily done in a sacrifice.)

श्रुत्यादिबलीयस्त्वाच्च न बाधः॥४७॥

[Objections raised in Sūtras 44 and 45 are further refuted.]

श्रुत्यादि (the Śruti and so on; the Śruti, the indicatory marks and the text, which have been shown in the Pūrva-Mīmāṁsā to be of stronger import than the subject-matter of the chapter), बलीयस्त्वात् (because of stronger import; as they are of greater force), च (also), न (no), बाधः (bar.)

Explanation—Also the Śruti, the indicatory marks and the text being stronger proofs than the subject-matter of the chapter (as professed by Jaimini), there is no bar to these fires constituting an independent form of meditation, rather than constituting a part of the ceremonial performance.

For the Śruti vide—

"ते हैते विद्याचित एव" (For translation vide Sūtra 46.)

For indicatory marks vide—

"एवंविदे सर्व्वदा सर्व्वाणि भूतानि विचिन्वीन्त।"

(All beings always prepare *fires* for him who meditates in this form.)

For explanatory text vide—

"विद्यया हैवैते एवंविदश्चिता भवन्ति।"

These fires are mentally conceived as such by the meditator by din of hist meditation in this form.)

अनुबन्धादिभ्यः प्रज्ञान्तरपृथक्त्ववत् दृष्टश्च तदुक्तम् ।।४८।।

[The argument in refutation of Sūtras 44 and 45 are continued.]

अनुबन्धादिभ्यः (from **अनुबन्ध** etc.; from the attendant performance and the reasons adduced in the previous Sūtra), **प्रज्ञान्तरपृथक्त्ववत्** (like the distinction of other forms of meditation), **दृष्ट** (is found), **च** (also), **तत्** (that), **उक्तम्** (said; is explained in the Pūrva-Mīmāṁsā.)

Explanation—From the import of the performances that are attendant on the main ceremony, and also from the reasons adduced in the previous Sūtra, it is clear that the fires, referred to in Sūtra 43, do not belong to the performances of the sacrifice, but to a separate and independent form of meditation (Agni-Vidyā), just in the same way as there are found in Śruti other forms of meditation, such as the Śaṇḍilya-Vidyā, Udgītha-Vidyā, Puruṣa-Vidyā, etc., which are independent of the ceremonial portion of the sacrifices described there. The fires being thus shown to be quite different from the ordinary sacrificial fire, an injunction, to the effect that these fires are to be meditated upon, is inferred, though there is no such injunction made in so many words. That such as inference is allowable, has been proved by Jaimini in his Pūrva-Mīmāṁsā by a Sūtra which means— "A passage given in the indicative mood should be interpreted as imperative (विधि), if it states something new, something other than an Anuvāda, *i.e.,* an illustration (vide Pūrva-Mīmāṁsā III, 5, 21.)

For reference in Śruti, vide the last quotation under Sūtra 46.

न सामान्यादप्युपलब्धेर्मृत्युवत् न हि लोकापत्तिः॥४९॥

[The argument in refutation of Sūtras 44 and 45 is continued.]

न (not), सामान्यात् (because of commonness; on the ground of their resemblance to the sacrificial fire), अपि (even), उपलब्धेः (as they are found *distinctly adapted to meditation*), मृत्युवत् (like death; analogous to the case of death), न (not) हि (for; as), लोकापत्तिः (transformation into the world.)

Explanation—Even on the ground of their resemblance to the sacrificial fire (vide Sūtra 45 last), those fires cannot be said to belong to the ceremonial performance, as they are distinctly found to belong to meditation. The case is analogous to that of Death in the two passages quoted below, one from the Śatapatha Brāhmaṇa and the other from the Taittirīya Saṁhitā; in the former the Spirit in the sun, and in the latter Fire, are represented as Death; and in this respect they resemble each other; but for the matter of that the Spirit is not the same as Fire. Again, when it is said 'This world is Fire' fire is not actually transformed into the world *above* (heaven.) Similarly, though the fires, referred to in Sūtra 43, have been stated to resemble the ordinary sacrificial fire, yet they need not do the business of the latter.

For reference in the Śatapatha Brāhmaṇa, vide:—

"स एष एव मृत्युर्य एतस्मिन् मण्डले पुरुषः।"

(The Spirit in that orb is Death indeed.)

Śatapatha Brāhmaṇa, Chap. X, 5, 2, 3.

For reference in the Taittirīya-Saṁhitā, vide—

"अग्निर्व्वै मृत्युः" (Fire indeed is Death.)

Taittirīya Saṁhitā, Chap. V, 1, 10, 3.

Also vide the Śruti showing that 'The world is Fire'—

"असौ बाव लोको गौतमाग्निस्तस्यादित्य एवं समिध्"

(The world *above* is Fire indeed, O Gautama, the sun is its fuel.)

Chāndogya, Chap. V, 4, 1.

परेण च, शब्दस्य ताद्विध्यं, भूयस्वात्त्वनुबन्धः ॥५०॥

[The argument in refutation of Sūtras 45 and 46 is concluded.]

परेणं (by the subsequent expression), **च** (also), **शब्दस्य** (of Śruti), **ताद्विध्यं** (that) nature, that the fires are intended for meditation), **भूयस्वात्** (because of abundance), **तु** (but), **अनुबन्धः** (statement along with *the ordinary sacrificial fire*.)

Explanation—By the subsequent expression also, the purport of Śruti is proved to be of that nature, namely, that the fires referred to in Sūtra 43, are intended for meditation; but the statement of them along with the ordinary sacrificial fire is due to an abundance of common matters with the latter.

By the subsequent expression, that the 'World is indeed piled up as Fire', in the chapter of the Agni-Vidyā, it is understood that the purpose of the text is the injunction of a mere form of meditation, and not of a ceremonial performance.

The subsequent expression is—

"अयं बाव लोक एषोऽग्निचितः" (The world is indeed that Fire piled up.)

एक आत्मनः शरीरे भावात् ॥५१॥

[A discussion begins as to whether the soul is to be meditated upon as he *is* in his state of bondage, or as he *should be* in his state of emancipation.]

एके (some *say*), आत्मनः (of the self), शरीरे (in the body), भावात् (because of existence.)

Explanation—Some say that the conditioned and embodied state of the self is to be meditated on, because the self exists in the body in such state. [This argument is advanced here by way of objection which is refuted in the next Sūtra.]

व्यतिरेकस्तद्भावभावित्वान्नतूपलब्धिवत्॥५२॥

[The statement in the preceding Sūtra is refuted.]

व्यतिरेकः (contrary to that stated in the preceding Sūtra), तद्भावभवित्वात् (because of attainment of that state, *i.e.,* because the object is to attain the free state), नतु (but the fact is not what is stated in Sūtra 51; but the above opinion cannot be maintained), उपलब्धिवत् (just like realisation of Brahma, *i.e.,* meditation must be on what is to be realised.)

Explanation—The self is to be meditated on as existing in his natural state, which view is contrary to that mentioned in the preceding Sūtra, *i.e.,* in his real free nature, but meditation must not be in his conditioned nature, existing, as he does, in his present prison-house; because a man becomes exactly what he intensely thinks to be (and the aim of the meditator is, no doubt, to be free), since the nature of the realisation of Brahma depends upon the nature of meditation.

अङ्गावबद्धास्तु न शाखा सु हि प्रतिवेदम् ॥५३॥

[After deciding that one should, at the time of meditation, think of himself as free and pure, Ācāryā Bādarāyaṇa now proeceeds to establish, that the forms of meditations connected with the ceremonial rites prescribed in the different branches of the Vedas, are equally to be interchanged.]

अङ्गावबद्धाः (*meditations* connected with parts *of sacrificial acts*), तु (but), न (not *to remain confined*), शाखासु (to the *respective* branches *of the Vedas*), हि (because), प्रतिवेदम् (*to be interchanged among all the* branches of the Vedas.)

Explanation—Meditations, connected with parts of sacrificial acts prescribed in particular branches of the Vedas are not to remain confined to their respective branches, but they are to be interchanged among all the branches.

As for instance, meditation on the word 'Om', connected with the Udgītha sacrifice in the Sāma Veda, and other similar meditations, are not to be confined only to those particular branches of the Vedas where they have been tought; but they are to be interchanged among all the branches, as the Udgītha and other similar meditations have been equally prescribed for all the branches of the Vedas. The details of the mode of meditation on 'Om', for instance, are fully stated in some branches and only partially in other, so the efficiencies of one branch should be made up by borrowings from the others.

मन्त्रादिवद्वाऽविरोधः॥५४॥

[The discussion commenced in Sūtra 53 is continued.]

मन्त्रादिवत् (as the incantations and the like), **वा** (or else), **अविरोधः** (no bar.)

Explanation—There is no bar to the process of meditation, mentioned in one branch of the Vedas, being transferred to all other branches; as the Mantras (incantations) and the like prescribed in one branch for certain rites, are freely transferred to all the branches for the same rite.

As for example, the incantation '**कुटरूरसि**' (thou art the grinding stone), prescribed in one branch of the Vedas for taking stone to grind rice, is acceptable in that rite everywhere; similarly the meditations prescribed in one branch of the Vedas may be transferred to other branches without apprehending any impropriety.

भूम्नः क्रतुवज्जयायस्त्वं तथाहि दर्शयति॥५५॥

[The Vaiśvānara-Vidyā is discussed here.]

भूम्नः (*meditation* of the Supreme Soul in His entire

universal form in the Vaiśvānara-Vidyā), क्रतुवत् (as in a sacrifice; like the aggregate of the parts of a sacrificial performance), ज्यायस्त्वं (prominance), तथा (thus), हि (for as), दर्शयति (*Śruti* shows.)

Explanation—Prominence should be given to the entire meditation on the Supreme Soul in the form of Vaiśvānara (*i.e.*, in the Vaiśvānara-Vidyā), and not to any particular part detailed thereof; just as prominence is given to the aggregate of the parts of a sacrificial performance, but not to any particular part thereof to the exclusion of the rest; for instance, the parts of the Pūrṇamāsa-sacrifice and the like, are described in different chapters but are collected together for performance in entirety. The Chāndogya Śruti, similarly prescribes the meditation of Vaiśvānara in its entirety without excluding any of His limbs or organs. There the King Aśvapati instructs Uddālaka and some other Ṛṣis (sages), that all the different limbs of Vaiśvānara (Brahma in His universal form),—such as are represented by heaven, sun, air, Ākāśa, world, earth and so on, should be taken in the aggregate and meditated as such. The Sūtra considers it rather prejudicial to the interest of the meditator to substitute any part for the whole. (Vide Chāndogya, chapter V, parts 11-18.)

For reference, as to the members of the body of Vaiśvānara, vide:—

तस्य ह वा एतस्यात्मनो वैश्वानरस्य मूर्द्धैव सुतेजाश्चक्षुर्विश्वरूपः प्राणः पृथग्वर्त्मात्मा सन्देहो बहुलो वस्तिरेव रयिः पृथिव्येव पादावुर एव वेदिर्लोमानि बर्हि र्हृदयं गार्हपत्यो मनोऽवाहार्य्यपचन आस्यमाहवनीयः।"

(Bright heaven is the head of this Vaiśvānara Self; the sun, who gives colour to all things, is His eye; the wind, blowing in all directions, is His Prāṇa; the pervading Ākāśa is the trunk of His body; the vast mass of water is His bladder; the earth is His foot; the sacrificial alter is His chest; Kuśa (grass) is the hairs on His body; the household fire is His thorax; the gastric fire is His mind; and the sacrificial fire is His mouth.)

Chāndogya, Chap. V, 18, 2.

For reference, as to the harmfulness of meditating on a part as the sole form of Vaiśvānara, vide—

औपमन्यव कं त्वामात्मानमुपास्स इति दिवमेव भगवो राजन्निति"
"मूर्द्धात्वेष आत्मन इति होवाच मूर्द्धा ते व्यपतिष्यद् यन्मां नागमिष्य इति।"

(*King As wapati asked* 'Whom dost thou, O son of Upamanyu, worship as *Vaiśwānara* Self?' 'Heaven *do I worship as Self*, my Lord' *answered he*. The king said 'This *heaven* is but the head of Self; thy head would have dropped down' hadst thou not come to me—*and received from me the fuller interpretation of Vaiśvānara*.)

Chāndogya, Chap. V, 12, 1 and 2.

नाना शब्दादिभेदात्॥५६॥

[This Sūtra states that though the object of meditation is the same everywhere, yet the forms and modes of meditation are very various.]

नाना (different, various), **शब्दादिभेदात्** (owing to difference of names etc.)

Explanation—The forms of meditation—such as the Śāṇḍilya-Vidyā, the Satya-Vidyā, the Dahara-Vidyā, the Vaiśwānara-Vidyā etc.,—are different owing to difference of names and processes; since each of them teaches the worship of the same Lord, but under a particular aspect, and meditations have been prescribed in various names and forms so as to suit different meditators.

विकल्पोऽविशिष्टफलत्वात् ॥५७॥

[This Sūtra determines which Vidyās are recommended for adoption in order to attain salvation; the Vidyās are, to name only the most important ones, Śāṇḍilya-Vidyā, Dahara-Vidyā, Upakośala-Vidyā, Vaiśvānara-Vidyā, Udgītha-Vidyā, Ānandamaya-Vidyā, Akṣara-Vidyā, etc.]

विकल्पः (option), **अविशिष्टफलत्वात्** (as the result of all the Vidyās is the same.)

Explanation—One may follow any Vidyā according to

his option, as the result of all the Vidyās is the same, namely, the realisation of Self.

In other words, the worshipper is welcome to choose any one of the Vidyās, and the goal is the same.

काम्यास्तु यथाकामं समुच्चीयेरन्न वा पूर्व्वहेत्वभावात् ॥५८॥

[The Sūtra shows an exception to the previous Sūtra, that more Vidyās than one may be followed, where the object is other than the realisation of Brahma.]

काम्याः (meditations adopted for some sensuous desire), **तु** (but), **यथाकामं** (according to one's desire or liking), **समुच्चीयेरन्** (may be conjoined), **न** (not), **वा** (or), **पूर्व्वहेत्वभावात्** (because of absence of the reason stated in the previous Sūtra.)

Explanation—Meditations, that are adopted for the fulfilment of some specific desire other than the attainment of Brahma, may be conjoined or not according to one's liking, *i.e.,* as many of them as one likes may be performed one after another; for in these meditations there is wanting the highest motive (**चरमपुरुषार्थ**)—the desire for salvation—stated in the previous Sūtra; the rewards of these meditations which are prompted by some worldly desires (**काम्योपासना**) are not the same, but are very various and are achieved in this or the next world; while the sole object of the meditations, specially meant in Sūtra 57, is the realisation of Brahma.

अङ्गेषु यथाश्रयभावः॥५९॥

[An objection is now raised to the effect that those Vidyās, which are parts of sacrificial rites, cannot be practised independently of those rites.]

अङ्गेषु (as regards meditations which are members of *sacrificial rites*), **यथाश्रयभावः** (becoming of the same nature as that to which they belong.)

Explanation—The Vidyās that are attached to sacrificial rites, are of the same nature as the rites themselves, *i.e.,* they are also integral parts of those sacrificial rites: Even as the Udgītha ceremony is a concomitant part of a sacrifice, the meditation, that is prescribed in connection with that Udgītha, is also a part of that sacrifice and has no independent existence of its own.

[This objection is supported by the following three Sūtras and subsequently refuted by Sūtras 63 and 64.]

शिष्टेश्च॥६०॥

[An argument, in support of the objection raised in Sūtra 59, is adduced.]

शिष्टेः (from the injunction in Śruti), **च** (also.)

Explanation—From the injunction in Śruti, as for instance, that 'One is to meditate on the Udgītha (the prayer in loud chanting prescribed in the Sāma-Veda); it is concluded that the Vidyā (meditation), dependent on the Udgītha-prayer, is also to be accepted as part of the sacrifice; as the Udgītha-invocation cannot be accomplished without the Vidyā (meditation) prescribed therein.

For the injunction in Śruti, vide—

"**उद्गीथमुपासीत्**" (One is to meditate on the Udgītha.)

Chāndogya, Chap. I, 1,1.

समाहारात् ॥६१॥

[Another argument, in support of Sūtra 59, is adduced.]

समाहारात् (because of recovery from pollution because of purification.)

Explanation—Śruti has shown, that if any mistake be committed by the hymn-singing priest in uttering the Udgītha then the Udgītha (of the Sāma Veda), thus defiled, is made whole by meditating on the Praṇava ('Om') of the Ṛk-Veda, meaning thereby that the Udgītha and the Praṇava are to be meditated on as one and the same thing.

The above injunction suggests that the meditation-part of the Udgītha is a compulsory concomitant of the sacrifice, otherwise why should it be expressly enjoined to be corrected if recited incorrectly ?

For reference in the Śruti vide—

"अथ स्वलु य उद्गीथः स प्रणवो यः प्रणवः स उद्गीथ इति होतृषदनाद्धैवापि दुरुद्गीथमनुसमाहरतीत्यनुसमाहरतीति।"

(What is Udgītha is Praṇava, what is Praṇava is Udgītha; this *meditation, on the oneness of the Udgitha and the Praṇava*, mends the Udgītha defiled *by any mistake committed* even on the part of the Hotā (the hymn-reciting priest) *in recitation of the Udgītha*.)

Chāndogya, Chap. I, 5, 5.

गुणसाधारण्यश्रुतेश्च ।।६२।।

[Another argument, in support of Sūtra 59, is adduced.]

गुणसाधारण्य (the commonness of property; that the Praṇava is the common property of the three Vedas), श्रुतेः (as it is found in Śruti), च (also.)

Explanation—It is found in Śruti that the Praṇava (Om-kāra, the mystic syllable 'Om') is the common property of the three Vedas; therefore it is an inseparable concomitant of the sacrificial rites prescribed in the Vedas; so the Vidyās also, being dependent on 'Om-kāra,' are concomitants of the sacrificial rites.

For the Śruti vide—

"तेनेयं त्रयीविद्यावर्त्तते" (By that *Praṇava* this three-fold Veda has its being.)

Chāndogya, Chap, I, 1, 9.

न वा तत्सहभावश्रुतेः।।६३।।

[This Sūtra refutes the contention raised in Sūtras 59-62.]

न वा (but no; but there is no settled rule regarding the

acceptance of the Vidyās to be indispensably connected with the ceremonial parts), **तत्सह** (with that; with the ceremonial parts), **भाव:** (connection), **अश्रुते:** (because there is no such injunction in Śruti.)

Explanation—But there is no settled rule regarding the acceptance of the Vidyās to be indispensably connected with the ceremonial parts with which they are prescribed; because there is no injunction in Śruti to prove such indispensable connection.

In refutation of the objection raised in the preceding four Sūtras, the framer of the Sūtras says that there is no binding rule that the Vidyā, depending on the Praṇava or on any part of a sacrificial rite is a necessary concomitant of the sacrifice; it may be dispensed with or retained at the option of the performer, with this difference that if Vidyā be associated with the rites, greater good will accrue; because though these parts themselves—such as the utterance of the Praṇava or the Udgītha hymn—have been enjoined by Śruti to be absolutely necessary for the sacrificial performances, yet Śruti does not insist that the Vidyā (meditation)—portion of the performance is a necessary adjunct of the performance. The act of meditation belongs to the mind; it is not absolutely necessary for the fulfilment of external sacrificies; meditation, therefore, though prescribed in connection with an external sacrifice cannot be said to be an invoilable act in that sacrificie, like the other (ceremonial parts;) *i.e.*, a sacrifice may be performed even without the meditation (Vidyā), prescribed therewith, merely by utterance of Mantras, singing of the Udgītha hymns, pouring of the clarified butter into the sacred fire and the like external rites, or the purpose of attaining particular desired objects; but the Vidyā or meditation on Brahma is productive of the realisation of the Lord. For this reason the Chāndogya and the Bṛhadāraṇyaka Śrutis, in describing the consequences of the Pañcāgani-Vidyā (the form of meditation by five fires), have taught that those, who follow the Vidyā-portion (*i.e.* the portion meditation), go by the path of gods (दैवयानम्), but those, who dispense with the Vidyā and only follow the external sacrifice of daily libation to the sacred fire (अग्निहोत्रम्) go by the path of the fathers (पितृयानम्.)

दर्शनाच्च॥६४॥

[This Sūtra is adduced in support of Sūtra 63.]

दर्शनात् (from Śruti), च (also.)

Explanation—This may also be inferred from Śruti.

In the Chāndogya Śruti it is said that the chief priest of a sacrificial performance, if possessed of this knowledge (of the process of meditation), saves the sacrifice, the sacrificer and all the priests. From the qualifying phrase 'If possessed to this knowledge,' it is clear that such knowledge is not indispensable, on the part of the priest, for the complete performance of the sacrifice, but it only makes the sacrifice more effective (vide the quotation and its translation under Sūtra 41 of this section.) Therefore, the Vidyā, dependent on a part of a sacrifice, is not an absolute constituent of that sacrifice.

For reference in the Chāndogya Śruti vide—

"मानवो ब्रह्मैवैक ऋत्विक्कुरुनश्वाभि रक्षत्येवंविद् ह वै ब्रह्मा यज्ञं यजमानं सर्व्वांश्च-ऋत्विजोऽभिरक्षति।"

(The mindful chief priest is the priest per excellence; as the horse saves the horseman, so the chief priest possessing such knowledge, saves the sacrifice, the sacrificer and all the priests.)

Chāndogya, Chap. IV, 17, 10.

SECTION—IV

In this section Ācarya Bādarāyaṇa establishes:—

(1) That the attainment of salvation is the direct result of Brahma-Vidyā, (2) that works or sacrifices are only indirect helps to meditation, by cleansing the heart; (3) that Karma (work) does not directly make for salvation (4) that the seeker of Brahma may even do away with Karma, and may attain salvation, solely by virtue of meditation on Brahma, and (5) lastly that even in that case, he should not give up the duties enjoined by the scripture.

Sūtras 1—16 show, by refuting the objections that may arise, that the highest end and aim of the individual soul, namely, the acquisition of Eternal Bliss is attained by the direct intuition (उपरोक्षानुभूति) of Brahma, and that Knowledge is distinct from, and superior to Work.

Sūtras 17—20 refute the contention of Jaimini, that salvation is attainable only by life-long performances of rituals and that renunciation of the world is forbidden by the scriptures. Moreover these Sūtras establish the author's own view that salvation is open to Saṇnyāsis (ascetics) as well as to householders, and that the prohibitory clause has been misread and misunderstood by Jaimini.

Sūtras 21 and 22 show that the meditation on the Udgītha (prayer in hymn in the Sāma-Veda) and such other Karmāṅga-Vidyās (*i.e.*, Vidyās prescribed in Śruti in connection with Karma or the sacrificial rites), are not intended to eulogise the Karma (sacrifice) in conjunction with which they occur; on the contrary, they are Vidyās (modes of meditation) directly enjoined to be performed in all seriousness, even independently of the sacrifices with which they stand connected.

Sūtras 23 and 24 say that the stories in the Upaniṣads are not to be placed in the same category as Pāriplava *i.e.,* recital of stories prescribed for the intervals of performing the horse-sacrifice, the former, on the other hand, are intended only to create an interest in the meditations illustrated thereby.

Sūtras 25 and 26 show that persons who are devoted to the meditation of Brahma and who have achieved Brahma-Jñāna (the knowledge of Brahma) need not fall back upon rituals and ceremonies; the rituals and ceremonies form the spade-work and prepare the ground for the advent of knowledge; but no work is compulsory after knowledge has originated.

Sūtra 27 teaches that persons, desirous of knowing Brahma, should have perfect control over their desires, passions and actions.

Sūtras 28—31. The permission of all foods, to the meditators of Prāṇa, in the Chāndogya Śruti, is not a general permission, but should be restricted to cases where danger to life is apprehended; since a clean food makes a clean heart, and this view has the sanction of both Śruti and Smṛti.

Sūtras 32—35. Persons, not desiring emancipation, are enjoined to perform works of permanent obligation (नित्यकर्म्म.) Persons, desirous of emancipation, should also perform sacrifices, as they help in the purification of the heart and in the dawning of Brahma-Jñāna. The same kind of work has been enjoined upon both the classes of people, namely those who are desirous of emancipation and those who are desirous of heaven; thus the conclusion is drawn that a house-holder, who is engaged in Brahma-Vidyā should also practice religious rites to make his faith firmer; but in the case of an ascetic, whose heart has become proof against sin, no such rites are necessary.

Sūtras 36—39. Even persons, not belonging to any of the four prescribed orders of life (the four being the student, the householder, the ascetic and the Saṅnyāsī), are entitled to Brahma-Jñāna; this is supported by Śruti and tradition. Knowledge may also arise in consequence of meritorious deeds done in previous births; thus widowers who have not married again and persons too poor to maintain family or otherwise disqualified for married life, have not been debarred from Brahma-Vidyā; it is, however better to be within the folds of the four orders of life (आश्रम) than to be outside them.

Sūtras 40—43 say that a person, once accepting a special vow, either to remain as a life-long student in his preceptor's house, or to become an ascetic, or a Saṅnyāsī, should not fall from it. There can also be no expiation for such lapses and consequently such fallen persons can have not right to Brahma-Vidyā. One, accepting the vow of abstention from sexual pleasure to be observed till the last day of his life (*i.e.*., Naiṣṭhika Brahmacārī) must not break it, there is no expiation prescribed for such a lapse. Some are of opinion that this breach is a minor sin, and not a grave one; but whether it be a minor or a grave sin, such persons are to be excluded and debarred from Brahma-Vidyā, as both Smṛti and custom condemn such a lapse; but Upakurvāṇa Brahmacāris (*i.e.*, Brahmacāris who have taken the vow of continence for a certain period only), are allowed to marry on only performing a certain rite.

Sūtras 44—45 (A) say, by comparing the opinions of the sages Ātreya and Auḍulomi, and by referring to Śruti, that meditation, connected with the subordinate parts of a sacrifice, is to be performed by the priest, but the fruit goes to the sacrificer, who purchases with a fee the priest's labour.

Sūtras 46—48 state that the qualifications helpful towards the acquisition of Brahma-Vidyā, are like necessary for members of all the orders of life, (Āśramas.)

Sūtra 49 teaches that a man, practising Brahma-Vidyā, shall have the simplicity of a child and make no display of his learning.

Sūtras 50 and 51 say that dawning of the knowledge of

Self takes place in this life, if there be no obstruction from any counteracting cause. There is no fixed time (whether in this life or in the next life), when the fruit of the knowledge, in the shape of emancipation, will appear; as Śruti has ascertained that emancipation takes place as soon as the chain of bondage slips off by the exhaustion of Prārabdha (the operative Karma.)

पुरुषार्थोऽतः शब्दादिति वादरायणः ॥१॥

[The result of Brahma-Vidyā is stated.]

पुरुषार्थः (object of human pursuit; *here* the chief object, *i.e.*, emancipation), **अत** (from this; from Brahma-Vidyā), **शब्दात्** (from Śruti), **इति** (this *is the opinion*), **बादरायणः** (the sage Bādarāyaṇa.)

Explanation—Man's chief object of pursuit, namely, salvation, follows from Brahma-Vidyā (meditation on Brahma), because Śruti says so; this is the opinion of the sage Bādarāyaṇa.

For reference vide—

ब्रह्मविदाप्नोति परम्" (He who knows Brahma, attains the Highest.)

Taittirīya, Chap. II, 1, 2.

शेषत्वात् पुरुषार्थवादो यथाऽन्येष्विति जैमिनिः॥२॥

[An objection is raised against Sūtra 1.]

शेषत्वात् (because of being only a concomitant requisite), **पुरुषार्थ** (**पुरुषार्थलाभवचन**) the statement of the attainment of the chief object of life *by Brahma-Vidyā*), **अर्थवादः** (exhortation); **यथा** (as), **अन्येषु** (in cases of other sacrificial materials), **इति** (this), **जैमिनिः** (the sage Jaimini.)

Explanation—The statement, that the reward of Brahma-Jñāna (knowledge of Self), is the highest good, does not mean that such knowledge by itself yields any real fruit; but the statement is only an exhortation to the performance of sacrifices. The knowledge of Self, says Jaimini, is useful only so far as it produces, in the performer, a belief in his extramundane existence to enable him to enjoy the rewards of his sacrifices. Thus, in the opinion of Jaimini, Self-knowledge can produce no fruit independently of the sacrifice with which it is conjoined. The statement that it yields any fruit by itself is only an exhortation to purification of the sacrificer. Like other material requisites of a sacrifice, the purification of the sacrificer is a necessary concomitant factor; for without this purification he would not be assured of his surviving the body and enjoying the fruit of his sacrifices in a brighter world after death.

[Jaimini's view, stated in Sūtra 2, are elaborated in Sūtras 3—7, which are refuted later on.]

आचारदर्शनात् ॥३॥

[The objection raised in Sūtra 2 is strengthened.]

आचार (practice), **दर्शनात्** (as it is found in Śruti.)

Explanation—From Śruti we learn that persons, like Janaka, after the attainment of the knowledge of Self, continue to perform religious sacrifices. The knowledge of Self is therefore only supplementary to the principal thing, sacrifice.

For reference in the Śruti vide—

"जनको ह वै वैदेहो बहुदक्षिणेन यज्ञेनेजे।"

(Janaka, the king of Videha, performed a sacrifice in which he gave away high remunerations to the priest.)

Bṛhadāraṇyaka, Chap. III, 1, 1.

तच्छ्रुतेः॥४॥

[The objection raised in Sūtra 2 is further strengthened.]

तत् (that; that knowledge is subsidiary and supplementary to sacrifice, **श्रुतेः** (from Śruti.)

Explanation—The statement that knowledge is subsidiary and supplementary to sacrifice can also be understood directly from Śruti.

For reference vide the Śruti—

"यदेव विद्यया करोति श्रद्धयोपनिषदा तदेव वीर्य्यवत्तरं भवति।"

(Whatever *sacrifice*, one performs with the aid of meditation, faith and knowledge, becomes all the more effective.)

Chāndogya, Chap. I, 1, 10.

समन्वारम्भणात् ॥५॥

[The objection begun in Sūtra 2 is continued.]

समन्वारम्भणात् (because of accompanying together; as they jointly follow the sacrificer to produce their effects.)

Explanation—As both, knowledge and work, of the departed soul follow him jointly at death to produce their effects, it is concluded that knowledge is not independent of work (sacrificial rites.)

"तं विद्याकर्म्मणी समन्वारभेते।"

(Both, knowledge and work, follow him jointly *at death to produce their effects*.)

Bṛhadāraṇyaka, Chap. IV, 4, 2.

तद्वतो विधानात् ॥६॥

[The objection, begun in Sūtra 2, is continued.]

तद्वतः (four one possessed of the knowledge of Self: तत्—that, the knowledge of Self; तद्वान्—one who is possessed of the knowledge of self; on who has acquired the knowledge of Self), विधानात् (because of injunction of work in Śruti.)

Explanation—Śruti enjoins the duty of performing sacrifice upon one who has already acquired the knowledge of Self; knowledge therefore must be considered supplementary to work.

Śruti enjoins, that after learning the Vedas and returning from the house of the preceptor one is to settle in household life and perform religious and secular duties; this shows that work is the direct object of Vedic injunctions and knowledge is only auxiliary to that work.

For reference vide the Śruti—

"आचार्य्यकुलाद्वेदमधीत्य यथाविधानं गुरो कर्म्मातिशेषेणाभिसमावृत्य कुटुम्बे शुचौ देशो स्वाध्यायमधीयानः।"

(On returning from the family of the preceptor after having studied the Vedas and having duly rendered all services to him, he is to return and settle, in a sacred place, amongst his relatives, and continue the study of the Vedas.)

Chāndogya, Chap. VIII, 15, 1.

नियमाच्च ॥७॥

[The argument, begun in Sūtra 2, is concluded here.]

नियमात् (because of compulsory injunction), **च** (also.)

Explanation—That work is the main object of life and knowledge is supplementary to it, is understood also from the compulsory injunction in Śruti to do household works, which are thus not left optional to the householder.

For reference in the Śruti vide—

"कुर्व्वन्नेवेह कर्म्माणि जिजीविषेच्छतं समाः"

(Let one with to live a hundred years here and perform all duties *both religious and secular.*)

Iśopaniṣad, 2.

अधिकोपदेशात्तु वादरायणस्यैवं तद्दर्शनात् ॥८॥

[Objections, raised in Sūtras 2—7, are now being refuted one by one. This Sūtra refutes Sūtra 2.]

अधिक (a Supreme Being), **उपदेशात्** (from the statement in Śruti), **तु** (but), **वादरायणस्य** (of Bādarāyaṇa), **एवं** (such *is the opinion*), **तद्दर्शनात्** (because there is teaching in Śruti *about such a Being*.)

Explanation—From Śruti it is known that Self (the knowledge of whom is the subject-matter of our present discussion) is stated to be One, Who is other than and superior to the individual soul, for whom are prescribed the social and religious duties. Hence the knowledge of this Self, on the part of the performer of a sacrifice, is not intended to confirm his faith in his surviving the body after death; on the contrary, the term 'Self' here stands for the Supreme Being, the realisation of Whom is the *Summum bonum* of life. This is the view of Bādarāyaṇa.

For reference in the Śruti vide—

"एष सर्व्वेश्वरः," "अन्तः प्रविष्टः शास्ता जनानां" "सर्वस्येशानः", "तं त्वौपनिषदं पुरुषं पृच्छामि," "सर्व्वे वेदा यत् पदमामनन्ति"

(He is the Supreme Ruler of all, entered into all hearts, Governor of all individuals, Lord of all; I want to know that Person Who is alluded to in all the Upaniṣads, Whom all the Vedas refer to.)

तुल्यन्तु दर्शनम् ॥९॥

[The refutation of the objections is continued; this Sūtra specially refutes Sūtra 3.]

तुल्यम् (of equal weight), तु (but), दर्शनम् (the declaration in Śruti.)

Explanation—There are indeed found in Śruti instances of sacrifices being performed by enlightened soul like Janaka, but there are also declarations, of equal weight, to the effect that performance of sacrifices is quite useless and redundant for the enlightened (*i.e.,* those who have known Brahma.)

So it cannot be asserted on the strength of the instances of Janaka and others like him, that knowledge is to be considered as secondary to the sacrifice.

For reference in the Śruti vide—

"किमर्था वयमध्येष्यामहे किमर्था वयं यक्ष्यामहे येषां नोऽयं लोकः"

(To what purpose should we study and to what purpose should we perform sacrifices, we who are seekers of this Brahma-Loka.)

असार्वत्रिकी ॥१०॥

[The refutation of the objections is continued. This Sūtra specially refutes Sūtra 4.]

असार्व त्रिकी (not universal; not applicable everywhere.)

Explanation—The statement of the Śruti, referred to in Sūtra 4, to the effect that the combination of meditation and sacrifice makes the sacrifice effective, is not applicable everywhere.

The above-mentioned statement of the Śruti does not refer to meditations in general, but only to the Udgītha Vidyā, which forms the subject-matter of the discourse concerned.

विभागः शतवत् ॥११॥

[This Sūtra specially refutes Sūtra 5.]

विभागः (division), **शतवत्** (like a hundred.)

Explanation—From the statement of the Śruti, referred to in Sūtra 5, to the effect that knowledge and works accompany the departed soul jointly, it does not follow that they produce a joint effect; but the statement rather indicates that they produce their respective effects separately; the division being just like a hundred rupees taken together, but divided separately between two persons according to their respective shares.

अध्ययनमात्रवतः ॥१२॥

[This Sūtra specially refutes Sūtra 6.]

अध्ययनमात्रवतः (of one who has only read *the Vedas*.)

Explanation—The quotation from Śruti, referred to in Sūtra 6, speaks of one who has only read the Vedas with the preceptor, but not of a person who has acquired the knowledge of Self by his studies and practices.

So this injunction for household duties is binding upon persons other than the seekers after Brahma by meditation and knowledge. All book-learned men are not earnest seekers after truth (विविदिषु.)

नाविशेषात् ॥१३॥

[The Sūtra specially refutes Sūtra 7.]

न (*compulsion does* not *apply*), **अविशेषात्** (because there is no special mention.)

Explanation—The compulsory household duties, referred to in Sūtra 7, are restricted to the ordinary run of men, the seekers after Brahma being exempted from them; because there is no specific mention of the latter in connection with that injunction.

Had it meant to include the searchers, the passage must have clearly and specially said so.

स्तुतयेऽनुमतिर्व्वा ॥१४॥

[This also refutes Sūtra 7.]

स्तुतये (for praise or commendation) **अनुमतिः** (permission, injunction), वा (or rather.)

Explanation—Or rather the injunction is intended to eulogise **विविदिषा** (search after knowledge); in other words, it is permissive injunction which adds to its glory.

The precept of the Śruti, referred to in Sūtra 7 and discussed in Sūtra 13, may be treated in another way also, namely, the injunction of doing works aims at glorification of the knowledge; in other words, the passage shows the glory of knowledge by stating that a person having the intuition of Brahman, may do all works and yet remain unaffected thereby; as can be understood from, the subsequent part of the same passage.

For the subsequent part of the passage, vide—

"न कर्म्म लिप्यते नरे" (The work does not tarnish the man.)

Iśopaniṣad 2.

कामकारेण चैके ॥१५॥

[The argument in refutation is continued.]

कामकारेण (according to his own liking), **च** (moreover), **एके** (some *Śrutis enjoin.*)

Explanation—Moreover, some Śrutis enjoins, that a person, who seeks the knowledge of Self, may renounce the world at will. Hence it is deduced that sacrificial rites, which are enjoined upon householders, are not binding upon the Seeker of Knowledge.

For reference vide the Śruti—

"किं प्रजया करिष्यामो येषां नोऽयमात्माऽयं लोकः।"

(What shall we do with offspring ? To us this Self is all this world.)

Bṛhadāraṇyaka, Chap. IV, 4, 22.

The household religious duties are evidently redundant for those who turn their back upon domestic and social entanglements for the sake of the dear Lord.

उपमर्द्दश्च॥१६॥

[The previous argument is continued.]

उपमर्द्द (complete annihilation; putting an end to all actions), **च** (too; again.)

Explanation—Again, far from being a part of work, Vidyā puts an end to all works—all obligatory duties.

For reference vide the Śruti—

"भिद्यते हृदयग्रन्थिश्छिद्यन्ते सर्व्वसंशयाः।
क्षीयन्ते चास्य कर्म्माणि तस्मिन् दृष्टे परावरे॥"

(Brahma, in both His superior and inferior aspects, being

realised, the knot of the heart [egotism] is cut down, all doubts are dispelled, and works are destroyed.)

Muṇḍakopaniṣad, Chap. II, 2, 9.

ऊर्द्ध्वरेतस्सु च शब्दे हि ॥१७॥

[The previous argument is continued.]

ऊर्द्ध्वरेतस्सु (in that stages of life where all the energies have an upward flow; the states of those who have renounced the world or turned recluse), **च** (moreover), **शब्दे** (in Śruti), **हि** (since.)

Explanation—Moreover knowledge, divorced from work, is enjoined to be sought for when all the energies have an upward flow, *i.e.*, in those Āśramas or stages of life in which one renounces the world and resorts to forest life. Since mention of such states is made in Śruti.

This shows that in a high state of life knowledge is to be sought for without the aid of work.

For reference in the Śruti vide—

"त्रयो धर्म्मस्कन्धाः.... सर्व्वं एते पुण्यलोका भवन्ति, ब्रह्मसंस्थोऽमृतत्वमेति।"

(There are three divisions of pious conduct,...all these *three classes of conduct* lead to the attainment of the sacred worlds—*the heavens or the abodes of the gods*; but one who dwells in Brahma *i.e.* devoted to Brahma, attains immortality, *i.e.,* salvation.)

Chāndogya, Chap. II, 23, I.

"तत् य इत्थं विदुर्ये चेमेऽरण्ये श्रद्धां तप इत्युपासत तेऽर्च्चिषमभिसम्भवन्ति।"

(Those who are acquainted with the secret of meditation by means of Five Fires, and also those who meditate in the forest with faith and austerity, attain the passge of light.)

Chāndogya, Chap. V, 10, 1.

परामर्शं जैमिनिरचोदनाच्चापवदति हि॥१८॥

[An objection to Sūtra 17, is raised.]

परामर्श (a passing allusion), **जैमिनिः** (the sage Jaimini), **अचोदनात्** (because there is no clear injunction in Śruti) **च** (also, rather), **अपवदति** (condemns), **हि** (clearly, certainly.)

Explanation—The sage Jaimini argues, that the passages in Śruti, regarding the stage of ascetic, are only a passing allusion of what sometimes happens in the world, and not by way of injunction; because there is no clear direction in Śruti to that effect; Śruti rather clearly condemns the life of asceticism.

The contention of the sage Jaimini is, that the passages, that may be brought forward to prove the superiority of an ascetic life, do not serve the intended purpose; they only state the fact that men sometimes have recourse to the order of an ascetic by renouncing the worldly life; but they do not indicate any injunction, because they contain no words in the form of injunction; on the other hand there are scriptural passages directly condemning the life of an ascetic.

For reference in the Śruti vide—

"वीरहा वा एष देवानां योऽग्निमुद्वासयते"

(An enemy to the maintainers of the gods is he, who does away with the sacrifical fire, *i.e., who gives up the life of a householder*.)

The allusion is to the belief that the gods are fed and supported by daily libations to the sacrificial fire.

अनुष्ठेयं वादरायणः साम्यश्रुतेः॥१९॥

[The objection, raised in Sūtra 18, is refuted.]

अनुश्रेयं (to be practised; to be followed), **वादरायणः** (the sage Bādarāyaṇa), **साम्यश्रुतेः** (on account of parallel statement in Śruti.)

Explanation—Ācārya Bādarāyaṇa opines, that the stage of an ascetic life is to be followed on account of parallel statements in Śruti in favour of both the stages of life, namely that of a householder, as well as that of an ascetic. In other words, the objection, raised against asceticism, may equally be levelled against the householder's stage, for there is also no direct injunction for the latter, in the Śruti under discussion. So asceticism is no less worth following than the householder's life.

विधिर्व्वा धारणवत् ॥२०॥

[The argument, commenced in Sūtra 19 to refute the objection raised in Sūtra 18, is continued.]

विधिः (injunction), **वा** (or rather) '**धारणवत्** (like the holding *of the sacrificial wood.*)

Explanation—Or the statement of the Śruti, referred to in Śruti 19, is rather to be understood in the light of an injunction and not of a mere passing allusion or a statement of fact, regarding the stage of an ascetic life. The case is analogous to that of the holding of the sacrificial fire wood, in offering liabations to the gods in the Mahāpitṛ yajña, above the ladle containing the libation; in this case, though there is no word indicative of direct injunction, the sage Jaimini himself concludes in his Pūrva-Mīmāṁsā that this statement—holding the sacrificial fire wood—carries the weight of an injunction [here '**धारयति**'(holds) is to be interpreted as '**धारयेत**' (ought to hold.)]

For reference to the Mahāpitṛ Yajña, vide—

"अधस्तात् समिधं धारयन्ननुद्रवेदुपरि देवेभ्यो धारयति"

(For *manes* or the fathers let one run on holding the sacrificial wood below *the ladle*, as one holds it above for the gods.)

For Jaimini's Sūtra vide—

"विधिस्तु धारणेऽपूर्व्वत्वात्।"

(But it is an injunction in the care of the holding, as it has not been enjoined anywhere before.)

[It is to be noted here, that there are also passages, in Śruti, which directly enjoin the stage of an ascetic life.]

For reference Vide

"ब्रह्मचर्य्यं समाप्य गृही भवेत्, गृहीभूत्वा वनीभवेत्, वनीभूत्वा प्रव्रजेत्, यदिवेतरथा ब्रह्मच्य्यादेव प्रव्रजेद् गृहाद्वा वनाद्वा।"

(Having completed the stage of the student life he is to become a householder; after having become a householder he is to become an ascetic in the forest; after having been an ascetic he is to roam about as a Saṁnyāsī (a wandering monk), or else he may roam about as a Saṁnyāsī either *directly* from his student life, or from the household-life, or from the forest-life.)

Jāvālopaniṣad, Chap. IV.

स्तुतिमात्रमुपादानादिति चेन्नापूर्व्वत्वात्॥२१॥

[This Sūtra states that certain texts forming parts of Vidyā, are not mere praises, but themselves enjoin the meditation.]

स्तुतिमात्रम् (mere eulogy; mere praise), **उपादानात्** (because of being the materials; because of their being supplements to the sacrificial rites), **इति** (this), **चेत्** (if); **न** (no, it is not so), **अपूर्व्वत्वात्** (because of their newness; as there are found no injunctions previous to them.)

[This Sūtra consists of two parts, namely, an objection and its reply. The objection-portion is:—**स्तुतिमात्रमुपादानादिति चेत्**; and the reply-portion is:— **न, अपूर्व्वत्वात्**.]

Explanation—If it be argued that the texts, indicative of Vidyās connected with sacrificial rites, are merely intended for eulogising those rites, by reason of their dealing with the sential materials of those rites; then our reply is, thus such an argument is not reasonable, as these texts treat of something quite new, not previously treated of anywhere else in Śruti, and therefore they should be regarded in the light of Vidhi (injunctions) rather than Anuvāda (glorifications.) For instance, the text dealing with the Udgītha-meditation which is connected with the sacrificial rite known as the Udgītha, treats of a matter quite new and not introduce before. Moreover, there has been no injunction for this meditation before this passage. Hence the text cannot be regarded as a mere Anuvāda of that injunction, but is itself indicative of the Vidhi for the Udgītha-meditation.

For the passage, reffered to vide—

स एष रसानां रसतमः परमः पराद्धर्योऽष्ठमो य उद्गीथः"

(The *Udgītha or 'Om'* is the best of all the essences *previously enumerated—the earth, the water, the cereals, the man, the speech, the Ṛk or metrical utterances, the Sāma hymns, and* the eighth and last, the Udgītha or 'Om' following in the order of their increasing importance.)

Chāndogya, Chap. I, 1, 3.

This 'Om' in the Udgītha-Vidyā is to be meditated upon in the light of the Supreme Soul.

भावशब्दाच्च॥२२॥

[The argument, commenced in Sūtra 21, is concluded.]

भावशब्दात् (from words indicative of existence of *injunction* in Śruti),] च (also, moreover.)

Explanation—Moreover, from words indicative of injunction in Śruti it is known that there is directed injunction for meditation on the Udgītha.

Hence it is concluded that the expression 'This is the best of all the essences', in the passage quoted under the preceding Sūtra, is not a mere laudatory expression, but it amounts to a part of the injunction for the Udgītha meditation.

For the direct injunction, referred to, vide—

"उद्गीथमुपामसीत।" (The Udgītha is to be meditated on.)

Chāndogya, Chap. I, 1, 1.

पारिप्लवार्था इति चेन्नविशेषितत्वात्॥२३॥

[The purpose of narration of stories in the Upaniṣads is stated in this Sūtra and in the next one.]

परिप्लवार्थाः (for the purpose of recitation by the priest to the sacrificer—**यजमान**—and his relatives for some days during the performance of the Aśvamedha or horse-sacrifice), **इति** (this), **चेत्** (if); **न** (no, they are not for that purpose), **विशेषितत्वाते** (because of specification; as specified stories and not others, have been prescribed for that purpose.)

[This Sūtra consists of two parts, namely, an objection and its reply. The objection-portion is:—**पारिप्लवार्था इति चेत्:** and the reply is:—**न, विशेषितत्वात्**]

Explanation—It may be said that narrations of stories in the Upaniṣads are intended to be recited by the priest, to the kind performing the Aśvamedha-sacrifice and his relatives, at intervals during the performance of the sacrifice. To this we reply that they are not for that purpose; as some specified stories (other than those narrated in the Upaniṣads), such as those of Vaivasvata Manu and others have been singled out for that purpose in Śruti.

For reference vide—

पारिप्लवमाचक्षीत...मनुर्वैवस्वतो राजा"

(*The priest is* to tell the prescribed stories *to the King and his relatives, one such story runs thus*—

The King Manu, son of Vivasvān---)

तथा चैकवाक्यतोपबन्धात् ॥२४॥

[The discussion, commenced in Sūtra 23, is concluded here.]

तथा (the case being so; the stories of the King Manu and others being specified for the purpose of recitation during the Aśwamedha sacrifice), **च** (also), **एकवाक्यता-उपबन्धात्** (being connected as the part of a whole teaching.)

Explanation—The story of King Manu and others being specified for the purpose of recitation during the Aśvamedha sacrifice (as stated in Sūtra 23), the stories stated in the Upaniṣads, such as those of the royal sage Janaka, of the sage Yājñavalkya and his wife, Maitreyī, of Jānaśruti etc., are to be connected with the teachings of the Upaniṣads as their parts. Consequently those stories are not meant to be treated as recitations adding to the merit of the sacrifice, but, on the contrary, are to be regarded as essential parts of Brahma-Vidyā. These latter stories are introduced only to facilitate an intelligent grasp of the subject.

For instance, in the story of Yājñavalkya and Maitreyī, Yājñavalkya says to Maitreyī:—

"आत्मा वा अरे द्रष्टव्यः श्रोतव्यो मन्तव्यो निदिध्यासितव्यः"

(The translation and reference are given under Sūtra 19, IV, Chapter I.).

अतएवं चाग्नीन्धनाद्यनपेक्षा ॥२५॥

[This Sūtra states that the seeker of Brahma may dispense with secrificial rites.]

अतएव (therefore; from the discussion it is deduced); **च** (also), **अग्नीन्धनादि** (fire, fire-wood and so on), **अनपेक्षा** (*has* not to depend on.)

Explanation—From the discussions made hitherto it is deduced that one, devoted to Brahma, has not to depend for his salvation, on fire, fire-wood and so on (*i.e.*, on sacrificial performances); these are superfluous to him.

As a person, devoted to the meditation of Brahma, is stated, in Śruti, to attain immortality and not any of the rewards arising from sacrificial rites, he is not required to have recourse to sacrificial works to be performed with fire, fire-wood and, so on.

For reference vide the Śruti—

"ब्रह्मसंस्थोऽमृतत्वमेति"

(One, devoted to Brahma, attains immortality.)

Chāndogya Chap. II, 23, 1.

सर्व्वापेक्षा च यज्ञादिश्रुतेरश्ववत्॥२६॥

[This Sūtra says that sacrificial works and the like are necessary for origination of knowledge.]

सर्व्वापेक्षा (necessity of all works *prescribed in the scripture*), **च** (also), **यज्ञादिश्रुतेः** (from the scriptural statement of sacrifices and the like), **अश्ववत्** (like a horse; analogous to a pony.)

Explanation—There is necessity of all works, prescribed in the scripture, for the origination of the knowledge of Self, as can be understood from the scriptural statement of sacrifices and the like; but knowledge, having once been attained, requires no help from external works for the production of its result, namely salvation. The case is analogous to a pony, whose help is required until the place of destination is reached; but it may be dispensed with after the journey has been accomplished.

For reference vide the Śruti—

"तमेतं वेदानुवचनेन ब्राह्मणा विविदिषन्ति यज्ञेन दानेन तपसाऽनाशकेन।"

(Brāhmaṇas seek to know Him by the study of the Vedas, and by sacrifices, gifts, penance and renunciation.)

Bṛhadāraṇyaka, Chap. IV, 4, 22.

शमदमाद्युपेतः स्यात्तथापि तु तद्विधेस्तदङ्गतया तेषामवश्यानुष्ठेयत्वात्॥२७॥

[A person, desirous of knowing Brahma, must take to the practice of the control of his passions, sensations and actions, and the like.]

शमदमाद्युपेतः (possessed of the control of the internal and the external Indriyas and the like), **स्यात्** (has to be), **तथापि** (still), **तु** (but), **तद्विधेस्तदङ्गतया** (as the practice of that is prescribed as a part of the acquisition of the knowledge of Self, **तद्विधे**—of the injunction about that; तदङ्गतया because of being a part of that; as it is prescribed to be a part of that), तेषामवश्यानुष्ठेयत्वात् (because they are certainly to be practised; because they are indispensable.)

Explanation—Though the performance of sacrifices and other works is considered necessary so far only as they are conducive to the knowledge of Self; still the seeker of Brahma-Vidyā must be re-inforced by habits of self-control, mastery over his passions and desires, etc., which are *sine quanon* of his success because they (the virtues) are certainly to be practised, being prescribed as a necessary concomitant of the acquisition of knowledge of Self.

For reference vide the Śruti—

"तस्मादेवं विच्छान्तो दान्त उपरतस्तितिक्षुः समाहितो भूत्वात्मन्येवात्मानं पश्यति।"

(Therefore a seeker of Brahma, having conquered the internal and external Indriyas, and being withdrawn within himself, patient and concentrated, finds the Self in his own self.)

Bṛhadāraṇyaka, Chap. IV, 4, 23.

सर्व्वान्नानुमतिश्च प्राणात्यये तद्दर्शनात्॥२८॥

[This and the subsequent three Sūtras show what kind of food is to be eaten.]

सर्व्वान्नानुमतिः (सर्व्व-अन्न-अनुमतिः, permission to take all food च (only), प्राणात्यये (in the event of danger of life), तद्दर्शनात् (as it is shown by Śruti.)

Explanation—Permission for eating all kinds of food is to be availed of only in the event of danger to life, as it has been shown by Śruti.

The Chāndogya Śruti says, that to him who meditates on Prāṇa, there is no food that is not eatable, *i.e.*, he may eat any food whatsoever; but it is not an injunction prescribed for all times, this is to be understood as a permission to be availed of only in the contingency of death from hunger; as has been shown by the same Śruti, chapter I, part 10, in the story of the sage, Uṣasti by name; he being famished saved himself by partaking of the beans left on the plate by a keeper of elephants, but would by no means accept the drink offered by the latter. The sage justified his conduct by saying 'I would not have lived, if I had not eaten the beans, but water I can do without at present.'

For reference vide the Śruti—

न ह वा एवंविदि किञ्चनानन्नं भवति।"

(To him who meditates on this *prāna,* there is no food forbidden.]

Chāndogya, Chap. V, 2, 1.

अबाधाच्च ॥२९॥

[The topic commenced in Sūtra 28 is continued.]

अबाधात् (as there is no contrary statement *anywhere in Śruti*), **च** (also; moreover.)

Explanation—Moreover, clean food should generally be taken, as there is no contrary statement, anywhere in Śruti, to the purifying effect of clean food.

There is nowhere any passage, in Śruti, contradicting the passage of the Chāndogya Śruti, which declares that clean food makes our nature pure.

For the passage of the Chāndogya, vide:—

"आहारशुद्धौ सत्वशुद्धिः।"

(A clean food makes a clean heart.)

Chāndogya, Chap. VII, 326, 2.

अपि च स्मर्य्यते॥३॥

[The previous topic is continued.]

अपि (also), **च** (moreover), **स्मर्य्यते** (is prescribed by Smṛti.)

Explanation—Moreover, Smṛti also has prescribed so in the matter of food. For the Smṛti vide—

"जीवितात्ययमापन्नो योऽन्नमत्ति यतस्ततः।"
लिप्यते न स पापेन पद्मपत्रमिवाम्भसा॥"

(He, who eats food procured from any place and every plac, when life is imperilled is not stained by sin, as a lotus-leaf *is not wetted* by water.)

From this it is inferred that generally clean food is to be taken in every case save and except the case of starvation.

शब्दश्चातोऽकामकारे॥३१॥

[The previous topic is discussed and concluded here.]

शब्दः (a passage in Śruti, a scriptural passage), **च** (also), **अतः** (hence; and again), **अकामकारे** (to prevent undue license: **कामकार**—(undue license.)

Explanation—And again there are also scriptural passages forbidding men to take undue liberty in the matter of food and drink.

The text, quoted in Sūtra 28, 'To one who meditates on this, there is no food forbidden', is a mere phrase in praise of Prāṇa (**अर्थवाद**), and not an injunction (**विधि**) like the injunction of self-control etc. (**शमदमादि**.) A permission should, never be mistaken for an injunction.

For a scriptural passage, referred to vide—

"तस्माद् ब्राह्मणः सुरां न पिवेत्।" (A Brahmin, therefore, must not drink wine.)

Kaṭha-Saṁhitā.

विहितत्वाच्चाश्रमकर्म्मापि॥३२॥

[This and the subsequent three Sūtras show who are required to perform sacrifices and do other prescribed duties.]

विहितत्वात् (as they are enjoined by the scripture), **च**

(moreover), आश्रमकर्म्म (the works prescribed for the different orders of life), अपि (also.)

Explanation—Moreover, नित्यकर्म्म (the permanent obligatory duties), prescribed for the different orders of life, should not be given up by one, who has not salvation for the immediate object of his pursuit. [Cf. Sūtra 26 of this section.]

To him the Śruti says—

"यावज्जीवमग्निहोत्रं जुहोति।"

(As long as he lives he must offer libations to the sacrificial fire.)

Taittirīya, Anuvāka 50.

सहकारित्वेन च ॥३३॥

[The topic commenced in Sūtra 32 is continued.]

सहकारित्वेन (as an auxiliary), च (and.)

Explanation—And those, who are desirous of emancipation, should also perform, religious rites as a help to Enlightenment [vide Sūtra 26 of this section.]

For reference in the Śruti vide—

"तमेतं वेदानुवचनेन ब्राह्मण विविदिषन्ति यज्ञेन दानेन तपसा।"

(For translation and reference, vide Sūtra 26 of this section.)

सर्व्वथापि तएवोभयलिङ्गात् ॥३४॥

[The previous topic is continued.]

सर्व्वथा (in every respect; in both the cases), अपि (also), ते (they; the sacrificial works), एव (certainly; and nothing else), उभयलिङ्गात् (because they are marked requisites from both standpoints.)

Explanation—In every respect, whether viewed as duties incumbent on a householder or as practices auxiliary to

Enlightenment, the sacrificial works, prescribed to be performed, are recognised to be the same and not different because they are indispensable requisites for both orders of life—as permanent duties for a householder and as auxiliary aids to meditation for a Sannyāsī.

अनभिभवं च दर्शयति ॥३५॥

[The previous topic is concluded here.]

अनभिभवं (invincibility), **च** (also), **दर्शयति** (Śruti shows.)

Explanation—Śruti shows also that knowledge becomes invincible by the practice of these religious rites.

By practising religious rites prescribed in Śruti, sins, which might otherwise get the better of knowledge, are subdued. Thus Śruti shows, that by performing religious rites, knowledge becomes brighter and clearer, being purged of all impurities or sins. The conclusion is that the householders, even if possessed of knowledge, should continue to perform religious rites, if only to consolidate knowledge; but upon ascetics, whose knowledge has already become invincible against sins, no such rites are binding.

For reference in the Śruti vide—

"धर्म्मेण पापमपनुदति"

(By performing religious rites one wipes away one's sins.)

Taittirīya Nārāyaṇa Anuvāka 5.

अन्तरा चापि तु तद्दृष्टेः॥३६॥

[This and the following three Sūtras show, what class of persons are entitled to Brahma-Vidyā, and whether persons, not holding any of the four prescribed orders life, but occupying a position intermediate between any two consecutive orders, are not debarred from the same.]

अन्तरा (*persons standing* between), **च** (and), **अपितु** (also) **तद्दृष्टेः** (as it is seen *in Śruti*.)

Explanation—And persons, standing between two consecutive stages of life, may also acquire knowledge, as, such instances are seen in Śruti.

Persons, not belonging to any one of the four prescribed orders of life, but standing apart (अनाश्रमी)—occupying a position intermediate between any two consecutive orders, are also entitled to Brahma-Vidyā, as is seen in the cases of Raikka, who is stated, in the Chāndogya Śruti (Chap. IV, 1), to be already blessed with Brahma-Vidyā, and of Vācacnavi, and others.

अपिच स्मर्य्यते॥३७॥

[The previous topic is continued.]

अपि (too, also), च (moreover), समर्य्यते (is stated in Smṛti.)

Explanation—Moreover, it is stated also in Smṛti that persons, not belonging to any one of the four prescribed orders of life, acquired Brahma-Vidyā.

It is on record in the Mahābhārata how Samvarta and others who paid no regard to the duties incumbent on the different orders of life, went naked and afterwards become great saints. The Great Bhīṣma is also an instance in point.

For direct sanction in Smṛti, vide—

"जप्येनैव तु संसिध्येद्ब्राह्मणो नात्र संशयः।
कुर्य्यादन्यन्न वा कुर्य्यान्मैत्रो ब्राह्मण उच्यते॥"

(There is no doubt that a Brāhmaṇa attains the final success only by the practice of continuously repeating the prayer [जप]; it matters little whether he performs other prescribed duties or not; one, who is friendly to all, is virtually a Brāhmaṇa.)

Manu-Saṁhitā Chap. II, 87.

विशेषानुग्रहश्च॥३८॥

[The previous topic is continued.]

विशेषानुग्रहः (special advantage; advantage acruing from extraordinary good works done in the previous life), च (also.)

Explanation—Persons, born with the special advantage of having made great spiritual progress in previous life, have every facility for speedy success (सिद्धि) in this.

Some persons appear to have been born as gifted with special merit in the shape of natural propensity towards attaining final emancipation; this occurs on account of their good works in the previous lives; they need not go through the prescribed duties of the different orders of life.

For reference vide the Smṛti—

"प्रयत्नाद् यतमानस्तु योगी संशुद्धकिल्विषः।
अनेकजन्मसंसिद्धस्ततो याति परां गतिम्॥"

(A devotee, persevering with steady application, being purged of all sins, and thus perfected through repeated births, attains the highest goal.)

Bhagavat Gītā, Chap. VI, 45.

अतस्त्वितरज्ज्यायो लिङ्गात् ॥३९॥

[The previous topic is concluded here.]

अतः (from this; than this; than the intermediate state mentioned above), **तु** (but), **इतरत्** (the other; the state of belonging to a prescribed order of life), **ज्यायः** (better), **लिङ्गात्** (from *such* indication in the scripture.)

Explanation—But the choice of and entrance upon any one of the four prescribed orders of life, is better than standing apart (**अनाश्रमित्व**); as can be understood from such indication in the scripture. For reference in the scripture, vide the Smṛti—

"अनाश्रमी न तिष्ठेत दिनमेकमपि द्विजः"

(Let a twice-born one stay not for even a day, outside the prescribed four orders of life.)

N.B.—Widowers who have not married again, persons who are too poor to marry and those who are forced by circumstances not to enter into wedlock, and have not yet renounced the world, come under the purview of Sūtras 36—39. They are however, ranked socially much lower than others who regularly discharge the duties of the four orders of life.

तद्भूतस्य तु नातद्भावो जैमिनेरपि नियमात्तद्रूपाभावेभ्यः॥४०॥

[This and the subsequent three Sūtras discuss whether persons, fallen from the vow of life-long Brahmacarya (studentship), of Vānaprastha (retirement to the forest life) or of Saṁnyasi (renunciation), are entitled to cultivate Brahma-Vidyā.

तद्भूतस्य (of one who has become that), **तु** (again), **न** (not, never), **अतद्भावः** (lapse from that stage) **जैमिनेः** (*according to* Jaimini), **अपि** (even), **नियमात्** (because of the strict rule), **तद्रूपाभावेभ्यः** (because there is no statement permitting it and because it is against custom, and so on.)

Explanation—Again, in the cases of persons who have once taken the vow of an ascetic, or the vow of retirement to forest, or the vow of life-long studentship, the Scriptures will not tolerate the lapse from that life involving, as it does, a wilful dereliction of duties; because there is no statement sanctioning such lapses, becauses it is against usage, and lastly because there can be no reasonable excuse for such lapse. This is the opinion of Jaimini too.

So such a person, if once fallen from his own order, cannot have any right for the culture of Brahma-Vidyā (vide Sūtra 43 next.)

For reference vide:-

"ब्रह्मचार्य्याचार्य्यकुलवासी....अत्यन्तमात्मानमाचार्य्यकुलेऽवसादायन्॥"

(One, who takes the vow, of life-long studentship in the house of his preceptor must live there till the last day of his life.)

Chāndogya, Chap. II, 23, 1.

Also:—अरण्यमीयान्न ततः पुनरेयात्।"

(Once retiring to the forest, one should never return to household-life.)

"सन्यस्याग्निं न पुनरावर्त्तयेत्।"

(An ascetic should not stir up the household fire again after having once renounced it.)

न चाधिकारिकमपि पतनानुमानात्तदयोगात्॥४१॥

[The previous discussion is continued.]

न (not), **च** (and), **आधिकारिकम्** (the chapter of the Pūrva-Mīmāṁsā on rights, previleges, and expiations), **अपि** (also), **पतनानुमानात्** (because Smṛti treats it as a fall), **तदयोगात्** (**तत्-अयोगात्**, as not deserving that; as not deserving expiation.)

Explanation—Expiations prescribed in the chapter of rights and privileges, of the Pūrva-Mīmāṁsā, are not also for the Naiṣṭhikas (those who have taken the vow to live and study for ever in the house of their preceptors); they are meant only for the Upakurvāṇas (those students who return to their home after finishing their education), because Smṛti declares that the fall of the former deserves no expiation.

In the Chapter of Pūrva-Mīmāṁsā, where there are injunctions regarding privileges, there is no expiation prescribed for a person, who slips from his avowed duty after he has taken the vow of Naiṣṭhika Brahmacarya (observing religious austerities and abstention from sexual pleasure to the last day of his life); such fall is also inferred, from the instructions in Smṛti, to be a very grave one; as there is no expiation added or prescribed for such fall.

The penance in the shape of the Nairta sacrifice, where it is required to pile up the household fire and to accept a wife, is enjoined in Pūrva-Mīmāṁsā only upon those persons who are to give up their Brahmacarya on the expiry of the limited period prescribed for them (Upakurvāṇa Brahmacāris)—who did not take up the vow for the whole period of life, but only for a certain period.

For reference in the Smṛti, vide—

"आरूढ़ो नैष्ठिकं धर्म्मं यस्तु प्रच्यवते द्विजः।
प्रायश्चित न पश्यामि येन शुध्येत् स आत्महा॥"

(I see no expiation, which might cleanse the self-destroyer who, belonging to any of the twice-born castes and having once entered on the duties of a Naiṣṭhika lapses from them.)

Āgneya XVI, 5, 23.

उपपूर्व्वमपित्वेके भावमशनवत्तदुक्तम॥४२॥

[The previous discussion is continued.]

उपपूर्व्वम् (**उपपूर्व्वक-पातकम्** (Upapātakam, a minor sin), **अपितु** (however), **एके** (some say), **भावम्** (possibility of expiation; expiability), **अशनवत्** (like the eating *of prohibited food*); **तदुक्तम्** (that has been explained *in Pūrva-Mīmāṁsā*.)

Explanation—Some say that a deviation from the vow taken by a Naiṣṭhika, is however, a minor sin, and so expiable, like the eating of prohibited food, such as wine or flesh. that Upapātaka (a minor sin) is an expiable sin, has been explained in the Pūrva-Mīmāṁsā of Jaimini, (Chap. I, 3, 8.)

बहिस्तूभयथापि स्मृतेराचाराच्च॥४३॥

[The previous discussion is concluded here.]

बहिः (outside; those, who break the vow, are to be excluded), **तु** (but), **उभयथा** (in either case, whether it be a grave sin or a minor sin); **अपि** (also, even), **स्मृतेः** (because of Smṛti), **आचारात्** (because of good custom), **च** (as well as.)

Explanation—But those, who break their vow, are to be excluded or debarred from Brahma-Vidyā in either case, whether it be a minor sin or a grave sin, as both Smṛti and custom indicate.

For the reference in Smṛti, vide the quotation and its translation under Sūtra 41 of this section.

स्वामिनः फलश्रुतेरित्यात्रेयः॥४४॥

[This Sūtra and the Sūtras 45 and 45A show whether the sacrificer (यजमान) or the priest (ऋत्विक्) should perform the meditation-part in those rites where meditation and sacrifice are both combined (कर्म्माङ्गाश्रित उपासना.)]

स्वामिनः (of the master; of the sacrificer or Yajamāna), फलश्रुतेः (from the declaration, in Śruti, of the reward in his favour), इति (thus), आत्रेयः (the sage Ātreya.)

Explanation—The sage Ātreya holds the view that the Yajamāna (sacrificer) should himself do the meditation connected with those rites where meditation and sacrifice are both combined (कर्म्माङ्गउपासना), such as the Udgītha-Vidyā, the Agni-Vidyā etc., and that the priest should take no part in the meditation; as Śruti declares that the reward of the performance belongs to the sacrificer, because his sacrifice becomes more effective, if combined with meditation.

For reference in the Śruti vide the quotation and its translation under Sūtra 4 of this section.

आर्त्विज्यमित्यौडुलोमिस्तस्मै हि परिक्रीयते ॥४५॥

[The previous topic is continued.]

आर्त्विज्यम् (the duty of the Ṛtvik or priest), इति (this), औडुलोमिः (the sage Auḍulomi, तस्मै (for that *labour*; for the purpose of that action), हि (as), परिक्रीयते (*his labour* is purchased, *for the performance, by payment of the sacrificial fee*.)

Explanation—The sage Auḍulomi, on the other hand, is of opinion, that the duty of meditation also devolves upon the priest whose consideration for the labour is the sacrificial fee (Dakṣiṇā.)

The labour of the priest is purchased by the sacrificer by paying the sacrificial fee for the whole performance, *i.e.*, for the purpose of performing the sacrifice together with meditation and all other parts connected with it and so the fruit of the whole performance, the meditation and all, done by the priest, is also attained by the sacrificer.

श्रुतेश्च॥४५(अ)॥

The previous topic is concluded here. This Sūtra has been noted by Ācārya Śaṅkara, but not by Ācārya Nimbārka or by Ācārya Rāmānuja.]

श्रुतेः (as Śruti declares so), **च** (also.)

Explanation—The fruit of the worships, that are performed by the priest, goes to the sacrificer; as Śruti also declares so.

This establishes the conclusion that the meditation, connected with the subordinate parts, of a sacrifice, is the duty of the priest.

For reference in Śruti vide—

"यां वै काञ्चन यज्ञे ऋत्विज आशिषमाशासत इति यजमानायैव तामाशासते॥"

(Whatever blessing the priests pray for at the sacrifice, they pray for the benefit of the sacrificer.)

Śatapatha Brāhmaṇa, Chap. I, 3, 1, 26.

सहकार्य्यन्तरविधिः, पक्षेण तृतीयं तद्वतो, विध्यादिवत्॥४६॥

[This Sūtra examines a passage of the Bṛhadāraṇyaka Śruti and concludes that continuous meditation is also to be considered as enjoined by Śruti for the realisation of Brahma. This and the following two Sūtras show that the scripture enjoins the four orders of life.]

सहकार्य्यन्तरविधिः (a separate auxiliary injunction; an injunction about another auxiliary observance), **पक्षेण** (in respect *of the two previous ones*), **तृतीयं** (the third), **तद्वतः** (of the person who has stepped into the stage of meditation), विध्यादिवत् (like the injunction of performing sacrifices and practising self-control, child like simplicity and acquiring learning.)

Explanation—The word 'मुनि' (Muni), of the passage quoted below, stands third in the order, the two previous ones being Pāṇḍitya and Bālya (erudition and childlike simplicity.) 'Muni' means a person who constantly meditates on Brahma. So constant meditation is the third auxiliary observance for one who is already possessed of Pāṇḍitya and Bālya; and as such, constant meditation is enjoined to be observed like the injunctions about sacrifices and control of the senses and so on (vide Sūtras 26 and 27 of this section.)

This Sūtra refers to a passage of the Bṛhadāraṇyaka Śruti, where, in reply to a question by one Kahola, the sage Yājñavalkya enjoins first, scholarly attainments, then childlike simplicity, and then, thirdly, continuous reflection (मननम्) co-operating with the two previous conditions, with a view to realisation of Brahma. Though there is no verb of injunctive or imperative force in the case of this third state, there is to be inferred an injunction to be understood like the injunctions in the other cases.

For the passage under reference vide—

"तस्माद् ब्राह्मणः पाण्डित्यं निर्विद्य बाल्येन तिष्ठासेद् बाल्यञ्च पाण्डित्यञ्च निर्व्विद्याथ मुनिरमौनञ्च मौनञ्च निर्व्विद्याथ ब्राह्मणः।"

(Therefore let a Brāhmaṇa, after he has done with his scholarship, stand in a child-like state; and after he has done with the child-like state and scholarship, *he may be* a Muni; and after he has done with Mauna and no Mauna, *meaning thereby all the three states mentioned above,* he becomes a Brāhmaṇa, *i.e., a person who has known Brahma.*)

Bṛhadāraṇyaka, Chap. III, 5, 1.

कृत्स्नभावात्तु गृहिणोपसंहारः॥४७॥

[This Sūtra states the reason why the householder is said,

in the Chāndogya Śruti, to be able to repair to the world of Brahma not to return again.]

कृत्स्नभावात् (because of the possibility of attaining Brahma-Vidyā in all the stages or orders of life), (indeed), **गृहिणोपसंहारः** (conclusion with the case of the householder.)

Explanation—The Chāndogya Śruti concludes by stating the case of the householder only; because there is possibility of attaining Brahma-Vidyā in all the stages of life, the case of the householder, as stated in the Chāndogya, being a typical one;—Brahma-Vidyā is attainable in all the orders of life, so the householder, too, is entitled to it, like any other person belonging to any other order. The statement of the household only, in the Chāndogya, is to be understood merely in the light of an illustration.

For reference in the Śruti, vide—

"स खल्वेवं वर्त्तयन् यावदायुषं ब्रह्मलोकमभिसम्पद्यते न च पुनरावर्त्तते।"

(He, *the householder,* conducting his life in this way, *concentrating all his senses upon self and abstaining from injury to any living being,* throughout his life, attains the world of Brahma and has not to return again to this world.)

Chāndogya, Chap. VIII, 15, 1.

मौनवदितरेषामप्युपदेशात्॥४८॥

[This Sūtra states that the scripture enjoins the observance of the duties of all the orders of life.]

मौनवत् (like constant meditation), **इतरेषाम्** (of the other *orders of life*), **अपि** (also), **उपदेशात्** (from *such* injunction in *Śruti*.)

Explanation—Like constant meditation (vide Sūtra 46 ante), there are injunctions also about the observance of the duties of the different orders of life as auxiliary to the advent of Brahma-Vidyā, since they have been enjoined by Śruti.

For reference in the Śruti, vide—

"त्रयो धर्म्मस्कन्धा यज्ञोऽध्ययनं दानमिति"

(There are three divisions of pious duties—sacrifice, study and making gifts.)

Chāndogya, Chap. II, 23, 1.

अनाविष्कुर्व्वन्नन्वयात्॥४९॥

[This Sūtra says that the perversity of a child is not meant by the word '**वाल्येन**'(by a child-like state) in the passage of the Bṛhadāraṇyaka Śruti quoted under Sūtra 46 ante.]

अनाविष्कुर्व्वन् (not displaying himself, not showing himself off), **अन्वयात्** (according to the context.)

Explanation—By the expression 'childlike state' in the Bṛhadāraṇyaka Śruti quoted under Sūtra 46, it is meant that the scholar should not display his pedantry, but behave himself like a child; because this meaning alone suits the context.

This Sūtra elucidates the meaning of the word '**बाल्येन**' (by a child-like state) in the passage of the Śruti quoted under Sūtra 46. By the expression 'child-like state', the passage means to say, that the scholar must not give himself airs, but behave just as simple child who has naturally no pride or vanity and does not strive to make a display of himself before others. Here the word does not mean the perversity of a child, but his simplicity and humility; because the passage must bear connection with the entire chapter on the ground of co-operating towards the principal matter, namely, the realisation of Brahma.

ऐहिकमप्रस्तुते प्रतिबन्धे तद्दर्शनात् ॥५०॥

[This Sūtra states whether the consequence of Brahma-Vidyā, which is the realisation of Brahma, is possible in this life or will wait till death.]

ऐहिकम् (taking place in this life), **अप्रस्तुते प्रतिबन्धे** (in the absence of an obstruction; if there be no obstruction by some other contrary work of which the effects are ready to operate), **तद्दर्शनात्** (as it is seen in Śruti.)

Explanation—If there be no obstruction by some counteracting cause, there is no bar to the attainment of Brahma-Vidyā and the consequent realisation of Brahma, in this life; otherwise it will follow in the next life on the removal of the obstruction. The realisation of Brahma in this life is seen materialised in Naciketā in the Kaṭha Śruti.

For reference in the Śruti, vide—

"मृत्युप्रोक्तां नचिकेतोऽथ लब्ध्वा विद्यामेतां योगविधिञ्च कृत्स्नम्।
ब्रह्मप्राप्तो विरजोऽभूद् विमृत्युरन्योऽप्येवं यो विदध्यात्ममेव॥"

(Thus Naciketā, receiving Brahma-Vidyā together with all the process of abstract meditation—explained by King Death, realised Brahma *in this life* and became pure and immortal; any other person too, who takes the same spiritual path, *may, likewise, attain the same and become cleansed and immortal*.)

मुक्तिफलानियमस्तदवस्थावधृतेस्तदवस्थावधृतेः॥५१॥

[The preceding Sūtra having shown when the advent of Brahma-Vidyā and Brahma-Jñāna (the knowledge of Brahma) takes place, this Sūtra states the time when salvation, the consequence of Brahma-Vidyā, will come.]

मुक्तिफालनियमः (*there is* no fixed time for the attainment of the goal of Brahma-Vidyā in the shape of salvation), **तदवस्था** (that state; the state of salvation), **अवधृतेः** (because Śruti has ascertained so.)

[The repetition of the last phrase indicates the termination of the chapter.]

Explanation—There is no fixed time for the attainment of the goal of Brahma-Vidyā in the shape of salvation, as Śruti has ascertained that the state of salvation is attained only after the obstructions have been removed.

The preceding Sūtra has shown that the attainment of Brahma-Vidyā and Brahma-Jñāna may take place in this life or afterwards; the present Sūtra shows that even the knowledge being acquired in this life, there is no rule that the fruit thereof, in the shape of salvation, is bound to follow in this life, as Śruti has stated that a person, on having acquired Brahma-Jñāna, will have to wait for the fruit till he is released from all bondage.

For reference vide the Śruti—

"तस्य तावदेव चिरं यावन्न विमोक्ष्येऽथ सम्पत्स्ये।"

(He is to wait so long as he is not released *from the obstructions,* and then he attains Brahma.)

Chāndogya, Chap. VI, 14, 2.

CHAPTER IV

SECTION—I

The framer of the Sūtras has already discussed the following subjects:—the nature of the Universal Soul, of the universe and of the individual soul; the relation of the individual soul and of the universe, to the Universal Soul; meditation on the Universal Soul, by which one attains emancipation; and the aspect of the Soul upon which the mind must be fixed at the time of meditation.

This chapter introduces a discussion on the subject of the emancipation of the individual soul.

The first section of the chapter treats of (1) the necessity of constant meditation, (2) the conception of the Universal Soul as the self of the meditator, (3) the light in which Pratīkas (symbols) are to be regarded, and (4) the position of the meditator, in this life, after he has realised Brahma.

Sūtras 1-12 show, by adducing evidences from Śruti and Smṛti, that meditation on Brahma must be constantly practised; that the meditator should conceive and preach the Lord as the self of the worshipper; but not to conceive the symbols, such as the mind, the Ākāśa, the sun and the like, as his self; that it would serve no purpose to think of Brahma in the light of material object of the senses, for it would be only to degrade the Infinite Lord to the status of sensuous object with all its limitations; Brahma being superior to everything that may be treated as a symbol, the symbol should be raised, higher in thought, to the level of Brahma, but Brahma should not be brought down to the level of the symbol; meditation on one's own self in the light of Brahma is the highest and most natural method of meditation (that is to say, one's self is to be reckoned as higher than any one of the symbols), the meditator should therefore raise himself to the level of Brahma by thinking himself as such, but should not bring Brahma lower to the level of his individual soul; and thus his narrower conception of self is replaced by the wider one of Brahma; that meditation is to be practised in a sitting posture: in the lying posture there is probability of slumber, and in the state of standing or walking there is probability of distraction of the mind; that concentration and tranquility of the mind being the chief objective in meditation the time and the place must be suited to that end; and that the habit of meditation should be kept up till the meditator's exit from the world.

Sūtras 13, 15 and 17 show that on the attainment of the knowledge of Brahma by a person, his previous merits and demerits (*i. e.*, good and bad works), of which effects have not yet begun to operate (*i. e.*, Sañcita Karmas) are cancelled; and the effects of his subsequent pious or impious works (if any) do not cling to him, but are inherited, at his death, by his well-wishers and evil-doers respectively. The previous works, on the other hand, of which the effects have begun to operate (Prārabdhas) are not annulled as soon as his enlightenment comes on; the existing body is the outcome of his Prārabdha and will drag on till this Prārabdha is exhausted; since his life force is not yet spent up, the Enlightened Soul lives and moves, but quite unaffected by the world's good and evil that the 'flesh is heir to'; and finally his wheel of life comes to a stand-still, since his Sañcita Karma has already been consumed by Brahma Jñāna. The wheel of life, which has been set in motion by the operative portion of previous Karma (Prārabdha), goes on whirling by the law of its own inertia, until it comes to a dead stop; the inoperative portion (Sañcita) being consumed by, Brahma-Jñāna, there is no other force remaining, to give it a fresh start, and to begin a new cycle of existence; the much desired release from bondage follows at once as a natural consequence.

Sūtras 16 and 18-19 show that seekers of Brahma-Jñāna should not abandon sacrifices, gifts and penances prescribed for their order of life (Āśrama), as these works are not antagonistic, but rather helpful, to the origination and consolidation of Knowledge; that religious works, combined with meditation, are more forceful than those divorced from meditation, because of the superior causal efficiency of the former with regard to the cognition of Self; persons seeking Knowledge should, therefore, perform religious rites for consolidation of the cognition of Self; and these persons, having the intuition of Brahma, become united with Him after death.

आवृत्तिरसकृदुपदेशात् ॥१॥

[This Sūtra states that constant practice of meditation is necessary.]

आवृत्तिः (repetition; practice of meditation on Brahma), **असकृत्** (not only once; frequent), **उपदेशात्** (because of instruction.)

Explanation—Frequent practice of meditation on Brahma is necessary, since there is instruction to that effect, in Śruti.

For the instruction vide the Śruti—

"आत्मा वा अरे द्रष्टव्यः श्रोतव्यो मन्तव्यो निदिध्यासितव्यः"

(Verily the Self is to be seen, *i. e*, *intuited,* to be heard, to be thought of and continually to be concentrated upon.)

Bṛhadāraṇyaka, Chap. II, 4, 5.

लिङ्गाच्च॥२॥

[The same topic is continued.]

लिङ्गात् (from Smṛti), **च** (also.)

Explanation—Smṛti also enjoins constant meditation on Brahma.

For the Smṛti vide—

"अथ चित्तं समाधातुं न शक्नोषि मयि स्थिरम्।
अभ्यासयोगेन ततो मामिच्छाप्तुं धनञ्जय॥"

(If on the other hand, O thou *Conqueror of wealth*, you cannot fix your mind firmly on me, then exert your will to get hold of me, *the Self*, by constant practice.)

Bhagavat Gītā, Chap. XII, 9.

आत्मेति तूपगच्छन्ति ग्राहयन्ति च॥३॥

[This Sūtra prescribes the process of meditation.]

आत्मा (self), **इति** (as this), **तु** (really), **उपगच्छन्ति** (approach, realise), **ग्राहयन्ति** (make others comprehend; instruct), **च** (also.)

Explanation—The teachers, in Śruti, are found to approach Brahma as their own self, and also to instruct others to do the same.

A person, desirous of emancipation, should, therefore, meditate in the way that the Lord is his own soul; in other words, he should think of himself as the Universal Soul. A person naturally thinks himself as different from Brahma; and that is the cause of his bondage. The intention, that the worshipper is essentially as the worshipped (Brahma) becomes clear by constant meditation of himself as identicial with Him; and this ultimately brings emancipation for the meditator—the worshipper.

For reference vide—

"**अहं ब्रह्मास्मि**" (I am Brahma.)

Bṛhadāraṇyaka, Chap. I, 4, 10.

Also vide—

"**एष त आत्मा सर्व्वान्तरः।**"

(This is thy Self dwelling within all—*on the background of every individual consciousness.*)

Bṛhadāraṇyaka, Chap. III, 4, 1.

[This अहंग्रह उपासना, meditation on one's own self in the light of Brahma—is recommended as the highest and the most direct way of realisation of Brahma.]

न प्रतीके न हि सः॥४॥

[This and the following two Sūtras examine the value of a Pratīka or symbol in worship.]

न (not), प्रतीके (in the symbol, such as the Ākāśa, the sun, the mind, *etc.*), न (not), हि (as), सः (he, the self.)

Explanation—But one cannot regard a symbol, such as the mind, the sun, etc., as his own self, as none of them is really the self.

Meditation on symbols, such as the mind, the Ākāśa, or the sun, etc., in the light of Brahma, are taught in Śruti. But the meditator cannot look upon them as his own soul, exactly in the same way as he can in the direct meditation of Brahma (vide the previous Sūtra); those symbols are mere material objects far inferior to his immaterial soul.

ब्रह्मदृष्टिरुत्कर्षात्॥५॥

[The same discussion is continued.]

ब्रह्मदृष्टिः (view in the light of Brahma), उत्कर्षात् (because of super-eminence.)

Explanation—To view the symbol as Brahma is quite proper, but by reversing the order, to view Brahma in the light of the symbol, is hardly justifiable, because of super-eminence of Brahma over the symbol.

It would serve no purpose to think of Brahma in the light of a limited thing; for it would be only to degrade the Infinite Lord to the status of a finite thing; Brahma being superior to everything that may be treated as a symbol, the symbol should be raised higher in thought to the level of Brahma; but Brahma should not be brought down to the level of the symbol.

आदित्यादिमतयश्चाङ्ग उपपत्ते॥६॥

[A particular instance is cited to confirm the preceding Sūtra.]

आदित्यादिमतयः (views in the light of the sun and the like), **च** (also), **अङ्गे** (in the subordinate part of *sacrificial rite*), **उपपत्तेः** (by reason of *the superiority of the sun and the like.*)

Explanation—In the part, known as the Udgītha prayer of the Udgītha-sacrifice, viewing the Udgītha in the light of the sun is justified for the reason of the superiority of the sun to the Udgītha.

In other words, the Udgītha should be raised higher in thought to the level of the sun, but not the sun be brought down to that of the Udgītha. In this way a meditator should raise himself to the level of Brahma by thinking himself as Brahma, but should not bring Brahma down to the level of the inidividual soul.

For reference vide the Śruti—

"य एवासौ तपति तमुद्गीथमुपासीत।"

(Let a man meditate on the Udgītha, assuming it to be he who shines yonder, *i. e., the sun.*)

Chāndogya, Chap. I, 3, 1.

आसीनः सम्भवात् ॥७॥

[A discussion on the posture of the meditator, while engaged in meditation, is now introduced.]

आसीनः (sitting), **सम्भवात्** (because of practicability.)

Explanation—Meditation is to be practised in a sitting posture, as in that case only true meditation is practicable.

In the lying posture there is probability of laziness and slumber, and in the case of standing or walking there is probability of distraction of the mind in its effort to maintain an erect position; but in the sitting posture, neither of the two contingencies is likely to occur. The sitting posture contributes to that composure of mind, which is the *sine qua non* of meditation.

ध्यानाच्च॥८॥

[An argument, in support of Sūtra 7, is adduced.]

ध्यानात् (as it is of the nature of concentration), **च** (also.)

Explanation—And Upāsanā (worship), being mainly of the nature of concentration, should be practised in a sitting posture, which is conducive to concentration.

Concentration being an uninterrupted and unintermittent current of thought sent towards a particular object, the sitting posture becomes indispensable.

अचलत्वं चापेक्ष्य ॥९॥

[The argument, in support of Sūtra 7, is continued.]

अचलत्वं (stability, steadiness), **च** (also), **अपेक्ष्य** (aiming at, pointing to.)

Explanation—The term 'Dhyāna' (concentration) is used in Śruti as aiming at steadiness. So concentration is to be made in a sitting posture, for it ensures steadiness.

With reference to the immobility of the earth in ordinary eye, the scripture fancies the earth as being engaged in concentration, as if it remains fixed in space in the act of pious meditation. It suggests that such a steady application of the mind can be attained by meditation only in a sitting posture.

For the fancied act of meditation, on the part of the earth vide—

"**ध्यायतीव पृथिवी** (As if the earth is engaged in meditation.)

Chāndogya, Chap. VII, 6, 1.

स्मरन्ति च॥१०॥

(The argument, in support of Sūtra 7, is concluded.]

स्मरन्ति (passage in Smṛti say), च (also.)

Explanation—Passages in Smṛti also corroborate the statement that meditation is to be practised in a sitting posture.

For reference in Smṛti vide—

"शुचौ देशे प्रतिष्ठाप्य स्थिरमासनमात्मनः।"

(Having fixed one's own seat steady in a sacred place.)

Bhagavat Gītā, Chap. VI, 11.

यत्रैकाग्रता तत्राविशेषात् ॥११॥

[This Sūtra deal with the time and place of meditation.]

यत्र (wheṇaver and wherever), एकाग्रता (concentration of mind), तत्र (then and there), अवशेषात् (for want of any special direction; as there is no special direction in Śruti.)

Explanation—Whenever and wherever concentration of mind is possible, then and there meditation may be practised; as there is no special direction, prescribed in Śruti, regarding the time and the place of meditation.

The time and the place of meditation should be selected only so far as they are favourable to meditation.

आप्रयाणात्तत्रापि हि दृष्टम् ॥१२॥

[This Sūtra says that Upāsanā (worship) is to be continued till death.]

आप्रयाणात् (till death), तत्र (then), अपि (also), हि (because), दृष्टम् (found *in Śruti*.)

Explanation—Worship is to be continued till death, because it is found in Śruti that the worshipper, continuing so till death, attains the world of Brahma after death.

For reference in the Śruti vide—

"स खल्वेवं वर्त्तयन् यावदायुषं ब्रह्मलोकमभिसम्पद्यते न च पुनरावर्त्तते।"

(For translation and reference vide Sūtra 47, Sec. IV, Chap. III.)

तदधिगमे उत्तरपूर्व्वाघयोरश्लेषविनाशौ तद्व्यपदेशात्॥१३॥

[The result of meditation, *i.e.*, the knowledge of Brahma, is now discussed.]

तदधिगमे (on the attainment of that; on the attainment of the knowledge of Brahma); **उत्तर-पूर्व्वाघयोः** (of the subsequent and the previous sins), "**अश्लेष-विनाशौ** (non-association and annulment); **उत्तरपूर्व्वाघयोरश्लेष-विनाशौ** (previous sins of a person are destroyed, and his subsequent sins can not cling to him), **तद्व्यपदेशात्** (because Śruti has declared so.)

Explanation—On the attainment of Brahma-Jñāna, previous sins of a person are destroyed, and his subsequent sins too cannot cling to him; because Śruti has declared so regarding a person who has attained the knowledge of Brahma.

For reference regarding non-association with subsequent sins vide the Śruti—

"**यथा पुष्करपलाश आपो न श्लिष्यन्त एवमेवंविदि पापं कर्म्म न श्लिष्यते।**"

(As water does not cling to a lotous-leaf, so no evil deed clings to him who has known this.)

Chāndogya, Chap. IV, 14, 3.

For reference regarding destruction of previous sins, vide:—

"**यथेषीकातूलमग्नौ प्रोतं प्रदूयेतैवं हास्य सर्व्वे पाप्मानः प्रदूयन्ते॥**"

(As the cotton of the Iṣīkā reed cast into fire, is burnt out, so are all his sins consumed.)

Chāndogya, Chap. V, 24, 3.

इतरस्याप्येवमसंश्लेषः, पाते तु ॥१४॥

[Discussion on the consequence of Brahma-Jñāna (the knowledge of Brahma) is continued.]

इतरस्य (of the one which is other *than sin*; *i.e.*, of piety),

अपि (also), एवम् (in this way, in the same way), असंश्लेषः (non-clinging; non-association), पति (at death), तु (indeed.).

Explanation—Piety also of a person does not cling to him on the attainment of Brahma-Jñāna, in the same way as sin; and when the same person dies, his salvation follows as a matter of course.

Like iniquity, righteousness is also a cause of bondage and stands in the way of emancipation; of a person having the knowledge of Brahma, all his accumulated (Sañcita) merits and demerits are annulled; thus his merits and demerits being completely inoperative, his Emancipation necessarily follows at death.

For reference that persons knowing Brahma shake off their virtues and vices, vide the Śruti quoted at the close of Sūtra 2, Section III, Chapter I.

अनारब्धकार्य्ये एव तु पूर्व्वे तदवधेः॥१५॥

[Discussion, on the consequence of Brahma-Jñāna, is continued.]

अनारब्धकार्य्ये (in the case of those works, the effects of which have not begun to operate), एव (only), तु (but), पूर्व्वे (the merits and demerits previously acquired and already mentioned in Sūtras 13 and 14), तदवधेः (because till that; because of waiting till death; as according to Śruti he has to wait for Emancipation till his death.)

Explanation—But annulment of pieties and impieties consequent upon Brahma-Jñāna, takes place only in respect of those accumulated works (Sañcita Karmas), whose effects have not as yet begun to operate; but annulment does not take place in respect of those works which have begun to operate (Prārabdha); they will continue to act till they are exhausted at the death of the Enlightened embodied soul.

Only those pieties and impieties, of which effects have not begun to operate before the acquisition of the knowledge of Brahma, are meant to be destroyed, as stated in the preceding Sūtras 13 and 14; but the works, of which the effects have already begun to operate in this life (Prārabdha Karmas), are not destroyed at once on the advent of Brahma-Jñāna, but will linger on till they are exhausted by enjoyment or suffering; on the exhaustion of the effects of all those works, death occurs, there remaining no motive force for the prolongation of life. The present life of a person has been called into existence only by his Prārabdha (the operative part of the effects of his previous works); and even if he happens to be elightened in the course of this life, his death cannot take place until his Prārabdha is exhausted. Sūtras 13 and 14 only mean, that his Sañcita Karmas (his merits and demerits, accumulated for ages and remaining inoperative for this life) are cancelled by Brahma-Jñāna.

For reference in Śruti vide:—

"तस्य तावदेव चिरं यावन्न विमोक्ष्यऽथ सम्पत्स्ये॥"

(For translation vide Sūtra 7, Section I, Chapter I.)

अग्निहोत्रादि तु तत्कार्य्यायैव तद्दर्शनात् ॥१६॥

[The Sūtra states that permanent obligatory works, enjoined by the Vedas for different Āśramas (order of life), are not to be given up.]

अग्निहोत्रादि (daily offering of oblations to the perpetually maintained fire, and similar other religious rites; daily sacrifices, gifts and penances etc.) तु (but), तत्कार्य्याय (towards that effect; towards the origination and fulfilment of Knowledge), एव (certainly), तद्दर्शनात् (as that is shown in Śruti; as Śruti says so.)

Explanation—In view of the acquisition of knowledge, a man shall not abandon daily sacrifices, gifts and penances, etc., as they are prescribed to be his duties; because these works are not antagonistic, but rather helpful, to the origination and fulfilment of knowledge; and because Śruti also says so.

Rites, with a motive for future fruition of the mundane desires and bodily enjoyments here or in the next world, are enjoined to be abandoned by a person who is desirous of Emancipation; but he is the perform them merely as his prescribed duties, so that they may exercise, a purifying influence on his heart and become a help towards the origination and consolidation of his knowledge.

For reference in Śruti vide:—

"तमेतं वेदानुवचनेन ब्राह्मण विविदिषन्ति यज्ञेन दानेन तपसाऽनाशकेन ॥"

(For translation vide Śutra 26, Sec. IV, Chap. III.)

अतोऽन्यापि ह्येकेषामुभयोः॥१७॥

[Now the question may arise—what about the works, other than the obligatory duties, done by the Enlightened person ? The present Sūtra gives an answer to this question.]

अतः (from these; than these obligatory ritualistic works, as spoken of in the preceding Sūtra), **अन्या** (other classes of works), **अपि** (also), **हि** (as), **एकेषाम्** (*the view* of some; some branches of Śruti states, **उभयोः** (*inheritance* of both, *good and bad works*.)

Explanation—Other than these obligatory ritualistic works, as spoken of in the preceding Sūtra, there is also a class of works, whose effects remain attached to the person till death, even when he has won his emancipation; at the fall of the body, as some branches of Śruti state, behind he leaves all his works, both good and bad, to be inherited by his friends and foes respectively, like his worldly properties to be inherited by his sons or relatives.

For reference of Śruti vide—

"तस्य पुत्रा दायमुपयन्ति सुहृदः साधुकृत्यां द्विषन्तः पापकृत्याम्।"

(For translation vide Sūtra 26, Sec. III. Chap. III.)

यदेव विद्ययेति हि॥१८॥

[The continuance of the obligatory duties, even after Brahma-Jñāna, is further strengthened in this Sūtra.]

यदेव (whatever), विद्यया (with the aid of meditation), इति (this), हि (as.)

Explanation—Whatever is done with the aid of meditation, becomes all the more effective, as Śruti says so.

Not to speak of ordinary persons, but even a person, desiring for the knowledge of Brahma, should perform works prescribed for his order of life (Āśrama), for the Śruti, alluded to in this Sūtra, says that a sacrifice, done with the accompaniment of meditation, becomes all the more effective; this passage of the Śruti does not mean that sacrifices without the aid of meditation are altogether useless; it only means that sacrifices combined with Vidyā (meditation), are superior, in force, to the same sacrifices not so combined, because of superior casual efficiency of the former with regard to the cognition of Self; the passage thus gives a hint that householders, having the knowledge, should continue to perform sacrifices and other religious rites for consolidation of the cognition of Self.

For reference vide the Śruti—

"यदेव विद्यया करोति श्रद्धयोपनिषदा तदेव वीर्य्यवत्तरं भवति।"

(For translation vide Sūtra 4, Sec. IV. Chap. III.)

भोगेन त्वितरे क्षपयित्वाऽथ सम्पद्यते॥१९॥

[The Sūtra concludes with the answer to the question, what becomes of the Prārabdha portion of the Enlightened Soul's work which has called his present life into existence ?]

भोगेन (by enjoyment and suffering), तु (but), इतरे (the other two sorts of works—good and evil), क्षपयित्वा (having exhausted), अथ (thereupon), सम्पद्यते (becomes united *with Brahma*.)

Explanation—The person, having obtained the knowledge of Brahma, becomes united with Brahma, after exhausting, by enjoyment and suffering, the effects of both the good and the evil works already in operation (Prārabdha.)

So there is no escape even on the part of the Enlightened Soul from the operation of law of Prārabdha, although his accumulated (Sañcita) Karma is cancelled by Brahma-Jñāna.

For reference vide:—

"तस्य तावदेव चिरं यावन्न विमोक्ष्येऽथ सम्पत्स्ये॥"

(For translation vide Sūtra 7, Sec. I, Chap. I.)

SECTION—II

This section is devoted to the mode of departure of the Enlightened and the unenlightened souls at the time of leaving the body.

Sūtras 1—6 show, by citing the authority of Śruti, that at the time of departure of the soul from the body (*i.e.*, at death), the Indriyas, namely the speech the eye and so on, merge themselves in the mind; as it is observed that these Indriyas discontinue their functions while the mind still continues to be active; that the mind, in its turn, after having absorbed within itself the functions of the external Indriyas, merges in Prāṇa (the vital energy) whose chief function is breathing, as it is observed at the time of death that while the function of breath yet continues, the functions of the mind are stopped; that Prāṇa, after having absorbed the mind, merges in the (embodied) soul; that the soul, after having absorbed Prāṇa and, with it all the Indriyas including the mind, is enveloped in the heat and the other subtle elements.

These six Sūtras describe the mode of departure which is common to all individual souls alike, enlightened or unenlightened.

Sūtras 7—11 state the extraordinary course of exit from the body taken by the Enlightened Soul, and say that immortality, *i.e.*, release from bondage, is enjoyed by him even in his lifetime long before life is extinct; that his subtle body outlives his gross body; and lastly that the vital heat, perceived in the gross body is not its own but is imparted to it by its survivor.

Sūtras 12 and 13 show, with the help of Śruti and Smṛti, that the Indriyas accompany the disembodied soul on its departure. Ācārya Śaṅkara makes here a distinction between the mode of departure of the absolutely Enlightened (सद्यमुक्ता) Soul and that of the relatively Enlightened (क्रममुक्ता) Soul. the soul of the absolutely Enlightened person is at once lost in the Universal Soul without undergoing translation to Brahma-Loka through the various stages of transition and the soul of the relatively Enlightened person, together with this mind and the external Indriyas, is translated to the world of Brahma stage by stage.

Sūtras 14 and 15 state that the subtle elements, forming the constituents of the subtle body, absolutely lose their identity in Brahma, so that all trace of their separate existence is lost in the One Homogeneous Whole.

Sūtras 16 and 17 say that through the influence of Brahma-Jñāna re-inforced by meditation, the opening of the veinule, leading from the heart to the head, is lighted up by the grace of the Indwelling Spirit; that through this veinule the soul comes out of the head and then following the direction of the solar ray, find its ultimate resting place in the Lord. Sūtra 16 throws out the hint, that in meditation one's own soul is to be thought of in the light of the Universal Soul dwelling within the heart.

Sūtras 18—20 show that there is no bar to the attainment of Brahma by Enlightened persons, who die at night, or in the dark lunar fortnight (Kṛṣṇa Pakṣa) or during the six months of Dakṣiṇāyaṇa (the period of the sun's motion from the summer solstice to the winter solstice.) There is a passage in the Bhagavat Gītā, alluding to the prevailing belief, that in the event of death happening at daytime, in the bright lunar fortnight (Śukla Pakṣa) and during Uttarāyaṇa (the period of the sun's motion from the winter solstice to the summer solstice), there occurs no return to this world, and in the event of death happening at night, in the dark lunar fortnight and during Dakṣiṇāyana, a return to this world is bound to follow. This does not mean that there is any hard and fast rule for the attainment of Brahma, so far as the time of parting is concerned; but the statement is only meant to be noted and remembered by the detached (**अनासक्त**) and attached (**आसक्त**) worshippers, so that they may shape their conduct accordingly, while on earth. There is indeed no bar to the Enlightened soul catching the ray of the sun, if he passes away even at night or in the dark fortnight or during the southern progress of the sun (Dakṣiṇāyana.) There are also clear statements in Śruti that the sun emits rays even during the night, and that of the Enlightened person the night also turns to day, that with him it is perpetual day.

वाङ्नसि दर्शनात् शब्दाच्च ॥१॥

[This Sūtra says that speech merges in the mind at death.]

वाक् (the speech), **मनसि** (in the mind), **दर्शनात्** (as it is generally seen or observed), **शब्दात्** (because of the statement of Śruti), **च** (also.)

Explanation—The power of speech merges in the mind at the time of the soul's departure from the body; and it is generally observed to be so; Śruti also confirms the statement.

When a man is at the point of death, it is generally observed that the function of the speech is stopped, while the mind yet remains active as can be understood from the movements of his eyes and from other gestures, which act for the speech; by means of his spech he endeavours to give expression to his feelings and desires; so the speech may be said to have merged in the mind at this stage; the statement of Śruti also lends support to that conclusion.

For reference in the Śruti vide:—

"अस्य सोम्य पुरुषस्य प्रयतो वाङ्मनसि सम्पद्यते मनः प्राणे प्राणस्तेजसि तेजः परस्यां देवतायाम्।"

(The dying man's speech, O my son, merges in the mind,

the mind in Prāṇa *or the vital force*, Prāṇa in the vital that and the heat in the Supreme Deity.)

Chāndogya, Chap. VI, 8, 6.

अतएव च सर्व्वाण्यनु॥२॥

[This Sūtra says that all the Indriyas merge in the mind at the time of death.]

अतएव (hence; for the same reason), **च** (also), **सर्व्वाणि** (all *the Indriyas*), **अनु** (**अनुगच्छन्ति**, follow.)

Explanation—For the same reasons (general experience and corroborative statement of Śruti) as stated in Sūtra 1, all the other Indriyas follow the speech, and merge in the mind at the time.

Like the Speech, it is observed that the eye and the other Indriyas discontinue their functions, while the mind continues to act; and the statement of Śruti also leads to the same conclusion.

For reference in the Śruti vide:—

"तस्मादुपशान्ततेजा, पुनर्भवमिन्द्रियैर्मनसि सम्पद्यमानैः"

(Therefore he whose vital heat has been abnormally lowered, comes to a new birth *with the subtle body. after death*, with all the Indriyas merged in the mind.)

Praśnopaniṣad, Chap. III, 9.

तन्मनः प्राण उत्तरात् ॥३॥

[This Sūtra states that the mind, with all the other Indriyas, merges in Prāṇa.]

तन्मनः (that mind *which has absorbed all the other Indriyas*), **प्राणे** (in Prāṇa, *the vital force*), **उत्तरात्** (as *instimated* by the subsequent clause *of the Śruti quoted in Sūtra 1*.)

Explanation—That the mind which has absorbed, within itself, the external Indriyas, is in its turn merged in Prāṇa, the vital force (whose chief function is breathing), as it is intimated by the subsequent clause of the Śruti quoted under Sūtra 1.

It is also observed in the case of persons about to die, that while the function of the vital force, *i.e.*, breathing continues, the functions of the mind are stopped.

For the subsequent passage vide—

"मनः प्राणे प्राणस्तजसि तेजः परस्यां देवतायाम्"

(For translation and reference vide Sūtra 1 of this section.)

सोऽध्यक्षे तदुपगमादिभ्यः॥४॥

[This Sūtra shows that Prāṇa, with the mind, attains the Lord of the Indriyas—the individual soul.]

स (he, Prāṇa), **अध्यक्षे** (in the ruler; in the individual soul who is the ruler of the body and the Indriyas), **तदुपगमादिभ्यः** (from the statement of the approach towards him and similar reasons; as this can be understood from the statement in Śruti that all the different phases of the vital force approach towards the soul as the time of death.)

Explanation—Prāṇa, after having absorbed the mind, joins the ruler of the body, namely the individual soul, this can be understood from the statement of Śruti saying that all the different phases of the vital force appraoch towards the soul at the time of death.

It is also known from another passage in the Śruti (quoted under Sūtra 1 above), that Prāṇa merges in Tejas (the heat.) So this Sūtra is to be understood in the way, that the vital force, joining the soul, assumes the form of Tejas (heat or light, the subtle essences of the element 'Fire'.)

For the statement of the Śruti that the vital force, in all its phases, approaches the soul at the time of its parting with the body, vide:—

"एवमेवेममात्मानमन्तकाले सर्व्वे प्राणा अभिसमायन्ति यत्रेतदूर्द्ध्वोच्छ्वासी भवति।"

(Thus Prāṇa, in all its phases, goes to the self at the last moment, when he is breathing hard preparing to expire.)

Bṛhadāraṇyaka, Chap. IV, 3, 38.

भूतेषु तच्छ्रुते॥५॥

[This Sūtra amplifies the previous one.]

भूतेषु (in the elements), तच्छ्रुतेः (तत्श्रुतेः, as that can be understood from Śruti.)

Explanation—The vital force, joining the soul, merges not only in Tejas, but at the same time in the other elements too, and this can be understood from Śruti, [It is said to merge only in Tejas, because Tejas is the predominating factor there.]

For the Śruti vide—

"पृथिवीमय आपोमयो वायुमय आकाशमयस्तेजोमयः।"

(*That soul is* united with the essence of the earth, of the water, of the air, of the Ākāśa and of the heat.)

Bṛhadāraṇyaka, Chap. IV, 4, 5.

नैकस्मिन् दर्शयतो हि ॥६॥

[Reasons are adduced to support Sūtra 5.]

न (not), एकस्मिन् (in one), दर्शयतः (both Śruti and smṛti show), हि (as.)

Explanation—Prāṇa, attending the soul does not merge in one element only, namely Tejas (the heat), as both Śruti and Smṛti have shown the impossibility of individual element's operation singly, without being united together.

For the Śruti vide—

"तासां त्रिवृतमेकैकां करवाणि"

(Quoted at length and translated under Sūtra 19, Section IV, Chapter II.)

"नानावीर्य्याः पृथग् भूतास्ततस्ते संहतिं विना।
नाशक्नुवन् प्रजाः सृष्टुमसमागम्य कृत्स्नशः॥"

(These, the separate elements, with their different potencies, became, without co-operation, powerless to create living beings, until they merged themselves in one another individually and collectively.)

Viṣṇu Purāṇa, Chap. I, 2, 52.

समाना चासृत्युपक्रमादमृतत्वञ्चानुपोष्य॥७॥

[After describing the general way of departure of all individuals in the first six Sūtras, the framer of the Sūtras now describes the special feature of the subsequent journey of the person blessed with Brahma-Jñāna.]

समाना (*the way is* common; the same as that of the others), **च** (also), **आसृत्युपक्रमात्** (until about to enter the Nāḍīs, *i.e.* the veinules: **सृतिः**—progress; entrance, **उपक्रमः**— commencement), **अमृतत्वं** (release from bondage), **च** (indeed), **अनुपोष्य** (without burning, *i.e.*, without severing the connection with the body and the Indriyas.)

Explanation—The mode of departure of an individual, who has got the intuition of Self, is also the same as that of the ordinary people, as described above in the preceding six Sūtras, till a different course, the special veinule is take by the former, who, indeed, has won his Release even in his lifetime without severing his connection with the body and the Indriyas, in the sense that his past sins are destroyed and future sins do not cling to him.

Śruti has described the departure of the Enlightened through a special veinule leading from, the heart to the head; until entrance into this special veinule, the manner of departure, as described in the previous Sūtras, is the same for all persons alike, whether enlightened or unenlightened.

For the progress through the special veinule, vide the Śruti—

**"शतं चैका हृदयस्य नाड्यस्तासां मूर्द्धानमभिनिः सृतैका।
तयोर्द्धमायन्नमृतत्वेति विश्वङ्ङन्या उत्क्रमणे भवन्ति॥"**

There are a hundred and one veins in the interior of the

heart, of which only one leads from the heart to the head; by that, progressing upwards, *the departing soul* attains immortality,—*i.e.*, *emancipation*; all the other Nāḍīs are for the egres *of the ordinary people—for undergoing bondage of frequently births and deaths.*)

Chāndogya, Chap. VIII, 6, 6.

For Release in the lifetime, vide the Śruti—

"यदा सर्वे प्रमुच्यन्ते कामा येऽस्य हृदि श्रिताः।
अथ मर्त्योऽमृतो भवत्यत्र ब्रह्म समश्नुते॥"

(As soon as all the desires, that fill the heart, are wiped off, a mortal attains Immortality and enjoys Brahma, *even* here *in this life*.)

Bṛhadāraṇyaka, Chap. IV, 4, 7.

तदापीतेः संसारव्यपदेशात् ॥८॥

[The Sūtra explains the special signification given to the word 'अमृतत्व' (Immortality), *i.e.*, Release in the previous Sūtra.]

तत् (that; Immortality or Release stated in the preceding Sūtra), आपीतेः (आ-अपीते; till the attainment *of the status of Brahma*, अपीतिः—attainment), संसारव्यपदेशात् (because Śruti states his concern with the world.)

Explanation—The word 'अमृतत्व' (Immortality or Release), as stated in the preceding Sūtra, is to be understood to be attained even without annulling bodily connections; because Śruti states that the Enlightened soul is to wait in his embodied state till he is released and attains the status of Brahma.

For reference in the Śruti vide:—

"तस्य तावदेव चिरं यावन्न विमोक्ष्येऽथ सम्पत्स्ये।"

(For translation vide Sūtra 7, Sec. I, Chap. I.)

सूक्ष्मं प्रमाणतश्च तथोपलब्धेः॥९॥

[This Sūtra states, that, on the disintegration of the gross body, there still remains the subtle body of the Enlightened soul.]

सूक्ष्मं (subtle *body*), **प्रमाणतः** (from testimony), **च** (also), **तथोपलब्धं** (because of perception in that way; as it is understood.)

Explanation—On the dissolution of the gross body of the Enlightened person, there still remains a subtle body, as it is understood by the testimony of Śruti.

Śruti mentions a dialogue between the god of the moon and the individual soul ascending through the northern passage of the solar rays; such a dialogue is not possible unless the latter possesses a subtle body like the god's.

For the dialogue referred to vide—

"तं प्रतिब्रूयात्, सत्यं ब्रूयात्"

(The Enlightened soul replies to him—*the god of the moon*—, and speaks the truth.)

Kauṣītaki, Chap. 1, 2.

नोपमर्द्देनातः॥१०॥

[This Sūtra supports Sūtra 7 by stating that immortality may be attained in this life.]

न (not), **उपमर्द्देन** (by the annulment *of the bodily connection*), **अतः** (therefore.)

Explanation—Therefore Śruti does indeed speak of immortality, but not by annulment of bodily connection.

As Śruti says that the subtle body accompanies the Enlightened soul, it is proved that immortality, spoken of in Sūtra 7, is attained without the annulment of bodily connection.

For reference in the Śruti vide—

"अथ मर्त्त्योऽमृतो भवत्यत्र"

(For the full passage and translation vide under Sūtra 7 of this section.)

This and the preceding Sūtras establish the theory of 'जीवन्मुक्ति'(a state of freedom unaffected by bodily concerns and mental entanglements, although the soul has not departed. from its bodily tenement.)

Ācārya Śaṅkara explains this Sūtra in the way that the subtle body is not destroyed by what destroys the gross body, such as burning and the like.

अस्यैव चोपपत्तेरुष्मा॥११॥

[This Sūtra states that the heat perceived in the gross body is not its own, but belongs to the subtle body.]

अस्य (of the subtle body), **एव** (certainly), **च** (also), **उपपत्तेः** (from proof furnished by *actual observation*), **उष्मा** (vital heat.)

Explanation—the normal temperature of the human body is certainly the inherent heat of the subtle body and this is perceived by the temperature of the skin, so that the proof is furnished by actual observation.

The subtle body imparts its own heat to the gross body and keeps it warm as long as it remains alive. When the subtle body leaves the gross body, the vital heat is no longer perceived in the latter; from this observation it is inferred that the heat really belongs to the subtle body, and not to the gross body.

For the Śruti vide—

"उष्म एव जीविष्यञ्छीतो मरिष्यन्"

(He is warm when living, cold when dying.)

प्रतिषेधादिति चेन्न शारीरात् स्पष्टो हि एकेषाम् ॥१२॥

[Here an objection is raised against the fact that the Indriyas accompany the Enlightened soul at death; and his objection is refuted.]

प्रतिषेधात् (as it is contradicted *by Śruti*) **इति** (this), **चेत्** (if *it be argued*); **न** (no, you cannot say so), **शारीरात्** (from the soul, the owner of the body), **स्पष्टः** (clear), **हि** (because), **एकेषाम्** (*the statement* of some Śrutis.)

[This Sūtra consists of two parts *viz.*, an objection and its reply. The objection-portion is:—**प्रतिषेधादिति चेत्**; the reply-portion is:—**न शारीरात्, स्पष्टो हि एकेषाम्**.]

Explanation—If it be argued that the Indriyas do not accompany the enlightened soul at death, but on the contrary, they remain with the body lately inhabited by the soul, as some Śruti denies the fact that they never part with the soul; then the reply is that the argument cannot stand, because there is no such denial although there may be some ambiguity as to whether the departure of the Indriyas is to be understood in the sense of parting with the soul or parting with the body; this ambiguity is, however, removed by a parallel statement occurring in some other Śruti, where the meaning is made clearer that Indriyas never part with the released soul when the whole party leaves the body.

From the passage of the Bṛhadāraṇyaka Śruti quoted below, it may, at first sight, appear that the Indriyas do not part with the body, but remain with it at death; but the expression of 'not parting' occurring there does not mean 'not parting with the body'; but it implies 'not parting with their lord, the embodied soul', as is clearly understood from the expression in the same Śruti of the Mādhyandina branch. According to the Mādhyandina branch there is a slightly different reading, as '**तस्मात् प्राणाः**' (Indriyas *from him*) instead of '**तस्य प्राणः**' (Indriyas *of him*), meaning that the Indriyas never part with the released soul but accompany him to Brahma-Loka.

For reference in the Śruti, vide—

अथाकामयमानो योऽकामो निष्काम आप्तकाम आत्मकामो न तस्य प्राणा उत्क्रामन्ति ब्रह्मैव सन् ब्रह्माप्येति"

(But *the Indriyas of the person* who has no desire, *and therefore,* is desireless and passionless, whose desires have all been fulfilled, whose only desire is to realise Self, the Indriyas of him never depart; he, having got the status of Brahma, becomes Brahma.)

Bṛhadāraṇyaka, Chap. IV, 4, 6.

But the reference in the Mādhyandina Śrutis is as follows—

"न तस्मात् प्राणा उत्क्रामन्ति"

(The Indriyas never depart from him—*from that person.*)

[Here 'तस्मात् प्राणा' used instead of 'तस्य प्राणा' of the former text is a clear indication that Indriyas and the soul are inseparable companions.]

So the denial of departure is clear in respect of the released soul and not in respect of his lately inhabited body.

Ācārya Śaṅkara has split up this Sūtra into two separate Sūtras: the first one is **"प्रतिषेधादिति चेन्न शारीरात्"**, and the second one is **'स्पष्टो ह्येकेषाम्;'** and his explanation of the first of these Sūtras is not different from that of Ācārya Nimbārka, as given above. The only difference is, that the first one of his two Sūtras is, according to him, put forward by way of objection, and the second one is its refutation.

Śaṅkara explains that the parting with the soul by the Indriyas has been denied; and that parting with the body has been affirmed in the first of these two Sūtras; this affirmation, that *also* the Indriyas of the Enlightened soul depart from the body, has been made by way of objection, which has been replied to by the second one of the Sūtras. So according to his explanation, the going out of the Enlightened soul's Indriyas from his gross body is not a fact; but they, with their lord—the released soul—are completely merged in the Universal Soul at death; after such merging of the soul along with the Indriyas, the body is then, according to him, disintegrated and resolved into its constituents and this is the kind of death for the Enlightened person. It is understood from the conversation between the sages Ārtabhāga and Yājñavalkya (Bṛhadāraṇyaka, Chap. III, 2, 11), that the departure and the journey of the soul at death, as stated in the Śruti, are not for those persons who have got the highest knowledge of Brahma but for those who are yet wanting in that consummation. One, who has known Brahma in His superior aspect, becomes united with the all-pervading Brahma; his actions and desirs are all destroyed, so there remains no reason or cause they may impel him to move from place to place or to take a long journey from the gross body to Brahma-Loka. Moreover, according to him, such expression of the Śruti, as "Here in this life he attains Brahma" (Bṛhadāraṇyaka, Chap. IV, 4, 7) becomes significant only when viewed from this standpoint. Ācārya Śaṅkara also makes a distinction between the two classes of meditators on Brahma: one classlook upon their own soul as the Attributeless Supreme Being, and this is the superior aspect of Brahma; and the other class look upon Brahma as possessed of qualities and attributes and related to this world of the senses. According to Śaṅkara this second aspect is illusory and unreal. The departure and the journey of the released soul can have a meaning only in reference to the second class of meditators.

The explanation by Ācārya Rāmānuja is also similar to that by Ācārya Nimbārka, as given above, but different from that by Ācārya Śaṅkara, whose views in this matter are strongly objected to by the followers of the other two Ācāryas mentioned above.

स्मर्य्यते च॥१३॥

[The previous discussion, on the progressive movement of the Enlightened soul, is continued.]

स्मर्य्यते (Smṛti says), **च** (also.)

Explanation—Smṛti also says to the same effect that the Enlightened soul departs from the body at death.

For reference in the Smṛti vide—

"जगाम भित्त्वा मूर्द्धानं दिवमभ्युत्पपात ह"

(But the soul went out bursting through the cerebral plexus and flew up to Heaven.)

Mahābhārata.

तानि परे तथा ह्याह॥१४॥

[This Sūtra shows that the minute elements, of the enlightened person, merge in Brahma, with the soul.]

तानि (those *minute elements*), **परे** (in the Supreme Soul, in Brahma), **तथा** (thus, so), **हि** (as, for), **आह** (*Śruti* says.)

Explanation—The minute elements of the constituents of the Enlightened person's body, such as vital heat etc., merge in Brahma, as Śruti says so.

For ante Śruti vide:—

"तेजः परस्यां देवतायाम्"

(For the full passage and translation, vide ante Sūtra 1.)

अविभागो वचनात् ॥१५॥

[This Sūtra shows the manner in which the minute elements merge in Brahma.]

अविभागः (non-distinction), **वचनात्** (from the declaration of Śruti.)

Explanation—When the parts (the minute elements) of the body of the Enlightened person, merge in Brahma, they do not retain their distinctive entity and become one with Brahma, as is understood from the declaration of Śruti.

For reference in the Śruti vide—

"एवमेवास्य परिद्रष्टुरिमाः षोडशकलाः पुरुषायणः पुरुषं प्राप्यास्तं गच्छन्ति, भिद्येते चासां नामरूपे, पुरुष इत्येवं प्रोच्यते । स एषोऽकलोऽमृतो भवति।"

(Thus these sixteen constituents—eleven Indriyas and five subtle elements—belonging to this seer, *i.e.*, the Enlightened disembodied soul, who reaches the *Supreme* spirit, lose their distinction and disappear in Him; their names and forms are abolished; they are spoken of as turned into the Spirit; and he becomes partless and deathless.)

Praśnopaniṣad, Chap. VI, 5.

तदोकोऽग्रज्वलनं, तत् प्रकाशितद्वारो
विद्यासामर्थ्यात्तच्छेषगत्यनुस्मृतियोगाच्च हार्दानुगृहीतः
शताधिकया ॥१६॥

[It has already been explained in Sūtra 7, that up to the entrance into the veinule the route of progress is the same for both the Enlightened and the unenlightened souls; there is the parting of the ways and it has also been explained that after death the subtle (Taijas) body of the Enlightened soul attains the status of Brahma.

Now the nature of departure, at death, of the Enlightened soul is separately dealt with.

तदोकः (his abode, the heart of the departing soul whence the Nāḍi No. 101 commences), अग्रज्वलन (the forepart *of the heart* being illumined), [तत् (तस्य, his; of the departing soul, ओकः (abode; the heart which is considered to be the abode of the soul at death), अग्रज्वलनं (the end of which is illuminated)] ततप्रकाशितद्वारः (the door of his egress being opened by Him, the Lord, तत्–तेन, by Him, by the Lord), विद्यासामर्थ्यात् (by virtue of his knowledge), तच्छेष-गत्यनुस्मृतियोगात् (owing to the application of constant thought to the progressive movement which is a secondary result of knowledge, तत्—तस्य, of that *knowledge*. शेषगतिः—the *progressive* movement which is a secondary result. अनुस्मृति—constant thought. योगात्—owing to the application), च (also), हार्दानुगृहीतः (favoured by Him who dwells in the heart.) हार्द—हृदयस्थ, (who dwells in the heart; the Supreme Soul), शताधिकया (by the one exceeding a hundred; by the hundred and first veinule; by the route No. 101.)

Explanation—By virtue of knowledge, and owing to the application of constant thought directed to the progressive movement which is subsidiary to that knowledge, the point of the heart which is the abode of the departing soul, is illumined, and through the grace of the Supreme Soul resident therein, the door or egress (the mouth of the veinule leading from the heart to the head, as stated in Sūtra 7 above) is thrown open; and the soul passes into the veinule numbered one hundred and one, (This veinule is the gate way of release, the other one hundred passages leading to bondage.)

This Sūtra and Sūtra 3 of Sec. 1, Chap. 4 distinctly inculcate the meditation of the Supreme Soul as residing in the heart. Cf. 'हृदि ह्येष आत्मा' (This soul certainly dwells in the heart.)

For reference vide the Śruti—

शतं चैका च हृदयस्य नाड्यस्तासां मूर्द्धानमभिनिः सृतैका"

(For the full passage and translation vide Sūtra 7 of this section.)

रश्म्यनुसारी ॥१७॥

[The description of progress of the Released soul, is continued.]

रश्म्यनुसारी (following the direction of rays, **रश्मि**—ray.)

Explanation—The soul, making its exit from the cerebral plexus (**मूर्द्धण्या नाड़ी**) takes the direction of the solar rays.

For reference vide the Śruti—

"यत्रैतस्माच्छरीरादुत्क्रामत्यथैतैरेव रश्मिभिरूद्ध्र्वमाक्रमते"

(As soon as *the soul* leaves this body, it takes its wing upwards along these very rays.)

Chāndogya, Chap. VIII, 6, 5.

"निशि नेति चेन्न सम्बन्धस्य यावद्देहभावित्वाद्दर्शयति च ॥१८॥

[An objection, to Sūtra 17, is raised and refuted.]

निशि (at night; by night), **न** (not; does not attain Brahma), **इति** (this), **चेत्** (if *it be objected*); **न** (no; the objection is not valid), **सम्बन्धस्य** (of the connection with his works), **यावद्देहभावित्वात्** (as long as the body exists); **दर्शयति** (*Śruti* shows), **च** (also.)

[This Sūtra consists of two parts, namely, an objection and its reply. the objection-portion is:—**निशि नेति चेत्;** the reply-portion is:—**न, सम्बन्धस्य यावद्देहभावित्वात्, दर्शयति च.**]

Explanation—If it be objected that the Enlightened soul cannot attain the status of Brahma if he happens to die at night (because there is no solar ray then for lighting his way and also because scripture condemns death by night, then the reply is:—No, the objection is not valid, because his connection with his works ceases with the body, *i.e.*, because his past works are destroyed and his future works do not cling to him; and the works, that have already begun to fructify (his Prārabdhas), bind him no longer. So, there being no binding force hampering his movement, the released soul is fre e to fly to his destinction, no matter he dies by day or by night. Śruti also shows it to be so.

The condemnation by scripture applies only to the bound and unenlightened soul.

For reference vide—

"दिवा च शुक्लपक्षञ्ज उत्तरायणमेव च ।
मुमूर्षतां प्रशस्तानि विपरीतं तु गर्हितम्॥"

(The day-time, the fortnight ofthe waxing moon, and Uttaraṇyaṇa, *i.e.*, the period of the sun's motion from the winter solstice to the summer solstice, are the fittest time for a dying man's passing away; the reverse *of the above mentioned time* is not commendable.)

Also vide—

"तस्य तावदेव चिरं यावन्न विमोक्ष्येऽथ सम्पत्स्ये"

(For translation and reference vide Sūtra 7, Sec. 1, Chap. 1.)

Ācārya Śaṅkara explains this Sūtra in the following way:—It may be argued that the would of an enlightened person, who dies at day-time, may follow the rays of the sun; but not so the soul of one who dies by night, when there is no sun and therefore the connection of the veinule and the rays is broken; ; but this is a mistaken assumption, because there lasts a constant connection between the vein and the rays as long as the body lives, as Śruti also says—

"नक्तमहरेवाभिनिष्पद्यते"

(Day he makes it in the night; *i.e., the sun emits rays even during the night.*)

Chāndogya, Chap. VIII, 4, 2.

अतश्चायनेऽपि दक्षिणे॥१९॥

[This Sūtra is a corollary drawn from the preceding Sūtra.]

अत: (therefore; for the same reason), च (and), अयने (during the sun's course),अपि (also), दक्षिणे (southern.)

Explanation—And for the same reason as stated in the preceding Sūtra, there is no bar to the attainment of Brahma by an Enlightened soul, who dies during Dakṣiṇāyana (the period of the sun's motion from the summer solstice to the winer solstice.)

योगिन: प्रति स्मर्य्यते, स्मार्त्ते चैते॥२०॥

[The argument in the two preceding Sūtras is strengthened here by further exposition.]

योगिन: प्रति (to those who practice meditation), स्मर्य्यते (are shown in Smṛti), स्मार्त्ते (for remembrance), च (and), एते (these two paths, *one of the gods and the other of the fathers*—Devayāna and Pitṛyāna.)

Explanation—And these two paths, one of the gods and the other of the fathers (Devayāna and Pitṛyāna), on death at particular times, are presented by Smṛti before those who practise meditation, so that they may bear in mind the different consequences of the two lines of work they adopt in their lifetime, *viz.*, (1) the practice of meditation and the realisation of Brahma, and (2) the performance of meritorious works with a view to sensuous enjoyments.

In the Smṛti (Bhagavat-Gītā), it is said, that in the case of death happening at day-time, in the bright fortnight and during Uttarāyaṇa there occurs no return to this world, and in the case of death happening at night, in the dark fortnight and during Dakṣiṇāyana, a return to this world occurs. This statement is meant to be noted and remembered by the detached (अनासक्त) and the attached (आसक्त), so that they may shape their conduct accordingly; and this does not indicate that there is really any special time or hard and fast rule for the Enlightened soul to leave the body—that he must die at such and such prescribed time in order to attain Brahma. the knowledge of the two paths is to be borne in mind by the Yogī as a safeguard against the fatal mistake of cherishing any earthly desire, while parting with this life.

For reference in the Bhagavat Gītā vide:—

यत्र काले त्वनावृत्तिमावृत्तिश्चैव योगिनः।
प्रयाता यान्ति तं कालं वक्ष्यामि भरतर्षभ॥२३॥

अग्नि ज्योंतिरहः शुक्लः षणमासा उत्तरायणम्।
तत्र प्रयाता गच्छन्ति ब्रह्म ब्रह्मविदो जनाः॥२४॥

धूमो रात्रिस्तथाकृष्णः षणमासा दक्षिणयनम्।
तत्र चान्द्रमसं ज्योतिर्योगी प्राप्य निवर्त्तते॥२५॥

शुक्लकृष्णे गती ह्येते जगतः शाश्वते मते।
एकया यात्यनावृत्तिमन्ययावर्त्तते पुनः॥२६॥

(I will tell you, O thou, the mightiest of the descendants of Bharata, of the times when the Yogis die to return *to this world*, and also the times when they die not to return; the fire, the light, the day-time, the bright lunar fortnight, the six months of Uttarāyaṇa are *the marks of* the path through which the worshippers of Brahma pass *after death* and attain Brahma; *again*, the smoke, the night, the dark lunar fortnight, and the six months of Dakṣiṇāyana, these are *the marks of* the path, through which the Yogī reaches the lunar world and returns to this life. These are the two eternal paths well-known to the world, one bright and the other dark; by the former the soul departs not to return, and by the latter it departs to return again.)

Bhagavat Gītā, Chap VIII, 23—26.

For the subsequent passage referred to, vide:—

"नैते सृती पार्थ जानन् योगी मुह्यति कश्चन।
तस्मात् सर्व्वेषु काल्लेषु योगयुक्ते भवार्ज्जुन॥"

(Knowing these two paths, O son of Pṛthā, the Yogī—meditator—becomes careful not to take a false step; therefore, O Arjuna, be constantly devoted to meditation.)

Bhagavat Gītā, Chap. VIII, 27.

This means that the meditator need not care for the considerations of time, as Śruti clearly states that the night to such a person turns into day—that with him it is always day.

For the cleary statement in the Śruti, vide:—

"नक्तमहरेव सम्पद्यते।"

(Night even turns into day *to them.*)

SECTION—III

This section describes the journey of the released soul on the way to Brahma, and takes up the thread of the story at the point where it was left in the preceding section.

Sūtras 1—5 tell how the Enlightened individual souls, on leaving their bodies, proceed by the way, known as the passage of the ray of light, etc., (अर्च्चिरादिमार्ग) better styled 'the path of the gods' (Deva-Yāna.)

As the first step on the way, they go to the deity of light, who leads them on, through his own sphere, to another deity—the deity of day, who, in his turn, leads the souls, through his own sphere, to the next deity—the deity of the waxing moon, and in this manner they are led, step by step, by the successive deities presiding over the sun and the moon, through their respective jurisdictions, till they arrive at the region of the deity of lightning; whence a Spiritual Being conducts them, successively through the worlds of the gods Varuṇa, Indra and Prajāpati, to the world of Brahma.

Sūtras 6-10 state the according to Ācārya Bādari, the Spiritual Being escorts the souls to the Personal Relative Brahma (अपरब्रह्म) and not to the Impersonal, Absolute Brahma (परब्रह्म) unconditioned by time and space; because the Personal Brahma (Iśwara), Who occupies a definite place, can be conceived to be the goal of a journey, whereas the Absolute Brahma, Who is present everywhere and is the inner Self of all, cannot be the destination of a journey. There is also an expression in Śruti denoting the limitation of this Relative Brahma by way of localisation and pluralisation (vide the term 'worlds'—ब्रह्मलोकान् in the Bṛhadāraṇyaka Śruti, Chap. VI, 2, 15.)

The Relative Brahma, Hiraṇyagarbha (Iśvara), is the first born, having sprung directly from the Absolute Brahma, Because of His close proximity to the Absolute Brahma, it is not unreasonable to apply the term 'Brahma' to this Personal God. At the general dissolution, when even the world of this Relative Brahma is re-absorbed in the Supreme Cause, the souls abiding therein, together with their Lord (the Personal Brahma), enter into the Absolute Brahma, never to return. This view has been demonstrated by quotations, both from Śruti and Smṛti.

Sūtras 11-13 show, that in the opinion of Ācārya Jaimini (the author of the Pūrva-Mīmāṁsā philosophy), the Spiritual Escort conducts the souls to the Absolute Brahma; because the Absolute Brahma is the principal and primary signification of the word 'Brahma' which signifies the Relative Brahma, only in a secondary sense; and there is the support of Śruti also in favour of this view.

Sūtras 14 and 15 conclude the discussion by referring to the view of Ācārya Bādarāyaṇa Vyāsa, the author of the Vedānta philosophy, who decides that the views of both Bādari and Jaimini are partially correct and partially faulty; in the event of the full admission of Bādari's view of a Personal God, the passage in the Śruti (that the emancipated soul, robed in brightest splendour, recovers his pristine form) becomes negatived; because the idea of a Personal God can hardly be reconciled with the idea of the soul's Own pristine form; and at the same time in the event of the full admission of Jaimini's view, (that only the meditators on the Absolute Brahma have the privilege of being conducted to the world of Brahma), the worshippers of the five fires (पञ्चाग्नि उपासकाः) will be excluded from that consummation. But the passage in the Śruti 'A person becomes in after-life what he resolves to be, while in this world'—leads to the conclusion that the meditator on the Relative Brahma proceeds at first to the Relative Brahma, and abiding with Him for long ages, at last is merged with his *fellows* and his Lord in the Brahma Absolute at the general dissolution; but he who meditates on the Supreme Brahma directly in his own self, attains the Supreme Brahma at once, *i.e.*, without having to pass through the world of the Relative Brahma and without needing the help of the Spiritual Escorts. By such conclusion all the statements of Śruti, in this connection, become consistent. the worshippers of Brahma by and through symbols, on the other hand, will enjoy their freedom unfettered only so far as the range of those symbols extends.

अर्च्चिरादिना तत्प्रथितेः॥१॥

[This Sūtra states that the emancipated soul proceeds, after death, by the path of the rays of light.]

अर्च्चिरादिना (by the rays of light and so on), **तत् प्रथितेः** (as it is well-known.)

Explanation—On leaving the body the departed emancipated soul proceeds by the path of the rays of light and so on, as detailed in the Chāndogya, the Bṛhadāraṇyaka and several other Śrutis.

For reference in the Chāndogya Śruti, vide—

(A) **"तेऽर्च्चिषमभिसम्भवन्त्यर्च्चिषोऽहरन्ह आपूर्य्यमाणपक्षमापूर्य्यमाण-पक्षाद् यान् षडुदङ्ङेति मासांस्तान्। मासेभ्यः सम्वत्सरं संवत्सरादादित्य-मादित्याच्चन्द्रमसं चन्द्रमसो विद्युतं तत् पुरुषोऽमानवः स एतान ब्रह्म गतय-त्येष देवयानः पन्थाः"**

(They attain to *the deity residing in* the ray of light, from the ray of light to the god of day, from the day to the fortnight of the waxing moon (Śukla Pakṣa), from the waxing moon to the half year of the suns northern motion (Uttarāyaṇa) and from that again to the year, from the year to the sun, from the sun, to the moon, from the moon to lightning; then a superhuman being conducts them to Brahma. This is the path of the gods.]

Chāndogya, Chap. V, 10, 1 and 2.

For reference in Bṛhadāraṇyaka, vide—

(B) "तेऽर्चिरभिसम्भवन्त्यर्चिषोऽहरन्ह आपूर्यमाणपक्षमापूर्यमाणपक्षाद् यान् षण्मासानुदङ्ङादित्य एति मासेभ्यो देवलोकं देवलोकाद् आदित्यमादित्याद् वैद्युदं तान् वैद्युतान् पुरुषो मानस एत्य ब्रह्मलोकान् गमयति।"

(They go to *the deity dwelling in* the ray of light, from the ray of light to the *god of* day, from the day to the fortnight of the waxing moon, from the waxing moon to the half year of the sun's northern motion, from that to the world of gods, from the world of gods to the sun, from the sun to lightning; then a spiritual being, coming *there*, conducts them from there through the worlds of Brahma.)

Bṛhadāraṇyaka, Chap. VI, 2, 15.

For reference in another Śruti, vide:—

(C) "स एवं देवयानं पन्थानमापद्याग्निलोकमागच्छति स वायुलोकं स आदित्यलोकं स वरुणलाकं स इन्द्रलोकं स प्रजापतिलोकं स ब्रह्मलोकं।"

(Having reached the path of the gods, he comes, *in turn*, to the world of Fire, to the world of Air, to the world of Sun, to the world of Varuṇa (the Nebular Region), to the world of Indra, to the world of Prajāpati, *and finally* to the world of Brahma.)

Kauṣītakyopaniṣad, Chap. I, 3.

वायुमब्दादविशेषविशेषाभ्याम्॥२॥

[The description of the path of the gods is continued.]

वायम् (the world of air), "अब्दात् (after the year), अविशेषविशेषाभ्याम् (because of non-specification and specification; because it is stated in general in one Śruti and in detail in another.)

Explanation—For the sake of consistency of the different versions of the Śruti about the description of the path of the gods, the sphere of Air is to be considered just beyond that of year, and below the world of Sun; because it is stated in the ordinary way in one Śruti and in detail in another.

The description of the path of the gods appears to be different in the different Śrutis; but this apparent discrepancy must be reconciled as all the texts are equally authoritative; so the steps named in one but omitted from the others have to be inserted in the latter, in order to fill up the gaps there. Now, it is found that the Kauṣītaki Śruti speaks of the world of Fire as the first step, which is the same as the ray of light of the Chāndogya; then the former mentions the world of Air before the world of Sun, having left out some steps between Fire and Air; these blanks have to be filled up by drawing upon the latter Śruti, which locates them between Ray and sun; these steps are:—Waxing moon, Northern sun and Year (vide quotation 'A' under Sūtra 1.) There is also in Chāndogya between year (or Deva-Loka) and Sun, a gap which has to be filled up by inserting Air; because its mention before Sun, has been made in the Kauṣītaki (vide reference 'C' under Sūtra 1); the Bṛhadāraṇyaka Śruti also mentions it in quite a specific way in one of its passages (see 'D' below.) As for the Deva-Loka (world of the gods) in the passage 'B' (Sūtra 1) quoted from the Bṛhadāraṇyaka this may be considered as identical with the sphere of the deity of the 'year' of the Chāndogya (on the ground that a year of this world of the ordinary mortals constitutes a day of the world of the gods.)

[Some are, however, of opinion that year and Devaloka are not identical, but are two consecutive steps, the latter being located immediately above the former.]

For reference of the specific mention in the Bṛhadāraṇyaka Śruti, vide—

(D) "यदा वै पुरुषोऽस्माल्लोकात् प्रैति स वायुमागच्छति तस्मै स तत्र बिजिहीते यथा रथचक्रस्य खं तेन स ऊर्द्धवमाक्रमते स आदित्यामागच्छति"

(When the person,—*the worshipper of Brahma*—goes away from this world, he comes up to Air, then Air makes room for him to pass through, like the axle-hole of a wheel; through this hole he mounts higher up and reaches Sun.)

Bṛhadāraṇyaka Chap. V, 10, 1.

तड़ितोऽधि वरुणः सम्बन्धात्॥३॥

[The enumeration of the stations of the journey is continued.]

तडितोऽधि (beyond Lightning; just above the sphere of Lightning), **वरुणः** (*the position of* Varuṇa, the position of the Nebular Region), **सम्बन्धात्** (because there is an intimate connection between Lightning and moisture.)

Explanation—The position of the world of Varuṇa (the Nebular Region) stated in the Kauṣītaki Śruti, is just above the world of lightning (stated in the Chāndogya); because there is an intimate connection between the one and the other.

In the description of the path of the gods, the position of the sphere of Varuṇa of the Kauṣītaki Śruti is to be regarded as next above the Lightning (Vidyut-Loka) of Chāndogya, there being very close connection between the two (flashes of lightning appear to come out of the rain-cloud.)

Therefore, to fill up the other gaps in the description of the Kauṣītaki, the worlds of moon and that of Lightning (of the Chāndogya Śruti) have to be inserted between the world of Sun and world of Varuṇa and to fill up in the Chāndogya, the worlds of Varuṇa, Indra and Prajāpati have to be inserted between the world of Sun and the world of Brahma. To sum up, the path of the gods may be thus mapped out:—

(1) Ray of light, (2) day, (3) waxing moon, (4) northern sun, (5) year—(the world of the gods), (6) air (7) sun, (8) moon, (9) lightning; then (10) Varuṇa-Loka (or the Nebular Region), (11) Indra-Loka, (12) Prajāpati-Loka; and finally, (13) Brahmā in Brahma-Loka.

This also suggests that the super-human being who is said to conduct the emancipated soul from the god of Lightning to Brahma, has to escort the soul through the other intervening worlds, namely Varuṇa-Loka, Indra-Loka and Prajāpati-Loka.

आतिबाहिकास्तल्लिङ्गात् ॥४॥

[The description of the path of the gods is continued.]

आतिबाहिकाः (conductors; deities conducting the departed soul), **तल्लिङ्गात्,** (as there is suggestive indication in Śruti to that effect.)

Explanation—The successive stations of the journey as described in Śruti, do not mean certain objects or spheres or localities merely, but the deities residing therein, conducting the departed soul through their respective spheres; as there is suggestive indication in Śruti to that effect.

In Śruti, a superhuman being is stated to conduct the departed soul from Lightning to Brahma; and thus there being a conductor during the subsequent course of the passage, it is suggested that Light, Day, Fortnight, Northern Sun, Year, Air, Sun, Moon and Lightning are also the earlier Ātivāhika Spirits (escorts of the emancipated pilgrim) in the earlier stages of his journey.)

उभयव्यमोहात् तत्सिद्धेः॥४अ॥

[This Sūtra has been noted by Ācārya Śaṅkara, and not by any other commentator; it is an argument in support of Sūtra 4.]

उभय (both *the road and the traveller*), **व्यमोहात्** (because of unconsciousness; being ignorant *of the passage*), **तत्सिद्धेः** (for the sake of accomplishment; as the success is a fact.)

Explanation—Both the road and the traveller being unconscious agents, the former being inanimate and the latter ignorant of the way, success in reaching the goal becomes an impossibility without the help of intelligent guides; as there can be no denying the accomplishment of the journey, there must be some conductor guiding the pilgrim.

If the light, the day and the other stations of the journey are taken only to mean those inanimate objects or some localities, they cannot be expected to show the way to a Stranger, the emancipated soul; for the success of the journey, there must therefore be some intelligent conductors to guide the traveller, through their respective jurisdictions, until he arrives at the world to Brahma.

वैद्युतेनैव ततस्तच्छ्रुतेः॥५॥

[This discussion on the journey is continued.]

वैद्युतेन (by the *superhuman* being who takes his charge from the god of lightning), एव (only), ततः (thenceforward), तच्छ्रुतेः (as Śruti states so.)

Explanation—Henceforth the Traveller is taken charge of by one and the same superhuman being from the custody of the god of lightning, until the party arrives at Brahma-Loka, as Śruti says so, passing on the way through the jurisdiction of Varuṇa, Indra and Prajāpati.

For Reference in the Śruti vide:—

"तान् वैद्युतान् पुरुषो मानस एत्य ब्रह्मलोकान् गमयति।"

(For the full passage and translation vide the second quotation under Sūtra 1 above.)

कार्य्यं बादरिरस्य गत्युपत्तेः॥६॥

[A discussion, is now taken up whether the soul is conducted to the Absolute Brahma (परब्रह्म) or the Relative Brahma—Brahma related to the creation—Personal God.]

कार्य्यं (the Relative Brahma or the Personal God, Who is related to the creation and is caused from the Supreme Brahma and Who is also known as Hiraṇyagarbha), बादरिः (the sage Bādari), अस्य (His; of Hiraṇyagarbha), गत्युपपत्तेः (as movement *on the part of the emancipated soul* is thus rendered possible.)

Explanation—The sage Bādari opines that it is not the Absolute Brahma, but the Relative Brahma, Hiraṇyagarbha, to Whom the soul is conducted by his escorts; for movement or progress is possible only to the Relative Brahma, He being conditioned by time and space, and not to Absolute Brahma, Who is Infinite and Omnipresent. Ācārya Bādari argues that the Absolute (Infinite and Attributeless) Brahma, Who is Omnipresent and is the inner Self of all, cannot be the destination of a journey, which is accomplished by passing through a series of limited spheres and worlds; therefore it must be the Relative Brahma (bound in time and space) to Whom the emancipated soul is taken by his conductors.

For reference in the Chāndogya Śruti vide—

"तत्पुरुषोऽमानवः स एतान् ब्रह्म गमयति"

(For the full passage and translation, vide the first quotation under Sūtra 1.)

विशेषितत्वाच्च ॥७॥

[An argument, in support of Sūtra 6, is adduced.]

विशेषितत्वात् (because of being specified in Śruti, च (also.)

Explanation—The destination, to which the departed souls are led by the superhuman being, is the conditioned (Relative) Brahma, because of His being so specified in Śruti; for, Brahma is there spoken of as *localised*, and the locality is also *pluralised*.

The statement of the Bṛhadāraṇyaka Śruti, that the emancipated souls, when departed, are conducted to the 'worlds' of Brahma (ब्रह्मलोकान्), shows that the Brahma, mentioned therein, is limited in His particular 'worlds' which can directly denote only some localities falling within the sphere of the law of causation; again the plural form 'worlds' also denote that the 'Brahma' residing therein may abide under different conditions and in different places, and so He must be the Relative brahma, and not the absolute Being, in whose case such specifications are absurdity.

For reference in the Bṛhadāraṇyaka vide—

"तान् वैद्युतान् पुरुषो मानस एत्य ब्रह्मलोकान् गमयति तेषु ब्रह्मलोकेषु पराः परावतो वसन्ति"

(A spiritual being, coming there, leads those souls who

have reached the sphere of Lightning, to the worlds of Brahma, and in those worlds of Brahma they live for ever more.)

Bṛhadāraṇyaka, Chap. VI, 2, 15.

सामीप्यात्तु तदुपदेशः॥८॥

[The argument, in support of Sūtra 6, is continued.]

सामीप्यात् (because of proximity; as he is in closest proximity to the Supreme Brahma), तु (but), तदुपदेशः (that designation; the designation 'Brahma'.)

Explanation—But the designation of Brahma is applied to the Personal God for His closet proximity to the Supreme Brahma, Whose earliest manifestation is He.

कार्य्यात्यये तदध्यक्षेण सहातः परमभिधानात् ॥९॥

[The individual soul's final absorpton in the Absolute Brahma is now stated.]

कार्य्यात्यये (on the dissolution of the world of the Relative Brahma), तदध्यक्षेण सह (in company of Hiraṇyagarbha, the Ruler of the world), अतः परम् (higher than this; the Supreme Brahma), अभिधानात् (from declaration of Śruti; as there is such declaration in Śruti.)

Explanation—On the disintegration (Pralay) of the world of the Relative Brahma of Hiraṇyagarbha, the whole body of the emancipated souls, in company of Hiraṇyagarbha, their Lord, are finally re-absorbed in the Supreme Being; as there is such declaration in Śruti.

For reference vide—

"ते ब्रह्मलोके तु परान्तकाले परामृतात् परिमुच्यन्ति सर्व्वे।"

(They all, who come to reside in the world of Brahma, attain the highest immortality and are finally released at the time of the re-absorption of the First Person—*Hiraṇyagarbha*.)

Taittirīya Nārāyaṇa X, 24.

स्मृतेश्च॥१०॥

[An argument, in support of Sūtra 9, is adduced.]

स्मृतेः (as Smṛti agrees with the view; according to Smṛti), **च** (also.)

Explanation—The view, expressed in the preceding Sūtra, is corroborated by Smṛti also.

For reference in the Smṛti vide:—

"ब्रह्मणा सह ते सर्व्वे सम्प्राप्ते प्रतिसञ्चरे॥
परस्यास्ते कृतात्मानः प्रविशन्ति परं पदम्॥"

(On the occasion of the general disssolution, when the First Person—*the Relative Brahma or Hiraṇyagarbha*—comes to His end, they all, if they have realised their Self, enter into the Highest Bliss, *the Supreme Being,* in company of Brahma *the First Born*.)

परं जैमिनिर्मुख्यत्वात् ॥११॥

[An objection to Sūtra 6 is adduced by presenting an opposite view.]

परं (the Supreme Soul), **जैमिनिः** (*the sage* Jaimini *opines*), **मुख्यत्वात्** (because that is the principal and primary sense of the word.)

Explanation—Ācārya Jaimini opines that the Brahma of the Brahma-Loka is the Supreme Soul, because that is the principal and primary sense of the word.

Jaimini says that the expression 'A superhuman being conducts the travellers to Brahma' (quoted under Sūtra 6), refers to the Supreme Brahma; for the word 'Brahma' principally and primarily means that Supreme Soul; it is sometimes used to denote the Personal God only in a secondary sense; and where a term may be interpreted both in its primary and secondary sense, preference is to be given to the former.

दर्शनाच्च ॥१२॥

[An argument, in support of Jaimini, is adduced.]

दर्शनात् (from Śruti), **च** (also.)

Explanation—Śruti also has directly stated that the Supreme Being and not Hiraṇyagarbha is the highest attainable goal.

For reference in the Śruti vide—

"परं ज्योतिरुपसम्पद्य स्वेन रूपेणाभिनिष्पद्यते।"

(*The emancipated soul*, robed in brightest splendour, recovers his pristine form.)

Chāndogya, Chap. VIII, 2, 3.

न च कार्य्ये प्रतिपत्त्यभिसन्धिः॥१३॥

[The argument, in support of Sūtra 11, is continued.]

न (is not satisfied), **च** (also), **कार्य्ये** (in the Relative Brahma), **प्रतिपत्ति** (realisation of Brahma), **अभिसन्धिः** (desire.)

Explanation—The desire for the realisation of Brahma, on the part of the meditator (as expressed in a passage of the Chāndogya Śruti), is not also satisfied by attainment of the Relative Brahma.

For the Brahma desired-for by the meditator, vide and Śruti—

"नामरूपयोर्निर्व्वहिता ते यदन्तरा तद्ब्रह्म तदमृतं स आत्मा॥"

(The Revealer of names and forms, within Whom are they, the *names and forms*, is Brahma; He is the Imperishable One, He is the Self.)

Chāndogya, Chap. VIII, 14, 1.

अप्रतीकालम्बनान्नयतीति वादरायण उभयथा दोषात्तत्क्रतुश्च ॥१४॥

[The discussion commenced in Sūtra 6, whether the soul is taken to the Absolute Brahma or the Relative Brahma, is concluded in this and the following Sūtra.]

अप्रतीकालम्बनान् (those who do not have recourse to symbols for the meditation of Brahma), नयति (takes, leads), इति (this), वादरायण: (the sage Bādarāyaṇa, the framer of the Sūtras), उभयथा (in both the ways; in the opinon of Ācārya Bādari (as stated in Sūtra 6-10) as well as in the opinion of Ācārya Jaimini (as stated in Sūtras 11-13), दोषात् as (is the form of meditation, so is the result; as is the will, so is the attainment), च (and.)

Explanation—The sage Bādarāyaṇa, the framer of these Sūtras, however holds the view that the escort conducts to the Absolute Brahma, the souls of those persons who did not have recourse to symbols for their meditation, but meditated directly on Brahma; as there is defect in both the opinions stated in the preceding Sūtras—in the opinion of Ācārya Bādari (as stated in Sūtras 6-10), and in the opinion of Ācārya Jaimini (as stated in Sūtrs 11-13); and that the destination is determined by the nature of meditation.

The great sage Bādarāyaṇa is of opinion that the decisions of both Bādari and Jaimini are partly correct and partly faulty. In the event of full admission of Bādari's view, that all the meditators on Brahma are led to the Relative Brahma, the passage in the Śruti (to the effect that 'the emancipated soul, robed in brightest effulgence, recovers his pristine form') becomes contradicted; and in the case of Jaimini's view being fully admitted, that only the meditators on the Supreme Brahma have the privilege of being conducted to Brahma-Loka (vide Sūtra 13 last), the worshippers of the five Fires (पञ्चाग्निउपासका:) and the like will be excluded. So in order to reconcile both the views it must be admitted that just as a person meditates in this world so he becomes after leaving this world, *i.e.*, his future goal is determined by the nature of his meditation while on earth—as is his will so is his goal; therefore he, who worships Brahma by and through a symbol, attains at first the Relative Brahma, and abiding with him for ever more, at last merges in the Supreme Brahma at the general dissolution, while he, who meditates directly on the Supreme Brahma *per se*, attains the Supreme Brahma at once (*i.e.*, without having to wait in the world of the Relative Brahma.)

For reference in the Śruti against the view of Ācārya Bādari, vide—

"परं ज्योतिरूपसम्पद्य स्वेन रूपेणाभिनिष्पद्यते।"

(For translation and reference vide Sūtra.)

For reference in the Śruti against the view of Jaimini, vide—

"य एवमेतद्विदुर्ये चेमेऽरण्ये श्रद्धां सत्यमुपासते तेऽर्च्चिषमभिसम्भवन्ति"

(For translation and reference vide the first quotation under Sūtra 31, Sec. III, Chap. III.)

For reference in the Śruti in favour of the conclusion in the present Sūtra, vide—

"यथाक्रतुरस्मिँल्लोके पुरुषो भवति तथेतः प्रेत्य भवति"

(A person becomes in after-life, what he resolves to be, while in this world.)

Chāndogya Chap. III, 14, 1.

विशेषं च दर्शयति॥१५॥

[An argument, in support of the conclusion arrived at by Bādarāyaṇa, is adduced here.]

विशेषं (a speciality; special rewards for special modes of symbol-worship), **च** (also), **दर्शयति** (Śruti shows; it is found in Śruti.)

Explanation—In respect of the mediators on Brahma by and through symbols, such as name, speech, mind etc., Śruti promises special rewards for worshippers of special symbols, which rewards, however, fall far short of the highest one—the atttainment of Brahma.

For reference to the rewards of symbol-worship vide—

"स यो नाम ब्रह्मेत्युपास्ते यावन्नाम्नो गतं गत्रास्य यथाकामचारो भवति"

"स यो वाचं ब्रह्मेत्युपास्ते यावद्वाचो गतं तत्रास्य यथाकामचारो भवति"

स यो मनो ब्रह्मेत्युपास्ते यावन्मनसो गतं तत्रास्य यथाकामचारो भवति"

(He, who worship Name as Brahma, or Speech as Brahma, or Mind as Brahma, wins his liberty unfettered within the sphere of Name or Speech or Mind respectively as long as and as far as it extends.)

Chāndogya, chap. VII, 1, 5, 2, 2; 3, 2.

SECTION—IV

This section deals with the condition and position of the Enlightened soul and his relation to the Supreme Soul, on his union with HIm after his Release.

Sūtras 1-4 state, on the authority of Śruti, that the Released soul, on attaining Brahma, is revealed in his own normal pristine form, and not in the form of a deity nor in any borrowed form; and thus being released from his late state of bondage, he abides in the glory of his Self, which is no other than Brahma; and though a part of Brahma, he perceives himself as assimilated to, and inseparable from, Him.

Sūtras 5-7 compare the views of the two sages, Jaimini and Auḍulomi, as to the ultimate form in which the Released soul emerges out of his previous state of bondage. Ācārya Jaimini thinks that the Released soul emerges from bondage, as endowed with the powers and attributes belonging to the Supreme Soul. The sage Auḍulomi holds the view that the Released soul manifests himself solely as pure consciousness. Ācārya Bādarāyaṇa Vyāsa, the author of the Vedānta philosophy, decides that both the natures, *viz.*, that of pure consciousness and that of possessing the powers and attributes of Brahma are manifested in the Released soul, and that there is no incongruity between the two natures; and Śruti supports both the views.

Sūtras 8 and 9 state that by the mere fiat of his will, the Released soul gets all his desires fulfilled; he thus becomes lord of himself and owes allegiance to none else, (except in matter of creation, preservation and destruction of the worlds, which form the exclusive function of Brahma Himself.)

Sūtras 10-16 compare the views of the two sages, Bādari and Jaimini, on the question whether the Released soul has any body and Indriyas of his own. The sage Bādari thinks that the Released soul possesses neither body nor Indriyas, while Ācārya Jaimini opines that he does possess a body with Indriyas. Ācārya Bādarāyaṇa Vyāsa decides that as Śruti contains indications of both kinds, the Released soul may exist in both conditions at his option; *i.e.*, when he wishes to have a body he appears in one, and when he wishes to be without it he has none. There is however, no hard and fast rule that the body, assumed by the Released soul, must be, in every case, created by his own will—he may sometimes have enjoyments by being united with a body created by the Lord, like the enjoyments, in dreams, of a living person. The divine will may however, make use of the Released souls as tools, through the instrumentality of which. It chooses to fulfil any of Its purposes. Besides, the Released Soul may put on any garb contrived by himself suited to take part in the fulfilment of that purpose. He has also the power of projecting himself into space just as the light of a lamb expands far off and is reflected from many things at the same time. He becomes omniscient and is never unconscious; what is stated in Śruti about specific non-cognition, or total unconsciousness, is either regarding deep sleep or regarding death, but not regarding the Released Soul in close union with the Lord.

Sūtras 17-22 show, on the authority of Śruti and Smṛti, that the Released Soul, united with the Universal Soul, becomes endowed with the powers and attributes on Brahma, except in the matters of creating, preserving and dissolving the worlds, and is privileged to enjoy all kinds of bliss available in diverse worlds; that he is no longer subject to mutations caused by births, deaths and so on, but he possesses for all time the supreme consciousness of being one with Brahma; that he attains equality with Brahma, only in respect of enjoyment, but not in respect of exercising authority in matters of creation etc.; and that he is not bound to return to this world and to undergo rebirths.

सम्पद्याविर्भावः स्वेन शब्दात् ॥१॥

[The Sūtra says that the Enlightened soul, after gaining the status Brahma recovers his original effulgent form proper.]

सम्पद्य (attaining, after attaining Brahma), **अविर्भावः** (manifestation), **स्वेन शब्दात्** (because of the word **स्वेन** 'meaning' 'his own'.)

Explanation—After attaining Brahma, the Emancipated soul appears revealed in his own natural form proper, as the Śruti uses the expression '**स्वेन**' (his own) with the term '**रूपं**' (form.)

The Emancipated soul, on attaining Brahma by the passage of the ray of light etc. manifests himself in his own natural form, and not in the form of a deity or in any form borrowed from elsewhere, as can be inferred from the word 'own' in passage of the Śruti.

For reference in the Śruti vide:—

"एष सम्प्रसादोऽस्माच्छरीरात् समुत्थाय परं ज्योतिरुपसम्पद्य स्वेन रूपेणाभिनिष्पद्यते"

(The Blessed soul, coming out of this body, robed in his finest effulgence, stands revealed in his own pristine glory.)

Chāndogya, Chap. VIII, 3, 4.

मुक्तः प्रतिज्ञानात्॥२॥

[The previous Sūtra is further elucidated.]

मुक्तः (freed; released), **प्रतिज्ञानात्** (from the promise.)

Explanation—The soul, referred to in the previous Sūtra, is recognised to be the *Released* soul; as is evident from the promise of Prajāpati to Indra, in the Chāndogya Śruti.

At the outset of the instruction imparted by Prajāpati to Indra and Virocana, the natural free state of the soul (beyond the reach of sin, death, decrepitude, sorrow, hunger, thirst and so on) has been pointed out; then Prajāpati promises to Indra that he would further explain the nature of the soul to him; and his closing remark only endorses what he promised at the outset and concludes with the repetition of the normal characteristics of the Released soul, which, now after his emancipation, stand fully revealed in their pristine gloiy.

For the normal character of the soul, vide the words of Prajāpati in the Śruti—

"य आत्मापहतपाप्मा विजरो विमृत्युर्व्विशोकोऽविजिघत्सोऽपिपासः सत्यकामः सत्यसंकल्पः सोऽन्वेष्टव्यः स विजिज्ञासितव्यः।"

(This soul is free from all imperfections, without decay, death, sorrow, hunger and thirst, and with desires and purposes that ever come true. He is to be sought for the inquired after.)

Chāndogya, Chap. VIII, 7, 1.

For the promise of Prajāpati, vide—

"एवं त्वेव ते भूयोऽनुव्याख्यास्यामि।"

(But I will explain this further to you)

Chāndogya, Chap. VIII, 9, 3.

For the concluding speech of Prajāpati, vide—

"परं ज्योतिरुपसम्पद्य स्वेन रूपेणाभिनिष्पद्यते।"

(For the full passage and translation, see under the preceding Sūtra.)

आत्मा प्रकरणात्॥३॥

[This Sūtra says that the individual soul recovers his own self as stated in Sūtra I.]

आत्मा (*the individual* soul), **प्रकरणात्** (because it is the subject-matter of the discourse.)

Explanation—He, who appears in his own pristine form after gaining the brightest effulgence, is no other being than the individual soul, because the subject-mater of the discourse is he himself.

अविभागेन दृष्टत्वात्॥४॥

[The released soul remains inseparable from the Supreme Soul.]

अविभागेन (inseparably), **दृष्टत्वात्** (as it is found so in Śruti.)

Explanation—The released soul, though a part of the Supreme Soul, perceives himself as inseparable from Him. Scriptures also state that there is nothing existing independently of and separately from the Supreme Soul; he now intuitively and clearly perceives to be true what he hitherto believed from the scriptures to be true.

Vide the Śruti—'**अहं ब्रह्मास्मि**' (I am Brahma.)

Bṛhadāraṇyaka, Chap. I, 4, 10.

Compare Sūtra 42, Sec. III, Chap. II, for the view that the individual soul is a part of the Supreme Soul.

ब्राह्मेण जैमिनिरुपन्यासादिभ्यः॥५॥

[The view of the sage Jaimini is stated in this connection.]

ब्राह्मेण (with properties belonging to Brahma; as possessed of the attributes of Brahma), **जैमिनिः** (the sage Jaimini), **उपन्यासादिभ्यः** (from the attribution in the beginning of the discourse, and the like.)

Explanation—Ācārya Jaimini thinks that the released soul emerges from bondage as endowed with the properties belonging to the Supreme Being Himself, as is understood from the attribution of those properties to the released soul, and also because he is described as freely moving about, enjoying himself, and the like.

For reference vide the Śruti—

"य आत्मापहतपाप्मा बिजरो विमृत्युर्व्विशोकः..."

For the full quotation and translation, see under Sūtra 2 above.)

Compare this with the instruction of Prajāpati to Indra in the same Śruti—

"स तत्र पर्य्येति जक्षन् क्रीड़न् रममाणः।"

(There he moves at large, enjoying himself, playing and making himself merry.)

Chāndogya, Chap. VIII, 12, 3.

"चिति तन्मात्रेण तदात्मकत्वादित्यौडुलोमिः॥६॥

[The view of the sage Auḍulomi is stated in this connection.]

चिति (in pure consciousness), **तन्मात्रेण** (solely), **तदात्मकत्वात्** (as that is its soul or essence), **इति** (this), **औडुलोमिः** (the sage Auḍulomi.)

Explanation—Ācārya Auḍulomi, on the other hand, holds the view that the released soul manifests himself solely as pure consciousness, since he is essentially of the nature of consciousness, his other properties, such as freedom from lomitations and imperfections (**अपहतपाप्मा**), wishes ever coming true (**सत्यकाम**), will-power never failing to be effected (*i.e.* Omnipotence) *etc.*, are only accidental.

For the Śruti vide—

"एवैवं वा अरेऽयमात्मानन्तरोऽबाह्यः कृत्स्नः प्रज्ञानघन एव।"

(Thus this self has neither inside nor outside, but is altogether massive intense consciousness.)

Bṛhadāraṛyaka, Chap. IV, 5, 13.

एवमप्युपन्यासात् पूर्व्वभावादविरोधं वादरायणः॥७॥

[The author's own view is now stated.]

एवमपि (in this way too), **उपन्यासात्** (owing to the representation, of the Released soul as Pure Consciousness, in Śruti), **पूर्व्वभावात्** (and owing to the attribution of the properties mentioned before), **अविरोधं** (there is no contradiction), **वादरायण:** (the sage Bādarāyaṇa, the author of the Vedānta-Sūtra.)

Explanation—Ācārya Bādarāyaṇa Vyāsa, the author of the Vedanta philosophy, decides, that though the Released soul has been described in this way too, *i.e.*, after the manner of Auḍulomi as Pure Consciousness, yet to the former are attributed also the properties mentioned previously in Sūtra 5. So the Released soul must be accepted to be of the nature of pure consciousness and also as possessed of those other properties. Thus the two apparently conflicting views are reconciled.

Ācārya Śaṅkara also explain this Sūtra in this way; but he adds that these accidental attributes can be affirmed of the Soul only in respect of His phenomenal aspect (**व्यवहारिक सत्ता**), and not in His noumenal aspect (**पारमार्थिक सत्ता**.) The Ācārya says that massive enjoyment and pure consciousness are the essence of Brahma, while omniscience, omnipotence *etc.*, are the properties of Iśvara (the Personal God), thus giving Iśvara subordinate position to Brahma.

सङ्कल्पादेव तच्छ्रुतेः॥८॥

[The powers and privileges, which a released soul acquires, are stated here.]

सङ्कल्पात् (by the exercise of will), **एव** (merely), **तच्छ्रुतेः** (**तत्श्रुतेः**, because Śruti says so.)

Explanation—By the mere fiat of his will the Released soul gets his desires fulfilled; because Śruti says so.

For reference in the Śruti vide—

"स यदि पितृलोककामो भवति संकल्पादेवास्य पितरः समुत्तिष्ठन्ति।"

(If he desires the vicinity or presence of the fathers, by the mere fiat of his will the fathers present themselves.)

Chāndogya, Chap. VIII, 2, 1.

अतएवानन्याधिपतिः॥९॥

[The previous topics is continued.]

अतएव (therefore; so), **अनन्याधिपतिः** (without any other lord; lord of himself .

Explanation—As the Released soul can carry into effect any of his desires by the mere fiat of his will he becomes the lord of himself, and owes allegiance to no other power.

For reference in the Śruti vide—

"स स्वराड् भवति" (He becomes lord of himself.)

Chāndogya, Chap. VII, 25, 2.

अभावं वादरिराह ह्येवाम्॥१०॥

[Here follows a discussion whether the released soul possesses a body or not.]

अभावं (*there is* absence of *a body and Indriyas*, he has no body nor Indriyas), **वादरिः** (the sage Bādari), **आह** (*Śruti* says), **हि** (as), **एवम्** (so.)

Explanation—The sage Bādạri thinks that the Released soul possesses neither a body nor Indriyas and bases his opinion on the authority of Śruti.

For the Śruti vide—

"अशरीरं बाव सन्तं न प्रियाप्रिये स्पृशतः।"

(He being bodies, nothing, pleasant or unpleasant, touches him.)

Chāndogya, Chap. VIII, 12, 1.

भावं जैमिनिर्विकल्पामननात्॥११॥

[A contrary view, to Sūtra 10, is adduced.]

भावं (*there is* existence *of a body and Indriyas*; he possesses a body with Indriyas), **जैमिनिः** (the sage Jaimini), **विकल्पामननात्** (because Śruti states of diversity; as it is stated in Śruti that he assumes diverse forms at his option. **विकल्प (विविध**

कल्पं; diversity in manifestation), **आमननात्**—(from statement in Śruti.)

Explanation—The sage Jaimini thinks that the released soul possesses a body with Indriyas, as it is stated in Śruti that he assumes diverse forms at his option.

For the reference vide the Śruti—

"स एकधा भवति त्रिधा भवति पञ्चधा सप्तधा..."

(He becomes one-fold, becomes three-fold, five-fold, seven-fold....)

Chāndogya, Chap. VII, 26, 2.

द्वादशाहवदुभयविधं वादरायणोऽतः॥१२॥

[A decision is given on the conflicting views noted above.]

द्वादशाहवत् (as is the case with the twelve-day sacrifice), **उभयविधं** (existing in both conditions *according to his option*), **वादरायणः** (Bādarāyaṇa Vyāsa), **अतः** (so; therefore.)

Explanation—The sage Bādarāyaṇa Vyāsa says that, because of his invincible will-power, the Released soul may exist in both conditions *viz.*, with a body or without a body, according to his option; as is the case with the twelve-day sacrifice.

In the opinion of Vyāsa, the author of this philosophy, the Released soul assumes a body when he wishes to do so; and when he wishes to be without a body, he has none; as the Soma-sacrifice extending over twelve days may be viewed either as an ordinary or as an extraordinary sacrifice; because both alternatives are indicated by Śruti.

तन्वभावे सन्ध्यवदुपपत्तेः॥१३॥

[An inference is drawn from the conclusion arrived at in Sūtra 12.]

तन्वभावे (in the absence of a body created by his own will, **तनु**—body) **सन्ध्यवत्** (like the *enjoyment in* dreams), **उपपत्तेः** (as it is reasonable.)

Explanation—Even if it be admitted that he may not possess a body created by his own will it is not unreasonable to expect that the Released soul, uniting at his option with a body specially created for him by the Lord, may enjoy himself therein; just as a dreaming person may experience pleasurable emotions in a body created by the Lord for the time being for his benefit.

There is, therefore, no hard and fast rule that the body, assumed by the Released soul must invariably be of his own creation.

[From these Sūtras it is evident, from the stand-point of Nimbārka, that even in the released state the individual soul's complete union with Brahma does not take place. Even in his released state Jīva may be said to be different from, as well as the same time with, Brahma.]

भावे जाग्रद्वत्॥१४॥

[Another inference is drawn from the conclusion arrived at in Sūtra 12.]

भावे (in the case of existence of a body *created by himself*), **जाग्रद्वत्** (*there may be enjoyment* just as in the state of wakefulness.)

Explanation—It is also possible for the Released soul to assume a body, contrived by himself to suit his purpose, by which he may, in communion with the Lord, experience enjoyments, similar to those of his wakeful state in corporeal existence.

This body, unlike the one in his dreaming state, may have an objective reality, such as one finds in his waking state.

When the Released soul assumes no body and Indriyas, his state may be viewed as analogous to that of a dreaming man, when wished-for objects have only a subjective existence in his mind. On the other hand, when he assumes a body with Indiryas, the things that that he perceives or wishes for, are objectively true, as in the wakeful state of his formerly embodied existence.

प्रदीपवदावेशस्तथाहि दर्शयति॥१५॥

[This Sūtra shows possibility, for the Released soul, of simultaneously possessing several bodies other than his own.]

प्रदीपवत् (just like *the expansion of light of* a lamp), **आवेशः** (penetration far and wide), **तथा** (so), **हि** (as), **दर्शयति** (Śruti shows.)

Explanation—The Released soul can perceive, from a great distance, what is passing in minds other than his own; just as the light of a lamp penetrates far and wide, though itself occupying a limited space; Śruti also shows so.

For the Śruti vide—

"**बालाग्रशतभागस्य..**" (quoted and translated under Sūtra 22, Sec. III, Chap. II.)

[Cf. in this connection Sūtra 23, Sec. III, Chap. II.]

स्वाप्ययसम्पत्त्योरन्यतरापेक्षमाविष्कृतं हि॥१६॥

[The range of knowledge of the Released soul is now discussed.]

साप्यय-सम्पत्त्योः (of deep sleep and death **स्वाप्ययः** deep sleep, **सम्पत्तिः**—departure from the body; death), **अन्यतर** (either of the two), **अपेक्षम्** (with reference to; with regard to; with an eye to), **अविष्कृतं** (fully revealed), **हि** (as, since); **आविषकृतं हि** (since his omniscience is fully revealed in Śruti.)

Explanation—It may so happen that even when in close union with the Supreme Soul, individual souls may remain quite unconscious of the blissful condition. Now, what the Śruti says about this unconsciousness is to be understood either with regard to one in the state of deep sleep, or with regard to one who is just leaving the body, but not with regard to one in the released state, when the soul retains full consciosunes, as Śruti has made it clear.

For reference, as to the full consciousness retained by the released soul, vide the Śruti—

"स वा एष एतेन दैवेन चक्षुषा मनसैतान् कामान् पश्यन्।"

(He, by gaining this celestial vision sees all these desired-for objects by his intellect.).

Chāndogya, Chap. VIII, 12, 5.

As to the unconsciousness in deep sleep, vide—

"अयं पुरुषं प्राज्ञेनात्मना सम्परिष्वक्तो न वाह्यं किञ्चन वेद नान्तरं।"

(This person *in deep sleep,* embraced by the All-knowing *Supreme* Soul, is quite unconscious of anything external or internal.)

Bṛhadāraṇyaka, Chap. IV, 3, 21.

"नाह खल्वयमेवं सम्प्रत्यात्मानं जानात्ययमहमस्मीति नो एवेमानि भूतानि।"

(This person in deep sleep, even knows neither himself—that I am this or that person, nor these created objected.)

Chāndogya, Chap. VIII, II, 1.

As to the unconsciousness at death, vide:—

"एतेभ्यो भूतेभ्यः समुत्थाय तान्येवानु विनश्यति।"

(He, rising from these elements perishes, as it were, along with them.)

जगद्व्यापारवर्ज्जं प्रकरणादसन्निहितत्वाच्च ॥१७॥

[The limitations of the Released Soul's power are stated here.]

जगद्व्यापारवर्ज्जं (excluding the actions regarding the universe; with the exception of the creation, preservation and destruction of the universe), प्रकरणात् (because of the general topic of the chapter), असन्निहितत्वात् (because they—the souls—have no place therein), च (and.)

Explanation—With the exception of the creation, preservation and destruction of the universe, other superhuman powers are acquired by the Released soul; because the Lord forms the general topic of the chapter, where the creation etc. of universe are discussed and because the souls have no place in that topic.

For reference vide the Śruti—

"यतो वा इमानि भूतानि जायन्ते"

(For the full quotation and translation, see under Sūtra 2, Section I, Chapter I.)

Ācārya Śaṅkara here makes a note that those, who through meditations on the Relative Brahma enter into a condition of equality with the Lord, do not acquire the power of creating the universe, and thus there remains some distinction between those Released souls and their Lord; but a meditator on the Absolute Brahma becomes, when released, completely assimilated to Brahma without retaining any trace of his personality and even individuality. But Ācārya Nimbārka's view is opposed to this: In his view, as shown in Sūtra 14, section III of this chapter, those, who meditate directly on Supreme Brahma and not on symbols as representing Brahma, attain directly the Supreme Brahma; but the meditators on symbols attain the Relative Brahma (Iśvara or Hiraṇyagarbha), and finally the Absolute Brahma (see Sūtra 14, Sec. III, Chap. IV); and according to him, the condition of the Released soul, after attaining the Absolute Brahma, is now stated in this section IV. Śaṅkara is a staunch supporter of the theory of absolute Monism; he would not tolerate any distinction between the Released soul and the Supreme Soul. According to Nimbārka, this Sūtra has made a distinction between the individual soul and Brahma, by giving the Released soul a subordinate position to Brahma, only so far as the creation *etc.*, of the universe are concerned. If Ācārya Nimbārka's interpretation be accepted as reasonable, it would lend support to the view of Dualism standing side by side with Monism (द्वैताद्वैतवाद), as expressed at the bottom of Sūtra 13 of this section.

प्रत्यक्षोपदेशान्नेति चेन्नाधिकारिमण्डलस्थोक्तेः॥१८॥

[An objection, to Sūtra 17, is raised and refuted.]

प्रत्यक्षोपदेशात् (from the direct teaching; from the expressed statement in Śruti), **न** (not *debarred from the power regarding the universe*), **इति** (this), **चेत्** (if); **न** (no), **आधिकारिकमण्डलस्थाः** (privileges belonging to the assemblage of the lords of the worlds; all sorts of bliss enjoyable in the worlds of the gods and that of Brahmā (**ब्रह्मा**); **आधिकारिक**—the master of a world, **मण्डल**—(assemblage), **उक्तेः** (as it is clearly stated in Śruti.)

[This Sūtra consists of two parts, namely, an objection and its reply. The object-portion is;—**प्रत्यक्षोपदेशान्नेति चेत्**; the reply-portion is:—**न, अधिकारिकमण्डलस्थोक्तेः**.]

Explanation—If it be objected, that from the express statements in the Chāndogya Śruti, the Released souls are known to be not debarred from possessing power of creation *etc.*, of the universe; the reply is, that this objection cannot stand; as it is clearly inferred from the statements in the Śruti that only the enjoyments, (and not the powers of creation *etc.*,) available in the worlds of the gods and in that of Brahmā (**ब्रह्मा**), are meant by the passage (in question) in the Chāndogya.

For the passages referred to in the Śruti vide—

"स स्वराड् भवति, तस्य सर्व्वेषु लोकेषु कामचारो भवति।"

(He becomes the lord of himself—his movements are unfettered in all the worlds.)

Chāndogya, Chap. VII, 25, 2.

"य इहात्मानमनुविद्य व्रजन्त्येतांश्च सत्यान् कामांस्तेषां सर्व्वेषु लोकेषु कामचारो भवति।"

(For them, who pass away after having realised in this life, the Self and these desired-for realities, their movements are unfettered in all these worlds.)

Chāndogya, Chap. VIII, I, 6.

विकारावर्त्ति च तथा हि स्थितिमाह॥१९॥

[The description of the status of the Released soul, is continued.]

विकारावर्त्ति (*becomes* incapable of transformation by birth, decay and death *etc.*, does not become subject to mutation by birth *etc.)* **च** (so), **हि** (as), **स्थितिम्** (status; condition), **आह** (*Śruti* says.)

Explanation—And the Released soul does not become subject to mutation by births, deaths and so on, as the purport of Śruti in respect of the status of the Released soul, appears to be so.

For reference vide the Śruti—

"रसो वै सः। रसं ह्येवायं लब्ध्वानन्दी भवति..."

"यदा ह्येवैष एतस्मिन्नदृश्येऽनात्म्येऽनिरुक्तेऽनिलयनेऽभयं प्रतिष्ठां विन्दते अथ सोऽभयं गतो भवति।"

("He—*the Lord*—is indeed Love and this *individual soul*, entering that Love certainly becomes filled with bliss...". "When this *individual soul* obtains a firm hold of Him, so as to be out of all danger,—Him, Who does not come within the range of vision, Who possesses no physical body, to Whom all speech is silent and Who cannot be confined to any particular locality, then alone his position is secure from all fear.")

Taittirīyopaniṣad, Chap. II, 7, 1 and 2.

दर्शयतश्चैवं प्रत्यक्षानुमाने॥२०॥

[An argument, in support of Sūtra 17, is adduced.]

दर्शयतः (show, declare), **च** (and; also) **एवं** (so; in the same way as stated in Sūtra 17, that the creation, preservation and destruction of the universe appertain to Brahma only), **प्रत्यक्षानुमाने** (direct knowledge and inference; both Śruti and Smṛti, **प्रत्यक्षं** —Śruti, **अनुमानम्**—Smṛti.)

Explanation—Both Śruti and Smṛti declare in one voice, that the function of the creation, preservation and destruction of the universe appertain to Brahma only.

For the Śruti Vide—

"स कारणं करणाधिपाधिपो न चास्य कश्चिज्जनिता न चाधिपः।"

(He—*the Supreme Soul*—is the cause *of all*, the Overlord of *Jīva*, the Lord of the senses; and there is no progenitor or lord of Him.)

Śvetāśvatara, Chap. VI, 9.

For the Smṛti vide—

"मयाध्यक्षेण प्रकृतिः सूयते सचराचरम्।

(Through me—her Lord, nature brings forth the animate and inanimate world.)

Bhagavat Gītā, Chap. IX, 10.

भोगमात्रसाम्यलिङ्गाच्च॥ २१॥

[The discourse, on the privileges enjoyed by the Released soul, is concluded.]

भोगमात्र (in respect of enjoyment only), **साम्य** (equality), **लिङ्गात्** (from the indication of Śruti), **च** (also.)

Explanation—From the indication in Śruti, it is gathered also that the Released soul has equality with Brahma in matters of enjoyment only (but not in matters of exercising power in creation *etc*.)

For the Śruti vide—

"सोऽश्नुते सर्व्वान् कामान् सह ब्रह्मणा विपश्चिता।"

(He enjoys all desires with the Omniscient Brahma.)

Taittirīyopaniṣad, Chap. 11, 3, 2.

अनावृत्तिः शब्दादनावृत्तिः शब्दात्॥२२॥

[The discussion on the privileges of the Released soul, is concluded here.]

अनावृत्तिः [non-return *to flesh*], शब्दात् (as it is understood from Śruti.) [The repetition indicates the termination of the chapter.]

Explanation—In the case of the Released soul, there is no apprehension of return (rebirth), since it is evident from Śruti.

For reference in the Śruti, vide—

"एतेन प्रतिपद्यमाना इमं मानवमावर्त्तं नावर्त्तन्ते।"

(Those, who proceed by this path, do not turn back to this mortal whirlpool.)

Chāndogya, Chap. IV, 15, 6.

Smṛti also corroborates this idea:—

"मामुपेत्य तु कौन्तेय पुनर्ज्जन्म न विद्यते"

(But on attaining me, O son of Kunti there does not recur a rebirth.)

Bhagavat Gītā, Chap. VIII, 16.

In the explanation of this Sūtra, Ācārya Śaṅkara says that the return of the meditators on Relative Brahma, has been denied herein by Ācārya Vyāsa; and that it must be admitted. with a stronger reason, that the non-return of the meditators on the Absolute Brahma is a settled fact.

Footnotes :

1. For the meaning of the word 'Akāśa' vide the glossary.
2. Self is said to pass through four states according to the stages of consciousness; the first is जाग्रदवस्था—the state of being wide awake, *i.e.*, being externally conscious of the world outside; the second is स्वप्नावस्था—the state of being in a dreamy or semi-conscious state, *i.e.*, being only internally conscious of a world of imagination; the third is सुषुप्ति—the state of sound sleep, the sub-conscious state,

when only a consciousness of undisturbed peace is experienced and the last is तुरीय, literally the fourth state, which is the state of perfect everlasting bliss, owing to full realisation of the highest self—the Union with Brahma, who is Vast—the Bliss infinite. Some (the Nirvāṇists) count also a fifth state, namely तुरीयातीत (meaning the state beyond the fourth one), when the individual, being wholly merged in the Universal Self, becomes one with the latter. The Non-Nirvāṇists, however, ignore this state, as being absurd and as meaning no bliss at all.

3. The three 'Guṇas' are Sattva (intelligence), Rajas (activity) and Tamas (ignorance.) These are said primarily to remain in a state of equilibrium, which constitutes the Primordial Matter or 'Pradhāna' of Sāṇkhya.
4. Vide the Bṛhadāraṇyaka. Chap. II, 2, 3.
5. This theory of pre-determination, however, leaves enough room for undoing or nullifying the results of previous birth by fresh acts of virtue in this life.
6. It may be added here that Chāndogya purposely omits Akāśa and Vāyu (वायु—air) from the list enumerated because it keeps in view the process of Tribṛtkaraṇa (combination of the three visible elements) instead of Pañcīkaraṇa (combination of five elements) which is elsewhere developed.

GLOSSARY

Avyākṛta	Non-manifest; undifferentiated.
Avyakta	Unrevealed to the senses; the unmanifested state of self; the causal body.
Ācārya	A teacher; a professor.
Adhvaryu	A priest who recites a portion of the Yajurveda in a sacrifice.
Āditya	The sun; Sun (the deity.)
Adṛṣṭa	The unseen; fate; the effect of actions waiting as a latent force to bear fruit in future.
Agni-Vidyā	The process of meditation taking fire as symbolising Brahma.
Agni-hotra	A Vedic rite requiring perpetual maintenance, by the twice-born (the first three castes of the Hindus), of a sacred fire to which oblations are made at stated times.
Āhavanīyāgni	A consecrated fire to which oblations are offered.
Aja	The Unborn (masculine);
Ajā	The Unborn (feminine); a she-goat.
Ākāśa	The first of one of the five primary

	elements; the subtlest of the elements filling all space. (It sometimes stands for the Universal Soul.)
Akṣara	The Imperishable. (It stands for the Universal Soul.)
Ānanda	Bliss
Ānandamaya	Bliss immense; All-bliss.
Anuśaya	The remnant of the meritorious work, unenjoyed in the world of the moon. (*vide* Sūtra 8, Section I, Chapter III.)
Anuvāda	Primarily, a re-statement of an already accepted exhortation; Secondarily, Eulogy; Glorification; an illustration.
Apāna	Peristaltic function: evacuation and micturition; one of the five functions of Prāṇa, the Life-Energy; one of the five vital forces.
Arcirādi Mārga	The path of which the first stage is rays, through which the Enlightened ascend to the world of Brahma after death. (This is also called the Path of the gods or the Northern Path.)
Asat	(Literally) that which is non-existent; that which yet remains to be manifested.
Asuras	(Literally) those who delight in sensual pleasures; the devils; the baser and lower propensities of the physical senses.

Aśvamedha-Yajña	A sacrifice in which flesh of a horse is offered as oblation.
Ātivāhikāḥ	Spirits or deities conducting the departed soul through the path of the gods.
Ātmā	Self; soul; [It stands sometimes for the individual soul (Jīvātmā) and sometimes for the Universal Soul (Paramātmā.)]
Āśrama	One of the four orders or stages of life.
Bahvṛca	A priest who recites a portion of the Ṛgveda in a sacrifice.
Bālya	Childhood; Child-like simplicity.
Bhūmā	The Vast; the Infinite; the Perfect [the word indicates the Universal Soul.]
Brahma	The Supreme Being; the Universal Soul.
Brahmā	Iśvara; Hiraṇyagarbha; the Relative Brahma; Brahma in His relation to the world.
Brahmacarya	The first one of the four orders of life; the student life; abstention from sexual enjoyment.
Brahma-Jñāna	The knowledge of Brahma; the realisation of Brahma.
Brāhmaṇa	A Brahmin by caste; one who knows Brahma; the explanatory portion of the Vedas; a section of a chapter of Śruti.
Brahma-pura	The city of Brahma, figuratively meaning the human body.

Brahma-Vidyā	Exposition of Brahma, and hence process of meditation on Brahma.
Caitanya	Consciousness.
Camasa	A ladle; a big spoon.
Caraṇa	A foot; a fourth part. (*vide* Sūtras 25-26, Section I, Chapter I); Conduct (*vide* Sūtras 9-11, Section I, Chapter III.)
Chāndogya	A priest who sings a portion of the Sāma Veda in a sacrifice.
Cinmaya	All-consciousness; All-intelligence; All-knowledge.
Cit	Consciousness; intelligence; knowledge.
Daharākāśa	The small cell within the heart.
Dakṣiṇā	The sacrificial fee paid to the priest for his labour.
Dakṣiṇāyana	The period of the sun's motion from the summer solstice to the winter solstice; the period of the southern motion of the sun.
Deva-Yāna	The path of the gods through which the Enlightened ascend to the world of Brahma after death.(This is also called the Arcirādi Mārga—the path indicated by the rays etc.)
Devas	The Bright Ones; the gods; the nobler and higher propensities of the senses.
Dhūmra-Mārga	The path of the smoke, through which an individual, after doing works of public utility or other good works, ascends to the region of the moon. (This is also called Pitṛ-yāna—the path of the Fathers.)

Dhyāna	Meditation; concentration of the mind.
Div	Heaven.
Dvija	The twice-born; the first three castes of the Hindus, who have got the initiation in Gāyatrī.
Gārhapatyāgni	The fire, kindled by a householder on his return from the preceptor's house at the expiry of the period of the first order of life (Brahmacarya.) [This fire is to be maintained perpetually till his death.]
Gāyatrī	A Vedic metre of six syllables; a hymn to the sun, or rather to the Creator of the Universe, contained in the Ṛg-Veda and repeated three times a day by a Brāhmaṇa after his investiture with the holy thread.
Gāyatrī-Vidyā	The process of meditation taking Gāyatrī as the symbol for Brahma.
Guṇas	The constituents of Pradhāna; such as Satva (intelligence), Rajas (activity) and Tamas (ignorance.)
Hiraṇyagarbha	The Universal Ego; the first manifestation of Brahma; the Personal God; the Relative Brahma; Brahma in His relation to the universe; Brahmā; Iśvara.
Hitā	The common name of several capillaries leading from the heart, where the individual soul enters in sound sleep.

Hotā	The chief priest in a sacrifice; the priest whose duty it is to utter the Vedic incantations and to offer libations to the sacrifical fire.
Indriyas	The senses and the dynamic centres of action.
Iśwara	The Personal God; the Lower or Relative Brahma; Hiraṇya garbha; Brahmā.
Jīva	An individual soul.
Jīvātmā	The individual soul as distinguished from Paramātmā, the Universal Soul.
Jyoti	Light.
Jyotiṣṭoma	A kind of Vedic sacrifice where flesh of animals is offered as oblation.
Kalpa	A design; a cycle of creation as designed by the Creator.
Karma	Work, sacrificial act; a sacrifice.
Karmāṅga-Vidyā	The process of meditation prescribed in Śruti as a necessary part of a sacrifice.
Karaṇas	Instruments of senses and actions.
Kartā	The doer; the agent; the master; the lord.
Kṛṣṇapakṣa	The dark lunar fortnight; the fortnight of the waning moon.
Kuśā	A kind of sacrificial grass.
Madhu-Vidyā	The process of meditation on Brahma taking the sun as a symbol for Him.

Mahān	The great.
Mahā-Ātmā	The Great Universal Ego.
Mahat	(According to Sāṅkhya) the prolific Nature, the primal evolution of matter, the Intelligence; (according to Śruti,) the Universal Ego.
Mantra	A sacred text; incantation.
Manu	The name of the king who was the first forefather of the human kind.
Mauna	The state of a Muni; the state of speechlessness in constant meditation.
Māyā	The mysterious power of Brahma in phenomenal emanation; the creative energy of Brahma; an illusion.
Mudrā	Interwining the fingers in religious worship; any gesture made by the fingers; any gesture.
Muni	One who remains speechless in constant meditation.
Nāciketa	Fire; (specially the fire, kindled by house-holder on his return from the first order of life (Brahmacarya), to be maintained perpetually till his death; same as Gārhapatyāgni.
Nāḍī	A veinule.
Naiṣṭhika-Brahmacārī	One who has taken the vow of life-long celebacy, residing in the house of his preceptor.
Om	The mystic name of Brahma.

Pañcāgni-Vidyā	Meditation by and through the five imaginary fires (for explanation *vide* under Sūtra 1, Section I Chapter III.)
Pañcīkaraṇa	Qintuplication; intermixture, in certain proportions, of all the five primary elements, namely Ākāśa, air, fire, water and earth, for the formation of the gross elements.
Pāṇḍitya	Erudition.
Paramātmā	The Universal Soul; the Supreme Soul.
Pāriplvava	Stories prescribed for recitation in the intervals of performing the horse-sacrifice.
Paurṇamāsa-Yāga	A particular kind of sacrifice performed in every full moon day.
Pitṛ-Yāna	The path of the Fathers, through which an individual soul on doing works of public utility or other good works ascends to the region of the moon after death to enjoy there the effects of his works. [This is also called Dhūmra-Mārga—the path of the smoke.]
Pradhāna	The Primordial Matter (of Sāṅkhya.)
Prakṛti	The Causal Nature.
Pralaya	Re-absorption in the cause; general dissolution.
Prāṇa	The life; the Life-Energy; the Chief Vital Force; respiration; the first one of the five vital forces.
Praṇava	The word 'Om' (ओम्) which is the

	shortest symbolical name of Brahma.
Prārabdha	The operative part of the consequences of one's previous works.
Pratīka	A symbol of worship.
Purītat	Pericardium (?)
Puruṣa	The spirit; an embodied person.
Pūrva-Mīmāṁsā	The name of the philosophy, by the sage Jaimini, regarding the portion of the Vedas on sacrificial works and other religious ceremonies.
Rajas	Activity; excitability; cause of pleasurable sensation.
Ṛṣi	A seer.
Ṛtwik	A priest appointed to perform some Vedic rites; a priest for performing rites related to the Ṛg-Veda.
Rudrākṣa	A kind of berries, of which the seeds are worn by some religious sects of the Hindus, as rosary around their necks, heads and arms etc.
Sādhaka	A person devoted to religious practices with a view to attain salvation.
Sādhanā	Practices with the view of salvation.
Samācāra	Name of the book containing the rules for the performance of Vedic rites.
Samāna	Assimilation; one of the five func-

	tions of Prāṇa, the Life-Energy; one of the five vital forces.
Saṁvarga-Vidyā	A particular kind of meditation.
Sañcita-Karma	A person's accumulated works, of which the consequences have not as yet begun to operate; the accumulated merits and demerits of a person, the consequences of which yet remain suspended.
Saṅnyāsī	An ascetic; a renouncer of the world.
Śāstra	Scripture; the body of rules for regulating conduct.
Sat	The Ultimate Reality; the Eternal Existence; the Real Being; the Real Thing.
Satva	Intelligence; stability.
Sava	Seven libations to one fire, prescribed to be performed by the Ātharvaṇikas (the students of the Ātharvaṇik school.)
Smṛti	The texts deduced from Śruti and kept in memory; traditions.
Soma	A sacrificial plant or its juice used in Vedic sacrifice.
Śraddhā	Faith; devotion.
Śruti	The Vedas including the Upaniṣads.
Śūdra	The fourth and lowest caste among the Hindus; one in a sorrowful mood of mind; [For explanation *vide* under Sūtra 39, Section III, Chapter I.

Śukla-Pakṣa	The bright lunar fortnight; the fortnight of the waxing moon.
Sūtra	An aphorism with minimum of words and maximum of sense; a tarse sentence.
Tamas	Ignorance; Perishability.
Tejas	Heat; the element Fire.
Tribṛtikaraṇa	Triplication; intermixture of the threee visible elements, namely, fire, water and earth, for the formation of bodies.
Udāna	Cerebration; one of the five functions of Prāṇa, the Life-Energy; one of the five vital forces; activity of the cerebral nerves.
Udgītha	A sonorous prayer, prescribed in the Sūma Veda, to be sung aloud,
Uktha	A metre of one syllable; a part of the Sāma Veda.
Upakurvāṇa-Brahmacārī	A student who takes the view of continence for a limited period only.
Upaniṣad	The secret of attaining Brahma; the knowledge of Brahma; a treatise dealing with the knowledge of Brahma.
Upapātaka	A minor sin.
Upāsanā	Worship; Divine Meditation.
Uttarāyaṇa	The period of the sun's motion from the winter solstice to the summer solstice; the period of the northern motion of the sun.
Vaiśvānara	The digestive fire; the gastric heat; the Universal Manhood

	(Brahma)—the sum total of the created beings; Brahma in the form of the Universe.
Vaiśvānara-Vidyā	The process of meditation on Brahma taking the digestive fire of the animal body as the symbol.
Vānaprastha	Retirement to the forest life.
Varuṇa-Loka	The Nebular Region; the region of the aqueous vapour.
Vāyu	Air.
Vedas	The most ancient, authentic and prehistoric scripture of the Hindus.
Vidhi	Injunction.
Vidyā	A process of meditation; a mode of worship; knowledge.
Vidyut-Loka	The region of electricity.
Vyāna	Circulation of the blood; one of the five functions of Prāṇa, the Life-Energy; one of the five vital forces.
Yajamāna	The performer of a Yajña; the sacrificer.
Yajña	A sacrifice.
Yoga	(Literally) union; abstract meditation for union with the Supreme Being; the name of the philosophy, by the sage Patañjali, teaching the process of union of the individual with the Universal Soul.
Yogī	One who practises abstraction; one who practises abstract meditation.

INDEX

O

P

R

S

X